Bandits and Bureaucrats

THE WILDER HOUSE SERIES
IN POLITICS, HISTORY, AND CULTURE

The Wilder House Series is published in association with the Wilder House Board of Editors and the University of Chicago.

A complete list of titles appears at the end of this book.

David Laitin and George Steinmetz, *Editors*

Bandits and Bureaucrats

The Ottoman Route to State Centralization

KAREN BARKEY

Cornell University Press

Ithaca and London

Cornell University Press gratefully acknowledges a grant from the Institute of Turkish Studies, Inc., which helped to bring this book to publication.

First published 1994 by Cornell University Press.
First printing, Cornell Paperbacks, 1997.

Printed in the United States of America

Library of Congress Cataloging-in-Publication Data

Barkey, Karen, 1958–
    Bandits and bureaucrats : the Ottoman route to state centralization / Karen Barkey.
        p.   cm.—(The Wilder House series in politics, history, and culture)
    Includes bibliographical references and index.
    ISBN 0-8014-2944-7 (alk. paper). — ISBN 0-8014-8419-7 (pb: alk. paper)
    1. Brigands and robbers—Turkey—History—17th century. 2. Outlaws—Turkey—History—17th century. 3. Peasantry—Turkey—History—17th century. 4. Patron and client—Turkey—History—17th century. 5. Patronage, Political—Turkey—History—17th century. 6. Bureaucracy—Turkey—History—17th century. 7. Turkey—History—Ottoman Empire, 1288–1918. I. Title. II. Series.
HV6453.T8B37   1994
364.1'09561—dc20   94-6099

Cloth printing   10   9   8   7   6   5   4   3   2   1
Paperback printing   10   9   8   7   6   5   4   3   2

To my parents

Contents

Preface   ix

Chapter 1   **Introduction**   1

Chapter 2   **The Context of the Seventeenth Century**   24

   The Legacy of the Classical Age   25
   The Ottoman Empire in Context   44
   The Crisis of the Seventeenth Century   48

Chapter 3   **Ottoman Regional Elites: Divided but Loyal**   55

   The State and Timar Holders   60
   The State and High-Ranking Provincial Officials   76

Chapter 4   **Ottoman Peasants: Rational or Indifferent?**   85

   Patron-Client Relations: Fictitious Landholders?   91
   Peasant Rural Organization   107

Chapter 5   **Celalis: Bandits without a Cause?**   141

   Peasant Alternatives   143
   The Manufacturing of Banditry   152
   Banditry as a Social Type   176

Chapter 6   **State-Bandit Relations: A Blueprint for**
              State Centralization   189

   A Political Invitation: May 1606   189
   Consolidation through Deal Making with Bandits   195
   Bargains and Force, 1590–1611   203
   The Politicized Rhetoric of Bargaining, 1623–1648   220

Chapter 7   **Conclusion**   229

Appendix 1   **The Study Area**   243

Appendix 2   **Primary Sources from the Ottoman Archives**   250

Bibliography   255

Index   275

Maps

The Ottoman Empire in Europe and Anatolia, 1451–1683, xiv

Western Anatolia, 245

Preface

BETWEEN THE RISE AND FALL OF EMPIRES, there is no stasis. For extended periods of rule, empires have held together diverse peoples through complex processes of incorporation and coercion. Controlling large expanses of territory has required adaptive imperial state strategies, often imposing great social costs. But those costs have also brought the benefit of diminished conflict. We need only look at the turmoil that has emerged with the decline of empires at both the start and the end of the twentieth century to be reminded of what empires have achieved in holding peoples together and keeping social conflict in check.

Analysts often focus on either the rise or the decline of empires, overlooking the dynamic process of imperial consolidation. Institutional change during imperial rule has frequently been misinterpreted as a sign of decline; any such change is taken to signal a failure or weakening of control. But consolidation of control requires varying adaptations. Empires have often accepted losses in one area to achieve gains in another. As a result, imperial rule is rarely stagnant or stable; in its variation, empires find strength. One-dimensional descriptions of "decline" that lasts half a millennium ignore the control maintained during such periods of rule.

Understanding how empires retain control requires examining the period of state centralization. The dynamic processes involved are often eclipsed by the attention paid to "state formation," with its narrow focus on the initial stages of imposed rule. We must look beyond the origins of empires to the shifting strategies used by the state to consolidate control.

To examine the mechanisms by which imperial states retain and strengthen their control over extended territories, I concentrate in this book on state-society relations in the Ottoman Empire during the seventeenth century, after the formation of the empire in the fifteenth century and before the decline in the nineteenth. Rather than interpret state maneuvers during this intermediate period as evidence of decline, I view them as evidence of a wily state responding to challenges as they emerge. Even the challenges themselves are not so much signals of a loss of state control as they are outcomes of state policies often purposefully designed to be amenable to official manipulation.

The central challenge to the Ottoman state during the seventeenth century came not in the form of peasant or elite rebellions but as banditry. Armed gangs, often decommissioned from the state's military campaigns, roved the countryside, available for hire and engaging in pillage. These bandits did not engage in rebellion per se, for they did not seek or find allies among the peasantry or elites interested in challenging the state. Ottoman strategies incorporated the peasantry and rotated elites, keeping both groups dependent on the state, unable and unwilling to rebel. The bandits themselves were also a creation of the state, emerging from its mercenary troops. Even after these troops had turned to banditry, they remained more interested in gaining resources from the state than in rebelling.

The interaction between the state and bandits is well demonstrated by a letter in the prime minister's archives in Istanbul. In May 1606, the Celali leader Canboladoğlu wrote to Ahmed I, offering his bandit armies as mercenaries for war, in return for the sultan's making Canboladoğlu governor of Aleppo and providing other positions for the bandit's deputies. Astonishingly, in the margin of the letter is a note, in the hand of the sultan himself. Ahmed I writes "This goes too far. Is it possible to give this much?" Clearly, the sultan was willing to engage in negotiations, quibbling over price rather than dismissing the bandit's demands out of hand. That the state was willing and able to control and manipulate these bandits through such deals, bargains, and patronage attests not to its weakness but to its strength. These bandits were not "primitive rebels," as Eric Hobsbawm romantically described them—just bandits. They were not so much enemies of the state as rambunctious clients.

In assessing the absence of peasant or elite rebellions and the manipulation of banditry, I am analyzing the dynamics of state centralization in the Ottoman Empire. In exploring the interactions of the state's political and military institutions and the social base of those institutions, I outline the processes of imperial rule and examine them in light of the experience of state formation in the Ottoman Empire. I have also found it useful to compare the Ottoman route to state centralization with those of the Chinese and Russian empires and the contrasting experiences of rebellion in France during the same period. In doing so, I hope to suggest a theoretical interpretation of imperial state centralization through incorporation and bargaining with social groups, and to enrich our understanding of the particular dynamics of Ottoman history.

This book would not have been possible without the support and wisdom of my teachers, colleagues, and friends over the years. I am particularly indebted to the unique combination of advisers I found at the University of Chicago. Theda Skocpol and William Julius Wilson inspired me to place my historical studies in a more comparative and theoretical context. Halil Inalcık with patience and wisdom opened the door to the intricacies of Ottoman history and paleography. They helped lay the foundations for this book.

In writing the book, I have benefited enormously from the advice and encouragement of Harrison White, Charles Tilly, and the editor of the Wilder House series, David Laitin. Throughout, Dan Chirot provided invaluable guidance and inspiration. Additional help was offered at various seminars at Columbia University's Center for the Social Sciences, and at Wilder House at the University of Chicago, by Ron Burt, Allan Silver, Herb Gans, Mark von Hagen, Mary Ruggie, Ed Mansfield, George Steinmetz, Hajdeja Iglic, and Andre Rus, Daniel Levy, among others. Significant contributions and support came from my friend Nader Sohrabi, who followed the project from its initial stages. Youssef Cohen's encouragement and advice on theory and organization were crucial. Linda Darling remained a valuable source of information.

I am also grateful for the financial support offered for this project. The American Research Institute in Turkey and the Council on Research and Faculty Development in the Humanities and Social Sciences at Columbia University provided grants. The Institute of Turkish Studies under the leadership of Heath Lowry provided support for the project at both its start and its conclusion.

I went to Turkey on three different occasions for this project. I first worked at the Topkapı Museum Archives and various libraries such as the Süleymaniye Library, then at the Başbakanlık Archives in Istanbul, and later at the Manisa Museum Archives. Initially, Mehmed Barlas, who was the editor-in-chief of Güneş, helped with access to the archives. I thank the staff and directors of these various archives for their assistance. At Istanbul University the late Bekir Kütükoğlu took time to acquaint me with several unpublished contemporary narrative sources. At both the

Topkapı and Başbakanlık archives, Ilber Ortaylı and Cornell Fleischer helped with sources and paleography, giving generously of their time to discuss my topic. In Turkey, I also benefited from the assistance and friendship offered by Halise Alkan, Ismail Çoşkun, Ahmet Kanlıdere, Recep Şentürk, and Namık Bozkurt. At the Manisa Museum, director Hasan Dedeoğlu gave me invaluable assistance and advice. Finally, Frida Gelburg helped with the literature in German. Michael Joyce provided yeoman service in editing my prose, and Roger Haydon did a fine job of shepherding the book through Cornell University Press.

Finally, this book would not have been possible without the love, support, and work of my family: my brother, Henri Barkey, and my parents, to whom it is dedicated. Not only did my parents offer love in abundance, but my mother filled in for me in Turkey in the best of diplomatic traditions, while my father patiently and conscientiously helped with the finishing touches. My husband, Tony Marx, dedicated himself to this project with extraordinary patience, commitment, and love. Without my family, I am sure that the Ottoman Empire would have conquered me as well.

KAREN BARKEY

New York, New York

Bandits and Bureaucrats

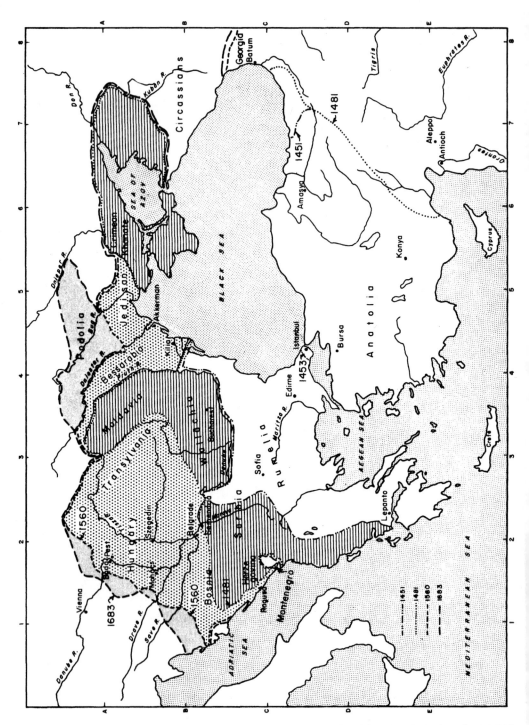

Map 1. The Ottoman Empire in Europe and Anatolia, 1451–1683. Reproduced from Jere L. Bacharach, *A Middle East Studies Handbook,* published by the University of Washington Press, copyright © 1987 by the University of Washington Press and used by permission.

I

Introduction

THE POWER OF THE WESTERN EUROPEAN STATE developed throughout the seventeenth and eighteenth centuries at the expense of established local forces and institutions, provoking various movements of opposition. Does this experience provide an exhaustive theory of a uniform global process? State making *did* often occur within the context of warfare between power holders interested in the expansion and consolidation of territory. To build armies for war, state makers needed to take resources from the population. Many times, onerous exactions and loss of administrative autonomy gave rise to fierce opposition, forcing the state to coerce and control more intensely. This pattern was pervasive, at least in western Europe, though with considerable variation. And because the western state is often considered the model for state formation, scholars tend to view this path of contested centralization and bureaucratization as the only possible direction for the development of the state. Analysts frequently assume that the formation of the strong and effective European state was the outcome of one well-established route of development, often provoking opposition, especially peasant rebellion. Other patterns are dismissed as anomalies, quaint variations, or indications of deficiencies on the part of other cultures and societies.

The western model does not exhaust all possible forms of state centralization, however. Analysis of the Ottoman Empire in the seventeenth century demonstrates that state development was neither unidirectional nor without variation. The power of the state necessarily grew not only at the expense of societal groups but also because the state incorporated or legitimized these groups and linked them to itself. Both traditional elites and various social elements arising from different social structures were incorporated, avoiding much of the contestation assumed in the European model of state making. Despite significant state consolidation and centralization, the Ottoman Empire did not experience the large-scale opposition and class conflict suffered by many western states. Even the pervasive banditry was less often crushed by force than it was managed by widespread bargaining. This interaction between state and society signals the differences in the outcomes of varying processes of state development.

In the Ottoman Empire there were no peasant or elite revolts. Even the bandits—who were seen as the major threat of the state—were used by the central authorities to consolidate their power. The state manipulated internal forces to its advantage, largely avoiding the disruptive contestations endemic in western Europe. The kings of Europe negotiated with elites but quickly took affront at challenges from outside the traditional order, reaching easily for the sword of state. The Ottoman sultans saw such innovative challenges instead as opportunities for bargaining, initially reaching into the state's revenues, distributing patronage to buy off or channel newly emerging opposition. Only later did the sultans resort to force. European challengers were broken; Ottoman challengers were first "house-broken."

In the seventeenth century, both Ottoman and western European state development resulted in strongly centralized authority, though in many ways the routes to this end ran in opposite directions. Most European states, especially France, moved from a more feudal pattern, based on indirect control by the nobility, to a more centralized pattern of direct state control by state-appointed officials. The Ottoman state started with a centralized pattern of direct control through appointed officials, then went through an interim period of mixed center-periphery control, and ended up developing a system of indirect control through local notables. Both states were attempting to consolidate their control over society and thereby redirect most of the resources toward the state. But the more feudal, corporate nature of European society differed from the centralized, prebendal Ottoman society. As a result, the European and Ottoman states had to pursue different styles of centralization.

The Ottoman state bargained and used banditry to consolidate its position and to maintain its predominance over society. In this book, I focus on three aspects in the process of developing state-society relations, comparing the western European case of state development with the Ottoman version of a similar political process. To begin, I explore how and why similar consolidation processes of warfare, taxation, and administrative imposition led to such differing outcomes in European and Ottoman state development. Second, I analyze the alternative paths of development of Ottoman society and the rise of banditry. Finally, I demonstrate how the state turned its relations with the bandits from potential confrontation to incorporation, as a prominent example of the Ottoman route to state consolidation.

States are never able to advance their own aims and strengthen their hold over the population without opposition. Everywhere, societal groups resent the incursion of the state, the billeting of armies, and the imposition of bureaucracy. Centralization threatens the interests of groups with entrenched local claims. Among them, traditional elites, nobles, and local magnates of various sorts represent the most likely groups to express these local interests. To prune local authority, administration, and control in taxation, in military matters, and in public security—the domains of the noble/magnate class—state makers manipulate traditional structures, capturing rights, privileges, and responsibilities within the central administration. For example, the French monarchy's selling of government offices weakened noble authority by enabling the state to rely on members of the bourgeoisie for administration. Abolishing offices, depreciating the significance of local administration, and changing the tenure of officeholders were mechanisms used to curtail local authority.

In the establishment of a unified, direct, and relatively homogeneous rule over a certain territory, state makers have to establish formal structural differentiation and an administration loyal to the center and staffed by officials independent of kinship, tribal, and other class or cultural groups. Representatives of the center are sent to the periphery and slowly overcome the rule of regional institutions and elites. For example, in France, although the *intendants* were not a group specifically assigned to the task of centralization, once their utility was discovered they were trained to direct and coordinate military and financial administrative tasks.[1] A similar process ensued in England when local magnates' and lords' authority was replaced by that of appointed governors and justices

---

[1]Perry Anderson, *Lineages of the Absolutist State* (London, 1979), p. 96. The *intendants,* mostly drawn from the *Maitres de requetes*—therefore educated lawyers—belonged to the *noblesse de robe.* The office of intendancy could not be bought and sold.

of the peace. Perez Zagorin tells of "the expansion of the gentry through the rise of families, the more than doubling of the titular peerage from 1603 to 1641, and the general increase of honors and titles" as indicators of this process.[2]

State making requires not only the centralization of administrative jurisdiction but also the demilitarization of regional power holders. States must acquire their own military, independent of elites. In England, the Tudor dynasty successfully demilitarized great lords by "eliminating their great personal bands of armed retainers, razing their fortresses, taming their habitual resort to violence for the settlement of disputes, and discouraging the cooperation of their dependents and tenants."[3] In a similar fashion, Richelieu and Louis XIII successfully destroyed noble strongholds, denouncing and censuring dueling and the use of firearms, thereby debilitating the toughest opponents of centralization. In both England and France such tactics secured for the state a monopoly of legitimate violence.

European states that extracted resources from the rural population also experienced widespread revolts against their actions. States that engaged in wars required cash to staff their armies and feed their soldiers. When states penetrated society with the intention of extracting resources and reshaping structures of control to reroute surplus directly to the state, without the help of intermediaries, rebellions took the form of antitax, antistate revolts, often seriously threatening the state. As Charles Tilly eloquently describes it, such exactions interfered with peasant life: "Warmaking and statemaking placed demands on land, labor, capital, and commodities that were already committed: grain earmarked for the local poor or next year's seed, manpower required for a farm's operation, savings promised for a dowry."[4] Especially when intervention took away surplus from both the cultivating and noncultivating classes, pruning away the autonomy of regional nobles and corporate associations, elites and peasants formed alliances against the state.[5] Small-scale revolts forced

---

[2]Perez Zagorin, *Rebels and Rulers, 1500–1660* (Cambridge, 1982), 1:74–75.

[3]Charles Tilly, "War Making and State Making as Organized Crime," in *Bringing the State Back In*, ed. Peter Evans, Dietrich Rueschemeyer, and Theda Skocpol (Cambridge, 1985), p. 174.

[4]Charles Tilly, *As Sociology Meets History* (New York, 1981), p. 121.

[5]Charles Tilly, *Coercion, Capital, and European States, AD 990–1990* (Oxford, 1990), p. 100. For similar arguments, see Roland Mousnier, "Recherches sur les soulèvements populaires en France avant la Fronde," *Revue d'histoire moderne et contemporaine* 5 (1958): 81–113, see also "The Fronde," in *Preconditions of Revolution in Early Modern Europe*, ed. R. Forster and J. Greene (Baltimore, 1970), pp. 131–59, and *Peasant Uprisings in the Seventeenth-Century*

states to make concessions, in the process reshaping forms of control and coercion. Those movements that widened led to civil wars, great popular uprisings, secession, and great power intervention. The English Civil War, the French Fronde, the revolts in Naples, and the French adventure in Catalonia are all incidents where the state was seriously threatened.[6]

Apart from regionally based rural rebellions, there was also localized banditry across Europe. Fernand Braudel writes, "Behind banditry, that terrestrial piracy, appeared the continual aid of lords," an indication that the nobility was attempting to disrupt state making through such innovative means.[7] Though European banditry never reached severe proportions during the seventeenth century, it did have an effect on state policies. France had imprinted on its collective memory the rampage that followed the Hundred Years' War, and as a result it never demobilized soldiers in sufficient magnitude to induce banditry. Instead Europe found a brilliant solution to the problem of demobilization: mercenary armies from abroad were hired to fight wars and then discharged outside the borders after the war. Mercenary armies were convenient, and their services were cheaper in the long run since they were paid only during wartime.[8] Although some of the troops still plundered as they were demobilized, the related problems never reached large proportions.[9]

Most centralizing states carry out their activities along general patterns of territorial consolidation, taxation, centralization, and bureaucratization, but they differ along the dimension of implementation. The type of

---

France, Russia, and China, trans. Brian Pearce (New York, 1970). The following texts and articles provide ample information on these rebellions: Yves-Marie Bercé, *Revolt and Revolution in Early Modern Europe* (New York, 1987); Zagorin, *Rebels and Rulers*; William Brustein, "Class Conflict and Class Collaboration in Regional Rebellions, 1500–1700," *Theory and Society* 14 (1985): 445–68; William Brustein and Margaret Levi, "The Geography of Rebellion: Rulers, Rebels, and Regions, 1500 to 1700," *Theory and Society* 16 (1987): 467–95, C. S. L. Davies, "Les révoltes populaires en Angleterre, 1500–1700," *Annales: Economies, sociétés, civilisations* 24 (1969): 24–60.

[6]Zagorin, *Rebels and Rulers*, 2:36–37.

[7]Tilly concurs with this idea in *As Sociology Meets History*, pp. 2–3, where he describes the adventures of the three noble brothers of Brittany, the Guilleris, who became the Robin Hoods of the early seventeenth century despite the fact that no one is entirely sure they gave to the poor.

[8]To hire mercenaries, the state would have to enter into a contract with a *condottiere* style military entrepreneur who would provide the army and pay the soldiers before the war. In Europe, famous mercenary armies existed and states tried to contract with them; France, for example, hired Swiss, Irish, German, and Scottish mercenaries. John Childs, *Armies and Warfare in Europe, 1648–1789* (New York, 1982), pp. 7–8; see also Tilly, *Coercion, Capital, and European States*, pp. 80–81.

[9]Tilly, *Coercion, Capital, and European States*, pp. 83–84.

centralization, and the degree and strength with which state makers implement their political agenda, depends on the nature of the organization and the resource structure of the social environment in which they attempt consolidation. The means of consolidation are shaped according to the organization, autonomy and resources of different social classes. In more agrarian settings, states must deal with nobles and cultivating rural classes; in more commercialized settings, state makers must maneuver among merchant capital, guilds, and city organizations. According to this distinction, Tilly acknowledges three broad types of state formation, with some internal variations. The first route, coercion-intensive, emerges when states, short of cash, set upon the landed populations and apprehend their surplus in the form of increased taxation. As examples, Tilly describes Russia and Brandenburg Prussia in their phases of tribute collection. The second route, the capital-intensive one, occurs when rulers operating within a capital-rich environment turn to the merchant classes for their resources. In a bargain struck between state makers and capitalists, resources are exchanged for protection. Finally, an intermediate mode, "capitalized coercion," occurred in France and England, exemplifying rulers' use of both coercion and capital.[10] The routes taken in France and England can be further specified. According to Michael Mann, states in medieval Europe were weak and set within what he characterizes as an "acephalous federation of a multiplicity of power networks" and a variety of social groupings, which exercised varying degrees of local autonomy. When states sought greater centralization, they grew dependent on populations for crucial resources, and were forced to develop symbiotic relations with their people. Depending on the form of resources available, two different types of European states emerged: in the absence of capital, the French state mobilized its population into a centralized military and developed a bureaucratic administration. In contrast, the English state developed through the use of capital, rather than coerced manpower, into a constitutional state.[11]

Within each mode of European state making, variation occurred according to state decisions regarding how best to manage its interests and maintain control over groups at the same time. Within the coercion-intensive mode, for example, Tilly notes variations among countries according to the extent of the nobility's ability to retain privileges. In Poland and Hungary, the nobility was extremely powerful and managed

---

[10]Ibid., p. 30.
[11]Michael Mann, *The Sources of Social Power,* Vol. 1: *A History of Power from the Beginning to A.D. 1760* (Cambridge, 1986).

to ward off the state's incursion, whereas in Russia and Sweden state makers were more successful at fully transforming and incorporating the nobility into their service.[12] Similarly, Tilly discusses variations in the two other types, stressing that differences exist between such cases as Britain, France, Prussia, and Spain which might otherwise be categorized together. They do share overall similarities in the use of coercion to crush provincial estates, and in the use of capital to ensure resources for military aims, but with different tendencies to move in one direction or another. Pursuing Mann's distinction, France more readily turned to coercion, whereas England more often proceeded along the capital-intensive approach.

Tilly's and Mann's analyses bring to bear an enormous amount of history to explain the variations observed on the European continent. The result is a continuum from coercion to capital-intensive modes. Social structures vary along strictly agrarian or mercantile modes, or their combination, with classes and states entering into conflict or alliances. The conflict or alliance outcome is different in each alternative. Differences that exist in the responses to centralization are important not only in their own right but also because they further shape the state as well as chart a course for future state action. For example, if state makers are able to recruit the nobility into their extractive operations, rebellions assume an antifeudal, antinobility character, diverted from direct challenges to the state. Whether the state recruits the nobility or not depends very much on the original structure of land exploitation. In the commercialized areas of France, the state recruited the nobility to help exploit the peasantry. The nobility was forced to collaborate with the state in efforts to tax and mobilize armies from within the rural classes. A similar entente developed between the Prussian and Russian states and their respective noble classes.

States are not always able to find allies among the nobility or peasants. During the seventeenth century, antifeudal rebellion was less common than antistate rebellion waged by class alliances. In cases like these, a landed nobility and a peasantry, both suffering from incursion by the state, ally to contest the intrusions. The French, Spanish, and English crowns experienced antistate revolts in numerous regions; France led in the number and intensity of these movements. The state's other alternative, that of allying itself with the peasantry at the expense of the nobility, also exists. But only where there are strong antagonisms between the peasantry and the nobility are state makers able to force a wedge between

[12]Tilly, *Coercion, Capital, and European States*, pp. 137–43.

these two groups. In the process, they reinforce the attachment of the peasantry to the state and strengthen the rural community, as in Burgundy in the late seventeenth and early eighteenth centuries.[13]

This type of state development through varying forms of contestation has been taken as the model of state development since it began occurring in many areas of western Europe about 1500. Internal conflicts often included coercion and deal making with landowners, members of the estates, and merchants with capital—the groups most likely to be involved in state making because they possessed economic and political resources. The European states then dealt with peasants, landlords, and a rising bourgeoisie, often through coercion. Response to societal resistance required accumulation of bigger and better military organizations. Overall, claims Tilly, "the history of European state formation runs generally upward toward greater accumulation and concentration, but it runs across jagged peaks and profound valleys."[14]

The process of increasing concentration of capital or coercion has been accepted by most sociologists and historians as the general theoretical case for state making. All other historical cases have been seen as insignificant deviations. The Ottoman Empire, however, despite fairly similar attempts at state consolidation and centralization, did not undergo antifeudal or antistate rural revolts. Of potential challenges, only banditry became a generalized phenomenon evoking a state response. This response was a process different from the European traditions of coercion and capital; state making by "public" co-optation, incorporation, and bargaining.

Banditry provided a fundamentally new context within which the Ottoman state proceeded with some of its most important functions, territorial consolidation and administrative control. In most of western Europe, the task of state consolidation was carried out through a process that mixed international war making, taxation, and co-optation of capital and landed interests, as the peculiarities of each region demanded. In the Ottoman Empire, state making—a process of continuous making and remaking—took on a different format: it was the outcome of negotiation and battle with internal bandit/mercenary troops, a process in turn shaped by international pressures.

The centrality of state-bandit relations in the Ottoman Empire suggests the relative lack of peasant or elite challenges such as rocked Europe. The traditional groups drawn into state making in Europe were not much in-

---

[13]Hilton L. Root, *Peasants and King in Burgundy: Agrarian Foundations of French Absolutism* (Berkeley, 1987).

[14]Tilly, *Coercion, Capital, and European States*, p. 28.

volved in the Ottoman process. Ottoman peasants, who were as affected by state centralization as their European counterparts, were not rebellious; on the contrary, they sought to leave the land rather than fight for it. They sought to adapt to their plight and found alternative means of survival, transforming themselves anew with more fluid identities, often with the encouragement of state institutions. Similarly, the landholding classes did not get involved in rebellion against the state. They continued their attempts at collecting rewards from within the state apparatus rather than in opposition to it.

The lack of traditional class opposition to state making, and the development of pervasive banditry and state bargaining with bandit/mercenary troops, presents a different context of state formation that needs to be analyzed and categorized in its own right. The Ottoman case is not just an interesting anomaly to be explained away; the peculiar nature of such conflict can be explained with the same variables that have been used to understand variation in western Europe. The difference lies in a new concept of state making that derives from careful analysis of state-society interactions and developments. I adopt a highly interactive analysis of social structure and state action that charts out how various structures shape state action and how state behavior restructures society, and I discover in the process an alternative mode of centralization that is different from, yet comparable to, those of western Europe. The difference lies in the peculiar combination of two factors that make up state-society relations in the Ottoman Empire: the social structure and the particular style of state centralization of Ottoman leadership. The patrimonial nature of the Ottoman state, the resulting prebendal structure of state-society relations, and the unique decisions the state took at particular historical junctures explain the divergence of the Ottoman case. I suggest that a similar pattern is evident in Russia and China, which together with the Ottomans offer a distinct model of state making through bargained incorporation rather than contestation.

Social structure and state action are the fundamental components of most studies of state formation. Social structure defines the ground in which states attempt to centralize. Tilly undertakes the analysis of social structural variation for western Europe, where he carefully distinguishes among different social classes, their relations, organization, and resources to identify alternative modes of state centralization. Yet the assumption is that state-society relations are structured in quite similar fashion in most of western Europe. This assumption needs, however, to be modified when one leaves the confines of western Europe to other locales where state-society relations did not emerge from the same sort of historical circumstances, or within the same cultural context. A full theory of state centralization and rural opposition must start by incorporating wider varieties of structural arrangements.

At the same time, variation in styles of centralization have to be accounted for. Again, in Tilly's work different periods of European history have engendered different styles of state centralization. The first two of importance to this work are the patrimonial, where "conquerors sought tribute much more than they sought the stable control of the population and resources within the territories they overran," and *brokerage*, where the bounded territory became the object of war and war was conducted by mercenaries from abroad.[15] In both these types of rule, the geopolitical and social structural conditions necessitated certain styles of action by the state, which acted on behalf of its interests based on its readings of societal forces. In this perspective, as well as in most of the western European–oriented literature of state formation, the state is accepted as an actor.[16] This implies variation in the level of state autonomy as well as in the state's responses. The goals of the various states are quite strikingly the same; their need to centralize, consolidate territory, fend off international enemies, and gain the quiescence of internal forces cannot be debated. Yet the manner in which they go about defending these goals depends on their particular interaction with societal classes, how they think they can manipulate them, and how they can alter the relations among classes in society. States are then actors that take into account the particular structure of society, their relationship of domination with this society, and the demands of the particular context. The decision-making process of the state is better informed by the more minute details and the nature of the structured relations and inequalities that exist in society. It is the two together, the particular nature of the social interaction and the manner in which the state sorts through and manipulates this structure, that matters.

[15]Ibid., p. 29.

[16]Here I follow Tilly and others in thinking and representing the monarchs, rulers, and sultans as the state, thereby reducing a more complex set of relations within the ruling apparatus to basically one single outcome, interest, or goal. And I adopt a Weberian definition of the state where a compulsory political organization with a territorial base is a state insofar as its administration maintains its claim to the monopoly of the legitimate use of force. Max Weber, *Economy and Society: An Outline of Interpretive Sociology,* ed. Guenther Roth and Claus Wittich (Berkeley, 1978). In the context of the Ottoman Empire, the state has not been well defined. I do not engage in much debate about what the Ottoman state was. Rather, I focus on the administrative decision making of this organization and pay attention to the sultan and the members of his imperial council.

The same issues of social structure and state action can be used to explain how the Ottoman state was able to deter societal groups from rebellion. Why did Ottoman peasants not engage in rebellious activity on their own or in alliance with other groups? State centralization in the Ottoman Empire, as elsewhere, proceeded at the expense of different classes, with elites and peasants as directly affected by the state action as in Europe. To clarify the lack of rural rebellions in the Ottoman Empire, we must focus on the social structure of society, and on the specific policies of the state that affected society, for both had a role in inhibiting collective action. It was not only the social structural arrangements of Ottoman society, the traditional relations of power and exploitation, but also the way the state made use of these arrangements and responded to crises that made it apparently impossible for the peasants to ally in rebellion.

The puzzle of "the missing rebellions to Ottoman rule" can be solved with a comparative eye on France. Looking carefully at French history during the period of consolidation—which Tilly terms "brokerage," mainly because of deals made with capitalists—one realizes that most antistate rebellions are in fact conducted by peasants in alliance with the nobility, who have been deeply hurt by centralization. Furthermore, these alliances occur where strong patron-client ties and organized community relations coincide with taxation and pruning of regional authority by the state. France combined a social structure favorable to rebellion with a centralizing state that infuriated both peasantry and nobility, facilitating their alliance.

The Ottoman Empire displays a different set of circumstances. During the same period of state consolidation, the Ottoman Empire combined a patrimonial system of rule with a brokerage style of centralization. On the one hand, according to established patrimonial rule, rebellion against the state was controlled and kept under check. On the other hand, a brokerage style of bargaining helped the state pursue its consolidation functions in the periphery. Accordingly, given patrimonial rule, rotation of state-appointed officials hindered strong patron-client ties, only to be intensified by the lack of local village-based organization and cooperation. State action also hindered elite cooperation by selectively promoting members of each category of elite, creating winners and losers within well-defined groups. Collective action was hardly a possible avenue for Ottoman classes: peasants were not organized, elites were split within their ranks, and peasants and elites had no preexisting basis for alliance. All the while, state interest in extracting rents and tributes continued.

A brokerage style of bargaining was necessitated by new social formations: bandit armies or pools of former mercenaries. These alternative "rebels" were largely created and fueled by the state. In response to state consolidation and the socioeconomic distress of the seventeenth century, peasants pursued alternative modes of survival, requiring a transformation of their identities. A variety of state institutions helped in the process. In the hard-hit rural regions of the empire, young landless males became vagrants; from vagrants, they became soldiers when the state offered them livelihood through enrollment in the relatively new musketeer armies, mobilizing and demobilizing them according to the needs of warfare. Participation in warfare meant organizing around army units, acquiring muskets, and earning daily wages. Demobilization meant losing daily wages while keeping organization and muskets. With demobilization, they changed identities once more from soldiers in the sultan's army to mercenaries available for hire. Under the best conditions, they were quickly remobilized by the state before they turned to banditry. Most often, however, they returned to the villages as bandits, burglars, or unemployed mercenaries looking for oxen, grain, or cash to steal, fields to plunder, or women to rape. Bandits also contributed to the lack of rebellious activity in rural regions. At the extreme, they represented an alternative form of employment for the young, the restless, the rebellion-prone. And distinct from this, bandits were the helping hands of anyone wishing to repress the peasantry: small-time tax collectors, regional magnates, state officials, and the state itself all used bandits when needed. As mercenaries ready for hire, bandits provided the retinues for control, coercion, and repression.

The rise of banditry, then, forced the state into new formats of consolidation. As the Ottoman state mobilized and demobilized mercenary armies without immediate attention to the consequences, banditry became a widespread phenomenon. Once banditry developed, the state both used it and was drawn into negotiations with its leaders. Banditry also became a potential agent in the hands of many regional officials, who used the brigands to suppress the peasantry. It is exactly this situation that the state manipulated to further legitimize its role in the eyes of the people. It used peasant complaints and demands that the state restore order in the provinces to clamp down on any regional officer perceived as threatening and to reinforce its image of the protector of the people. Peasant demands and state responses became the main legitimizing literature for Ottoman rule, with the state gaining loyalty by crushing, often enough, the same bandits it had employed. The resulting state legitimation was disseminated through many forms, from state orders to popular rescripts, literature, and folk stories. Ottoman sultans sent central officials to handle the disturbances and, when necessary, they empowered the peasantry to protect itself. Although not a preferred solution, the peasantry was armed when the menace of local officials intensified. This measure unintentionally added more potential bandits to the pool, since protection meant arming and organizing those men in the village who were not actively involved in cultivation. But this in turn required and justified further centralizing intervention, achieved almost regardless of whether bandits were employed, crushed, or both.

Clearly, the relations between the state and bandits varied significantly from region to region. In regions relatively close to the seat of power, excesses of local militarization were more easily remedied by force. In more remote regions far from state control, banditry became a relatively organized phenomenon which, although not directly threatening to the state, willy-nilly involved it in a process of negotiation. The type and amount of negotiation was heavily influenced by geopolitical contingencies. Small-scale banditry was often used as a rationalization for further policing and control, but it also led to more organized banditry, which succeeded in forcing the state to bargain, co-opt, or fight, and therefore consolidate. Bandits forced the state to negotiate; yet the Ottoman state held strongly to the principle of negotiation by inclusion, presenting itself as the sole center for rewards and privileges. It therefore developed a style of centralization that emphasized bargaining and at least temporary incorporation. Examining nearly a century of bandit unrest in Anatolia suggests a view of state development that explores the nature and intensity of the militarized banditry that occurred and discovers the ways banditry contributed to the processes of state consolidation and centralization.

This form of state development was clearly distinct from the western models. It was, however, closer to the Russian and Chinese experience of state centralization, where some of the characteristics of strong central states engaged in a continual process of centralization were also evident. For the Russian Empire, centralization and incorporation have usually been discussed in two distinct contexts: the incorporation of the European lands, for which military diplomatic means were employed; and incorporation of the eastern lands, where regions were lured into becoming part of the empire.[17] Yet even the European consolidation was different

---

[17]Marc Raeff, "Patterns of Russian Imperial Policy toward the Nationalities," in *Soviet Nationality Problems*, ed. Edward Allworth (New York, 1971), pp. 22–42; David D. Laitin, Roger Petersen, and John W. Slocum, "Language and the State: Russia and the Soviet

from those patterns observed in the West. The most important feature of the Russian Empire was the creation of a service nobility out of semi-independent landlords, transforming a potentially decentralized empire into a strong central entity, resembling prebendal rule in that it lacked strong independent feudal lords and intermediate bodies more common in the West. The service nobility, which was relatively open to newcomers, established a tradition of incorporation into the state elite that the state then could use as its bargaining tool.[18]

The Russian pattern of state formation through bargaining is best demonstrated in the history of Cossack incorporation. The Russian state was able to absorb and transform the Cossack elites by co-opting them into the Russian gentry. This was accomplished through a process quite similar to that of the Ottomans. The Cossacks, a frontier people buffering Muscovy from the Tatars, developed a depot for vagrant peasants, bandits, and mercenaries. Through dealings that continued for more than a century, the Cossacks were incorporated into the Russian state. The key to their incorporation, as was the case in the Ottoman Empire, was the perception of the Russian state as the center of favors and rewards for the members of an elite.[19] The result was the transformation of the Cossack captain into the Russian gentryman, with an increasing differentiation within Cossack ranks because not everyone benefited directly from this incorporation. But the differentiation within Cossack ranks resulted from a more western process. Russian centralization and bureaucratization under continuous warfare on western frontiers in the mid-seventeenth century engendered peasant discontent, flight, and migration of large numbers of Russian peasants into Cossack territory, where they fueled rebellions such as those of Razin and Pugachev.[20] As Cossack social structure differentiated, two processes occurred simultaneously: on the one hand, the upper inhabitants of the Don, or "House-owning Cossacks," were being incorporated through government incentives and services, and the lower inhabitants of the Don, or "the Naked Ones," were being incorporated through rebellion and defeat in their opposition to the crown.

Union in Comparative Perspective," in *Thinking Theoretically about Soviet Nationalities: History and Comparison in the Study of the USSR*, ed. Alexander J. Motyl (New York, 1992), p. 137.

[18]Mousnier, *Peasant Uprisings*, pp. 162–64.

[19]Bruce W. Menning, "The Emergence of a Military-Administrative Elite in the Don Cossack Land, 1708–1836," in *Russian Officialdom: The Bureaucratization of Russian Society from the Seventeenth to the Twentieth Century*, ed. Walter McKenzie Pintner and Don Karl Rowney (Chapel Hill, N.C., 1980), pp. 130–33.

[20]Paul Avrich, *Russian Rebels, 1600–1800* (New York, 1972).

Just within one region, then, we see mixed modes of centralization that emanate from different social structures, different social groups, and their perceived interests.

China is perhaps the empire that shares most closely with the Ottoman Empire a history of banditry and state-society interactions mediated by banditry and militarization in a variety of fashions. In the sixteenth and seventeenth centuries, the strong Chinese state encountered movements in which peasants and bandits seem to have acted in concert against state consolidation. Especially those bandits who were organized along military lines were incorporated into the state's defense system. Incorporation into the Chinese army both contained rural disruption and added armies to the Chinese forces, much as was the case in the Ottoman Empire. Later in the mid-seventeenth century, however, the Chinese state started losing its ability to incorporate these bandits, who acquired leadership and came to threaten the center. In 1635 there were at least thirteen bandit chiefs representing seventy-two bands intent on breaking up China into their own areas of rule. The breakup did not occur, though from then on the history of struggle between local militarization and the state went hand in hand with centralization. Numerous revolts combined militarized bandits, local militia captains, and bandit chieftains whose actions developed as an extension of everyday forms of competition and struggle for resources. Elizabeth Perry demonstrates well, through the study of the Nien and the Red Spears in Late Imperial China and the Republican period, how the particular symbiosis of the environment, social structure and state action developed these different rural formats which allied in rebellion and confronted the state. Predatory or protective in their aims, rooted in village-level organizations, these bandits turned to challenge the state, fighting both its various impositions and as foreign intervention.[21] China experienced more revolts, but the local forms of militarization and banditry were comparable to the more incorporated groups in the Ottoman Empire.

The history of Chinese state making, with its fits and starts, is suggestive. Local militarization, banditry, and rebellion in China were elements of a complex and varying process of state consolidation. Prasenjit Duara describes this process as "involutionary," in that the ability of the state to

[21] Elizabeth J. Perry, *Rebels and Revolutionaries in North China, 1845–1945* (Stanford, 1980); Philip A. Kuhn, *Rebellion and Its Enemies in Late Imperial China: Militarization and Social Structure, 1796–1864* (Cambridge, Mass., 1980).

tax increased while its local control decreased.[22] State making proceeded with growing turmoil on the local level, much as was evident during different periods in the Ottoman Empire and in Russia. In all three, social structure threw up local militants which the state had to incorporate to solidify its control. What looked like turmoil was part of the process of state making.

When compared to Europe, the Ottoman, Russian, and Chinese states were much more encompassing of societal elements. For our purposes, state development in the Ottoman Empire demonstrates many of the patterns briefly explored in Russian and Chinese history, only more distinctly and intensely. In many ways, it resembles what Duara calls involuntary: the Ottoman state increased its control over Ottoman society by leaps and bounds, and not in all realms at the same time. As society appeared chaotic under the spell of banditry, the state found ways to incorporate bandits and increase its sphere of control. At the same time, as it devised methods of increasing taxation, it let intermediaries exercise authority until it could sap their power for good. It managed and played off different groups, responding to and curtailing their orbit of influence while keeping all groups dependent on the state. A state-centered culture was embedded in the structure of society by state action, with everyone from elites to bandits dependent on state-servicing patronage.

Ottoman development between 1550 and 1650 occurred through different processes, with different groups entering into negotiations with the state, and therefore different channels and deals emerging. Even when some of the traditional groups were in interaction with the state, the outcome was not traditional. For example, when the state responded to the needs of the peasantry, it took action that led to low-level militarization of the countryside, fueling the phenomenon of banditry and therefore creating new negotiating partners. Or, for example, the reorganization of provincial assignments, which at first sight seems comparable to France in the use of central officials to handle regional administration, turned out to be quite different in style and outcome. The process entailed phasing out the smallest land units and their landholders, achieving larger units, and entrusting them to men from the center. This was not the same as eliminating all the powerful intermediaries in the process of tax collection and administration. In the Ottoman context, under certain conditions the policy led to a snowballing increase of intermediaries. Moreover, in a most

---

[22]Prasenjit Duara, *Culture, Power, and the State: Rural North China, 1900–1942* (Stanford, 1988), p. 73.

unconventional manner, when large bandit armies starting roving around the countryside, the Ottoman state sat down at the bargaining table with them. Bargaining between bandits and the state, again, would seem an anomaly in the western European model of state centralization. Yet the imperative was the same: states have to be the only military power in their territory. The Ottoman state struck bargains with the bandits, who were not as threatening to the state as were the regional power holders of France. The bandits represented alternative centers of militarization that were dealt with in the old patrimonial style, through incorporation and reward.

The peculiarities of the Ottoman case are not peculiarities after all; the variation in state building we observe primarily in the Ottoman and other similar cases emerges from wider variation in state-society relations than we see in the European. Social structure and state action exerted a complex impact on state-society relations which shaped modes of centralization. Variations in social structure (feudal versus prebendal, as the current example) and variation in state action need to be scrutinized for the further development of models of state centralization. Embedding these two variables into a state-society format means a promise of careful attention to the manner in which the distinct aspects of social structure and of state action interact with each other—how state action is determined by structural constraints as well as how state action attempts to alter and shape societal formats.

This book develops the literature on state centralization and social movements. I argue that the process of state development is diverse and that this diversity is contingent on the specific nature of social structures and the realm of possible actions on the part of the state. States develop and centralize essentially by entering into conflict, negotiation, and accommodation within the existing configuration of forces in society. I therefore spend time disentangling the specifics of the established relationship between the state and society in the Ottoman Empire to demonstrate the manner in which this created alternative paths of action for the Ottoman state which were not available to other western European states. These theoretical concerns lead us to scrutinize Ottoman history carefully.

I make two historical claims that originate in theoretical debates on state formation and collective action. First I claim to illuminate an era of Ottoman history that has been largely neglected as a transitional—and therefore unsettled and unknown—period. Second, I contend that the history of Ottoman banditry has to be moved away from romantic models of "primitive rebellion" toward a more realistic representation of who these brigands really were. Between the strong, centralized empire able to threaten Europe at the doors of Vienna and the weak, decentralized "sick man of Europe" preparing to be chopped up by a superior Europe, the intermediary period tends to be ignored. Yet this period is crucial because it enlightens comparison to both the "rise" and the "decline" of the empire. Analysis of this period demonstrates that some of the state's practices during its strength were not necessarily the best practices for effective long-term rule. It also suggests that the decline, which is supposed to have lasted for centuries, was not really a decline. The history of the seventeenth century shows that state rulers were testing practices of rule, adapting to the society, and attempting to consolidate and centralize their power at the same time. They learned from their mistakes; they eliminated some practices while consolidating others. They by no means gave up; rather, they adapted to a new world order quite well. Variation did not represent weakness. In the process, state development went through the "jagged peaks and profound valleys" Tilly so aptly describes, yet with a different centralized outcome.

It is not inadvertent that I have chosen this period of Ottoman history to address state strength and consolidation. The early periods of state formation would have provided an easier context. I chose the time when most European states were also consolidating. Their stories were different because they encountered entrenched interests and rebellions that threatened the very foundation of their existence. The Ottoman Empire also encountered resistance, but a resistance that demanded to be incorporated and was willing to be included in the system. The rebels of the Ottoman seventeenth century were status-seeking rebels. They desired positions in the Ottoman administration. Since the Ottoman rulers did not feel as threatened by such internal forces, they chose to respond to them on a temporary, deal-based fashion, setting the development of the Ottoman state off on a different route. Nevertheless, it was not a weak state, unable to handle opposition. The Ottoman state was very much aware of the weakness that could result from overexpansion and sheer size. It was forced to devise a more flexible approach to governance, compensating for some of its natural geopolitical flaws. Flexibility meant strength, not weakness.

Related to the issue of state strength is that of unilinear development. Reflection on processes of state formation also suggests that state development is rarely unilinear or uniform. In fact, the increasing number of case studies on western state formation demonstrate that the process is much less glorious than western Europeanists have made it out to be. In the western experience, state formation is perceived as a struggle between state and society, yet it is more or less an evolutionary process in which the state gains increasing strength. More generally, however, it is a process that is often stalled, halted, and reactivated according to both international and internal political conditions. Different societies have different societal formats, and the interactive processes between the state and these formats present variations on the process of state formation. Some societies may be incorporated smoothly, others may pose serious threats to states, leading to near revolutionary outcomes. To this theoretical debate, the Ottoman case has much to add. The Ottoman state experienced severe setbacks during centralization, necessitating regrouping and rethinking.

The question of state breakdown, unfortunately, continues to be a sore spot in the history of seventeenth-century Ottoman history and analysis. Although historians have become aware of the deleterious effects of decline theory, its effects still linger. More recently, sociologist Jack Goldstone has joined the historians in arguing for numerous breakdowns of the Ottoman state. Eager to extend comparative sociology to the relatively unexplored shores of the Middle East (and rightly so), Goldstone forces Ottoman history of the early seventeenth century into his model. The result is a misreading of the period that attributes key developments to only weakly related variables. To say that the Ottoman Empire experienced setbacks is not to say that it experienced breakdown. The existence of contending forces in society does not necessarily mean state breakdown; and it does not necessarily mean total loss of control on the part of the government. We need to analyze the type of contention and the solutions to this contention before we can make generalizations about the breakdown of the state.[23]

States break down, for Goldstone, when they lose their effectiveness or are hampered by elite competition and revolt, as well as by popular revolt and violence. A major goal of this book is to show that the Ottoman state instead effectively regulated social classes to contain their possible rebellion. I demonstrate that elites were not rebellious against the state. They

[23]Goldstone links population shifts in early modern Eurasia to state breakdown. He argues that the destabilizing effect of population growth leads to the breakdown of state institutions that are too rigid to adapt to change. His analysis of demographic changes are only marginal to our interests. Yet as this book shows I do not agree with either the interpretation of the Ottoman institutions as too rigid or the analysis of the Ottoman seventeenth century as a time of periodic state breakdown. See Jack A. Goldstone, *Revolution and Rebellion in the Early Modern World* (Berkeley, 1991).

remained competitive within and across their ranks, having been subjected to intense manipulation by the state. Similarly, there were no popular revolts; the banditry that spread across the countryside was a by-
product of state making and war making and was absorbed into the fabric
of the state. Where the culture of seeking state office and sharing in state
power is very strong, contention can take the form of conservative and
state-reinforcing appeals for incorporation, not to be confused with challenges to state rule. Jockeying for positions within the state apparatus
takes different forms according to the position and status of the contender. Whereas for those within the system there are a variety of ways of
improving their status, those outside the system have to seek confrontation. Therefore, there may be moments in state development when alternative social forces force the state to the bargaining table and the state and
society are competing within the same primary domain, that of the use of
physical force. These are the forces of those outside, entering through
confrontation and later deal making. The state is, however, still a viable
actor that only strengthens itself through constructing the right deal.[24]

I also distinguish this phase from that of multiple sovereignty in which
the "government previously under the control of a single, sovereign polity
becomes the object of effective, competing, mutually exclusive claims on
the part of two or more distinct polities."[25] In such cases, the state is being challenged by contenders who want to capture the government; it is a
revolutionary situation. A state-society confrontation instead implies that
the state and other groups are competing for access to resources, taxation,
and control and are using similar means—yet the authority of the state is
not directly challenged. There are no demands for overthrowing the state.
This is, I contend, a situation that easily arises exactly during periods of
consolidation because they are prime times of conflict, bargaining, and
accommodation. Accordingly, I use state-society confrontation to denote
times when the state is forced to bargain with both societal elites and popular groups.

Understanding the nature of state consolidation also helps to correct a
misinterpretation of a series of bandit uprisings during this period of the
Ottoman Empire. Whereas most scholars see these uprisings as the result
of the deteriorating economic conditions and state violence, I describe

---

[24]The state that reemerges after the breakdown, according to Goldstone, is a different
one. Yet he gives no reason to think of the Ottoman state in different terms after the seventeenth century; *Revolution and Rebellion*, p. 10.

[25]Charles Tilly, *From Mobilization to Revolution* (Reading, Mass., 1978), p. 191.

them as more of a by-product of state centralization.[26] Following Eric Hobsbawm, most scholars have seen banditry through romantic lenses and argued that bandits are rural rebels in search of ways to help the peasantry. I describe the same bandits as the real malefactors of rural society. They hurt the rural community in several ways: they inhibited its potential for collective action; they plundered its resources and actively participated in its coercion by local power holders. These agents of the local strongmen could not have been benevolent. Bandits were neither necessarily nor often enemies of the state. By demonstrating the origins, the intent, and the consequent demise of these bandit groups in rural society, I present a less romantic image of the bandits. In doing so, I outline processes of rural revolt, clarifying the distinction between class-based movements that threaten the structural arrangement in society and a banditry that attempts to benefit from the existing structural arrangements in society. The bandits, in the final analysis, have no reason for the destruction of those structures of inequality from which they benefit.

There are three particularly relevant features of the Ottoman seventeenth century: the lack of class-based collective action on the part of the peasantry, the development of a pool of bandit mercenaries, and the consolidation of the state through state-bandit bargaining. All three were part of an ongoing process of state consolidation and centralization, a process unlike that in western Europe. Ultimately, these features can be explained through the interaction between the state and the peculiar organization of societal groups.

In the first part of the book I scrutinize the causal connection between state centralization and rural rebellions. In this context, I show how both the nature of state-society relations in the more patrimonial structure of the Ottoman state and the decisions made by the state during the process of centralization hindered rural rebellions. In Chapter 2 I describe the Ottoman social structure and the nature of state-society relations as established by the key research of Ottoman observers and historians. I also provide a context for the early seventeenth-century world system and the general conditions of economic and demographic change that constituted its crisis. Chapters 3 and 4 investigate why Ottoman peasants did not rebel in response to the increasing conditions of centralization and warfare. In

[26]Anton Blok, *The Mafia of a Sicilian Village, 1860–1960: A Study of Violent Peasant Entrepreneurs* (Prospect Heights, Ill., 1974), makes a similar argument to explain the development of the Sicilian Mafia when a centralizing state was unable to eradicate the existing local networks of power, therefore leaving room for landlords to recruit the future mafiosi, who in turn were able to formulate alternative social organizations.

Chapter 3 I focus on the conditions that led the regional elites to competition, division, and inability to coordinate collective responses against the state. In Chapter 4 I analyze the inability of peasants to engage in collective action—their inability to ally with other affected regional classes and their own internal organizational obstacles. In each of these chapters I consider a medley of social structural constraints in light of specific state action, giving each variable interactive weight. This analysis demonstrates that the specific nature of the social structural arrangements and the implementation of state policies inhibited class-based movements.

In the second section of the book I investigate the causal connections among state action, patrimonial societal relations, and banditry. In this context, I show how both the nature of state-society relations in the more patrimonial structure of the Ottoman state and the decisions made by the state during the process of centralization led to the rise and development of banditry. Chapter 5 demonstrates that banditry did not pose a serious threat to the state; on the contrary, it was a by-product of state policies and was quickly appropriated by the state for purposes of state consolidation and peripheral control. I also differentiate the bandits from other rural classes; bandits had multiple, fluid identities (ex-peasants, landless vagrants, students, soldiers, mercenaries, bandits). The process by which they became part of a collectivity with horizontal ties presumes that the linkages of each individual to his own reference group were cut. Therefore I argue that banditry was an artificial social construction and it did not represent a threat to the state in the traditional sense since it did not attempt to destroy the social structure; it simply wanted to derive as much utility from it as possible. The bandits manipulated the interstices of the system; they had no proclaimed ally or enemy and no significant ideology.

In Chapter 6 I show how bandit collectivities were formed and how the state used its own creations for state consolidation. This chapter recounts the history of state-bandit bargains and the manner in which the state either co-opted bandits into the system and consolidated a region or fought them through internal warfare and consolidated through their defeat. In each situation, I analyzed state decisions for their geopolitical content. Finally, Chapter 7 ties together the analysis in a theoretical conclusion.

Embedded in these statements is one general conclusion: the Ottoman Empire was not seriously challenged in the manner of the European states, where class-based collective action (of a single class or a coalition of classes) occurred and directly challenged the system of rule. In Europe, especially in France, a demarcated social structure with clearly defined classes with strong positions, identities, and interests meant that challenges to the state arose from within the established lines of communication and channels of interaction between state and society. In the Ottoman Empire, the inability of groups to organize along class lines and challenge the state from more or less simple interest-based principles of collective action resulted in the Ottoman state's not being seriously challenged by societal forces. Therefore, the necessary social reorganization did not come until much later, when elites finally had enough regional power bases to slowly secede from the center. Ottoman disintegration was not the result of a sudden and tumultuous breakdown; it was the result of a process of chipping away at the edges—a slow and in fact nonrevolutionary process of decentralization. In the long run, it left the core aware of its exposed and stripped center. "Revolution from above" then ensued in order to salvage what was left of this gargantuan edifice.

2

The Context of the Seventeenth Century

B Y THE BEGINNING OF THE SEVENTEENTH CENTURY, Ottoman state and society mixed features from the Classical Age and adaptations to recent world systemic changes. On the one hand, the foundations of state-society relations and the structure of Ottoman rule at the center and in the provinces shifted as a series of adjustments brought about certain relaxations of control and a certain fluidity that allowed movement in and out of otherwise closed units. At the same time, the state adhered to the ideals of centralization while redefining the ways it might be achieved. On the other hand, the legacy of the sixteenth century throughout Eurasia resulted in the crisis of the seventeenth century: the Ottoman Empire experienced an unsettling demographic transition; it endured fluctuations in the monetary system; it labored under the effects of the price revolution; and, finally, it watched the West emerge as a stronger adversary than before. Both state and society adapted to reinvent conduits of transformation: the state adapted its institutional mechanisms to cope with these changes within the realm of Ottoman dogma. Both central and regional institutions were restructured to improve doing what states do best: extract resources, organize armies, and spread tentacles of control over society. Society responded in different ways, either fully engaging the state or disengaging from the state in search of alternative solutions. It is in this context of adaptation to both the existing set of arrangements and the international context of change that the Ottoman state undertook various actions vis-à-vis elites, peasants, and bandits. It is therefore important to study the structure of state-society relations in the Ottoman Classical Age as well as the context of the changing world system. It is even more important to understand the new world system since it equally affected Europe and Asia. Nevertheless, the results of the transformations partially triggered by these changes were very different in these two settings.

The Legacy of the Classical Age

Massive empires of the Ottoman type often alternated dangerously between creating strict rules and letting environmental variations, local standards, and precedents establish the pattern of rule. Or better yet, descriptions of such empires present respectively images of oriental despotism or arrested patrimonial evolution with little institutional development of the state.[1] Reality fell short of both extremes. No hard and fast rule dictates how to run an empire; often a structure lent itself to manipulation by individuals who occupied its various administrative levels. All too often, historians have studied these structures with little attention to their flexibility, interpreting each and every instance of deviation as a particular case. This is very much how the Classical Age has been represented by many contemporary and modern scholars.[2]

The greatest achievement of the Ottomans by the time of the Classical Age was building an empire with a bureaucratic administration that extended beyond the immediate patrimonial realm. This empire was able to govern effectively a vast expanse of territory, with diverse communities dominated by local power holders not overly eager to surrender their privileges. In this attempt at consolidation and control, the Ottomans created a military and administrative structure that was able to infiltrate the remote areas of the empire. More important, they engineered a system in which the allegiance of members of the military and administrative apparatuses was practically unchallenged. The state made these men for its own purposes and rewarded them through its own channels, tying their livelihood, rewards, and status to itself through methods of divide and rule. This was partly the reason for the long-lasting success of the state; even as economic and military ills hit them, officials looked for rewards from the state and tried to advance within the state apparatus rather than challenge it.

[1] Susanne Hoeber Rudolph, "Presidential Address: State Formation in Asia—Prolegomenon to a Comparative Study," *Journal of Asian Studies* 46 (1987):731–46.

[2] The exception to this failing is that of Halil Inalcık, whose Ottoman history has been written as an institutional history yet with outstanding detection and understanding of how these institutions change and adapt to different circumstances. See Inalcık, *The Ottoman Empire: The Classical Age, 1300–1600* (New York, 1973).

As the Ottomans developed, a complex compact between state and society gradually incorporated all potentially autonomous elites and organizations into the state. This appropriation set the stage for the peculiar route of the Ottoman centralization throughout the sixteenth and seventeenth centuries. The story of the Ottoman Empire can be told as that of the transformation from a rather small house of nomadic conquest into an established house of rule relying on strong patrimonial guidelines. During this transformation, which lasted approximately from the fourteenth to the sixteenth century, the Ottoman house of rule managed to shape a variety of internal forces to its own will, sometimes by offering deals, sometimes by forcing migration, and at other times through sheer coercion. Whatever the means employed, the end result was to tie all potential regional elites and potential corporate entities strictly and solely to the state without allowing them the freedom of autonomous organization.

That the Ottoman Empire achieved fairly uniform centralization is all the more remarkable given regional diversity and varying geopolitical pressures. Control over the periphery always requires more energy and resources than managing core regions of an empire. Overextension therefore usually produces some form of indirect rule in the faraway provinces. The core of the empire, the Balkans and Anatolia, had more or less uniform administrative arrangements for land tenure, taxation, and other fiscal policies whereas the rest of the empire, the periphery, experienced indirect rule. The outlying areas of the empire thus enjoyed some degree of autonomy in the mixture of pre-Ottoman with Ottoman practices. Forms of land tenure and taxation were adaptations of various practices derived from regional and central sources. Consequently, the borderlands revealed different state-society arrangements: groups behaved according to the dictates of this new blend of institutions, even though they were securely bound to the central state apparatus.

Although different state-society arrangements preserved social control in diverse regions, a general principle of rule was applied throughout, which rendered even indirect rule more controlling than it would otherwise have been. State control was exerted through ties from the periphery to the center, segmenting elites and common people, all of whom were responsive to the center but not to each other. Relations with the center were strong, while those among groups and communities were weak; this weakness was maintained by such practices as rotation of regional offices. Sociopolitical and economic links of patronage and trade all extended from the periphery to the central state. Because links within the periphery were weak, social disorganization became the pattern in Ottoman provinces. Şerif Mardin, who has well demonstrated the lack of corporate entities in Ottoman society, describes such state-created diffuseness as having hindered the development of autonomous bodies.[3] Accordingly, it is necessary not just to describe institutions and groups in society but also to explain the manner in which the state manipulated them and created diffuse and fluid identities.

The question of state action has often been confused with that of intentionality. I clearly provide the Ottoman state with agency, but I do not argue that all state practices were deliberately or accurately calculated by state officials to achieve increased control. Often, various narratives of state action exist simultaneously because many diverse events that may or may not be causally connected occur all at once. Nevertheless, what gets chosen as the actual narrative of state action is that which seems most rational for gaining state goals and imputes perfect intentionality to state actors. That is because it is easier to relate events in a temporally and causally connected fashion and attribute straightforward intentions to individuals. But to those actually carrying out actions, events often look as if they have been pieced together in quite an ad hoc fashion.

The state that emerged was to maintain a strong patrimonial-bureaucratic form with a specifically Near Eastern and Islamic cultural meaning. Each of these aspects—the patrimonial and the bureaucratic—had an enormous influence on how society was shaped. The patrimonial aspect centered around the household and the rule of the sultan, who, as the head of the household, presided over the dynasty (his family), the ruling class constituted of his slaves, his flock (the people), and the territory of the empire as his "dynastic patrimony."[4] The bureaucratic aspect meant the extension of specialized means of bureaucratic administration, which developed early and extended beyond the limited realm of the household. The ideological came to the aid of the geopolitical aspects in the form of the ideal of *gaza*, whereby the realm of Islam was to be expanded through Holy War. The contribution of each of these aspects was enhanced and united in the larger political scheme: the general understanding of "the reign of justice within a circle of equity."

It is this cognition of the circle of equity contextualized into the patrimonial-bureaucratic state with Islamic and Near Eastern overtones that I think constituted the political culture of the Ottoman empire. The

[3] Şerif Mardin, "Power, Civil Society and Culture in the Ottoman Empire," *Comparative Studies in Society and History* II (1969): 269.

[4] Carter Findley, *Bureaucratic Reform in the Ottoman Empire: The Sublime Porte, 1789–1922* (Princeton, 1980), p. 7.

general understanding was that justice provided the major counterbalance to absolute authority.[5] Accordingly, this circle had eight propositions: "a state requires a sovereign authority to enforce rational and Holy Law; to have authority a sovereign must exercise power; to have power and control one needs a large army; to have an army one needs wealth; to have wealth from taxes one needs a prosperous people; to have a prosperous subject population one must have just laws justly enforced; to have laws enforced one needs a state; to have a state one needs a sovereign authority."[6] Halil Inalcık sums up the implications of this well: "Justice, in this theory of state, means the protection of subjects against abuse from the representatives of authority and in particular against illegal taxation. To ensure this protection was the sovereign's most important duty. The fundamental aim of this policy was to maintain and strengthen the power and authority of the sovereign, since royal authority was regarded as the cornerstone of the whole social structure."[7]

The propositions of this theory of governance define the terms of the compact between state and society. Although the state was supreme, responding to the needs of societal groups remained important to its wellbeing. The state propagated the ideals of the circle of justice, including the guarantee of state protection, at every opportunity, in every manifesto, and in countless symbolic actions. To comprehend the mechanics of this rule we need to consider the form and content of the Ottoman state.[8]

Centralization in the Ottoman Empire from the time of Mehmed II (1451–81), the chief architect of central control, meant both a centralization program—a strong state and stringent control of the periphery—and the establishment of rules and regulations by which the consolidation was to be maintained. In the process, from the time of Mehmed II to that of Süleyman, the state was transformed to include a more encompassing and bureaucratic notion of itself. The period of Mehmed II was the embodiment of a "centralist program which inevitably called for a strong treasury: eliminating potential rivals to the throne from within the Ottoman family through fratricide if needed, enforcing Ottoman superiority over other Turkish principalities in Anatolia, curbing the power of 'old fami-

[5]Cornell Fleischer, "Royal Authority, Dynastic Cyclism, and 'Ibn Khaldunism' in Sixteenth-Century Ottoman Letters," *Journal of Asian and African Studies* 18, nos. 3–4 (1983):201.

[6]Joel Shinder, "Early Ottoman Administration in the Wilderness: Some Limits on Comparison," *International Journal of Middle Eastern Studies* 9 (1978): 499.

[7]Inalcık, *The Ottoman Empire*, p. 66.

[8]I cannot present the Ottoman state in all its complexity, institutions, and processes of rule in this chapter. I discuss only those institutions and mechanisms that are most relevant to the arguments of this book.

lies' which could grow into an aristocracy, establishing the courtly eti-
quette and lifestyle of an absolute monarch, creating an administrative
structure based primarily on *kuls*, assigning *kul* troops a larger role in
warfare, and most conspicuously, conquering Constantinople."[9] Manip-
ulations ranged from incorporation through marriage to incorporation
through coercion.[10] At the same time, Mehmed the Conqueror for the
first time in Ottoman history proclaimed law codes that established more
firmly the regulations and statutes concerning government and the people. These decrees based on sultanic law (*kanun*) and traditional regulations (*örf*) did not refer to and were different from the religious Islamic
law (*şer'iat*). They established the rule of the sultan and the role of the
state in this process of rule. Sultanic codes developed and established
the power of the state even more forcefully during the reign of Süleyman
the Magnificent, known also as "the Lawgiver." Throughout this period
the codification of provincial regulations was one of the main ways of incorporation and centralization. Sultan Süleyman, the consolidator par excellence, ruled "for forty-six years with justice, and took special care to
nurture the men of religion, poets, bureaucrats (*ehl-i kalem*), and military
men who were the primary supporters of the state."[11] It is in fact during
the reign of Süleyman that the concept of the state gained larger significance, becoming more than the sultan himself or even the individuals who
staffed the bureaucracy. The state was transformed into an institution
governed by the sultan's household and an extensive bureaucracy, where
intricate negotiations, decision making, and politicking became the rule
rather than the exception.[12]

[9]Cemal Kafadar, "When Coins Turned into Drops of Dew and Bankers Became Robbers
of Shadows: The Boundaries of Ottoman Economic Imagination at the End of the Sixteenth
Century," Ph.D. diss., McGill University, 1986, p. 51.

[10]As Rhoads Murphey explains, marriage became a common practice for ensuring the
allegiance of state-level central as well as provincial leaders who were deemed to be crucial
to the sultan's rule: "The malleability of these top-level bureaucrats was guaranteed by the
bonds of filial obligation imposed through marriage to princesses of the royal line." The
practice was institutionalized by the reign of Süleyman I (1520–66), and the most important
grand viziers of the time were also the sons-in-law (*damad*) of the sovereigns. See Murphey,
"The Historical Setting," in *The Intimate Life of an Ottoman Statesman, Melek Ahmed Pasha
(1588–1662)* (New York, 1991), p. 32. Murphey also attributes the center-provincial marriage
ties to the need for centralization and neutralizing potentially quarrelsome elements. These
marriages established kinship ties between the important families of the provinces, and the
central government provided the means to co-optation, wealth, and power.

[11]Fleischer, "Royal Authority, Dynastic Cyclism," p. 212.

[12]That the Ottoman state moved from a patrimonial to a more rational-bureaucratic
structure has been demonstrated by Inalcık at various times; see Halil Inalcık, "Osmanlı
Hukukuna Giriş: "Örfî-Sultanî Hukuk ve Fatih'in Kanunları," in *Osmanlı Imparatorluğu,
Toplum ve Ekonomi* (Istanbul, 1993), pp. 319–41. He further discusses the implications of such

During expansion and consolidation it was necessary for the state to weave together the various populations of nomads, peasants, merchants, and artisans into a common entity and purpose—that of contributing to the welfare of state and society. Conquest also introduced to the Ottomans the previously autonomous and powerful local power holders, who had to be integrated into the system and convinced to relinquish at least part of their revenue to the new state. With the conquest of the Balkans and then the Arab lands, new cultural and religious groups had to be incorporated, settled, and respected in their different identities, inducing them to contribute to the welfare of the empire. The ruling class was to realize these needs in their function as warriors and administrators. The ruling class described by Inalcık, "called *askeri*, literally the 'military', includ[ing] those to whom the Sultan had delegated religious or executive power through an imperial diploma, namely officers of the court and the army, civil servants, and *ulema*,"[13] was the class created by the state for the purposes of the state and would remain faithful to the sultan since they depended on him for their privileges. The *askeri* class was to be differentiated from the *reaya*, "comprising all Muslim and non-Muslim subjects who paid taxes but who had no part in the government" and who were specifically excluded: "it was a fundamental rule of the Empire to exclude its subjects from the privileges of the 'military'. Only those among them who were actual fighters on the frontiers and those who had entered the *ulema* class after a regular course of study in a religious seminary could obtain the sultan's diploma and thus become members of the 'military' class."[14]

The *askeri* class,[15] endowed with the sole right to bear arms and to receive revenues and land grants, was also the embodiment of the sultan's

---

a transformation from a Weberian perspective in arguing that the bureaucracy developed its own internal solidarity, justifying its actions as being for the good of both religion and the state. See Halil Inalcık, "Comments on 'Sultanism': Max Weber's Typification of the Ottoman Polity," *Princeton Papers in Near Eastern Studies* 1 (1992): 63–64.

[13]Inalcık, "The Nature of Traditional Society: Turkey," in *Political Modernization in Japan and Turkey*, ed. Robert Ward and Dankwart Rostow (Princeton, 1964), p. 44.

[14]Ibid. This societal distinction and its implications have been described by Shinder, who discusses the different theories of the state regarding the Ottoman Empire. He represents the political differentiation used by Lybyer and Wittek versus the more sociocultural model of Inalcık and Itzkowitz in which the differentiation is more elaborate, while still maintaining the primary ruling class–subject class dichotomy. See Shinder, "Early Ottoman Administration in the Wilderness," pp. 499–501.

[15]Here I use the term "class" carefully since debates have belabored this point. The *askeri* was clearly a class in the economic sense because of its particular position in the productive

absolute power. Although absolute royal authority belonged to the sultan only, this authority was exercised in his name by this class of men who were his own creation, his slave-servants. The palace that acted as the central headquarters of the state housed these slave-servants, trained and educated them in the Ottoman customs, and channeled them into the military or administrative routes according to their skills. In the process, the sultan assured that the *askeri* would be loyal to him and help him protect his absolute rule. Wars and slave markets gave way to the more standardized *devşirme* as the source of slaves. Here, under local supervision Christian villagers were to surrender all their male children between the ages of eight and twenty, who were brought to Istanbul where their Ottomanization began.[16] In the words of one author, "So perfectly did the Palace School mold aliens of widely divergent race and creed to the Turkish type, and so thoroughgoing was the process of assimilation, that there are on record few instances of rebels and renegades among officials educated within its walls."[17] Muslim subjects were excluded from this process because it was believed that they would abuse their position, whereas Christians who were given a chance to rise in an alien system would become zealous at the task of maintaining it.[18] Moreover, it seems that, as in most other Islamic empires, an attempt was made not to disturb agriculture by pulling the peasantry into the army and to use in their stead

---

apparatus of Ottoman society, and it did reproduce itself within that position. Partly because of its origins and partly because of the strength of the Ottoman state, the *askeri* was not autonomous.

[16]Inalcık, *The Ottoman Empire,* p. 78.

[17]Barnette Miller, quoted in Metin Kunt, "Ethnic Regional (*Cins*) Solidarity in the Seventeenth-Century Ottoman Establishment," *International Journal of Middle Eastern Studies* 5 (1974):234. There is, however, a certain amount of controversy around the issue of whether the *devşirme* was the main cause of the loyalty of the slave-servants in the Ottoman Empire. Some of the controversy regards whether these men cut off their connections to their original lands and families or kept an interest in the future of their homeland. Whereas H. A. R. B. Gibb and Harold Bowen argue that these children were totally cut off from their parents and their regions, Albert Howe Lybyer disagrees and defends the thesis that at least some of them might have kept their initial associations and their belief in Christianity. See Gibb and Bowen, *Islamic Society and the West* (Oxford, 1957), 1:43,[l] and Lybyer, *The Government of the Ottoman Empire in the Time of Suleiman the Magnificent* (Cambridge, Mass., 1913), pp. 68–69. Kunt in "Ethnic Regional (*Cins*) Solidarity," added to this literature by demonstrating that, when these slave-servants reached positions of power and privilege, they frequently reestablished contact with their area of origin, even spoke the language and wore the garb of their original homeland. This demonstrates that they kept some loyalty to their homeland, but it does not demonstrate that they were thereby not loyal to the sultan.

[18]Inalcık, *The Ottoman Empire,* p. 78.

slaves who themselves were less involved in the economic production process of the empire.[19]

From early times, the Ottomans maintained the *askeri* class by blending a meritocratic system with sultanic favoritism to enhance the position of descendants or reward preferred clients. Max Weber emphasized the more discretionary aspect of rule in the patrimonial system: "The ruler's favor or disfavor, grants and confiscations, continuously create new wealth and destroy it again."[20] Ottoman historians, on the other hand, have praised the system for its favoring of upward mobility based on talent and ability. As the polity moved away from patrimonialism, merit or professional networks and solidarity gained importance as determinants of status.[21] In fact, although there is no doubt that the better skilled were given a chance, it is not entirely correct to conceive of the Ottoman system as meritocratic. In the workings of the *devşirme,* the system of merit was established and continued throughout one's career. In the central as well as the provincial system, those who did well were rewarded with better positions and more opportunities for the acquisition of wealth and status. This was the perception of many travelers in the Ottoman Empire in the sixteenth century especially. For example, Ogier Ghiselin de Busbecq attests to this in his Turkish letters. But, especially at the palace, positioning and important connections also helped tremendously to get oneself noticed. In times when patrons quickly fell in and out of favor, it became important to manipulate connections even more carefully. Metin Kunt demonstrates this well in his story of the Derviş Mehmed Pasha, who ended up as a successful grand vizier. Derviş Pasha not only established ties with his superiors and his patrons; in fact, he made his first move by establishing ties with a man with whom he shared a patron. The importance of this tie was that this man had just been appointed to a state position. Derviş Pasha's acumen, then, was in his ability to connect with another client of the same patron, then appointed to a state position.[22]

---

[19]They were not excluded from these activities either. Slaves were used in trade and in large agricultural enterprises. It was usually freed slaves who participated in trade and became commercial agents in long-distance trade. In the case of agriculture, slave labor was used when regulations about the *reaya* forbade their use on large estates (*çiftliks*). See Inalcık, "Servile Labour in the Ottoman Empire," in *The Mutual Effects of the Islamic and Judeo-Christian Worlds: The East European Pattern,* ed. Abraham Asher, Tibor Halasi-Kun, and Bela K. Kiraly (New York, 1979), pp. 25–52.

[20]Max Weber, *Economy and Society: An Outline of Interpretive Sociology,* ed. Guenther Roth and Claus Wittich (Berkeley, 1978), 2:1099.

[21]Stanford J. Shaw, *History of the Ottoman Empire and Modern Turkey* (Cambridge, 1976), and Lybyer, *The Government of the Ottoman Empire.*

[22]Metin Kunt, "Derviş Mehmed Paşa, Vezir and Entrepreneur: A Study in Ottoman

The servant elite was characterized by its utter lack of autonomy. This slave-servant system that provided the sultan his military and administrative instruments—a central janissary army, other central troops, all bureaucratic officials, and the members of the imperial council—also prevented independent policy and action. The state-created attributes of this slave-servant system ensured that the ruling class could not develop an autonomous identity and institution outside the state itself. Membership in the *askeri* was allowed according to established criteria. These were then individuals who were sustained through state interaction and acquired their status through the state. Having no independent basis of power or wealth of their own, they remained subservient and, as Carter Findley aptly argues, their post in life was much different from their European counterparts in both medieval and modern times. Accordingly, no corporate institutions such as were common in Europe were ever to develop in the Ottoman Empire.[23]

The lack of a corporate body—which I here confine to the elites—manifested itself in the difficulties of acquiring power, wealth, and status independently from the state and in the numerous checks and counterchecks on each official's discretionary power. For example, accumulation of wealth and status did not confer political power on individuals; only the state conferred political power. On rare occasions, members of the ruling class acquired wealth and power as it was bestowed by the ruler.[24] Furthermore, the practice of confiscation (*musadara*) guaranteed that no individual would accumulate a fortune that could turn him into a potential contender.[25] Important central and regional positions were held in check by other equally important and centrally assigned positions. Even the grand vizier, who was "the absolute deputy in the exercise of his [the sultan's] political and executive authority" and the foremost military commander, did not exercise unchecked power. Besides the men of religion, the head of the finance department and the leader of the janissary corps were positions used to check the power of the grand vizier.[26] This central system thus included within itself individuals whose self-interested in-

---

Political-Economic Theory and Practice," *Turcica* 9 *(1977):* 197–214.

[23]Findley, *Bureaucratic Reform in the Ottoman Empire*, pp. 14–15.

[24]Ibid., p. 15.

[25]The practice of confiscation has been explained by Rifaat Abou-el-Haj, "The Ottoman Vezir and Paşa Households, 1683–1703: A Preliminary Report," *Journal of the American Oriental Society* 94 (1974): 446, n. 36, and by Gilles Veinstein, "Trésor public et fortunes privées dans l'empire ottoman (milieu XVIᶜ–début XIXᶜ siècles)," *Actes des journées d'études Bendor* (1979), p. 122.

[26]Inalcık, *The Ottoman Empire*, pp. 95–96.

stincts were held in check, but state interests were given free rein within the governing body of the imperial council. This system of rule extended into provincial government, where it was replicated on a smaller scale. At the same time, under the confines of this system, a cohesive whole was maintained at the level of the imperial council. The concept of rule through consultation (*müşavere*) bound together the sultan, members of the state (*ulu'l-emr*), and religious leaders in an attempt to reach coherent, state-level decisions.[27]

Among the most important institution of the patrimonial system of rule was the janissary army, a standing infantry corps maintained by the treasury until it was abolished by the state. As Weber argued for patrimonial systems in general, the Ottoman sultan maintained an army paid for by him, at his command, and which could be used against society itself. The janissary corps was the typical patrimonial institution ensuring the sultan's safety. It functioned as his private army, independent of the subjects of the realm, and joined the sultan at his side in war.[28] The janissaries were not the only central army. Other central troops, such as the Six Cavalry Divisions making up the *kapıkulu* military division, also bred and maintained at the center, were the sultan's servile elites. In many ways, the central army was devised to protect the sultan's household and offset provincial power holders, whether from various older established dynasties or from tribesmen swept in by invasions.[29]

Yet the state-janissary relationship was not an untroubled one. As the sultans imposed their will on these military men, the changing means of warfare gave the janissaries more bargaining power vis-à-vis the state. Control of the janissaries, because of their location at the seat of power and their quick-to-challenge nature, could be difficult. One of the main challenges occurred mainly because army-state relations interfered with the fiscal side of centralization. For example, Mehmed II, who understood clearly the demands of centralization and the necessity of a solid fiscal policy—which would reinforce his ability to pay this army—was also forced to debase the currency (*akçe*) at his accession to the throne and later during his reign on a routine basis. This was done with the understanding that such policies were detrimental to the janissaries and that they were likely to fight them.[30] As a result of the hardship experienced,

[27]Murphey, "The Historical Setting," p. 34.

[28]Weber, *Economy and Society*, 2:1015–19.

[29]Shinder, "Early Ottoman Administration in the Wilderness," p. 514.

[30]Kafadar explains this very well in his work. He argues that a strong treasury meant that the sultan could be independent because he could use his treasury to maintain his main

the janissaries struck a bargain with Beyazıd II not to debase the coinage at his accession to the throne.[31]

The struggle between the sultan and his immediate patrimonial army rekindled during the reign of Murad III (1574–95), in 1589, when the members of the *kapıkulu* army revolted against the policies of the main fiscal architect of the sultan, his friend and companion the governor-general (*beylerbeyi*) of Rumelia, Mehmed Pasha. The new sultan's centralization policies combined with the hardships of war on the Iranian border and the subsequent debasement of the coinage all acted to trigger the revolt. The rebels demanded Mehmed Pasha's head and warned the sultan to accede to their demands, but the revolt subsided quickly and contemporary narrators affirm that the sultan was never really threatened. The rebels had simply condemned the concept of two powerful men at the center. The soldiers did not alter their allegiance to the center; they opposed the notion of two centers.[32] Over time the bargaining power of the central army steadily increased, until finally the sultan's realization of its increased autonomy and power led to the janissaries' demise.[33] Yet it is fair to say that, during the period under study here, their size grew to the detriment of other troops, especially as the European wars required more and more firepower.[34] The central army celebrated its heyday, and the state made sure it glowed in this brilliance.

If the central army was the permanent patrimonial arm of the ruler, the provincial army, composed of a mixture of local military power holders incorporated at the time of the conquest and others sent out from the center, was the representative of the Ottomans' glory in the provinces. In relations between center and periphery, the central army rivaled the regional

---

army, the janissaries. Yet this very fiscal policy of the state could not be maintained unless it hurt the janissaries directly, since it meant the debasement of the *akçe* as a regular measure of filling up the treasury. Kafadar argues that Mehmed II made use of recoinage and debasement as a regular component of his fiscal policy. See Kafadar, "When Coins Turned into Drops of Dew," pp. 51–54.

[31] Ibid., p. 53.

[32] Kafadar uses the poem of a rebel to indicate this controversy: "Can two kings rest in one palace? Or in one home reside two lions? In short, accept either him or us, o lord! Two sultans cannot employ so many slaves." Ibid., p. 223, n. 129.

[33] The destruction of the janissaries occurred in 1826 during the reign of Mahmud II. But even earlier Selim III had been able to bypass the janissaries by erecting a new army, the *nizam-ı cedid*, to replace these seditious military elements with increasing say in government affairs. See Stanford Shaw and Ezel Kural Shaw, *History of the Ottoman Empire and Modern Turkey*, Vol. 2.

[34] Whereas the corps counted 10,000 men in 1480, by the end of the seventeenth century it counted nearly 54,000 men. The cavalry, on the other hand, declined in size and importance in this last century. Inalcık, *The Ottoman Empire*, p. 83.

armies, the central bureaucracy countered the regional, and within the different administrative regions of the empire military, administrative, and policing functions were disputed by different power holders. These rivalries and disputes were designed to pit different groups against each other in competition for state rewards, that is, to maintain a state-controlled contest in society. Each of these confrontations, of the state with its own units and of intrasocietal units, enhanced the autonomy of the state.

Provincial officials at all levels were rotated to prevent the establishment of any privileged house away from the center. In this system—which Weber terms prebendal—[35] the land did not belong to the cavalrymen or the governors; it belonged to the state, which administered it carefully. In 1528, about 87 percent of the land was state-owned (*miri*).[36] Brief tenure in office, facilitated by state ownership of land, was certainly an effective mechanism of central control.[37] Generally, provincial officials were assigned to a different location every three years to prevent them from acquiring clients loyal to themselves and, by implication, disloyal to the sultan. Thus the system prevented the establishment of any legal relation between the landholder and the land. Yet, by allowing the sons of landholders to get land grants (often in regions other than their fathers'), this class was able to reproduce itself in some fashion.

The cavalry army, the essence of the Ottoman provincial system, consisted of prebendal land (*timar*) holders and their retinues. The timar system was based on the allocation of land to members of the cavalry in return for service in the provincial army. The exchange was simple: the state allocated a specified plot of land comprising a certain number of villages to the cavalryman, who collected the taxes from its peasantry, ensured his livelihood, and raised a retinue for war. The timar holder therefore had to prepare for battle and administer the villages under his jurisdiction.[38] Successful warriors were rewarded by larger domains. In addition to war making, the state assigned the tasks of rural administration, security, and policing to provincial officials.

The timar holders made up a class with the proviso that it existed and remained functional as individuals who saw their fortunes tied to the state that manipulated their tenure arrangements. In this sense, to borrow a

---

[35]Weber, *Economy and Society,* 2:1077–79.

[36]Inalcık, *The Ottoman Empire,* p. 110.

[37]Weber also emphasizes this point in his discussion of patrimonial rule and the control of potential contenders to power; see *Economy and Society,* 2:1043.

[38]Inalcık, *The Ottoman Empire,* p. 108.

term from Marx, they remained a class-in-itself.[39] In terms of their own interest as a class, the tımar holders were not well positioned, since they were formally linked to the state and not to other tımar holders. Individual fortunes were entirely contingent on the state: individual members were rewarded for prowess at war, were dismissed, rotated, or even cast out of the system. The system as such worked because rewards kept the officials content. In other words, the logic of the system was presented in terms of the acquisition of larger domains; the more successful the warrior, the larger his domain. Tımar holders were thus induced to aspire to larger domains and perceived the rotation system as meritocratic rather than controlling. As Irène Beldiceanu-Steinherr and others have made clear, this worked especially well when the empire was expanding and tımar holders were ready to move for better and more land.[40] But this circumstance was to change in the mid-seventeenth century.

The larger provincial system replicated the tımar along different levels. The provincial army was put together by a district official (*subaşı*), claimed by the district governor (*sancakbeyi*), and went to war under the command of the governor-general (*beylerbeyi*). Each of these officials was granted revenues from land and taxes in accordance with rank and accomplishment. The governor-general, who held the military command of the troops, convened a provincial council that largely mirrored the central one. He met regularly with the legal, financial, and administrative functionaries of the provinces. With the help of his two tımar officials, he advised the central state on tımar appointments, providing a certificate (*tezkere*) for deserving soldiers or reporting those deserving of punishment.[41] He was naturally provided with enough autonomy to advise the central state on local conditions and men deserving promotion, but this status did not translate into any independent initiative, because both his treasurer and his judge were central appointees whose loyalty and interests were also directed to the state.[42] Similar arrangements were made regarding the lower-level officials subordinated to the governor-

[39]I refer here to the distinction between a class-in-itself and a class-for-itself, the second representing the class that is able to act in its own interests.

[40]Irène Beldiceanu-Steinherr, "Loi sur la transmission du tımar (1536)," *Turcica* 11 (1979):78–102.

[41]For information on the function of the *beylerbeyi*, see Ibrahim Metin Kunt, *The Sultan's Servants: The Transformation of Ottoman Provincial Government, 1550–1650* (New York, 1983), pp. 26–29; Inalcık, *The Ottoman Empire*, p. 117; Douglas Howard, "The Ottoman Tımar System and Its Transformation, 1563–1656," Ph.D. diss., Indiana University, 1987, pp. 82–83.

[42]Gyorg Kàldy-Nagy, "XVI. Yüzyılda Osmanlı Imparatorluğunda Merkezi Yönetimin Başlıca Sorunları," *Tarih Araştırmaları Dergisi* 7 (1969): 49–55.

general. The district governors who administered the original units of
rule, the *sancaks*,[43] also recommended individuals for the granting and
dismissal of tımars and formed the link between the state and the *sancak*
as well as among units.[44]

The provinces were also administered and controlled by judges, part of
the larger literati (*ilmiye*) class whom Inalcık defines as "a privileged
group whose status and hierarchy was based on the level of certified
knowledge in the Islamic sciences."[45] A hierarchically organized, semiautonomous bureaucratic apparatus under the control of the sultan, this
group bestowed unique judicial authority on its members. At its top was
the *şeyh-ül-islam*, the most prominent and powerful member of the ulema,
followed by the chief justice of Rumelia and Anatolia. These men were in
turn followed by various ranks of judges (*kadıs*) ranging from the judge of
Istanbul to the small-town judges resident across the empire. The kadıs
assigned to regional posts were to employ law only for the administrative
purposes of the state.[46] These representatives of the sultan practiced in the
provinces according to secular (*kanun*) and religious (*şeriat*) law. In accordance with the traditional rule of patrimonialism, "Ottoman law attached great importance to precedent and gave wide discretionary powers
to the judges, whose decrees (*ferman*) frequently instruct simply to act in
accordance with the law that is customarily applied."[47] This was also quite
different from legal practice in western Europe, where rational law developed independent of the administrative purposes of the state.

Judges were administrators and adjudicators; they also managed to in-
tegrate various dissimilar forces in Ottoman society. As Madeline Zilfi
maintains, "In these [judges] and in the strength of their ideological ties
to the official center, the ulema of the hierarchy, lay the guarantee that
Ottoman society would preserve not only its Sunni identity but its cen-

---

[43]Kunt, *The Sultan's Servants*, p. 14. These are the units for which provincial rules
and regulations were drawn up. The cadastral surveys were also conducted for each unit
separately.

[44]Kunt, *The Sultan's Servants*, pp. 23–25.

[45]Inalcık, "The *Ruznamçe* Registers of the *Kadıasker* of Rumeli as Preserved in the Istanbul Müftülük Archives," *Turcica* 20 (1988): 251–75.

[46]This is not to say that the Islamic religious establishment was insignificant. Overall it
"represented the greatest power within the state independent of the grandvizier," as well as
forming an organized religious hierarchy fulfilling religious and civil duties of administration. At the top, the *şeyh-ül-islam* interpreted religious law (*şeriat*) and only slowly managed
to increase his power *within* the government. Not only did he gain and maintain jurisdiction
of the religious and legal establishment, he also fought for independence from state officials,
especially the grand vizier. Inalcık, *The Ottoman Empire*, p. 96.

[47]Kunt, *The Sultan's Servants*, pp. 74–75.

trist and legalitarian character as well."[48] This network of trained Islamic scholars helped counter the independent and heterodox religious forces in the hinterland. Judges and other members of the ulema represented a distinct alternative to Sufi orders, which attracted the people, directing them toward heterodox belief and sometimes oppositional politics. The Sufi orders—some of which were heterodox in belief—were probably the most potentially organized force in society and were neutralized by the state either through co-optation of their leadership or through the counterforce of the Sunni religious establishment.[49] Another important integrative function of the judge was the intermediary position he could assume in the interaction between peasant and landholder, settling disputes to serve the interests of regional stability. Because both landholder and judge were state officials, this intermediary position integrating the peasant directly into the realm of the state made for tension between the sultan's servants. Their relationship was envenomed by the fact that the state gave both the military-administrative and the religious-administative authorities overlapping powers; often the timar holder or his deputies exercised their penal authority without regard to the judge,[50] thereby increasing the amount of diffuseness and confusion in the system. Crossing the line between the two parallel administrations, as when judges became district governors or governor-generals, potentially increased the competition and tension between regional power holders.[51]

The relationship between the government and the judges was not immune to conflict either, since tension between these was also established in the practice of rotation and the dependence of these officials on the state for their positions, rewards, and interim pay when they were out of office. Although the main argument for the establishment of a rotation system among the ulema seems to have been the drastic increase in the number of judges, the practice seems to have started early enough to also be seen as a regulation system. Data from the appointment registers dem-

[48]Madeline Zilfi, *The Politics of Piety: The Ottoman Ulema in the Postclassical Age (1600–1800)*. Studies in Middle Eastern History 8 (Minneapolis, 1988), p. 26.

[49]The Bektashis as well as the Mevlevis were tied to the state. The Bektashis were incorporated as the chaplains of the janissaries and the Mevlevis "acquired the right to gird a Sultan with a holy sword upon his accession." Ira M. Lapidus, *A History of Islamic Societies* (Cambridge, 1988), p. 326. Inalcık makes a similar argument about the incorporation of the different heterodox orders into the political center.

[50]Gibb and Bowen refer to this problem as well. They argue that the result was the creation of "a series of conflicting and overlapping jurisdictions." *Islamic Society and the West*, 1:128.

[51]Ibid., 1:117–18.

onstrate that judgeship was limited by a fixed period of tenure. The re-script of 1597 makes it clear: "A new candidate (*mulazim*) shall not be appointed before he completes three years (of waiting).... The cadis [judges] of small towns shall be in possession of their post for two full years."[52] As Inalcık concludes from the registers, the duration of judge-ship at a post kept decreasing; it went from three years to two and then to twenty months, and by the eighteenth century the period had been re-duced to eighteen months.[53] Rotation as it applied to judges had a det-rimental effect on both the judges and their constituencies, because judges who held their positions for a specified period of tenure were practically taken off the payroll by being put out of office for a certain period of time before reentering the system. The period out of office was seen as one during which the judge would be able to work with his mentor, increas-ing his knowledge to qualify for a better position.[54] As in the case of other provincial officials, rotation was assigned a meritocratic meaning, making it palatable to those who endured its hardships. And hardships were com-mon, since when the judge relocated he remained unable to draw income in the form of court dues, and the lifestyle and the requirements of cere-monial attendance in Istanbul were quite costly. To make financial sur-vival possible, judges resorted to bribery, exploitation, and manipulation of the rural population to gain extra income before they went on rotation.

The patrimonial state performed its task of elite control and shuffling so that elites were constrained by their lack of autonomy, and their de-pendence on the state for office, awards, and status and brought into a seemingly natural competition which Weber saw as determined by the "quasi-jurisdictional limitation of the powers of office."[55] How could similar control of potential societal organizations such as cities, guilds, village, and tribal associations be maintained?

The most important organizational aspect of the Ottoman Empire, as Mardin claims, was the absence of "civil society."[56] The state was able to incorporate a variety of groups—whether occupational, religious, or eth-nic—into its domain, bypassing the intermediate structures that gave so-ciety an independent existence. The absence of private property is one of the crucial aspects of this relationship. Such intermediate structures as "corporate bodies with autonomous jurisdiction . . . formed the institu-

[52]Inalcık, "The *Ruznamçe* Registers," p. 261.
[53]Ibid.
[54]Ibid., pp. 261–65.
[55]Weber, *Economy and Society,* 2:1029.
[56]Mardin, "Power, Civil Society," p. 264.

tional base of civil society in the West."[57] In general, the presence of many associations does not signal civil society either; often when trade associations or peasant communal associations are formed, they desire to solve the daily problems of production, distribution, and trade. Accordingly, they end up fostering localism. On the other hand, when these associations become larger than the local concerns, they come under the scrutiny of the state and run the danger of being captured by it. Civil society should be arrived at from the right balance of associations, networks of affiliation that contain the state as well as constrain it. This was never the case in the Ottoman Empire. Civil society did grow in western Europe, and one of the most important developments to come out of this institutional base in Europe was the relatively stronger self-governing towns that had an enormous impact on the rise of the West.[58] The components of the Ottoman narrative are different.

In the Ottoman lands, the state subjugated economic activity to political considerations. It strongly regulated economic activity, controlled and manipulated cities, created them and restricted their associational, commercial, and political activities.[59] In return, it promised control of trade routes, transportation, and security in the hinterland. The main reasons for this regulation ranged from the enrichment of the treasury to the provisioning of the cities, especially of Istanbul, the seat of power. It was the need to feed Istanbul that forced the state to organize production and distribution into a vast integrated economic system that encompassed the entire empire.[60]

Control of the cities and merchants and regulation of the price mechanisms (*narh*) were the center's main channel to ensure that the people were fed and the elite content. The elites in particular were of concern to the state because they received fixed incomes and were therefore dependent on stability in the market. As Cemal Kafadar explains, the *narh* was not a haphazard institution of irrational state price control; rather, it was

[57]Ibid.

[58]Ibid. See Weber, *Economy and Society;* Daniel Chirot, "The Rise of the West," *American Sociological Review* 50 (1984): 181–95; Reinhard Bendix, *Nation-Building and Citizenship* (Berkeley, 1977). I am also indebted to Naomi Chazan for this understanding of civil society.

[59]Mardin, "Power, Civil Society," p. 264. Inalcık explains that this was in accordance with all Near Eastern empires, where the state would be actively involved in building and revitalizing cities, towns, and villages, as the historian al-Tabari described and rationalized for the Sassanids. This was because the authorities believed that the welfare of state and society was dependent on the close regulation of economic and agricultural activity. These would feed the people and fill the treasury. See Inalcık, *The Ottoman Empire,* p. 140.

[60]Ibid., p. 145.

a carefully devised system based on extensive data collected about the market and its movement. Furthermore, the evolution of these regulations from the time of the early conquerors to the rigorous establishment of law codes on market supervision (*ihtisab kanunnameleri*) by Mehmed II and then Beyazid II was part of centralization.[61] Since before market control markets had to be created, especially in newly established cities, policies of forcible settlement were at the core of this state need. Mehmed the Conqueror is famous for his forced settlements of minorities into Istanbul to stimulate trade and commerce in his new capital.

The guild was the economic institution most likely to capture autonomy for itself. H. A. R. B. Gibb and Harold Bowen, looking for similar associational and corporate identities as in Europe, argue that guilds in the Ottoman Empire were fairly organized. Remnants of the more powerful thirteenth- and fourteenth-century Anatolian city professional societies, which developed out of a tradition of Islam and specific codes and ethics (*futuwwa*), were incorporated into the government realm of authority with centralization. On whose initiative were the Ottoman guilds formed, that of merchants and craftsmen or of the state? Opinions vary. While Mardin, Ira Lapidus, and Gabriel Baer argue that guilds were not formed at the initiative of their members, Inalcık describes the guilds as similar to western ones and contends that they were formed in a similar fashion. In the Ottoman Empire, the strong Islamic tradition of *hisba*, which affirmed the concern of the ruler for his people, meant that merchants and artisans would not be allowed to maximize their profits.[62] Most occupational groupings in the Ottoman cities were organized into "corporate bodies to enforce economic discipline and facilitate administration."[63] These bodies had the authority to execute the important internal affairs of the guilds, while for external business they were under the obligation to comply by the strong rules and regulations established by the state and traditional practice. *Hisba* was a long-established tradition that gave the state the power to interfere in the market mechanism and redirect it for the supposed good of society. There is therefore little doubt that the guilds were in fact less than autonomous organizations within society. They might have started with greater autonomy and have lost it with the centralization of the state.[64]

---

[61]Kafadar, "When Coins Turned into Drops of Dew," pp. 118–24.

[62]This is not accepted by all scholars; see Lapidus, *A History of Islamic Societies*, p. 330.

[63]Ibid. On the question of *hisba*, Barkan and Inalcık differ.

[64]Inalcık, in fact, acknowledges that guilds lost the autonomy they once had. See *The Ottoman Empire*, and "Capital Formation in the Ottoman Empire," *Journal of Economic History* 29 (1969): 97–140.

Religious and ethnic minorities were other separate groups with potential autonomy, at least in their internal affairs. Especially in the major cities, Jews, Greeks, and Armenians had been established as communities, with internal jurisdiction of their affairs, and had managed to order their relationships with the outside world through both their leaders and a series of local arrangements.[65] Yet, again, they were never given autonomy for more than internal issues of community government. And even then new research suggests that the government kept a close eye on the internal legal affairs of the communities, so much so that we see in the court records that minorities made extensive use of the Muslim courts.[66] Although these communities seemed to be independent decision-making units, their decisions were all internal and not relevant to the organization of society, to production in society, or to the potential interaction between classes. They were decisions regarding internal religious administration, community maintenance, election of leaders, and the patterned interaction with the state. They did not affect any other group in society.

Gibb and Bowen refer to other institutions related to rural and tribal organization and argue for the autonomy and community organization of these as well. There are a few key difficulties with this representation. On the one hand, the Ottoman state no doubt attempted to incorporate the periphery as it was conquered and to establish its domination over these territories. On the other hand, it did so by incorporating or sending elites to administer for them, relying on an intricate vertical chain of command that ended with the rural producer. In the process, it tied, through a distant loose association, every unit to a center, and every center to a slightly larger central unit. The end result of this chain of association and surrendering of surplus to the state was the extreme isolation of the individual

---

[65]Aron Rodrigue shows how this relationship worked. The degree of corporate autonomy these groups had as well as the boundaries of their relationship with the state have been the subject of an interesting controversy among historians. Some have argued for a formal, structured, and closely regulated setup with each minority group forming an integrated and cohesive community, the *millet*. See Kemal Karpat, "Millets and Nationality: The Roots of the Incongruity of Nation and State in the Post-Ottoman Era," in *Christians and Jews in the Ottoman Empire*, ed. Benjamin Braude and Bernard Lewis (New York, 1982), 1:141–69; Shaw, *History of the Ottoman Empire*. Others have argued that there was no strict system by which minority affairs were regulated; rather, as Rodrigue puts it, these were "a series of local arrangements" overseen by the state authorities; Rodrigue, *French Jews, Turkish Jews: The Alliance Israélite Universelle and the Politics of Jewish Schooling in Turkey, 1860–1925* (Bloomington, 1990), p. 29. For the original debate, see Benjamin Braude, "Foundation Myths of the *Millet* System," in *Christians and Jews in the Ottoman Empire*, ed. Braude and Lewis, 1:69–88.

[66]Rodrigue, *French Jews, Turkish Jews*, p. 29. He also cites many other pieces of work in the literature that attest to this point. This is also corroborated by the case study I have conducted of the Manisa court records, which indicate heavy reliance of minorities on the Muslim court, not only in interfaith issues but also in the internal affairs of their community.

community, which was more bound by vertical than horizontal ties. Research has demonstrated that, even if village councils existed, rural organization was sorely lacking.[67]

To conclude, Ottoman state-society relations made the state's interests predominant and determined how society was organized. Traditional social structures were preserved insofar as they did not interfere with the sultan's rule and were incorporated and reshaped when they exhibited potentially autonomous strength. The central state apparatus dealt with peripheral contention in typical patrimonial fashion, through incorporation. The center was omnipotent; it was protected by a central patrimonial army of loyal slaves and it ruled the periphery through a prebendal corps of regional state officials, who if not similarly loyal were at least securely tied to the state through their social and economic interests. The center also gained its strength through its accepted flexibility, its ability to adapt to the various geopolitical variations it encountered. It was on this system of control and flexibility that the crisis of the seventeenth century was superimposed, and it is the central apparatus of this system that implemented changes in order to readjust its system of rule. It is important, then, to examine the changes the world system underwent during the late sixteenth and early seventeenth centuries and the impact on Ottoman state-society relations.

The Ottoman Empire in Context

By the middle of the sixteenth century, the Ottoman state had asserted its place in history; the reign of Süleyman the Magnificent had ensured the fear and respect of other kingdoms. The Ottomans were a force to be reckoned with, and no major European power was about to deny or challenge this politically. Rather, internal developments in Europe, mainly economic and technological, altered the international stage to challenge Ottoman boldness and strength. Two sets of questions need analysis here: first, the source of the Ottomans' strength and of their image of infallibility; second, the nature of the changes that contact with the western world and its particular crisis initiated in the realm of the Ottomans. Ma-

---

[67]For arguments about formal organization and informal association and control in the Ottoman society, see Gibb and Bowen, *Islamic Society,* 1:159. For the lack of rural organization see Inalcık, "Köy, Köylü ve Imparatorluk," *V. Milletlerarası Türkiye Sosyal ve Iktisat Tarihi Kongresi, Tebliğler* (Ankara, 1990), pp. 1–11; Karen Barkey, "Rebellious Alliances: The State and Peasant Unrest in Early Seventeenth-Century France and the Ottoman Empire," *American Sociological Review 56* (1991):699–715, and "The Uses of Court Records in the Reconstruction of Village Networks: A Comparative Perspective," *International Journal of Comparative Sociology 32* (1991): 196–216.

terial abounds on the glory of the early centuries, but there is a severe dearth of analysis regarding the crisis of the late sixteenth and early seventeenth centuries. It should also be pointed out that in popular understandings the crisis of the seventeenth century caused the decline of the Ottoman Empire after the Süleymanic period. I argue two points: that we do not really know the extent of the damage caused by the crisis, and that the Ottoman state did not deteriorate so severely as to justify talk of decline.

The success of Sultan Süleyman (1520–66) in international and domestic arenas was based on his ability to balance the conception of a grand empire abroad with stability and cohesion at home. This he achieved through campaigns against East and West begun at his accession to the throne and through reforms meant to strengthen the legal system.[68] From the conquest of Belgrade in 1521 to the numerous wars with the Hungarians and Persians to the maritime wars in the Mediterranean, the Ottomans incorporated new areas into the empire, areas that were both geopolitically essential and economically lucrative. The geopolitical instinct of control and consolidation took precedence, however. For example, one of the new sultan's first goals was to conquer Rhodes, whose knights were considered a menace to the control of the Eastern Mediterranean and a roadblock on the way to the newly conquered colonies of Egypt and Syria.[69] The wars with Hungary and Iran were to some extent wars of expansion, but even more they were wars of consolidation. In an attempt to consolidate his hold over the conquered territories of the West, Süleyman promoted discord in European lands, for example, by supporting the Protestant movements in France and Germany.[70]

By the end of Süleyman's reign, the Ottoman Empire had reached the comfortable geographic limits of expansion.[71] Thereafter, conquest and incorporation seemed to level off, as the ability of armies to reach the frontiers in good time diminished. An example is provided by the failure

---

[68]Among his numerous campaigns in the West, we can cite the conquest of Belgrade in 1521, Rhodes in 1522, the battle at Mohacs against Hungary in 1526, and the two indecisive campaigns waged against Vienna in 1529 and 1532. Conflict with Hungary was to be taken up later by means of naval warfare in 1534, followed by naval warfare against Venice. The rest of the reign is similarly filled with wars at the western front. Against the East, Süleyman undertook two major offensives: in 1534 Tabriz and then Baghdad were consolidated; a second, later campaign lasted long and remained unfruitful.

[69]V. J. Parry, "The Reign of Sulaiman the Magnificent, 1520–66," in *A History of the Ottoman Empire to 1730*, ed. M. A. Cook (Cambridge, 1980), pp. 79–80.

[70]Halil Inalcık, "State and Ideology under Sultan Süleyman I," in *The Middle East and the Balkans Under the Ottoman Empire: Essays on Economy and Society* (Bloomington, 1993), pp. 70–94.

[71]Bernard Lewis, *The Emergence of Modern Turkey* (Oxford, 1975), p. 24.

of the Persian campaigns Süleyman undertook toward the end of his reign. By the time armies reached the front, the campaign season was almost over and the armies were decimated. Nevertheless, during the late sixteenth century the Ottoman Empire fought wars successively on two fronts, on both the Safavid and the Habsburg borders—with Iran from 1579 to 1590 and with the Habsburgs from 1593 to 1606. The wars with Iran continued into the seventeenth century, on a full scale from 1588 to 1610 and on a smaller scale (expeditions to Erivan and Tabriz) from 1634 to 1638. Each sultan who came to the throne attempted a conquest or two in the East as well as advances in the West. During the second half of the sixteenth century, gains were interspersed with losses; the conquest of Cyprus (1570) was immediately followed by the losses of the Ottoman fleet at Lepanto (1571).

Ottoman internal policy related and intimately resembled international policy. Süleyman carefully carried out a program of consolidation and centralization, establishing rules and regulations for the government. From the development of a sophisticated registration and taxation apparatus to its elaborate bookkeeping techniques, the Ottoman state put together a strong centralist bureaucracy under Süleyman's rule.[72] Centralization and bureaucratization went hand in hand to extend the reach of different departments into the Ottoman realm. The finance department provides a good example of bureaucratization whereby the finances of the government grew to be operated by "a hierarchy of salaried scribes working in functionally differentiated groups according to regularized procedures."[73] In a further exhibit of development, the financial institution became highly flexible and adapted to the changing conditions of the empire.

Together with centralization, absolute patrimonial rule became entrenched with a blend of justice and authority. Resistance to the sultan was rarely tolerated, and high-ranking officials were often dismissed for dissenting opinions. Furthermore, under the centralist policies of the time, resistance from various groups was put down and rebellions were contained.[74] Despite the occasional harshness of imperial rule, Süleyman

---

[72]Ibid., pp. 34–35.

[73]Linda T. Darling, "Adaptations in Administration: The Ottoman Fiscal System," in *Political Economies of the Ottoman, Safavid, and Mughal Empires*, ed. Tosun Arıcanlı, Ashraf Ghani, and David Ludden. Forthcoming.

[74]I am referring here to the revolt of Canberdi al-Gazzali, the governor of Damascus, who tried to liberate the newly conquered territory of Syria and restore the Mamluk kingdom in

acquired the reputation for being the most just among Ottoman sultans. This was exemplified by the various edicts he sent to local authorities curtailing their power and ensuring the fair treatment of the peasantry.[75] Also, his rule allowed some provincial officials to remain in office for long periods of tenure, thereby decreasing exploitation of the peasantry. In short, the success of Süleyman's reign within Ottoman society was due mainly to his ability to control officials as well as turn them into loyal members of the Ottoman elite while preserving the policy of *adalet-istimalet*, that is, of restraint in taxation and exploitation.[76]

Whereas the Süleymanic era was the most rigorous time of consolidation, it was also the time when a certain flexibility in the system of rule became obvious as Süleyman himself tampered with the rules to adapt to international and local geopolitical circumstances. Strains of various kinds, exigencies on the part of vital segments of the ruling apparatus, had been present throughout the reign of Süleyman. The system, however, adjusted to incorporate them. For example, already during Süleyman's time the tımar system had started to lose its original constituency. People from outside the corps (*ecnebis*) were infiltrating the system and obtaining appointments. During the Persian campaign of 1534–35, when peasants fought in the war and were accorded tımars as reward, Süleyman assented and granted them an exemption. Later, however, he repealed this order and banned peasants from the tımar corps.[77] The reason may have been that too many peasants were leaving their land to join the wars, gaining tımars, and enhancing their status. What was good for the peasantry— the opportunity for upward mobility—ended up being detrimental to society; depopulation and decreased production ensued because peasants were the main producers. As a result, the experiment with moving the peasantry in and out of the military was halted, demonstrating that the system was not as rigid as doomsday pamphleteers described it.

The pamphleteers, who represent a major source of information for the sixteenth and seventeenth centuries, were disheartened by the flexibility of the Ottoman system of rule. In their observations, they made two basic

---

1527. Around the same time, from 1526 to 1528, revolts of *şeyhs* associated with Turcoman nomads were suppressed by Süleyman's forces. See Shaw, *History of the Ottoman Empire*, 1:87–93.

[75]Inalcık, in "State and Ideology," p. 75, mentions a 1521 order to kadıs in the provinces specifying the court fees to be exacted from the population.

[76]Ibid., 70–94.

[77]Julius Kàldy-Nagy, "The 'Strangers' (*Ecnebiler*) in the Sixteenth Century Ottoman Military Organization," in *Between the Danube and the Caucasus: A Collection of Papers*, ed. Gyorgy Kara (Budapest, 1987), p. 168.

mistakes: First, they referred to the Süleymanic era as one in which all segments of the society worked perfectly and the word of the law dominated;[78] this is incorrect since many analyses of the period demonstrate the system's flexibility and its manipulation of the code in order to maintain the health of society. Second, they attributed all problems of the seventeenth century to the internal changes of rule—the lack of strong leaders, the corruption and unpredictability they themselves were experiencing in their careers. Advice literature—the genre with which these pamphleteers became identified—located decline in the major political, economic, and military transformations of the empire. The sultan's decreasing interest in state affairs, irregular and unmeritocratic appointment of grand viziers, reduced effectiveness of the army, and ad hoc measures to fill the treasury were identified as the major causes of decline. Every major institution of the empire was described as being in a state of disrepair.[79] The focus on the internal rather than the international crisis demonstrates the shortsightedness of some of these bureaucrats and pamphleteers.[80] Nevertheless, the internal predicament the Ottomans faced was a product of the seventeenth-century crisis, which was omnipresent across Eurasia, and of the changes in economic and military relations between West and East.

The Crisis of the Seventeenth Century

There seems to be some agreement on the topic of a general crisis that struck the Asian and European continents in the late sixteenth and early seventeenth centuries. But although the crisis has been well documented in its manifestations, its causes have remained a focus of contention. It is often disputed which among these changes were the most crucial: the demographic and economic, or the political? The demographic changes

[78]See, for example, Koçi Bey, *Risale,* ed. Zuhuri Danışman (Istanbul, 1972).

[79]Bernard Lewis, "Ottoman Observers of Ottoman Decline," *Islamic Studies* 1 (1962): 71–87. In this article Lewis outlines two of the major treatises of the time, the *Asafname* of the Grand Vezir Lütfi Pasha and the *Risale* of Koçi Bey, as well as an essay titled "The Rule of Action for the Rectification of Defects" by Katip Çelebi.

[80]This is corroborated by Kafadar's analysis, which demonstrates that the pamphleteers concentrated, for example, on state-induced devaluations of the currency, especially during the times of accession, rather than on the price revolution, which was by far the more serious phenomenon. The price revolution was induced from the outside, whereas the periodic devaluations by the state at the accession of the sultan to the throne were internal mechanisms of filling up the treasury. See "When Coins Turned into Drops of Dew," p. 110.

were vast increases of the population in Europe and Asia starting in the early 1500s and leveling off only at the beginning of the seventeenth century. The economic changes in these areas were triggered by increases in prices during the same period. Further, in Europe, the demise of political institutions, the loss of power of major rulers, and popular revolts of various forms have been incorporated into the crisis framework.

The existence of some sort of crisis has been documented for the Ottoman Empire as well. The data on demographic and economic changes in the Ottoman Empire are scarce; only recently have regional details been filled in and greater accuracy gained. In the Ottoman Empire, as in the western world, the population in the sixteenth century seems to have doubled. If we take Ömer Barkan's figures for the empire as a whole, we have a population of 30 million people.[81] The economic and political dimensions of this crisis are not as clear cut, although three related issues stand out: monetary fluctuations, the price revolution, and state economic policy. The relationship between these issues as well as their cumulative effect has to be analyzed.

One of the first issues scholars connected to state action was that of the wide-ranging monetary fluctuations in the empire. From all accounts, these fluctuations began with the influx of silver from the New World, brought in by the increasing number of traders who entered the Turkish lands to buy goods. The influx of silver is said to have affected the Ottoman akçe, pushing it into a course of uncertainty. The structure of Ottoman commercial equilibrium was further affected because the cash that entered the empire usually did not stay put, instead moving on to Persia through the silk trade and from there to India to pay for spices and luxuries.[82] The continual debasement of the akçe has been seen in the context of this lack of structural equilibrium. According to Barkan, "the Ottoman Empire, caught up in the current of a great international inflation, tried ineffectually to counter its difficulties with devaluation. Devaluation, however, led to even greater dislocation of prices, and the empire was dragged from one financial crisis to another, unable to move against

[81]Ömer L. Barkan, "Essai sur les données statistiques des registres de recencement dans l'Empire Ottoman au XVe et XVIe siècles," *Journal of the Economic and Social History of the Orient* (1957):9-36. Fernand Braudel has similarly researched the population growth of the Ottoman Empire in the sixteenth century. He has come up with a smaller total of 22–26 million, which he seems to think fits better with the whole of the Western Mediterranean. See *The Mediterranean and the Mediterranean World in the Age of Philip II* (New York, 1972), 1:398.

[82]Cemal Kafadar, "Les troubles monétaires de la fin du XVIe siècle et la prise de conscience ottomane du déclin," *Annales: Economies, sociétés, civilisations* 2 (1991): 381–400.

the strong current that held it."[83] But Haim Gerber aptly demonstrates that this debasement was no more than the state's response to lowered treasury reserves and the impending need to pay soldiers. Furthermore, he shows that debasement was basically irrelevant to international trade, undermining explanations that have thrown all these factors together.[84]

Why was the treasury experiencing lowered reserves?[85] There are many answers, most not fully satisfactory. Were taxes being collected adequately? Both Goldstone and Gerber have suggested that the state was unable to collect taxes as well as it did in the fifteenth and sixteenth centuries. They have, however, no data to show this to be the case.[86] Linda Darling's research suggests that at least for most of the seventeenth century the finance department adjusted rather rapidly to devise alternate ways of increasing tax revenues.[87] Other arguments have been made about the amount of taxes and dues that did not see the state treasury and were instead skimmed by regional officials, especially governor-generals.[88] More important were the monetary setbacks resulting from changing international trade routes and the decreased role of the Ottoman state in the appropriation of trading benefits, which, as Gilles Veinstein reminds us, hurt the treasury substantially. The use of the Cape route for trade harmed the finances of Syria and Egypt, provinces that figured prominently in the revenues of the Ottoman state.[89] Added to these explanations is the impact of *celali* rebellions, which made it impossible for tax collectors to send cash back to Istanbul.

Geopolitical reasons are among the most important for the state's inability to increase its revenues. The changing nature of warfare at a time of increased wars of consolidation and territorial unity devastated the

[83]Barkan, "The Price Revolution of the Sixteenth Century: A Turning Point in the Economic History of the Near East," *International Journal of Middle Eastern Studies* 6 (1975): 14.

[84]Haim Gerber, "The Monetary System of the Ottoman Empire," *Journal of the Economic and Social History of the Orient* 25 (1982): 308–24.

[85]This is demonstrated by Barkan's figures. Whereas the 1527/28 budget recorded a surplus of 71,354,114 akçes, the 1581/82 budget showed 2,071,967 akçes. By the end of the seventeenth century, budgetary deficits would become drastic, amounting to as much as 45,000 akçes. Barkan, "The Price Revolution," p. 17. For detailed analyses of these budgets, see Barkan, "Osmanlı imparatorluğu bütçelerine dair notlar," *Istanbul Üniversitesi Iktisat Fakültesi Mecmuası* 17 (1955–56): 193–224.

[86]Gerber, "The Monetary System of the Ottoman Empire," p. 323; Jack Goldstone, *Revolution and Rebellion in the Early Modern World* (Berkeley, 1991), pp. 366–67.

[87]Darling, "Adaptations in Administration," pp. 1–36.

[88]Gerber, "The Monetary System of the Ottoman Empire," p. 323.

[89]Gilles Veinstein, "Trésor public et fortunes privées," p. 122. See also Barkan, "The Price Revolution," pp. 3–28; Mustafa Akdağ, *Türk Halkının Dirlik ve Düzenlik Kavgası* (Ankara, 1979).

state treasury. The Ottoman state engaged in many wars that did not always lead to conquests and hence to booty and lands and people to tax. These campaigns drew valuable resources from the state, the people, and the land. In the war with Iran, the state was obliged to spend the income of adjacent provinces such as Aleppo, Diyarbekir, and Erzurum, provinces that normally contributed significant amounts to the central treasury.[90] Also, new techniques of warfare devised by the enemy required their imitation in the empire. Whereas Europeans were moving toward hand gunpowder weapons like muskets, the Ottomans still held on to their major cavalry army, the *sipahi,* and simply added some regiments of soldiers equipped with firearms. When the Ottomans lost their ability to fight effectively against their European enemy, now equipped with firearms, they revamped their armies and their manner of fighting. The resulting composition of the armies required more cash, putting more and more strain on the treasury.

The price revolution is a second issue that has drawn the attention of all major scholars of the Ottoman Empire. This price hike that accompanied monetary fluctuations has been interpreted in various ways. The development of European industry and commerce no doubt had an important impact on the Ottoman economy. But the price revolution, which affected Asia as well as Europe, was also related to some extent to the increasing amount of money in circulation.[91] New interpretations have stressed the relationship between population growth, inelasticity of agriculture, and a resultant increase in prices, especially for wheat.[92] Whether because of the European impact or because of demographic factors, the economy of the late 1500s started experiencing a price increase that leveled off only toward the middle of the seventeenth century. Mustafa Akdağ presents data that attest to the fact that by 1609 wheat and sheep prices had risen to twenty times their price in 1520. The prices of cloth and other commodities like oil increased at least fivefold during the same period.[93] Barkan emphasizes the development of the "North Atlantic economy" as the major

[90]Barkan, "The Price Revolution," pp. 18–19.

[91]This point has been argued by numerous scholars for western Europe and by Barkan and Inalcık for the Ottoman Empire; see Barkan, "The Price Revolution," pp. 12–13; Inalcık, "The Ottoman Decline and Its Effects upon the Reaya," in *Aspects of the Balkans, Continuity and Change: Contributions to the International Balkan Conference, UCLA,* 1969, ed. H. Birnbaum and S. Vryonis (The Hague, 1972), pp. 348–49. Leila Erder and Sureiya Faroqhi make a similar argument in "Population Rise and Fall in Anatolia, 1550–1620," *Middle Eastern Studies* 15 (1979): 322–45.

[92]Goldstone, *Revolution and Rebellion,* pp. 360–62.

[93]Akdağ, *Türk Halkının Dirlik ve Düzenlik Kavgası,* p. 463.

causal linkage in the price revolution,[94] whereas a more monetarist view was proposed by Inalcık, who connects the influx of silver to the mechanism of inflation.[95] Kafadar, on the other hand, argues that the Ottoman Empire was ready for an inflationary push because of population growth, urbanization, expansion of commerce, and the increased moneterization of the empire. It seems that most of the factors cited above—population growth, foreign merchants' practices, and the influx of silver—had dire consequences for Ottoman state and society. If the state had to alter its taxation practices to increase the amount of revenue flowing to the treasury, or debase the akçe and thereby risk the wrath of the salaried employees of the state, society in its various groupings also paid a price. Most groups, except merchants, were severely hurt by the price increases, and peasants were hurt by the new tax collection practices and by the institution of tax farming.[96]

A third source of discussion in this debate is the role of the state. Here the argument is that the economic crisis that afflicted the Ottoman lands would probably have taken quite a different turn had the Ottoman state been able to relax its economic regulations. The crux of the problem was that Ottoman rulers were used to regulating the economy in order to maximize their revenues, to protect those classes of elites with fixed incomes, and to fulfill the needs of the internal markets. Various measures of filling the treasury were common: devaluation of the currency, taxation of the productive classes, and assessments from the trading of goods within the boundaries of the empire.[97]

As Europe developed, it encroached on the Ottoman Empire, forcing changes to which the state-controlled economy was unable to respond. Both Murat Çızakça and Mehmet Genç attribute the ensuing economic troubles of the Ottomans to the mercantilism of Europe as opposed to the policies of fiscalism and provisionism of the Ottoman Empire. Çızakça has documented the increasing imports into the Ottoman Empire of silk

---

[94]Barkan, "The Price Revolution," pp. 3–28.

[95]Inalcık, "Impact of the Annales School on Ottoman Studies and New Findings," *Review* 1 (1978): 69–96.

[96]Kafadar, "Les troubles monétaires," p. 389.

[97]Inalcık and others have pointed out the importance of the trade routes for the Ottoman treasury; from the silk exchanges that occurred in Bursa to the spice trade in Egypt, the Ottomans gathered riches from the customs duties. See Inalcık, "The Ottoman Economic Mind and Aspects of the Ottoman Economy," in *Studies in the Economic History of the Middle East*, ed. M. A. Cook (London, 1970), pp. 207–18, "Bursa and the Commerce of the Levant," in *The Ottoman Empire: Conquest, Organization, and Economy* (London, 1978), pp. 132–47, and "Capital Formation in the Ottoman Empire."

and woolen cloth, which caused a decline in local production as the sales of raw material increased.[98] In the words of Genç, "As a consequence of the system of provisionism the Ottoman state manipulated only with the exportation and usually did not interfere with importation. When the state did interfere with importation it was usually to encourage its volume, with fiscalist considerations."[99] Similarly, Benjamin Braude has documented the decline of Salonica's cloth industry. He too attributes these changes partly to the Ottoman state's lack of interest in economic policy. The Ottomans, he argues, were far more interested in the military aspects of state building and ignored the economic aspects that would have led them to protect their merchants and offer them incentives. He deplores the lack of an Ottoman protectionist policy because it led to the demise of many industrial centers.[100]

The Ottoman Empire at the turn of the seventeenth century, then, was hit by the effects of two related phenomena, and the state took action to incorporate and deal with these changes. In Europe, the crisis revived the European economy, altered the means of warfare, and renewed the commitment to encroach on lands conquered by the Turks. In the Ottoman Empire, the results were mixed. This crisis did not necessarily mean decline, however. The crisis was managed. The Ottoman state readapted to conditions of crisis, finding alternative ways of drawing surplus from its society and in the process, sometimes, controlling and consolidating even more than before. The internal economic and military constraints of the Ottoman system of rule set in motion a series of internal state responses quite different from those in Europe. The bureaucracy in its diverse offices adapted to maintain tax flows by altering fixed taxation to a more variable basis, changing the emphasis on certain taxes, exploiting cash revenue, and changing tax collectors. State officials devised these measures by paying careful attention to the state's particular relationship with each class in society while maintaining internal control and centralized administration. State-related and military goals were never forsaken for economic and commercial reorganization. Rather, the state tried to centralize and control each class by manipulating its own peculiar tie to that class. In

---

[98]Murat Çizakça, "Price History and the Bursa Silk Industry: A Study in Ottoman Industrial Decline, 1550–1650," *Journal of Economic History* 40 (1980): 533–50. Also see Çizakça, "Incorporation of the Middle East into the European World-Economy," *Review* 8 (1985): 353–77.

[99]This quotation, from an unpublished manuscript, is printed in Çizakça, "Incorporation of the Middle East," p. 370.

[100]Benjamin Braude, "International Competition and Domestic Cloth in the Ottoman Empire, 1500–1650: A Study in Undevelopment," *Review* 2 (1979): 437–51.

the process, it altered the determining conditions prevalent for the provincial elites by keeping them dependent on the state and by drastically increasing their intraclass competition and struggle. The seventeenth century left the provincial elites more divided than ever, incorporating within their ranks winners and losers. The combined effect of elite struggles and increased state exploitation left the peasantry at a similar loss regarding their interests. Their already isolated and fragmented communities were unevenly populated, and their weak ties to the landholders were further severed. Where they stayed, peasants acquired new landlords, unwilling to relieve their plight. Finally, as banditry emerged from the fetters of the rural communities with the generous help of the state, state makers used it to further regain strength and emerge aloft Ottoman society.

3

Ottoman Regional Elites: Divided but Loyal

M OST OF THE CLASSIC EUROPEAN LITERATURE on state consolidation concentrates primarily on the relationship between
the state and societal elites. Elite discontent and elite struggles, or intraelite competition, have been the overarching themes.[1] In
Europe, the state's centralizing efforts resulted in the opposition of disgruntled elites. In France, those elites who perceived themselves as losing
their privileges used their alliances with the peasantry to fight against an
aggressive and intrusive state. In other cases, as in England, a crown unable to regulate internal struggles and external commercial pressures was
further incapacitated by elite competition. In both these cases, the elites
were initially independent and autonomous, and their loss of privileges
through political and commercial causes turned them against the crown.
The history of European state formation is notable for the prominent role
of elite struggles against the state, with elites determined to stop short
this newly emerging center of power.

Unlike western European elites, Ottoman prebendal elites were unable
to oppose the state seriously. Even though the state precipitated internal
competition within their ranks and aggravated the conditions of their livelihood, because of their initial dependence and loyalty they continued to
search for solutions from within the state. Ottoman elites in the early sev-

---

[1]Charles Tilly, *The Contentious French* (Cambridge, 1986); William Brustein, "Class Conflict and Class Collaboration in Regional Rebellions, 1500–1700," *Theory and Society* 14
(1985): 445–68; Richard Lachmann, "Elite Conflict and State Formation in 16th and 17th
Century England and France," *American Sociological Review* 54 (1989): 141–62; Roland
Mousnier, "Recherches sur les soulèvements populaires en France avant la Fronde," *Revue
d'histoire moderne et contemporaine* 5 (1985): 81–113.

enteenth century did not look for solutions to the ills they experienced by rebelling against the state and challenging the structure of the state and society. If they rebelled, they did so to demand that they be incorporated into the state's privilege structure once again. This was true for both established elites of the provincial system and the newly recognized, strategically important bandit leaders. They were not interested in breaking the lineage of the Ottoman house of rule. This point clearly sets apart the conflicts within the Ottoman realm from the European and therefore has implications for the development of the state in both areas. Indeed, by the time the Ottoman elites started threatening the state, the structure of society was already altered to look more like the European feudal one.

The inability of the elites to oppose the Ottoman state during the century of consolidation and centralization has two causes. First, as explained in Chapter 2, Ottoman elites were trained by the state and tied their fortunes to it. Moreover, state manipulation ensured that they would lack autonomy. As these elites were hit by economic and political crises, often concurrently, they were unable to disassociate their future from that of the state. They searched for state-oriented solutions because traditionally both their status and livelihood were tied to the state. This was true of both the central and regional military, bureaucratic, and judicial elites. Even the short-lived challenges of the central troops were directed toward the state's privilege structure. A second factor disabling elite opposition was that the state, in response to the sociopolitical and financial demands of consolidation, created a provincial situation in which concerted, organized opposition was practically impossible. Even though the provincial actions of the state may not have been fully intentional or calculated, a regional policy can be pieced together. This regional policy played havoc with elites.

In this chapter, I argue that the main consequence of this regional policy was the creation of multiple layers of winners and losers among the elites. Within each group of provincial officials, the state managed to divide in such a way as to set landholder against landholder, governor against governor, and governor-general against governor-general. In the general atmosphere of competition, elites were unable to organize for concerted action against the state.

As in every centralizing state, the Ottoman government was also primarily interested in reinforcing provincial positions as well as deepening provincial loyalty. This latter decision required increasing central appointments in the provinces. As a result the main policy decision of the state turned out to reinforce the higher ranks of officials to the detriment of the lower ranks. This is because the simplest way to implement this decision was through the appointment of central officials to higher level regional positions, a function the central state kept firmly in its grip. When the lower levels of the provincial hierarchy lost at the expense of the higher levels, losers appeared in every category of officeholder. As a consequence—intended or unintended—elites were so divided that they were unable to ally against the state, and the manner in which the state divided them kept them faithful to the traditional arrangement of expecting rewards from the state. Thus, while Ottoman elites were systematically incapacitated, the state enjoyed autonomy from potential opposition and continued its consolidation activities, choosing and picking which segments of groups it would incorporate. This impotence on the part of elites was also reflected in their inability to make common cause with other societal groups, potential allies who could have aided in a struggle against the state.

How can we understand the framework of the state at this turning point in Ottoman history? I argue that the state at this time was neither the state of Süleyman the Magnificent nor that of decline. It was a state undergoing serious adjustment to the new conditions of internal and international existence. For all the success of the Ottoman state, state managers did not carefully follow a strong, calculated agenda of centralization. Rather than an overall principle of rule or a policy of centralization and control, state officials were far more interested in day-to-day difficulties. Although not necessarily clear in the historiography of this period, state managers made decisions of central and provincial control that were best suited to the international crisis and internal conditions. Precisely because of the need to respond and adapt to the demands of the new international order, there was no easily identifiable, clear-cut state policy between 1550 and 1650. Overall, the larger goals of state formation remained the same over the years; it was the implementation of these goals that did not follow a consistent path. Rather, implementation seemed to vary from period to period and from region to region. The Ottoman state followed a policy of crisis management, of temporary fixes to sometimes temporary problems. As a result, decisions that may seem chaotic were in fact quite rational responses to actual day-to-day events in the provinces.

My analysis in this chapter is divided into two main sections: one deals with the lower-level provincial officials, the landholding cavalry, and the other deals with the higher-level provincial officials, the governors and governor-generals.[2] Markedly different fates were experienced by each of

---

[2]See Appendix 1 for a description of the two provinces under study. Appendix 2 concentrates on the data: the registers, their format, and the sampling methods. Unless otherwise noted the data analysis in this chapter comes from the following BBA Tımar Ruznamçe Registers: 37, 46, 59, 676, 681, 685.

these groups, and variation occurred within the groups. My first set of data, from the period 1572–82, demonstrates a rather regular pattern with few deviations. The second set, from 1654–55, illustrates the change and the existence of a medley of decisions on the part of the state. My argument is constructed from a mix of narratives of the period, historical analyses, and data on provincial assignments. This latter is the clearest to interpret. Since the control of elites was carried out through their official positions, the transformation of rule in this period is most easily and best detected in the state's central and provincial appointments.

Narratives of the period differ according to their goals. Some belong to the chronicle genre, written at the turn of the sixteenth century, while others are political pamphlets written expressly to influence the sultan. This pamphlet literature, constructed in contrast-oriented fashion, displays the glorious achievements of the past, distinguishing them from the perceived decline and disintegration of the state. Their advantage for us lies in the description of the state and societal groups during the time of glory and as their relationship began to change. Their disadvantage lies in their teleology and personal biases.[3] A more traditional group of historians have taken the work of these pamphleteers at face value, transferring to our time the same understanding of an empire in decline. These scholars strike a similar note in their search for clear-cut policies on the part of the Ottoman state, seeking to categorize the state after the Classical Age as one either in decline[4] or in the process of incorporation into the world system.[5]

[3]Contemporary pamphleteers criticized most of the new policies which were different from those of the "classical period." Thus, for example, Koçi Bey wrote against the practice of *reaya* (he calls them *ecnebi* [foreigners] in this context) getting hold of tımars. This, he argues, was contrary to prior government practice and therefore wrong, and it brought about the decline of the tımar institution. Koçi Bey, *Risale,* ed. Z. Danışman (Istanbul, 1972), pp. 54–55. See also the work of an unknown author, *Kitab-i Müstetab,* ed. Yaşar Yücel (Ankara, 1974). See also Ayn-i Ali Efendi, *Kavanin-al-i Osman der Hülasa-yi Mezamin-i Defter-i Divan,* ed. Tayyib Gökbilgin (Istanbul, 1979), and the *Telhisat,* from an anonymous author, edited by Rhoads Murphey, "The Veliyyuddin *Telhis:* Notes on the Sources and Interrelations between Koçi Bey and Contemporary Writers of Advice to the Kings," *Belleten* 43 (1979): 547–71. One should also include in this list another famous treatrise, Aziz Efendi, *Kanun-name-i Sultani li Aziz Efendi,* ed. and trans. Rhoads Murphey as *Aziz Efendi's Book Of Sultanic Laws and Regulations: An Agenda for Reform by a Seventeenth-Century Ottoman Statesman,* Sources of Oriental Languages and Literature no. 9 (Cambridge, Mass., 1985).
[4]Bernard Lewis, "Ottoman Observers of Ottoman Decline," *Islamic Studies* 1 (1962): 71–87.
[5]Immanuel Wallerstein, "The Ottoman Empire and the Capitalist World Economy: Some Questions for Research," *Review* 2 (1979): 389–98.

Another way of seeing this phase of Ottoman history is as a time of periodic challenges followed by numerous recoveries, in the course of which the state developed and manufactured new ways of harnessing society to achieve its own goals. The Ottoman state was unquestionably confronted by a series of crises, and the effects of the crisis of the seventeenth century were real enough. And there were societal responses to the upheavals of the time: the rebellion of 1589 by the members of the elite central cavalry, the rebellions of the *celalis* (1596–1610), and the 1703 rebellion by a section of the central troops. But these reactions never led to a complete loss of control on the part of the government. These challenges to the state did not entail the overthrow of one dynasty for another. Instead, state officials engineered new ways of control and incorporation, which were sometimes devised in a more ad hoc fashion than at other times. The Ottoman state did not lose control over society; it may have had to readjust its various institutions to adapt to novel conditions. The point here is to understand state policies as responses to specific historical situations and social structures, as well as to explain how they affected different segments of the population.

The more analytic historical studies that focus on state decisions vis-à-vis elites in the late sixteenth and early seventeenth centuries contribute to this image of the Ottoman state. Metin Kunt's *Sultan's Servants*—with a focus on the early seventeenth century—analyzes the policies of the state vis-à-vis the provinces by studying appointment registers for governors and governor-generals and shows that the state tended to appoint central government men to provincial posts. Kunt aptly demonstrates that during this time the state had the power to implement greater central involvement in provincial affairs and improve the quality of governance.[6] Rifaat Abou-el-Haj, shows—for the last decades of the seventeenth century—the increased importance of vizier households, creating a different balance in the structure of state power.[7] Both works, for different parts of the seventeenth century, present different data sources to assess state's strength. Given that the Ottoman concept of state underwent a profound transformation in the middle of the sixteenth century—the state becoming larger

---

[6] I. M. Kunt, *The Sultan's Servants: The Transformation of Ottoman Provincial Government, 1550–1650* (New York, 1983), pp. 77–93.

[7] Rifaat A. Abou-el-Haj, "The Ottoman Vezir and Paşa Households, 1683–1703: A Preliminary Report," *Journal of the American Oriental Society* 94 (1974): 438–47. I am well aware of the attacks launched by Abou-el-Haj against Metin Kunt. These attacks are unconvincing since Abou-el-Haj uses a different time period in his analysis and also employs an overly restrictive definition of the state.

than the individual of the sultan who represented it—both assessments of state decisions based on the center and the immediate vizierial elites make sense. In both cases, a larger state institution was in action, rather than a sultan, a grand vizier, or a few lower-level vizierial elites. Given the larger institution, the Ottoman state demonstrated shifts and changes in state power but not a decline.

Contemporary literature has also stressed the struggles within the palace, the intrigues of the women—the mother of the prince on the throne and the women who had sons from the sultan—and other palace officials and viziers. As V. J. Parry describes for the period just before Murad IV and later as well, "there was faction and intrigue, too, amongst the officials of the central régime, especially amongst the viziers, the number of whom was to rise as high as nine. These dignitaries, striving to attain the highest office in the empire, the grand vizierate, often aligned themselves with other elements engaged in the quest for power."[8] He continues to argue that at this time the ulema, the men of religion, were also intimately involved in the quest for power and influence. The influence peddling of this period in Ottoman history does not automatically disprove arguments about the strength of the state. Rather, it shows that decision making was contested from within the state and that many members of the state apparatus were trying to climb the ladder of internal state mobility and thereby acquire influence. Grand viziers were overwhelmingly successful at this task.

While the contested sources of various decisions within the state might be fascinating to analyze, my purpose here is to consider the state as an integrated set of institutions that exhibited a variety of policies resulting from exchange, debate, and political rivalries. The policies and their impact are of more interest to this work.

The State and Timar Holders

In Chapter 2 I described the timar system and concluded that the nature of their relations with the state made it practically impossible for timar holders to constitute a class-for-itself. This, I argued, was one of main reasons for their inability to act against the state. In addition, the transformation of the timar system in the late sixteenth century, which resulted

---

[8]V. J. Parry, "The Period of Murad IV, 1617–1648," in *A History of the Ottoman Empire to 1730*, ed. M. A. Cook (Cambridge 1980), p. 136.

from state actions ranging from neglect to manipulation, increased competition within their ranks, further incapacitating this group of provincial elites.

The timar system in both contemporary and modern histories has been discussed as the first Ottoman institution to disintegrate, and its very disintegration has been linked to the decline of the empire as a whole. The advice literature identified the problem as the fact that timars were being handed out to those outside the system rather than to the sons of timar holders. Contemporary observers such as Mustafa Ali argued that the fiefs were "all reserved for mercenaries [*levends*] and for the slaves of the great [*ekabir kulları*]." In the words of Douglas Howard, "The anonymous author of *Kitab-i Müstetab* wrote that they were 'the prerogative of the vezirs,' that by approaching a ten-*aqce* scribe, they name the slave girls in their households, their beardless youths and slave boys, even their cats and dogs, everyone of them being designated by a name, are awarded a diploma for a *zi'amet* or *timar*." In another colorful image, Koçi Bey contended that the ranks of the timars were filled by "those who were johhny-come-latelys, those who said 'there is profit here,' who could not distinguish good and evil, those who had no legitimate connection, those who by origin or stock were not possessors of *dirliks*, some of them city boys and some of them peasants, a bunch of commoners, not useful for anything.[9]

This picture is not entirely correct. The timar system was first modified by state managers as well as by those who gained their livelihood from this institution. It was not immediately abandoned. It continued in its old forms, together with other adaptive variations that made sense for the period, attesting to the strength of the system. This is not to say that the timar holders were not affected—that they went on to secure their livelihood in a relatively undisturbed fashion. On the contrary, they were the section of the elite that was most hurt. The timar holders were the most easily manipulated of the elite groups; they had the most to lose from the economic crisis, and they were heavily dependent on the state as well as on their reproduction through continued warfare along traditional lines. The changes in the manner of fighting, the devaluation of the coinage, and the transformation of land into tax-farming operations affected them deeply. In their vulnerability as a group, they turned on each other, and by the end of the period under consideration the main mechanism for ac-

[9]For all these quotations and translations, see Douglas Howard, "The Ottoman *Timar* System and Its Transformation, 1563–1656," Ph.D. diss., Indiana University, 1987, pp. 21–22.

quiring a timar was to evict other timar holders from their land by smear campaigns designed to discredit those with land; fellow landholders were slandered, accused of deserting the battlefield or of not showing up at all. In the process, the largest timar holders—those with connections and the ability to fight in war—were saved, while the others perished. Also, as this dismantling of smaller prebends was going on, state officials were distributing small timars to peasant soldiers, upstarts with no connections as a reward for action in the battlefield. The state thus allowed both the dismantling and the original distribution of smaller plots of land to take place at the same time. This brief exposition indicates not only that this institution was key to the transformation that occurred but also that its history—both in the actions of its members and in the actions of the state—is much more complex that any historian or pamphleteer was willing to disentangle.

In this section, I use timar appointments as an indicator of state involvement in the future of the timar holder class in general. The changes in the decisions made by the state regarding this group indicate well the need on the part of the state to balance the demands made by technological transformation in the West, monetary restraints, and the existence of a large class of men whose livelihood was dependent on the central government. Three significant periods demonstrate the thinking behind the policies that were implemented. I review data on timar appointments for the periods 1572–82 and 1654–55. Between these periods, in 1632–34, Sultan Murad IV ordered a reorganization and revamping of the provincial system, so a comparison should reflect this intermediate procedure.

The timar holder was usually a mounted soldier (*sipahi*) who had been granted a fief in return for his services at war. Governors (*sancakbeyi*) received grants much larger than the regular timar holders yet functioned in administrative terms in much the same fashion; they held grants varying between 200,000 to 600,000 akçes per annum. Governor-generals (*beylerbeyi*) received grants of even greater value: 600,000 to 1,000,000 akçes per annum. The timar holders, in contrast, received on average 2,000 akçes per annum. The highest yield for a timar holder was 20,000 akçes.[10] The cavalryman who was granted a fief was to administer it for his livelihood and had to maintain a small unit of fully armed horsemen—the number of whom depended on the income of the cavalryman.

[10]Halil Inalcık, *The Ottoman Empire: The Classical Age, 1300–1600* (New York, 1973), p. 115. Parry, "The Successors of Süleyman," in *A History of the Ottoman Empire to 1730*, ed. Cook, p. 105.

Early on, the power to bestow timars on such individuals rested with the provincial governor, who granted to each deserving sipahi a diploma of possession.[11] With Sultan Süleyman's centralizing decree of 1531, a restraint was placed on the provincial governor's power to bestow such grants: he was now allowed to decide about the smallest timars, but the larger ones, as well as the initial timars, were to be bestowed centrally.[12] The provincial governor kept some influence in that he was still supposed to provide information about the applicant. This reduced role of the provincial governor signals the increased centralization of the Süleymanic era, whereby the periphery provided information on local affairs and the center weighed the information and set policy.[13] It is based on this particular transformation that we are able to study timar appointments and use them as indicators of state behavior vis-à-vis timar holders.[14]

The first period under consideration, 1572–82, by most accounts had already witnessed the initial decay of the timar system. If the literature is correct, the data should show an increasing number of men from outside the military institution, with no credentials, assigned to these fiefs. It would also have to demonstrate a mixture of old and new trends, rotation, for example, together with appropriation of smaller units by larger ones. The second period under consideration, 1654–55, should, according to most Ottoman intellectuals and historians, demonstrate a timar system in ruins. Yet between these two periods Sultan Murad IV undertook to reorganize the provincial system in an effort to reassert the control of the center. Therefore, the results of the investigation are even more important. They show whether the central state really reorganized or not, and

---

[11]Howard,"The Ottoman *Timar* System," pp. 100–102.

[12]I have used both original and published versions of this decree. I thank Linda Darling for lending me a copy of the original: *Kanun-name-i Osmani bera-yi Timar Daden*, Bibliothèque Nationale, Paris, A. F. Turc 41. Also, Tayyib Gökbilgin, "Kanuni Sultan Süleyman' in Timar ve Zeamet Tevcihi ile Ilgili Fermanları," *Tarih Dergisi* 22 (1968): 35–48. See also, Parry, "The Successors of Süleyman," p. 105.

[13]According to Howard, this did not really alter the central system: "The development of bestowal procedure in this period shows a clear diminution of the significance of the provincial administrative apparatus in the bestowal process. This need not imply, however, that the *timar* system underwent a process of centralization in this period." Howard does not, however, provide convincing arguments as to why this is not centralization; see Howard, "The Ottoman *Timar* System," p. 123. On the contrary, Inalcık argues that this tightening of the appointment procedure meant centralization and that appointment and dispossession were both held in the control of the state, see *The Ottoman Empire*, p. 114.

[14]Howard delineates the process by which the central administration was involved in timar bestowal. He demonstrates how, with each step of the way—the petition, the certificate, and the diploma—the central administration initiated action or had to be activated; see "The Ottoman *Timar* System," pp. 105–13.

to what degree the actions of the state were true to the stated goals of Murad IV.

A cursory comparison of these two periods immediately reveals differences in the types of tenure available. There was a considerable rise in the number of the larger tenures (*zeamet*) in the second period. In the first period, only 10.3 percent of the entries in the sample were zeamets, while in the second period nearly 30 percent were zeamets. The data show that in the seventeenth century the tımars were being swallowed up by larger units, some of which were zeamets.[15]

Analysis and comparison of the two periods yield interesting insights into the changes in the tımar system. During the first period, the system fit quite well with the descriptions of its classical functioning. The tımar and zeamet holders more or less adhered to the patterns of bestowal, promotion, rotation, and dismissal. I present results for the tımars since the zeamets basically replicate the trends. Most of the tımar holders were regular members of the cavalry corps engaged in the routines of transfer and acquisition of new land. In fact, 75 percent of those who appear in the registers were tımar holders, new members or older ones. Only 16 percent were members of the military outside the cavalry coming in from central appointments. But even these appointments do not seem very significant; most were salaried soldiers, and just a handful were more senior in rank (*çavuş*). Most of the tımar entries refer to regular transfers or the addition of more land to already existing tımars. Often these increases were

---

[15]An alternative explanation for this rise in the number of larger units in the registers of the second period is that up to the end of the sixteenth century there were other registers (especially, *tahrir defterleri*) where has, zeamet, and tımar lands were being recorded, and that the registers under consideration (*ruznamçe defterleri*) were specialized in bestowal information for tımars. In the second period, the *tahrirs* had fallen into disuse and therefore the zeamets were being registered in the *ruznamçe* registers. From a *tahrir* register, I found the area of Aydın to hold 582 tımars and 51 zeamets in 1572. From a *yoklama defteri* (military recruitement register) dating from 1655, I found 181 tımars and 17 zeamets in the region of Aydın; here the zeamets represent 8.6 percent of the total. It should be noted that these numbers represent the tımar holders who came to campaign (129) and those who remained as *harçlıkçı* (representatives to collect the taxes for the tımar holders on campaign) (52). The campaign referred to is that of Crete, which had been on the Ottoman agenda on and off since 1644 and which was not fully conquered until 1669. Thus these are still not accurate numbers, since the registers do not give any information about the tımar holders who chose to remain at home and pay a fee instead. I checked this problem in the *ruznamçe* registers; the Aydın sample showed one case of a tımar holder deserting the front and two cases where the tımar holders opted to pay a yearly fee rather than go to war on the island of Crete. Thus, I think it is reasonable to argue that there was quite a significant decline in the number of tımars in the region of Aydın, with a slight increase in the proportion of zeamets. See BBA Tapu Tahrir 516 (1572) and 786 (1655). The first is a register catalogued as regular tımar, while the second is catalogued as military.

granted when tımar holders were of service during campaigns (39 percent). Sons of cavalrymen received 19.5 percent of the bestowals.

Despite the lack of attention paid to the question of rotation by modern historians, I believe that rotation was one of the key elements of the tımar system. It maintained a regular movement of provincial officials, controlling their activity. The tımar holders got their land (additional villages or sometimes new estates) from members of the corps who went on rotation. The registers indicate that the officials who were rotated (*feragat* or *azl*) theoretically added their land to a pool of revenues to be used for other rotation bestowals. During three snapshots of one year each, 1572, 1576, and 1582, an average 45 percent of officials were rotated. The regulations cite that tımar holders were obliged to give up their tımar for a certain period of time, during which they remained estateless. There is little information as to what the cavalrymen on rotation did. Trade and warfare seem to be the two options referred to in the registers. Yet, despite the hardships of rotation, the registers also imply that tımar holders went on rotation of their own will; this could be so either because of the formulaic use of the terms in the records or because tımar holders really believed they could get better tımars by going on rotation. Consequently, rotation still worked rather well at the end of the sixteenth century and there were relatively few complaints about it. This does not seem odd in light of the fact that 39 percent of those sampled obtained better tımars because of service (*yararlık*). Furthermore, the dearth of complaints against the practice of rotation in the advice literature points to the degree to which it must have been accepted.[16]

As well as rotation, the absence of inheritance was also used for control. The attempt to discourage the formation of strong patron-client ties in the provinces was bolstered by the overarching lack of private, and thus inheritable, lands. In accordance with the rules of the Classical Age, sons of tımar holders could obtain units of smaller sizes. Sixteen tımars that were handed out to sons of tımar holders represented 59 percent of the new tımars. Among these sixteen bestowals, two got exactly the same unit as their fathers, while eleven received different ones. In this second category, three sons were established on other tımars in the same district (Aydın if the father was from Aydın and Saruhan if the father lived in Saruhan), while nine were given tımars in other districts of the province of Anatolia. Hereditary tımar assignments in the same area were quite in-

---

[16]Howard points out that Mustafa Ali bitterly complained about the hardships of rotation yet never argued that it should be dismantled, "The Ottoman *Tımar* System," pp. 89–90.

significant for this period and this region. They remained the result of special arrangements between state makers and landholders. Furthermore, the few cases I was able to follow in this period yielded an average tenure of 2 to 3 years in one area, thereby confirming the notion that timar holders were rotating fast enough not to establish roots in any one area.

By the mid-seventeenth century, the backbone of the Ottoman land system was undergoing change. The second period shows differences with regard to the individuals who received these tenures and to the manner in which these tenures were secured. Competition for the well-established, wealthy timars and zeamets became widespread. For one thing, the procedure of finding a timar and requesting it was to a much greater degree in the hands of the cavalrymen. In our sample, 42 percent found their timar and asked to have it approved. Another 18.4 percent acquired their timar by contesting someone else's right to have land. The increased competition between landholders for fiefs and larger fiefs yielded stories of frenzied slander and vilification. Timar holders were accused of not going to war, deserting during a campaign, and all sorts of moral infractions. This practice was common among both landholders and outsiders in search of land. Moreover, since the early seventeenth century Anatolia had experienced the flight of peasants to the highlands as well as to cities;[17] in some regions a shortage of labor pushed landholders to try to obtain the fiefs of others rather than establish timars in other regions.

Competition and conflict among the ranks of the landholders increased with state decisions to dismiss those cavalrymen who were no longer useful to Ottoman needs. In fact, cavalrymen experienced competition from men of lower rank as well as from grandees and central officials. The importance of service in war was stressed by making timars conditional on participation in war and by rewarding any soldier of unknown social origin with a timar if he fought for the Ottoman army. A majority of those in the register did not have established titles or occupations. Of those, 64.7 percent were upstarts returning from war, finding themselves a piece of land and requesting a timar from the central authorities for the first time. The state's willingness to grant these men tenures reinforces the argument that the state, having benefited from the services of the musketeers, was willing to reward them with land. There is some speculation as

[17]Leila Erder and Suraiya Faroqhi, "Population Rise and Fall in Anatolia, 1550–1620," *Middle Eastern Studies* 15 (1979):322–45.

to who these individuals were. From the admonitions of the contemporary pamphleteers, it seems clear that they were of peasant (*reaya*) origin, youths displaced by agricultural and demographic change.[18]

At the other end of the spectrum, high-ranking military officials from the center (especially *çavuş* and *müteferrika*) also acquired land. Increasingly, central appointments were made by the government to reward important clients, family members, and others. Whereas in the first period the military officials who received timars were low-ranking ones, in the 1650s pashas were given zeamets of considerable size and *çavuşes* received positions as *gedik* (special tenure with life-long privileges). As some groups took over tenures from the state, other groups, often the more deserving in traditional terms, tended to lose their rights. For example, in this period sons of landholders who received land grants were scarce: only three cases are reported, two of whom received their father's timar.

As the state reassessed its position on this provincial system and its inability to win wars with Europe, it made use of the land in a less systemic and less traditional fashion to reward those who had provided their services during warfare as well as those high-ranking officials whom the state makers wanted to keep happy. This task had been simplified because greater numbers of landholders either deserted or died leaving timars vacant (*mahlul*).[19] Therefore, the system was transformed into a sort of fund on which the state drew when in need. As a result, the timar became increasingly competitive for the original members, who were obliged to contend with the state in order to function in the system. As practices of bestowal changed, those who held land strove to keep it for as long as possible. Therefore, when timar or zeamet holders received a holding, they tried to hang on to it by paying a yearly fee (*bedel*) to the state. Often timar holders ended up paying yearly fees ("her sene vaki olan bedeli eda edip Girid seferine memur değil iken"), avoiding war and turning their

---

[18]Mustafa Âli accuses: "But there are many foreigners [ecnebiler] and incapable upstarts and wealthy men, who, having become salaried retainers to the *paşas* and *beğs* of Yemen and Egypt and Syria, have in some fashion gained a military appointment and stipend [dirlük]; see Cornell Fleischer, *Bureaucrat and Intellectual in the Ottoman Empire: The Historian Mustafa Âli (1541–1600)* (Princeton, 1986), p. 208.

[19]From his research in the district of Aydın, Howard argues that there is a greater likelihood that many more sipahis were dying on campaigns. Moreover, the maritime wars the Ottomans engaged in always drew heavily from the western coastal region, and therefore the Aydın sipahis (and in our case the Aydın and Saruhan sipahis, might have been hit very hard during the last decades of the sixteenth century; see "The Ottoman *Timar* System," pp. 181–82.

land into some sort of tax farm.[20] Longer tenures resulted, announcing a new era of land structure.[21]

In sum, the 1650s demonstrate the results of a new, more opportunistic policy of the state: there were fewer timars but a greater likelihood of remaining on the same timar. This was usually done by turning timars into quasi-tax farms. Furthermore, it is clear that two strikingly different pools were being drawn from in the awarding of timars: at the top, central military officials, men close to the center, were being rewarded for one reason or another;[22] at the bottom, peasants and vagrants were assigned timars as a reward for fighting. These men were valuable, since they provided a service for the state, and they were also dangerous, since otherwise they might join the armies of the landless and the poor. As a result, original beneficiaries were pushed out to accommodate groups that otherwise posed a greater threat to the state.

Why were the original cavalrymen unable to retain their land as well as their status? The most profound damage to the cavalry army and thereby to the timar system was inflicted by the increasing need to fight new types of war on both the European and eastern borders. On the one hand, expansion into new territories necessitated fortresses and garrisons equipped with soldiers using firearms. On the other hand, especially on the western front, the new enemies were the Christian arquebusiers, who in the words of Ogier Ghiselin de Busbecq ridiculed the once fearless Turkish soldiers: "Our pistols and carbines, which are used on horseback, are a great terror to the Turks, as I hear they are to the Persians also."[23] The cavalrymen thus had to either learn to use firepower or be phased out as one of the important military segments of the Ottoman army. In fact, Grand Vizier Rüstem Pasha tried to persuade the cavalrymen to fight with pistols as they rode on their horses. As Busbecq relates, this was practically impossible: "The Turks were also against this armature, because it was slovenly (the Turks, you must know, are much for cleanliness

[20]I am grateful to Halil Inalcık for alerting me to the meaning of these documents.

[21]Although Howard did not examine his data in light of these points, he did find that average tenure for these years is 10 years 3 months, "The Ottoman *Timar* System," p. 175.

[22]Bistra A. Cvetkova provides similar data in her own study on the origins of the feudal system in the Ottoman Empire. She finds *çavuşes*, *müteferrikas*, and scribes getting timars in the region of Skopije. Similarly, in the region of Sofia for the period 1609–18, she reports many timars or zeamets of considerable revenue being held by palace men of the same ranks; see Cvetkova, "L'évolution du régime féodal turc de la fin du XVIe jusqu'au milieu du XVIIIe siècle," *Etudes historiques à l'occasion du XIIe congrès international des sciences historiques Vienne* (Sofia, 1965), 2:183.

[23]*The Turkish Letters of Ogier Ghiselin de Busbecq*, trans. E. S. Forster (Oxford, 1927), pp. 123–24.

in war), for the troopers' hands were black and sooty, their clothes full of of spots and their case-boxes, that hung by their sides, made them ridiculous to their fellow-soldiers, who therefore jeered at them, with the title of *medicamentarii.*"[24]

From the time of Süleyman to the early seventeenth century, the need for musketeers was acknowledged but only partially resolved. Busbecq tells us that Grand Vizier Rüstem Pasha unsuccessfully added two hundred horsemen armed with pistols to his force during the Persian campaign of 1548.[25] Even during the 1593–1606 war against the Habsburgs, demands were issued from the front to the center for additional musket-bearing troops in order to cope with the German infantry. In a letter published by Cengiz Orhonlu, Grand Vizier Mehmed Pasha makes this plea: "In the field or during a siege we are in a distressed position, because the greater part of the enemy forces are infantry armed with muskets, while the majority of our forces are horsemen and we have very few specialists skilled in the musket. . . . so the tüfeng-endaz [equipped with a fire-arm] Janissaries, under their *agha*, must join the imperial army promptly."[26]

The relative reluctance of cavalrymen to switch to guns empowered the janissary corps. Whereas timar holders were reluctant to fight with muskets, troopers on western fronts were successful and soon requested to join campaigns where the sultan sent the janissary army to fight, to train more musket-bearing infantry corps, and even to get the cavalry to adapt and use firearms.[27] Obviously, musket-bearing armies (whether additions to the janissary corps or *reaya* recruits) cost substantially more than a self-maintained army like the timar-holding cavalry based in the provinces. Despite that, the janissary corps increased from nearly 8,000 men in 1527

[24]Ibid.

[25]Halil Inalcık, "The Socio-Political Effects of the Diffusion of Fire-arms in the Middle East," in *War, Technology, and Society in the Middle East*, ed. V. J. Parry and M. E. Yapp (London, 1975), p. 198.

[26]Although I have used the series of letters published by Orhonlu, this particular translated section comes from Inalcık's "The Socio-Political Effects of the Diffusion of Fire-arms," p. 199. See Cengiz Orhonlu, *Osmanlı Tarihine Aid Belgeler: Telhisler (1597–1607)*, Istanbul Üniversitesi Edebiyat Fakültesi Yayınları, no. 1511 (Istanbul, 1970), document 81.

[27]The reports from the battlefront published by Cengiz Orhonlu present this information well. Document 60, for example, is a letter written by Grand Vizier Yemişçi Hasan Pasha, who alerted the sultan that if by March five to ten thousand men equipped with firepower did not show up at the Hungarian front where he was engaged in battle, there could be trouble; see, Orhonlu, *Telhisler*, pp. 51–52. In this and another letter (no. 114) the grand vizier requests that the sultan send the governor of Menteşe to the Hungarian front. He is to bring with him a large number of men equipped with muskets, ibid., p. 98. These letters are also used and reprinted in Inalcık, "The Socio-Political Effects of the Diffusion of Fire-arms," p. 199.

to 53,499 in 1669. Its expansion was felt not only in the major cities, but also all over the provinces. Increasingly, the corps was assigned to maintain law and order in provincial towns. Members settled, intermarried and became an integral part of provincial society. Their increased number and influence empowered them, so when they were assigned provincial positions they often abused their power.

The timar holders responded only minimally. Not only were they not trained to use firearms, but their income was not sufficient to reequip themselves and their men for the new style of war. Their disdain for this kind of warfare originated with its association with the methods of the rival army, the janissaries. The timar holders' inability to change was enhanced by inflation in the economy, which decreased their capacity to adapt. Thus, many of the small timar holders, stricken by poverty, opted out. An interesting contrast to this situation was the ease with which the peasantry was able to buy guns. Partly as a reaction to these needs and partly as a response to the threat of vagrant youths, bandits, and robbers in the villages, the state had relaxed the restrictions on the production, purchase, and use of firearms, thereby making weapons available to the people. Ironically, peasants bought firearms and equipped themselves to enter the military, while the cavalry opted out of the military (see Chapter 5).

The first indications of these changes appeared after the Battle of Mezö-keresztes in 1596. When at the end of the war, after his victory against the Habsburg army, Grand Vizier Çağalazade Sinan Pasha gathered his army, he declared all missing cavalrymen deserters (*firaris*) and carried out a policy of dispossession and confiscation of their land and privileges. Many timar and zeamet holders were named in the Register of Deserters (*Firari Defteri*) prepared at the time. The actions of the grand vizier are revealing. In light of previous losses at the beginning of the war at Mezö-keresztes, the grand vizier understood the need for changes in the makeup of the Ottoman army. Therefore, dismissing those who deserted, appropriating their wealth, and redirecting it were among of the first measures considered by the state vis-à-vis the timar holders. Historical sources do not indicate concerted action against all timar holders. The grand vizier simply attempted to remove those who proved inefficient and replace them with individuals who promised to make more effective use of the land.[28]

---

[28]The Battle of Mezö-keresztes has been discussed by several historians, comtemporaries of the war as well as recent scholars. The most interesting study is that of Akdağ, who has studied the Register of Deserters. He finds out that there were very few timar holders with

From the battle of Mezö-keresztes until the accession of Murad IV to the throne in 1623, the tımar system remained in a state of flux and received little attention due to the increasing power of the janissaries and palace cavalry, the armies that managed the execution of Sultan Osman II (1622). The tımar holders were used during the wars, although complaints about their inability to adapt were often repeated. In fact, during his reign Osman II seems to have harbored plans to remilitarize the Ottoman army with an Anatolian peasant-based militia. After his tragic death, a final bid was to be made during the reign of Murad IV (1623–40) to restore the parts of the tımar system still functioning. The attempt would not have been worthwhile if the system had totally crumbled by then. The number of tımar holders in 1610 ranged from 20,000 to 30,000.[29]

The endeavor to reorganize the tımar system was part of Murad IV's centralization policy and show of force at every level of central and provincial authority. In the first part of his reign, the Ottomans lost Baghdad to the Safavids (1624); from then on, their attempts to recapture it met with little success. At his accession, Murad IV had to deal with large-scale banditry in the provinces, especially that of Abaza Mehmet Pasha, whom he successfully co-opted into the Ottoman military. The sultan also faced deep divisions in the central government and infighting among state officials—infighting that became even more severe when the central army mutinied in favor of one or another official, sometimes forcing the sultan to deliver his officials into their murderous hands.[30] The severity of the internal and international problems faced by Murad IV made the immediate reorganization of the empire's institutions necessary.[31]

---

less than 6,000 akçes income in the register. Instead, the majority comprised tımar and zeamet holders with large revenues (between 20,000 and 60,000 akçes) who had not been going to war and whose estates could be used to establish many more individuals. Akdağ argues that these estates were divided up and given to janissaries, smaller tımar holders, and various low-level military men; see Akdağ, *Celali Isyanları (1550–1603)* (Ankara, 1963), p. 188. See also Mustafa Naima, *Tarih-i Naima* (Istanbul, 1283/1866–67), 1:165. See also the translation of this volume by Charles Fraser, *Annals of the Turkish Empire from 1591 to 1659 of the Christian Era* (London, 1832), pp. 92–93.

[29] Ayn-i Ali Efendi, "Kavanin al-i Osman," p. 76.

[30] I am referring here to the animosity between the then grand vizier Hafız Pasha and the central troops. This led to Murad IV's handing him to the troops gathered outside the palace and his being executed. See Ismail Hakkı Uzunçarşılı, *Osmanlı Tarihi* (Ankara, 1983), 3:1.180–85.

[31] The main sources I have used for the reorganization that went on during the time of Murad IV are Mustafa Naima's *Tarih-i Naima* and Howard's "The Ottoman Tımar System." Whereas Naima presents a detailed narrative of the events that preceded the reorganization and of the emergency session of the imperial council, Howard provides a more structured explanation that puts the events into the context of the tımar system. I therefore rely heavily

In 1632, Murad IV convened an emergency session of the imperial council (*ayak divanı*). This meeting was to include all the high-ranking dignitaries of the empire: the grand vizier, the *şeyh-ül-islam*, the *kadıaskers* of Rumeli and Anatolia, the *ağas* of the janissaries and of the palace cavalry, and all the viziers, ulema, and elderly and wise men of the councils.[32] The sultan first consolidated his own immediate entourage (the grand vizier and the imperial council), then went on to reprimand the leadership of every corps in the empire in the hope of regaining their loyalty. Mustafa Naima narrated with vivid detail the biting rhetoric of Murad's speeches against each section of the state apparatus and their humiliation as with each reprimand they were forced to plead with the sultan, pronounce their oath of allegiance, and hope to be spared from execution. The chief troublemaker, Grand Vizier Receb Pasha, was put to death, and the sultan refused to pay the palace army divisions the additional payments (*hidmet*) they had come to expect. A cleanup operation proceeded, begun with the janissaries and the elite cavalry and going on to encompass magistrates and the *ağas* of other military corps. Those deemed impossible to reform were executed. The army was handled through bargains that forced the leadership to rid the ranks of known rebels in return for the granting of the extra payments, rescinded soon after.

The economic crisis and its consequences also forced the state to confront financial issues directly—in two ways, both of which had an impact on the old elites. First, it altered the system of taxation, and, second, it changed those responsible for the collection of taxes. As was mentioned earlier, one immediate provincial strategy was to phase out those timars which were no longer paying for themselves. But more important, revenue flow into the treasury demanded reconfiguration of administrative offices to retrieve old taxes better and devise new taxes as well. Indirect methods of taxation like the timar had to be replaced with direct taxes. Two taxes, the *cizye* and the *avarız*, underwent drastic revamping so that more of these taxes could be collected, and more efficiently.[33] New elites appeared on the provincial scene when tax collection was handed over to men from palace cavalry units and even more to palace personnel and

---

on his interpretation. Overall, as I checked through Naima's and other narratives of the time, I agreed with Howard's interpretation and therefore used it with confidence.

[32]Howard, "The Ottoman *Timar* System," p. 204.

[33]New registers dating from this period show this clearly. Linda Darling mentions three such surveys: a survey of Chios in 1633, another one of Tikveş from 1640, and a register of Cyprus from 1642; see "Adaptations in Administration," p. 23.

other central officials.[34] Later, toward the end of the seventeenth century, the solution would be reliance on the tax-farming system.

At the provincial level, reorganization and consolidation followed the central procedure. The goal of this reorganization was to salvage the remnants of the land tenure institution by emphasizing only those features relevant to the seventeenth century. Reorganization did not mean a return to the traditional system of land tenure; rather, it meant adaptation to new conditions, to international and internal contingencies that impacted on this institution. Strategically, it was formulated in the language of and in accordance with the established law (*kanun-i kadim üzere*) and therefore made palatable to the more traditional element in society.[35] Awareness of the increased power of the janissaries, as well as the empire's military goals (such as the reconquest of Baghdad), must have influenced Murad to attempt full-scale reorganization of the provincial system and its main asset, the sipahi army. This was a courageous and certainly difficult move given the state of demoralization of the tımar holders. The Veliyyuddin *Telhis* recognized Murad IV's attempts at reorganization and pointed to the importance of creating a balance between these two armies, the cavalry and the janissary, in order to obstruct any bid at more power on the part of the janissaries.[36]

Reorganization necessitated intensive and far-reaching inspection: "In the past, all of the possessors of *zi'amets* and *tımars* dwelt and resided in the provinces in which their *tımars* were located. When a campaign or other service was ordered, all of them were present in the province of the alay begi. With regard to wars and conflicts for the faith, through their many endeavours praiseworthy conquests became possible. At present, however, no inspection has been made of possessors of *zi'amets* and *tımars* for some time, and with everyone dwelling and residing wherever they wish, the above groups have fallen into disorder."[37]

Murad appointed Hüseyin Pasha, a veteran vizier, to the task of reorganizing the Rumelian provinces by gathering all holders of tımars and zeamets, examining their documents, and granting renewals to all deserving cavalrymen. The latter were those holders of fiefs who lived in their district and responded to the call to arms of their military field com-

---

[34]Ibid., p. 26.

[35]This is well expressed by Howard in "The Ottoman *Tımar* System," p. 211, where he studies the directives provided to the vizier Hüseyin Pasha, who was appointed to reorganize the land system.

[36]Murphey, "The Veliyyuddin *Telhis*," pp. 552–53.

[37]Howard, "The Ottoman *Tımar* System," p. 210.

mander (*alaybeyi*).[38] The governor-general of Anatolia, Mehmed Pasha, was asked to carry out similar procedures. In Anatolia alone 5,312 diplomas (*berats*) of tımar holders were renewed under this procedure.[39] The requirements of this reorganization were clear. The two men responsible for this process were to ensure that the tımar holders lived in the district of their land and that they attended the campaigns. A new registration reset the rules of tımar appointments and maintenance and provided a basis for assessing the number and extent of vacant tımars that could be used by the state.[40] The registration had the important function of determining the extent to which the institution was useful and could be adapted to a new environment.

The degree to which the reorganization of the tımar system was a quick solution is illustrated by the requirements of the sultan and his council. Their immediate goal was to establish as many people as possible on tımars, to increase the size of the provincial army. The new information on who could obtain tımars made no mention of an obligation to distribute tımars to sons of tımar holders, thereby opening the door for outsiders who participated in war to be rewarded with land. In this reorganization, the old rules for the granting of tımars were not to be applied. One of the directives from the center clarifies the point:

> Those who are possessors of *zi'amets* and *tımars* in the province of Erzurum were inspected, according to their *diplomas* and documentation. It was ordered that in accordance with regulations, a certificate should be given to those registered one *aqça* in excess of the base, who are present under the standard of the *alay begi* and resident in the province. When a vacancy occurs, or when it becomes necessary for any other reason, the *zi'amet* or *tımar* should be bestowed on those who petition from among *the salaried personnel of the cavalry divisions and from among the other servants of my threshold, and on those petitioners from among the meritorious youths, who though they are not petitioners from among the salaried ones, have evidence (of their merit) in their possession, with the understanding that they are resident in the province of their service.*[41]

These guidelines are all the more interesting since they clash with the advice of contemporary pamphleteers, who were more interested in reviving the old rules and regulations. When the pamphleteers asked for the

[38]Ibid., pp. 211–12.
[39]Murphey, "The Veliyyuddin *Telhis*," p. 554, n. 9a.
[40]See Howard, "The Ottoman *Tımar* System," p. 221.
[41]Ibid., pp. 215–16, emphasis added.

reorganization of the timar system, they wanted timars to be distributed to the sons of sipahis. Any bestowal became illegitimate in their eyes if it provided outsiders with fiefs.[42] The Veliyyuddin *Telhis,* for example, points out the disorganization of the process of bestowal; many timars were vacant, but many were also, disputed. In Murphey's translation: "Taking advantage of the confusion vezirs were able to assign timars to members of their own household even when these timars were not vacant or when their tenure was disputed."[43] If we look, however, at the directive quoted above, we see the state handing out timars to individuals who were in theory not eligible. The provincial military establishment was now open to members of vizier households, salaried personnel, members of regional military units (*bölüks*) and fearless youth. It was expected that especially the adventurous and armed vagrants would swell the ranks of the military.

The effects of such policies are seen in our data and relate to the period after Murad IV's reforms. As I pointed out earlier, the number of timars bestowed on individuals of unknown origin having military skills increased considerably in the seventeenth century. Equally important were the timars handed out to high-ranking military men from the palace. The inspection procedure relating to them is not so clear. In response to requests from Hüseyin Pasha, the state answered that members of the *harem* who held timars or zeamets should be dispossessed. However, members of the royal family should not be dispossessed and should not be expected to participate in wars.[44] Pashas, their sons, and other central military personnel were to attend the inspection, and if their documentation was in order their diplomas were to be renewed.[45]

Thus, the timar system was not left to rot. The traditional group of timar holders who used their swords and despised firearms were evicted to give way to individuals willing to use more modern techniques. These now vacant timars and those that were already empty were consolidated and assigned to soldiers and their retainers.[46] This does not necessarily

---

[42]This is seen in Koçi Bey, *Risale,* as well as in the Veliyyuddin *Telhis* collection published by Murphey.

[43]Murphey, "The Veliyyuddin *Telhis,*" p. 551.

[44]Howard, "The Ottoman *Timar* System," p. 217.

[45]Ibid., p. 212.

[46]Howard explains why some timars were empty using Akdağ's "Great Flight" argument that there was no revenue to collect since all the peasants had fled the cultivated lowlands. I take up the notion of the "Great Flight" in Chapters 5 and 6. For Howard's explanation, see "The Ottoman *Timar* System," pp. 221–22.

mean that Murad IV's reform was completely successful in the military reorganization of the provinces. The data for 1654–55 clearly show that the typical timar and zeamet holders who stayed behind and paid the *bedel* were still very much part of the scene. They were the larger timar and zeamet holders who could afford to pay yearly fees. They were, however, transformed into quasi-tax farmers. The state permitted tax farming in order to enjoy the economic benefits of such an arrangement.

Overall, the changes were instituted to swell the ranks of the provincial armies, to create a loyal force in the provinces, and thereby to ensure participation in wars. The state successfully exploited land that had been abandoned by distributing plots to anyone who had participated in campaigns—nameless soldiers or important officials connected to the government. For those units where timar and zeamet holders still made a living and paid off the state, the status quo was maintained. This was done primarily because of the income it brought the treasury. The purpose, then, was to reactivate a crisis-ridden institution in order to milk it of its resources. In the process, however, not all timar holders were losers; some continued on, especially the wealthier ones.[47] This situation was enhanced by competition within the group over the increasingly difficult task of finding and keeping adequate land without joining wars that were devastating to the cavalry units.

The State and High-Ranking Provincial Officials

The Veliyyuddin *Telhis* provides the following clues about the higher levels of the provincial system: "The governor generals should be guaranteed the revenues assigned to them in the accounting registers [*icmal defteri*] and protected from the diversion of these revenues to other purpose whether through assignment as freehold property [*mülk*] or to meet the expenses of maintaining a garrison [*ocaklık*]. . . . provincial governor generals should be given long-term appointments. Without permanent secure positions, the beys are liable to resort to injustice and when injustice prevails the people are in discomfort and the country is in distress and disorder."[48] Some of the advice given here certainly seems to have been

---

[47]The problem with this assertion is that we do not have any other data on this question. Our only indication is the fact that there were timar holders who did not go to war and stayed on by paying the state.

[48]Murphey, "The Veliyyuddin *Telhis*," pp. 549–50.

taken into consideration. During the early seventeenth century, the main provincial concern outside the timar institution was the role and stability of the governor-generals. Their maintenance cost other groups in the provinces dearly. While the governor-generals were provided with ways to survive the economic crisis, other less important members of the provincial hierarchy were phased out. The governor was the main victim of a new provincial division of labor.

The reorganization of the provinces was meant to consolidate a loyal elite in charge of the newly reconstituted military and to maintain the cash flowing to the central treasury. As already examined, this goal was certainly achieved in the lower ranks of provincial officialdom. The state used the timar holders for its own purposes, keeping some on their land, dispossessing others, and replacing them with alternative contenders, either those with cash or those with military abilities. A similar policy of immediate military and monetary reinforcement with regard to the other major officials in the provinces, the governor-general and the governor, was introduced in the context of central appointments.

The governor and the governor-general, notable officials of the provincial hierarchy, were creatures of the state, appointed by the central administration to keep the provinces dependent on and cooperative with the center. Provincial administrators came from the palace service and were clearly loyal to the center. With increasing territorial gains the provincial establishment experienced formal differentiation. Territorial expansion and the requirements of bureaucratic control necessitated units of administration larger than the *sancak,* the original Ottoman unit of conquest. Therefore, many *sancaks* were united under a province, and governors were placed under the jurisdiction of governor-generals. Both officials functioned as representatives of the state with military and administrative duties in the provinces. Their income was secured through their *has* holdings: taxes, dues, and all other payments made on land and various commercial holdings. Apart from their official income, they also secured unofficial sources as booty and income from money lending, trade, and various speculative activities.[49] Their ability to accumulate vast resources while being far removed from the central administrative control was checked only through the practice of confiscation (*musadara*).

As the high-ranking regional officers of the patrimonial center, provincial officials were important to the sultan, who made sure their loyalty was sustained through their palace indoctrination, slave (*kul*) status, rotating

[49]Kunt, *The Sultan's Servants,* p. 54.

appointments, and the benefits accrued from membership in the state apparatus. In return, they represented for the state an administrative, centralizing force as well as a source of military reserve since they were required to maintain a number of retainers depending on their income. Thus, much like the timar class (only on a larger scale), they maintained a retinue and participated in warfare. The crisis of the seventeenth century altered the compact between the state and the provincial officials.

These officials were of great value in the sixteenth century, but their power diminished as the state started adapting to the international crisis and redefining its own centralization goals within the new world context. Similar to the timar holders, the governors were both directly and indirectly affected by the state's decisions. An investigation into the appointments of governors and governors-generals shows that both groups were affected, albeit differently. The consolidation carried out by the Ottoman state regarding the higher levels of the provincial system affected elites at many different levels. On the one hand, there was a consolidation of larger units to the detriment of the smaller ones; governors and their original appointment units tended to disappear, leaving provincial control to the governor-general. This type of consolidation brought about inter-elite conflict, competition between governors and governor-generals for the larger, lucrative assignments. On the other hand, the elimination of some positions led to vast intraelite conflict, since within each group some officials tended to benefit while others lost out. These points are similar to those made earlier about the timar holders, among whom a group of winners and a group of losers could be identified. Furthermore, governors were thrown into competition not only within their ranks but with other officials as well.

The consequences of the reorganization by the state were twofold. It reinforced a few select positions concentrated in fewer well-administered provinces with trusted central officials. The belief was that a few good men could do the job better if the state maintained its support for them and kept them satisfied. For these positions, patronage and the sultan's household affiliations gained in importance. Also, the method of direct cash contributions from the province to the center functioned well with the better-known clients of the state. The rest of the provincial officials were adversely affected. The major outcome of this period was the incapacitation of most elites in Ottoman society, who were torn by internal conflicts while steadily losing their means of livelihood. As they came to expect promotions, clients of the state were appointed to positions that made further mobility impossible. Under these circumstances, it is impossible to expect any alliance against the state. In fact, these conflicts are important since they are also linked to the inability of the peasantry to ally with elites; this helps explain the lack of cohesive collective action on the part of any of the provincial groups.

Appointment registers and contemporary accounts represent the best sources on provincial change. The registers disclose the nature of state action since *sancak* as well as *beylerbeyi* appointments were made by the state. This is why contemporary pamphleteers also addressed their grievances regarding appointments to the sultan. One of the complaints of the Veliyyuddin *Telhis* has to do with the changes in the appointment of the governor-general. The author of this *telhis* argues that the governor-general should be appointed for longer periods of time, since "without permanent secure positions, the beys are liable to resort to injustice and when injustice prevails the people are in discomfort and the country is in distress and disorder."[50] From this statement, we understand that one of the major problems of the seventeenth-century provincial governors was the kinds of appointments they had and how they were able to maintain themselves in these positions.

The best study of provincial officials up to now has been provided by Kunt. His prosopographic study of provincial officials focuses on precisely the period of transformation, 1550–1650. In an attempt to understand the changes in the provinces of the Ottoman Empire, he analyzes the late sixteenth- and mid-seventeenth-century appointment registers and tries to follow the careers of many of the officials. The transformation he records is critical to an understanding of this period.

Kunt discovers that in the sixteenth century training and knowledge about posts were very important. State decisions about who to send to the provinces and who to promote followed a clear pattern of learning and merit. He finds that 67.8 percent of zeamet holders became governors and 85.7 percent of governors became governor-generals. Career moves directly from the center to the periphery were much less common: 32 percent of the palace officers (*kapıkulu*) became governors and 14.3 percent became governor-generals. In this system, value was placed on training in the provinces; central palace education was not enough; one had to go through the ranks in the provincial system to qualify for advancement. For example, it was important that governors in the frontier provinces be from the ranks of the lesser officials of those same provinces.[51] This was

[50]Murphey, "The Veliyyuddin *Telhis,*" p. 549.
[51]Kunt, *The Sultan's Servants,* p. 63.

not always the case for lesser officials (such as the timar *defterdarı* or timar *kethüdası*), who seem to have been appointed from the center to the provinces directly.

According to Kunt, during the seventeenth century the course of official appointments changed drastically. His study demonstrates that in the latter period only 25.4 percent of the zeamet holders became governors and only 26.9 percent of the governors were promoted to the position of governor-general. As opposed to this, an increasing number of members of the palace military and the page organizations were appointed to these posts. In this second period, 49 percent of the governors appointed were from the central administration.[52] A comparison of the two periods suggests that in this new period of state-provincial relations the state may have been jeopardizing its provincial interests in order to respond to some immediate central question. The situation is not clear; data about the decision making of the state would be necessary to understand the reasoning behind certain appointments. Kunt tells us, however, that three-quarters of the central appointments to the provinces were kept to the interior regions. This indicates that the concern about sending untrained personnel to the province was still genuine; at least border regions were protected from the potential damages of palace personnel.

Another interesting aspect of the transformation, according to Kunt, relates to duration in office. From the sixteenth to the seventeenth century the duration of appointment shrank considerably. In Kunt's assessment, governors remained within the same region while their appointments became shorter and shorter. He argues that by the 1580s especially by the 1630s long terms (3 years or more) in office were rare. Provincial governors were not only hurt by short terms of office, but they also suffered from longer and longer rotation periods out of office. The findings are similar for governor-generals. Similar trends of regionalism are seen in their case, and the time spent in office was drastically lower. For example, close to 60 percent of the governor-generals of the Ottoman provinces in the 1630s were dismissed within one year of appointment. The governor-generals, however, were taken seriously by the center. They were reappointed fairly quickly and were assigned the revenues of *sancaks* as fodder money (*arpalık*) during their periods out of office.[53]

From these results Kunt argues that the provincial system was losing its primary importance and that state officials were gaining increasing con-

[52]Ibid., p. 64, Table 4.5.
[53]Ibid., pp. 70–76.

trol over the provinces. He maintains that "central government officials came to take over provincial administration positions at higher ranks; the province replaced the district as the main administrative unit; patronage relations and household affiliations became dominant factors in the polity."[54] Using some of the same sources, I have carried out an analysis of appointments in the *beylerbeylik* of Anatolia in general and in the provinces of Aydın and Saruhan in particular. For some questions, I broadened the analysis to other districts as well.[55] For the period from the 1560s to the 1630s, I examined changes that affected the course of officials' lives. However, a close analysis shows that we cannot really find a particular pattern of state behavior in these changes. Instead, it seems more logical to argue that the lack of pattern, the lack of predictability, is what made provincial officeholding so precarious and turned it into a businesslike enterprise. Similarly, Murphey argues that "the office of the *beylerbeyi* had come to be regarded no longer as a sacred trust, but as a financial investment involving large expenditures for bribes and favors [*ca'ize*] during the appointment process, to be recouped during the tenure of office."[56]

The changes discovered by Kunt in the appointments of governor-generals also appear in my analysis. For the district of Anatolia, all governor-generals in the sixteenth century were governors before promotion; in the seventeenth century, this picture changed. Not only were there relatively few (25 percent) regional appointments, but those appointments were from among other governor-generals. No governors were promoted to the rank of governor-general in the district of Anatolia. Moreover, the duration of office was quite short in the second period, varying around one year. The increased time out of office is evidenced by the number of provinces given out as fodder money. For the district of Anatolia, in a period of 9 years *sancaks* were handed out as *arpalık* fifteen times. Some of these *sancaks* seem to have been separated as *arpalık* domains; they changed hands often and remained in this status for long periods of time.

[54]Ibid., p. 95.

[55]For this analysis I used three appointment registers: BBA Maliyeden Müdevver 563 (1568–74), BBA Cevdet Dahiliye 6095 (1632–41), and BBA Kamil Kepeci 266 (1632–41). Although I wanted to use registers from the 1654–55 period, they were not available. Apart from Aydın and Saruhan and the district of Anadolu, I have enlarged the sample to twelve other districts: Budun, Rumeli, Bosna, Ozu, Temeşvar, Kantire, Şam, Van, Eğri, Adana, Haleb, and Erzurum. For comparative purposes I chose districts from both eastern Anatolia and the Balkans.

[56]Rhoads Murphey, "The Functioning of the Ottoman Army under Murad IV (1623–1639/1032–1049): Key to the Understanding of the Relationship between Center and Periphery in Seventeenth-Century Turkey," Ph.D. diss., University of Chicago, 1979, 1:279.

The *sancak* of Saruhan, for example, was handed out five times as *arpalık* during these 9 years. In terms of a pattern for the lives of governor-generals, the example of Gürcü Mehmed Pasha is instructive. He was in office as governor-general of Anatolia for 2 years 9 months (the longest appointment in this period), then went without office for 2 years; he then returned to the same district but remained there for a very short time. One can recognize the need for extra resources when officials were out of office so often and so long.

Another means of gaining revenue during periods of rotation was by engaging in trade or other lucrative business. The activities of Derviş Mehmed Pasha are suggestive. He was appointed to the district of Baghdad during the reign of Murad IV. Once in Baghdad, he engaged in trade and agriculture and started rebuilding the city. He is described as having cleared large segments of land for further cultivation and setting up numerous businesses in baked goods, sheep trade, and luxury goods. It seems that he gained 40 million akçes in one year from these endeavors. This was no doubt necessary, since his troops and immediate entourage amounted to 10,000 people.[57] Such was the life of the successful provincial governor-general.

The fate of the governors was both more complex and more painful. In general, governors were more used to being shuffled around. There were no drastic changes between the two periods in regional arrangements. In the district of Anatolia, nearly the same number of governors (36 and 35 percent, respectively) came from other provinces in the two periods. While there was more reshuffling within Anatolia in the first period, this seems to decrease, only to be taken up by central appointments in the second period (25.5 to 11.5 percent).

Governors were hurt by two different state practices: increasing the number of provinces handed out as fodder money, and making duration in office more erratic. Allocation of provinces as *arpalık* had a drastic effect on the governors, who were effectively pushed out of the system. As districts were handed out as *arpalık*, fewer districts remained for governors to be assigned to. A particular governor whose province was just turned into an *arpalık* might or might not be reassigned. Also, since the empire was no longer expanding, new districts were not being added on. To add insult to injury, the state continued assigning provinces to new officials from the palace. In all aspects, then, the world of the governor

---

[57]I. M. Kunt, "Derviş Mehmed Paşa, Vezir and Entrepreneur: A Study in Ottoman Political-Economic Theory and Practice," *Turcica* 9 (1977):197–214.

was shrinking. In fact, Kunt also argues that, as the governor-general gained power, he was given more revenues (as *arpalık* or *zamime* [additions]) from the governors' estates.[58]

Centralization and bureaucratization worked differently at different times. With expansion, many subunits had been gathered to form one larger unit; later subunits were wiped out so larger units could rule free of entanglement. While the appointment of trusted central officials to these positions might in the short run consolidate center-periphery ties, in the long run it opened the door to the rule of a few strong and wealthy governor-generals. The seventeenth century therefore represented the passage to the rule of strong governor-generals. In the resulting shuffle, the governor was dispossessed. There were actually several reasons for what might seem an unintended consequence of state policy.

During the Classical Age, when the tımar system flourished and formed a viable military force in the Ottoman Empire, the immediate commanders of the tımar holders, the governors and their field commanders (*alaybeyi*), were crucial in maintaining the tasks of coordination and control. Later on, with the dissolution of the original tımar system, the role of the governors was reduced. The regional field commander who managed to cut himself a corner of the new market by promoting untitled warriors for posts as tımar holders remained active. The governor was not that lucky. He was hit by the deterioration of the tımar system as well as the rampant inflation of the late 1600s. Faced with a state in need of an increasing amount of cash, the governor saw his office phased out. The reason was clear and simple: it made sense to eliminate unnecessary individuals who drew on revenues the state could instead distribute as political favors or as tax farms. The state began with offices of governor handed out to central military officers—such as pashas, *kapıkulu,* and imperial captains[59]—and continued with the more lucrative business of tax farming. There is one more reason why the state could in fact see little harm in the disruption of the province. The larger unit, the *beylerbeylik,* had developed into an even more powerful military unit. This is because governor-generals had over time developed large retinues, in fact armies of mercenaries whom they would bring to fight for the state when necessary. Therefore, the state's military needs in the provinces were largely met by the governor-generals, which left the governor with little to do.

---

[58]He finds, for example, that "Bihke in Bosnia, Semendire in Budin, Sigetvar in Kanije, Filek in Eğri, and Bayburd in Erzurum all lost their *sancak* status in the 1630s"; see Kunt, *The Sultan's Servants,* p. 90.

[59]Ibid., p. 65.

The uncertain fate of the governors was visible in other relevant decisions made vis-à-vis their positions. In fact, the lack of state policy was painfully clear on many points, including how long officials were to remain at a certain post. Whereas in the first period under investigation the time in office varied between one and two years, in the second period governors either remained in office for long periods (4 years) or for very short periods (less than a year). This is proof of the state's lack of a policy concerning the governors, especially because when they managed to remain for long periods of time, they did so by fierce struggles. Since not all governors were eliminated at the same time, a warlord kind of struggle erupted for the remaining positions. For instance, one governor went twice to different provinces, claiming them as awarded by the state, but he was not able to seize possession of his posts because stubborn governors would not leave their posts. During the second incident the wandering governor was ambushed and killed by his competitor.[60] This seems to be the tragic end of many officeless individuals in search of land and revenues.

To recapitulate, an investigation into the appointments of the primary provincial officials (governors and governor-generals) demonstrates that, overall, governors lost out under the pressure of state manipulation of the regional scene. While not all governors lost, fierce struggles jarred the countryside. And, overall, governor-generals won under the state's concerted effort to use them as the main bureaucrats and centralizers of the provinces. This process led to the rise of a strong quasi-entrepreneurial class with its own sources of income, its own army of retainers, and thus every basis for future autonomy.

[60]Ibid., pp. 89–90.

4

Ottoman Peasants:
Rational or Indifferent?

A FEW DAYS BEFORE THE MIDDLE OF THE MONTH OF ŞABAN 1063
(1653), Ibrahim left his village of Alibeyli, traveled across the Çal
Mountains and the plain of Manisa, a journey of at least a couple of days, and came to court in Manisa to request an explanation from
the kadı regarding relentless increases in taxation. He emphatically argued that he did not believe there could be a sultanic order to collect so
many taxes and therefore requested documents of proof regarding taxation. With this demand he demonstrated his suspicion of the local tax-
collecting officials and his faith in the justice of the sultan. Unwilling to
question the higher authority of the sultan and trusting that the "circle of
justice" was functioning properly, he accused local officials of abuse. He
was shown the latest imperial orders demanding new and varied taxes and
returned home, disappearing from the historical records.

Ibrahim did not rebel in alliance with his fellow peasants, or with his
rural patrons, for that matter. Unable to pay taxes any longer, he might
have left the village and joined bands of vagrants in search of a livelihood.
Instead, Ibrahim chose to complain. He undertook a long journey to
court, faced the local judge, and presented his grievances. He might have
couched his complaints in language suitable for the court, never doubting
the justice of the sultan but questioning lesser officials.[1] In fact, he was

[1]James Scott, *Domination and the Arts of Resistance: Hidden Transcripts* (New Haven,
1990), argues that both the powerful and the powerless have a public and a hidden language;
that the powerless express themselves differently in the presence of authority than in the
presence of equals or nonthreatening others. Yet, according to Scott, they know very well the
source of their exploitation; they choose to present an image of submission for fear of mak-

probably correct in accusing the regional officials of corruption. The judge effectively reinforced Ibrahim's sense of exploitation by showing him proof of sultanic orders. Yet the important point remains that he was willing to undertake a long journey to clarify matters over which he probably had little control.[2] Moreover, the court made Ibrahim's actions possible by creating an alternative route for channeling complaints and setting into motion a mechanism by which some regional conflict could be alleviated.

Why didn't Ottoman peasants rebel? Given that the socioeconomic situation of the peasantry had clearly deteriorated under the pressure of population growth, state centralization, and the dramatic increases in the exactions of state and regional power holders, the question begs an answer. Most European countries that experienced the seventeenth-century crisis had witnessed revolts by their rural populations. Since the Eurasian continent experienced similar crises and since agrarian structures predominated in these areas, it is fair to ask why rebellious activity was absent in the Ottoman lands. Peasants in the seventeenth-century Ottoman Empire did find themselves confronted with increasing hardships related to population growth, economic distress, and heightened exploitation by state and other regional political elites. Most elites who staffed the central and regional hierarchies of power were in some sense guilty in the debacle of rural Ottoman relations. But peasants were either incapable of or uninterested in rebellion.

This chapter is not about the "hidden transcripts" of the weak. It is mostly about the constraints on peasant action. It is difficult to understand the "hidden transcripts" of peasants or the reasoning behind individual peasant behavior in historical contexts. Fortunately, it is relatively easier to determine the constraints on explicit peasant action given the manner in which central and regional rule were organized and the organizational and ideological opportunities and resources in the villages.

State action can provide the incentives for collective action. A state that is centralizing can infuriate the peasantry as it intrudes further and further into their lives. As emerging statesmen make war and bureaucrats tax

---

ing it even more difficult for themselves. And the powerful put on public displays of power and pomp to convince the powerless of their domination. What is not clear, however, is the degree to which the existence of "public transcripts" hinders collective action.

[2]We know the journey was long since we know the location of the village of Alibeyli. We also have information about a request villagers from Alibeyli made to the government that a market be established in their region since the travel to Manisa was so long and onerous. Feridun Emecen, *XVI Asırda Manisa Kazası* (Ankara, 1989), p. 269.

the people to finance statesmen, peasants are recruited into the army and are taxed heavily for purposes of war. In the process, Charles Tilly argues, peasants see most of their economic subsistence and their savings for social and cultural functions disappear. They revolt.[3] Most of the Moral Economy arguments would also support the notion that increased state interference and commercialization of agriculture lead to irritating changes in the modes of peasant subsistence.[4] Commercialization of agriculture directly affects peasant potential for rebellion through its effect on class relations.[5] Samuel Popkin would agree, since state action and commercialization offer peasants incentives for participatory action, which when frustrated leads to rebellion.[6]

In Theda Skocpol's presentation, when the state collapses, controls on the peasant population effectively collapse as well, presenting opportunities for rebellion.[7] Here it is the inability of the state to control, the retrenchment from the provinces, that provides the peasantry with the sense that it is time for opposition. Eric Wolf's classic study of twentieth-century revolutions also keys the peasants in as actors whose perceptions of their opportunity is changed when central regimes collapse or weaken.[8] To classify these diverse circumstances, one needs to assess state actions, which might be repeated in times of formation or collapse and which create opportunities for collective action. For example, such state action might increase the opportunities for alliances between aggrieved classes; this sort of outcome might appear in times of either breakdown or potential strengthening.

In this study, state action is seen in interactional relation to the social structure. In this sense, the system of rule as established in the past impinges on the opportunities and constraints on provincial groups, providing them with boundaries of action. At the same time, state policies geared to responding to crises, controlling provinces, and extracting ben-

[3]Charles Tilly, ed. *The Formation of National States in Western Europe* (Princeton, 1979); *As Sociology Meets History* (New York, 1981); *The Contentious French* (Cambridge, Mass., 1986); *Coercion, Capital, and European States, AD 990–1990* (Oxford, 1990).

[4]James Scott, *The Moral Economy of the Peasant* (New Haven, 1976); Eric R. Wolf, *Peasant Wars of the Twentieth Century* (New York, 1973); Joel Migdal, *Peasants, Politics, and Revolution: Pressures toward Political and Social Change in the Third World* (Princeton, 1974).

[5]Barrington Moore, *Social Origins of Dictatorship and Democracy: Lord and Peasant in the Making of the Modern World* (Boston, 1966).

[6]Samuel Popkin, *The Rational Peasant: The Political Economy of Rural Society in Vietnam* (Berkeley, 1979).

[7]Theda Skocpol, *States and Social Revolutions: A Comparative Analysis of France, Russia, and China* (Cambridge, 1979).

[8]Wolf, *Peasant Wars.*

efits also alter established relations between state and social groups, providing new opportunities and constraints. State action, then, cannot be studied and understood in a vacuum; it requires analysis of societal arrangements.

Although we are used to thinking of social structural conditions that are likely to lead to peasant rebellions, we usually do not think in terms of social structures inhibiting collective action. To the degree that the structure of society is constituted to facilitate the formation and organization of opposition movements, providing them with resources and communication channels to disseminate ideas, strategies, and solidarities, rebellions are more likely to occur.[9] Collective action can be carried out by an aggrieved group when they have organized as a collectivity, and when they have accumulated enough resources and mobilized around key issues to wage a struggle.[10] In the absence of one or a few of these requirements, groups either are ineffectual or need to ally with other societal groups to reinforce their assets. In light of the relative lack of resources peasants can draw on, researchers have acknowledged the importance of potential allies for peasant collective action.[11] In the absence of resources, peasants can reinforce their claims only by allying with groups with similar claims. For groups to enter alliances, they have to share at least some grievances and be in regular contact so as to exchange information and assess the benefits of an alliance.

Peasant rebellions did not occur in Ottoman society because of the inherent qualities of the Ottoman social structure and the manner in which the Ottoman state chose to manipulate these qualities under stressful socioeconomic conditions. A combination of state action in the periphery,

---

[9]Variations of this theme have been offered in the literature of collective action as well as that of peasant rebellion. Charles Tilly, for example, built a model of collective action specifically emphasizing the variables of organization, resources, and mobilization under conditions of repression or facilitation; see *From Mobilization to Revolution* (Reading, Mass., 1978). Jeffery Paige labors over the types of structural arrangements of agrarian regimes, class relations, and the nature of the conflict that they engender, *Agrarian Revolution* (New York, 1975). Scott, Wolf, and Migdal concentrate on patron-client relations but also on communities and their characteristics in the explanation of peasant movements; see Scott, *Moral Economy;* Wolf, *Peasant Wars;* Migdal, *Politics and Revolution.*

[10]Tilly, *From Mobilization to Revolution.*

[11]John Walton, *Reluctant Rebels: Comparative Studies of Revolution and Underdevelopment* (New York, 1984). See also Roland Mousnier, "Recherches sur les soulèvements populaires en France avant la Fronde," *Revue d'histoire moderne et contemporaine* 5 (1958): 81–113; William Brustein, "Class Conflict and Class Collaboration in Regional Rebellions, 1500–1700," *Theory and Society* 14 (1985): 445–68; and William Brustein and Margaret Levi, "The Geography of Rebellion: Rulers, Rebels, and Regions, 1500 to 1700," *Theory and Society* 16 (1987): 467–95.

the structure of society, and the inability to rally other classes to their cause rendered the peasantry unable to act in rebellion against the state. Five different aspects of state action and structures of interaction explain the lack of peasant rebellion: (1) structures of control and alternatives of control; (2) rotation of officials and potential community leaders; (3) organization of production, labor, and rural life; (4) alternative organizations outside production; and (5) rural networks of trust and trade. The first points are closely related. Ottoman society exhibited structural features of control that severely hindered collective action on the part of a single group or a few in alliance. The ordering of groups in function and in rhythms of action which brought them together for specified periods of time, under controlled circumstances, became detrimental to the formation of alliances across social groups. The lack of private ownership of land enabled the state to rotate its landholding elites, incapacitating them in many ways. Moreover, different groups were more or less kept separate in their daily routines and controlled by a state attempting to remain all-powerful above the various configurations within society. To the degree that different classes mixed, but did not really combine, and to the degree that they mixed and were mutually competitive and conflictual, alliances across classes were not to be found.

The structure of rule called for several other secondary relationships that modified the primary patron-client relationship. These relationships, also partly keyed as patron-client ones, tended to further diminish the strength of the cultivator-noncultivator relationship. A variety of noncultivators acted as agents or quasi-agents of the state by collecting taxes and administering the provinces, so interrupting the cultivators' contact with their patrons. Even more important among these officials was the local judge, who with authority provided by the state to oversee rural administration penetrated the dyadic cultivator-noncultivator relationship. The fact that the local judge was tied to both peasant and state, providing an alternative route of action for the aggrieved peasantry, transformed the odds of collective action.

In the absence of allies, peasants can make a difference, at least locally, by organizing active village societies. Peasants organize collective action when the rural social structure, the organization for production, alternative organizations outside production, and rural networks, from trade to measures of self-help and traditional and cultural occasions, bring them together in regular interaction. For example, French villages, with such institutions as the *terroir*, the church, and Sunday mass, rank high on the level of cohesion. The Ottoman provinces had few integrative institutions, partly because of the highly fluid nature of the groups moving back and forth between stages of agriculture and nomadism, and partly because of the competitive and conflictual nature of certain institutional arrangements in the rural setting.

I argue in this chapter that, despite the socioeconomic crisis of the seventeenth century and the increased exploitation of the state, Ottoman peasants were unable to become rebellious because of several structural barriers that were well entrenched in state-society relations. Furthermore, I demonstrate that most of the alternatives pursued by the peasantry were built into the system and maintained part of its fluidity as well as its resiliency against collective action. Peasants had a variety of options including rebellion, increased cultivation, and migration out of the village. Generally, rebellion is but one option among many and, in fact, is probably the most difficult and onerous. Therefore, before embarking on drastic confrontation with the oppressor, the oppressed may pursue avoidance ploys.[12] Among the most prominent are flight, renomadization (with accompanying changes in the mode of production), and migrations to distant highlands inaccessible to power holders. In the Ottoman Empire, migration to the cities, temporary employment opportunities, and religious schooling became attractive possibilities, especially for young unattached men. Peasants also made use of periodic settlements and the extra land these offered for occasional cultivation, and when conditions worsened they reverted to nomadism. They tried to adapt, but a rapacious state often caught up with them, registered them on other settlements, and forced them to pay additional taxes. For every peasant alternative, state agents, tax collectors, and officials with various claims devised a novel response. Alternatives, then, became temporary solutions practiced by some in the game of one-upsmanship with the state and its officials.[13]

This chapter in many ways operates at two levels. On the one hand, I present simple and clear arguments about structures of control and odds for collective action, reconstructing the macro-to-micro linkages that hindered the development of cohesive intragroup and intergroup alliances. On the other hand, I blur this clear picture by depicting the nature of alternative forms of survival that provided an escape hatch for some of the peasantry.

[12]Michael Adas, "From Avoidance to Confrontation: Peasant Protest in Precolonial and Colonial Southeast Asia," *Comparative Study of Society and History* 23 (1981): 217–47. James C. Scott, *Weapons of the Weak: Everyday Forms of Peasant Resistance* (New Haven, 1985).

[13]Halil Inalcık, "Adaletnameler," *Belgeler* 2 (1965): 49–145.

Patron-Client Relations: Fictitious Landholders?

Historically, European peasants rebelled against either the landholder class or the state, often allying with the nobility against the latter. Where rebellions occurred against the state, peasants and lords shared both an interest in allying against the state and the opportunity structure for forming such an alliance. They were engaged in long-standing tenure arrangements, with shared interests and a history of social and cultural dealings. Similar conditions were missing in the Ottoman case.

I take the necessary condition for peasant rebellion against the state to be that both parties, peasants and elites, must have an interest in alliance and rebellion. As I argued in Chapter 3, despite the hardships Ottoman elites were subjected to beginning in the late sixteenth century, they seem to have remained uninterested in rebellion. And, as I argued in Chapter 2, it is possible that Ottoman peasants who were affected by the various economic and demographic crises of the same period could have had an interest in rebellious activity. Yet, the argument in this chapter is that the opportunity structure for alliance was missing. Assuming an interest in rebellion—at least on the part of the peasantry—three main structural features of control rendered an alliance between the peasantry and the elites practically impossible. First, because of the organization of production, the peasant did most of his work for the family unit alone. Second, the rotation of the landholder, his frequent assignment to military campaigns, and the resulting lack of long-term investment in the land or the peasant impeded the development of a strong relationship between rural partners. To distance cultivator and noncultivator farther, the institution of the court provided the peasant with the alternative of making official complaints to the local judge. This introduced into the dyadic rural relationship a third party, diminishing the strength of the original relationship. These three particular structural features of patron-client relations determined a different course of action for the Ottoman peasant, one that did not allow for rural alliances in open armed rebellion against the state. Therefore, at a time when most of western Europe witnessed rebellions in which peasants and nobles joined against an increasingly intrusive state apparatus, there were for Ottoman peasants no allies to be found.

The Absentee Landholder

When the tımar holder Halil Bey of Bekir, Burunörümcek, and other villages sent his agent to collect taxes, the peasant Veli B. Mehmed refused to pay and in court complained that he had already paid a considerable amount (130 ölçek of wheat, 42.5 ölçek of barley, 11 ölçek of oats, and also some chickpeas) a few months earlier. When other peasants joined in to corroborate the story, the court ascertained that an imposter, Solak Mehmed Ağa, had collected grain in these villages. Peasants had duly delivered the grain because the impostor held an imperial diploma, later ascertained to be false (1650–51).[14] In Ottoman-style patron-client relations, peasants did not even know their landholders well enough to distinguish them from impostors! In another court record, typical of many others, a tımar holder who was never around his villages requested the local judge to set aside his revenues at harvest time. A note added by a diligent scribe describes this tımar holder as renowned for his absence—partially due to his military duties, but also because of frequent squabbles with the peasants of various villages (1654–55).[15]

What do these stories imply about lifestyles of patrons and clients, their interactions, and the mutual dependence that develops in regular bounded patron-client relations? The peculiarities of prebendal officeholding need to be considered in explaining the lack of strong bonds between tımar holder and peasant. Strong bonds manifest themselves in personal contact or functional dependence. The lack of strong personal contacts between patrons and clients needs to be analyzed within the context of the landholder's activity. Personal contact was severely limited by the nature of land ownership, the temporal and spatial organization of the tımar, and the military obligations of the tımar holder. Rotation every three years was the mainstay of this strategy. It was reinforced by the military duties of the tımar holder, which ensured prolonged absences from the land during campaigns, and the scattering of tımar assignments, which prevented regional officials from consolidating their command over a few villages or a region. The limited impact of the functional dependence between peasants and landholders also derived from the multitude of officials who intruded on this already porous dyadic relationship. An army of other officials contracted by the state or the landholder himself transformed the economic relations of surplus extraction, often taking them over. As a result, we are hard pressed to find the dense mesh of mutual economic and social needs that characterized French patron-client relations prior to the successful alliances of the seventeenth century.[16]

[14]The case is taken from the Manisa court registers (2 Zilhicce 1061), Register 102, case 95.
[15]Manisa court records (21 Ramazan 1065), Register 106, case J30.
[16]Karen Barkey, "Rebellious Alliances: The State and Peasant Unrest in Early Seventeenth-Century France and the Ottoman Empire," *American Sociological Review* 56 (1991): 699–715.

Several features of the Ottoman landholding system were consequential to patron-client relations. Among these were the absence of land ownership and the rotation of landholders. Prebendal in nature, the system was organized around a politico-administrative unit; those assigned a prebend maintained a retinue of soldiers and joined in wars in return for the privilege of taxation and administration of the land. In the absence of real ownership of land, the tımar remained an administrative and political unit, the representative of which was the transient tımar holder, who maintained a rather superficial interest in it. The tımar holder was the representative of the state, bestowed with certain privileges, among which tax collection was of primary importance. The nature of his superficial interest in the land coupled with the keen interest in taxation of peasants provided contradictory results in regular land exploitation. On the one hand, their lack of direct interest in the land made holders able to collect taxes in regular and predictable fashion, benefiting their retinues and therefore benefiting the state with well-maintained armies. On the other hand, their disinterest made the system impersonal enough that no solidarity would emerge between rural classes. The interests of these two groups thus rarely coincided: without doubt, even though the family farm unit was conceived as a production unit, it remained so only for the peasant. It never was so for the tımar holder, who remained apart from agricultural production and far more interested in collecting taxes and maintaining a retinue that would join him at war.

Except for harvesting and taxation times, peasants and landholders had little interaction. A complete image of the tımar holder's life—resembling, say, what we know of the English or French lord's manor life—is missing, making it difficult to reconstruct the nature and strength of rural ties. Although Mustafa Akdağ says that the tımar holder chose the central village (*başkariye*) to live in, we have practically no clue as to what this choice entailed.[17] More important are the demands on the landholder. Responsibility for a large household impressed on him the necessity of land revenues. His household can be compared to a large extended family with kin and military members. According to the law, for every 3,000 akçes of revenue the tımar holder was to bring to war one armed man (*cebelü*).[18] Thus, depending on the size of their holdings, tımar holders

---

[17]Mustafa Akdağ, *Türkiye'nin Iktisadi ve Içtimai Tarihi* (Ankara, 1979), 2:374.

[18]Different sources give us different information. While Halil Inalcık says that a *cebelü* was required for every 3,000 akçes, Nicoarà Beldiceanu asserts that that was true for every 2,000 akçes. See Inalcık, *The Ottoman Empire: The Classical Age, 1300–1600* (New York, 1973), p. 113; and Beldiceanu, *Le tımar dans l'état ottoman (début XIVe–début XVIe siècle)* (Wiesbaden, 1980), pp. 87–88.

might have up to ten armed men to feed and maintain. These men might have been recruited from among the peasantry, but mostly they were recruited from among slaves and the sons of other cavalrymen.[19] In addition, Halil Inalcık speculates that the tımar holders must have had agents to help them in their tax-collecting duty.

For himself and his family, the tımar holder had access to a plot of land or other revenues such as orchards or gardens (*hassa çiftlik*). Although there is no clear information about this, it is logical to assume that the family must have lived on or close to that plot. If the tımar holder did not want to work the land himself, he could either rent it out or make arrangements with peasants for some sort of sharecropping, thereby engaging with a segment of the peasantry.[20] Rare were the cases in court records where peasants complained about labor conditions on *hassa* lands, pushing us to ask how relevant a category this was. In fact, it seems that the practice died out by the end of the sixteenth century.[21] The decline of these special lands for the tımar holders suggests that they did not have time to attend to them, did not live permanently close to them, and stood to derive more benefits from directly exploiting peasant labor on the general tımar land.

The spatial organization of the tımar land both hindered alliances and kept the potential for class conflict under control. The tımar revenue comprised shares of land (*hisse*) scattered among different villages in a district. There was a careful attempt not to assign large chunks of contiguous land

[19]This information is not certain; see Beldiceanu, *Le tımar dans l'état Ottoman*, p. 88.

[20]Ömer L. Barkan, "Çiftlik," in *Islam Ansiklopedisi* (Istanbul, 1945), p. 394. The landholder could use the three days a year of corvée labor owed to him by the peasant; Beldiceanu, *Le tımar dans l'état Ottoman*, p. 56. Also, Inalcık points out the use of the *hassa çiftlik* for rice cultivation and the corvée labor for forcing the *reaya* to work on their land. What seems to have been to the tımar holders' advantage was the regulation that *reaya* working on such lands were to pay tithes much higher than normal (one-fourth instead of one-eighth) and also the ability of the tımar holder to oblige the peasant to pay corvée labor equivalents in cash as well as in days of labor; see Halil Inalcık, "Rice Cultivation and the Çeltükci-Re'aya System in the Ottoman Empire," *Turcica* 14 (1982): 69–141.

[21]The land registers from both Aydın and Saruhan show that some of these *hassa çiftliks*, separated for the tımar holder, were in fact disappearing. Either independently or through administrative fiat these lands were sold or assimilated into peasant holdings; M. A. Cook, *Population Pressure in Rural Anatolia, 1450–1600* (London, 1972), pp. 74–75. Ömer Barkan argues that with military conquests and extended campaigns, landholders were unable to attend to their *hassa* lands and therefore got rid of it; see "Tımar," in *Islam Ansiklopedisi* (Istanbul, 1945), p. 305. Inalcık, on the other hand, sees the case more as the transfer of land tımar holders had previously appropriated from the peasant. Under state supervision, then, the *hassa* lands were returned or resold to the peasant; see "Çiftlik," *Encyclopedia of Islam* (Leiden, 1965), 2:33.

and villages to the same holder. The state assigned the tımar holder a series of villages in a province to tax and administer, but these villages were
not located close to each other. In fact, villages were divided among different holders. The format of both the *tapu tahrir* registers and the *ruznamçe* registers demonstrates this well. For example, we learn that from
among the 113 tımar holders who had land in 1572–73 in the district of
Manisa, 58 had a share in one village, 17 had shares in two villages, 15 had
a whole village, and 4 had one whole and a share of another village. Earlier, in 1531, from among 88 tımar holders, 32 had one full village and 11 had
one full and one share of another village assigned to them. Study of the
ruznamçe registers (tımar bestowal registers) shows that overall tımar
holders were assigned villages from within the same district (*nahiye*) yet
from different regions in the particular district. This strategy made it difficult for landholders and peasants to assemble and ally in groups. On the
one hand, tımar holders could not easily assemble their clients, who were
often separated by significant distances. This situation was in sharp contrast to that for French nobles, who were able to recruit loyal peasants in
their fight against the state.[22] On the other hand, when conflictual relations between peasants and landholders existed, class struggles were also
difficult to organize. Peasants who knew each other on the basis of living
in the same or in contiguous villages did not necessarily deal with the
same landholder. And, since peasants from the same village were bound
to different landholders, they had no direct common enemy to ally
against. Therefore, in most cases of peasant-landholder conflict, individual peasants were pitted against individual landholders.[23]

Campaign activity severely restricted landholder participation in rural
life. The tımar holder spent most of his time on campaign, which for the
Ottoman army started in March and usually ended in October. If the campaign extended into the winter, or the troops wintered over far from
home, the system of tax collection was disrupted. The tımar holder could
count on the help of his agent if he employed one. Often, though, tımar
holders on extended campaigns would organize and send some among
them home to collect revenues for the rest. When these men (*harçlıkçı*)

[22]The example of the duc de Montmorency, whose clients followed him to fight and protect the liberties in their province, is an interesting digression from the general pattern. The
duc de Montmorency was a larger estateholder who owned more scattered land than most
of the smaller lords with their well-circumscribed territory. See Roland Mousnier, *Peasant
Uprisings in the Seventeenth Century: France, Russia, and China* (New York, 1970), p. 42.

[23]Frequent cases in court records vary along these lines; for example, a peasant woman
came to court to constrain the tımar holder from using her orchard, inherited from her
brother; a tımar holder went after individual peasants who were unable to pay their taxes.

arrived in the villages, they needed and expected the cooperation of the kadı for access to tax registers, as well as in the tax collection itself.[24] The peasant, therefore, sometimes did not meet his tımar holder for a year or more, having to deal instead with other officials such as agents, judges, or cavalrymen returning from war on the special mission of tax collection.

This problem seems all the more serious when we consider the movement of the tımar holder during his life. As was discussed in Chapters 2 and 3, one of the salient points of the patrimonial system was its attempt to keep officials both loyal and dependent on the ruler's household. One way of maintaining loyalty was the rotation of various officials. The implications for the tımar official were an unstable life, inability to put down roots in one area, and probably for the small tımar holders misery and hardship during periods of dispossession. Nor were the implications for the peasant bright.

According to this system of rule, the tımar holder did not spend his life on the same land for the duration of his productive career as a military official. As the occupant and beneficiary (*mutasarrıf*) of a tımar, the landholder was a temporary user of the grant, replaced for various reasons, among the most significant being death or rotation.[25] Accordingly, we have to ask two major questions in order to figure out the movement in provinces that impeded the development of strong patron-client ties: What happened to the tımar when the cavalrymen died? What happened during the lifetime of the tımar holder?

Was the tımar system hereditary, so that at the death of the cavalryman his son automatically continued the exploitation of the specific unit? The question of inheritance has troubled most scholars of Ottoman land tenure.[26] No doubt there was variation and adjustment of the system after the inception of the Ottoman system of rule, with much depending on the relative strengths of the two bargaining sides—the state and the estab-

[24]Stanford J. Shaw, *History of the Ottoman Empire and Modern Turkey* (Cambridge, 1976), 1:127. Gilles Veinstein, "L'hivernage en campagne: Talon d'achille du système militaire Ottoman classique," *Studia Islamica* 58 (1983): 109–48.

[25]Accordingly, tımar bestowals were made from two types of vacancies: a first list of tımars that became vacant because of the death of the cavalryman, and a second list of tımars that became vacant as a result of the cavalryman going out on rotation. The first list in fact included all those who lost their tımars because of desertion or retirement.

[26]Inalcık and Filipovic discuss the variations in the system of tenure as peculiarities; Inalcık, *The Ottoman Empire*, p. 115; Nedim Filipovic, "Bosna-Hersekte Tımar Sisteminin Inkişafında Bazı Hususiyetler," *Istanbul Üniversitesi Iktisat Fakültesi Mecmuası* 15 (1953–54): 168. Irène Beldiceanu has argued that during the reign of Murad I (1362–89) the concept of hereditary tımars was accepted but only as an exception to the rule; see Beldiceanu-Steinherr, "Loi sur la transmission du tımar (1536)," *Turcica* 11 (1979): 78–102.

lished dynasties, which were not about to accept rotation out of their land. Therefore, the more permanent tenures were left in the hands of the relatively powerful landed elite established before Ottoman consolidation.[27] Also, from then on, inheritance was used as a strategy to provide those deemed important to the state with special deals. Since according to the regulations the timar holder did not own the land and was not supposed to develop roots in any area, we should assume that in principle his son was not able to inherit his father's timar. In fact, the general rule seems to have been that at his death the timar holder transferred his status to his son, but not his land; the son would receive a land grant smaller than his father's and not necessarily in the same area. The appointment registers from the area of Aydın show that the "truly begotten son" could get a timar at the death of his father as long as he proved the family relationship.[28] Analysis of western Anatolian transfers of land from father to son shows that sons of timar holders were usually assigned timars in different regions, and that this practice became even more frequent in the seventeenth century. In the province of Aydın, for the period 1563–64, 12 of 30 sons of timar holders who were assigned land received it in the same area as their father's. The rest were assigned to other districts in Anatolia. For the period 1654–55, 50 of 51 sons were assigned to districts other than their father's, scattered around Anatolia.[29] My own research, using the same data as Howard and adding data from the province of Saruhan, reaches a similar conclusion for the late sixteenth century. During 1572–82, 31 percent of the timars were handed out as new timars from the same

[27]Beldiceanu-Steinherr argues that the hereditary timar existed in the Ottoman Empire from the very inception of the state in Anatolia. This, she argues, happened because the established families in Anatolia kept their land in their hands forever. This regional argument makes sense for those few established and powerful families from Anatolia who were able to bargain more successfully and remains restricted to the provinces of Karaman, Germiyan, Canik, and İç El. Furthermore, the strong rule of Mehmed II (1451–81) altered this position, since he gave more prominence to the policy of rotation and movement among timar holders; Beldiceanu-Steinherr, "Loi sur la transmission du timar," pp. 89–90.

[28]In the case of the data provided by Howard, the number of these cases in Aydın is not very large. For the years 1563–64, 29 percent of all transactions and 64 percent of new assignments were to sons of timar holders. For the years 1576–77, 18 percent of all transactions and 50 percent of new assignments were to sons of timar holders. For the years 1588–89 Howard found data only on the new assignments. The percentage of those assigned to sons was quite small, only 19 percent. The total transactions include cavalrymen on rotation or those who have gotten better timars, assignments to men in the service of the central provincial government, and sons of deceased timar holders. For the data, see Douglas Howard, "The Ottoman *Timar* System and Its Transformation, 1563–1656," Ph.D. diss., Indiana University, 1987, pp. 167–73.

[29]Ibid.

pool. Among these, 59 percent were handed to sons of timar holders. From among those sons who obtained timars, only 12.5 percent were assigned the same timar, whereas 68.75 percent were assigned different timars. Of these different assignments, 82 percent were outside the district of residence of the father. Although the conditions of transfer changed much after Murad IV's centralization, the same pattern of land assignment for sons remained valid for the second period (1654–55).[30]

The young cavalryman in charge of his relatively small timar unit could not assume that he would spend his life in relatively stable tenure on the land. He would brave war, participate in rotation, and perhaps earn larger and larger holdings to one day equal his father's. Assuming heroism and a successful military career, his increasingly larger timars would be assigned to him from among a second pool, those reserved for rotating state officials. Most historians of the Ottoman Empire agree that the state perceived its best interest to lie in the rotation of the timar holder about every three years.[31] Accordingly, a cavalryman would have to go out on rotation at the latest three years after the original acquisition.[32] In this system, every timar holder was to give up his land rights for a certain period of time, during which he would not hold a grant. The longest period a timar holder would spend without a grant would be 7 years, since regulations asserted that after 7 years timar holders would revert to peasant status and thereby lose all their privileges. During three snapshots of one year each, 1572, 1576, and 1582, an average of 45 percent of the officials were rotated. In the second period, rotation diminished in the sense that it was no longer an individual renouncing his timar but rather rapacious timar holders with no land grant alleging breach of conduct by their landholding rivals and attempting to displace them. As a result, the rotation schedule fluctuated from just a few months to over 5 years.[33]

Echoing a theme from a previous chapter, the effect of the monetary crisis on peasants and landholders was to abridge their relationship

[30]BBA Ruznamçes 37, 46, 59, 676, 681, and 685.

[31]Beldiceanu-Steinherr, "Loi sur la transmission du timar," pp. 83–84, and Beldiceanu, Le timar dans l'état ottoman, pp. 66–67. They obtain this information from the transfer documents themselves. It does not seem to be written in the codes of law. Both Beldiceanu and Beldiceanu-Steinherr argue that the timar assignment could be revoked at any time after three years of exploitation.

[32]This could be either a government decision or a voluntary one. The language of the rotation differentiated between the two options since both dismissal (azl) and renunciation (feragat) were used to designate rotation. The state imperial registry scribes used these terms to mean a regular process; see Howard, "The Ottoman Timar System," p. 86.

[33]BBA Ruznamçes 37, 46, 59, 676, 681, 685. Howard, "The Ottoman Timar System" p. 175, calculates rotation in the late sixteenth century at every 32 months on average and argues that in the early and mid-seventeenth century the time in tenure increases drastically to 10 years.

further. Both suffered from the vagaries of the empire's monetary and inflationary transformations. Tımar holders saw their financial and administrative capacities reduced to the point where they were unable to conduct business as usual. Their decreased authority derived from peasant flight and from the increasing frequency of campaigns that kept them away for long stretches of time. Court cases corroborate this lack of authority: tımar holders who had difficulty making their clients comply ended up in court.[34] A rescript of the time (1648) describes the loss of authority on the part of the tımar holder; the peasants no longer respected their landholder; they still paid their taxes, but they were strict about limiting his stay in villages or performing services for him.[35] Although continuity of traditional practice was an important component of patron-client ties in the Ottoman Empire, the early seventeenth century brought about confrontation and a serious need for arbitration during the fleeting moments of cohabitation.

In sum, if peasant and landholder were relatively distant from each other during the Classical Age, by the mid-sixteenth century they had grown totally apart. From the various applications of rotation to the distress of the elites, especially in the early seventeenth century, the dyadic relationship between peasant and landholder became increasingly fragmented. The tımar holder's position bred insecurity because he rotated posts frequently, stayed away at war, and remained dependent on peasants and other officials for his livelihood as a member of the provincial administration. The peasant's position remained fragile because he was squeezed by an economic crisis and because his landholder was often displaced. The peasant, whose usufructuary rights on the land were hereditary, did not see his landholder very often, and the spatial and temporal dimensions of this particular patron-client relationship ensured that the little interaction that transpired was ridden with tension.

Chains of Local Brokerage: Tax Farmers and Other Officials

In the absence of solid comparable data, it is practically impossible to ascertain the degree of peasant exploitation and compare it across different land regimes. Rather, the arguments made in this section concentrate

---

[34]Manisa court records, Registers 11, 102, 104. For Register no. 11, documents 5 and 6 are good examples of tax and land disputes, respectively.

[35]Suraiya Faroqhi, "Political Activity among Ottoman Taxpayers and the Problem of Sultanic Legitimation (1570–1650)," *Journal of the Economic and Social History of the Orient* 35 (1992): 26–27.

on the nature of linkages and ties, and their frailty, to show how under crisis structural weakness was enhanced.

Scholars of the Ottoman Empire have repeatedly used the rescripts of 1550–1650 to investigate the different abuses of the peasantry by such officials as governor-generals, military commanders, tax farmers, and judges.[36] No one has made the more important point that these abuses were often delivered through a chain of patronage, whose painful links were experienced by the peasantry, thus weakening patronage ties rather than reinforcing them. Peasants often appealed to the court to break these chains of rural dependence. Therefore, I argue that the number and the demands of the different officials who penetrated the dyadic patron-client relation became as important as the weakness of the relation itself. In fact, other tax collectors, tax farmers, or intermediaries to whom governors and landholders farmed out their rights further weakened the relationship between the landholder and the peasant. They also contributed to increased exploitation of the peasantry.

The best illustration of this chain of exploitative patron-client relations comes to us in the context of a love story. In 1650 the complaints of an enraged father at the court of Manisa inadvertently illuminated the case of a chain of tax collection from which many peasants had suffered. The father complained that a group of bandits had befriended his daughter, capturing her out in the woods. Among them, one Ali B. Başir was targeted. Not only was this good-for-nothing bandit in love with the girl, but he also happened to be the lowest-ranked agent in a chain of tax collection starting at the top with the deputy lieutenant governor (*mütesellim*) of Saruhan, Abdülkadir Ağa B. Abdülkerim. This latter had commissioned a certain notable (*ayan*) of Manisa, Ahmet Ağa, to become his agent, who in turn had entitled Ali B. Başir, a well-known local bandit (*eşkiya*) to do the job for him.[37] Contracting out revenues to bandits became increasingly more frequent as tax collection grew burdensome. As chains extended, many deputees of various arrangements (*mütesellim, mübaşir, emin, amil,*) hired intermediaries whom peasants dealt with or encountered at court. Interestingly enough, despite the fact that such high-ranking officials as governors and governor-generals hired out others to collect the petty dues, they easily invaded villages with their retinues and demanded

[36]Inalcık, "Adaletnameler"; Cezar, *Osmanlı Tarihinde Levendler* (Istanbul, 1965); Akdağ, *Celali Isyanları* (Ankara, 1963), and *Türk Halkının Dirlik ve Düzenlik Kavgası* (Ankara, 1975); Faroqhi, "Political Activity."
[37]Manisa court records (22 Zilhicce 1061), Register 102, document 45.

more levies and imposed more burdens.[38] The greater the number of intermediaries, the greater was the likelihood of each swindling the peasant.

Tax farming was another intermediary form of revenue collection that manifested itself between the state and the peasantry as well as between high-ranking regional officials and the peasantry. An intermediate regime between land ownership and prebendal revenue contracting, it entailed a different set of linkages among peasant, tax farmer, and the state. As it developed, tax farming maintained arrangements that were profitable to a strong state where contracts were handed out, regulated, and discontinued as state officials' perceived their needs. As the state lost strength in the next century, tax farming took on the characteristics of life-term tenures (*malikanes*). Both timar holder and tax farmer, in fact, were agents of the state or agents of state officials. Yet their interest in the labor of the peasant differed. The tax farmers paid money in advance to the state for the privilege of taxation, and they were determined to recuperate at least as much if not more rather quickly. The timar holder's exploitation was the result of his disengagement from the productive process because of his military and administrative duties, whereas the tax farmer's exploitation was the product of his keen interest in the product of peasant labor. The latter group was much closer to the traditional absentee landlord class of western Europe.

Tax farming was instituted in the early empire for collection of the revenues of sultanic lands (*havass-i hümayun*), which constituted a substantial 35 percent of the arable land in 1527.[39] Revenues were collected by either salaried officials (*emin* and *kethüda*) or tax farmers. Tax farming (*iltizam*) was the simple sale of state income sources to private individuals who would offer the state a fixed amount of money for the taxation rights to certain plots of land; it was carried out through a bidding system in which the state sold the rights to the land for a period of 1 to 3 years. Mehmed Genç, using Ömer Lütfi Barkan's 1527–28 data on the state treasury, argues that approximately half the tax income that entered the treasury came from tax farming.[40]

A relatively stable and immediate source of income for the state, tax farming gained importance as the sixteenth century wore on and the state

[38]Inalcık, "Adaletnameler," pp. 83–84.

[39]Abdul Rahman Abdul Rahim and Yuzo Nagata, "The Iltizam System in Egypt and Turkey: A Comparative Study," *Journal of Asian and African Studies* 14 (1977): 179–80.

[40]Mehmet Genç, "Osmanlı Maliyesinde Malikane Sistemi," in *Türkiye Iktisat Tarihi Semineri, Metinler/Tartışmalar*, ed. Osman Okyar (Ankara, 1975), p. 234.

treasury grew dependent on it. Yet tax farmers were far from beneficial to the rural population. Tax farms were originally granted for a year or two. Yuzo Nagata argues that, when the state became aware of the damage such short-term leases caused the land system, it tried to extend the lease to three years.[41] This might also have been a ploy to increase the revenue. In any case, there is no denying the impact of this system on the peasantry. The suffering of the peasant was documented in many sultanic decrees that tried to eliminate injustice on the part of tax farmers: Inalcık documents the abuses of these tax farmers and argues that the method of tax farming had spread to all state positions and was increasing rapidly as the state treasury developed shortages. To add insult to injury, bribes were also received at all levels of the appointment process.[42]

Not confined to the state, tax farming infiltrated every level of rural relations. Governors, district governors, and other regional officials who held land grants, sometimes even tımar holders, depended on tax farmers to collect their revenues from the population. This brings us back to a previous argument that most of the cases of rural abuse concentrate on relationships between peasants and agents of various levels of importance. There is no doubt that peasant subsistence was seriously endangered by these demands. I also believe that such intermediaries, as better known faces in villages, tended to further reduce the substance of ties between peasants and tımar holders.

Patronizing the Court: An All Too Frequent Trick or an Ordeal?

"The reaya were undoubtedly in a happier position than the serfs of medieval Europe, the main difference lying in the fact that the Ottoman peasant lived under the protection of a centralized state and its independent legal system."[43] Although this image of legal relations in the countryside is correct and certainly part of the general wisdom, the actual dynamics of the relationship between courts and peasants have not been fully analyzed. Seen from the top, the institution of the court was part of the extension of control over the provinces, a process that continued into

---

[41]Rahman and Nagata, "The Iltizam System," p. 181.

[42]Halil Inalcık, "The Ottoman Decline and Its Effects upon the Reaya," in *Aspects of the Balkans, Continuity and Change, Contributions to the International Balkan Conference*, UCLA 1969, ed. H. Birnbaum and S. Vryonis (The Hague, 1972), pp. 341–42.

[43]Inalcık, *The Ottoman Empire*, p. 112.

the late seventeenth century whereby courts were established in newly conceived districts (*kazas*). Seen from the bottom up, it perpetuated an important tradition of complaint in the empire and in Islamic societies generally. Seen from the eyes of the individuals who belonged to it, the court remained contradictory.

The institution and the judges each had negative effects on the ability of peasants to forge alliances with rural groups. The court system as established throughout the Ottoman lands was the main alternative for direct contact with the state, and complaint to the state, about local conditions. Ottoman peasants made frequent use of the courts, which functioned to deflect anger away from local tax-collecting patrons and acted as a safety valve for the Ottoman state. Peasants as well as nomads in rural society used local courts as a recourse against those who abused their livelihood and privileges. Especially for the peasant, the court was the main foundation of mediation between himself and the timar holder. It also weakened the tie between landholder and peasant, hampering their potential efforts at alliances.

The actions of judges should be examined in light of their dependence on the state as well as their network of rural relations. The state used the court to preserve control over two social classes while simultaneously controlling the judges themselves. Rotation and dependence on the state for positions maintained court officials' allegiance to the central government and also discouraged peasant-judge alliances. For the local judges, being subject to a system of rotation meant reestablishing themselves every few years. The strain created by such movement must have been the cause of various abuses and corruption. Neither the judiciary's lack of independence nor the perpetuation of abuses by its members diminished its popular legitimacy. The court remained one of the few stable institutions in the Ottoman rural setting whose functions transcended the infractions of individual members. I propose that we look at the position of the local judge in both micro patron-client relations an the more macro rural social structure.

Parallel to the military-administrative chain of command existed the judicial-administrative chain, which ended up in the central towns with the kadı, who administered the law for the state. Through their active participation in rural affairs, since they handled the court cases for a central town and all its surrounding villages, judges became important to both the state and the local population. Accordingly, most royal decrees (*fermans*) were written jointly to the governor-general or governor and to the kadı, in his capacity as the legal representative of the state.[44] In the provinces, the kadı mediated disputes between peasants and arbitrated between peasants and tımar holders or various other officials, intermediaries, and agents. He represented the closest and most reliable recourse for the peasant, short of going to the Porte and asking the imperial council for an audience.[45] Courts were the main rural mechanism for redressing wrongs. Judges were authorized to resolve matters in court or to mediate between the state and the people by writing up the necessary petitions. Often, in matters referring to the abuses of the tımar holder or other local state officials, the kadı took action against the officials. Similarly tımar holders and other state officials who encountered resistance from the peasantry had recourse to the judge.[46] Despite the reliance of local state officials on the court, the tımar holder and the kadı competed for administrative power and privilege and tried to impinge on each other's territory. As the sheer number of court cases demonstrates, the peasant must have considered the court his primary refuge from the vagaries of land tenure. The numbers of peasants who utilized the court is impressive, particularly since a fee was required to have cases resolved in court. Peasants apparently considered making the trip to the central town or paying the court fee a worthwhile endeavor.[47]

Patronage of the court is consequential to collective action. The existence of the court as a semi-independent institution located outside the traditional patron-client relationship encouraged the peasantry to see it as an alternative structure for rural action. And to the degree that the kadı remained, at least in perception, autonomous from the landholding elite and the state, his role as a mediator and alleviator of social and collective tension would last.[48] The existence of this semiautonomous institution thus eased the tensions that might have led to collective action.

The argument can be substantiated in comparative perspective. In France, for example, where the seignorial judge was the appointee of the

[44]Uriel Heyd, *Ottoman Documents on Palestine, 1552–1615: A Study of the Firman According to the Mühimme Defteri* (Oxford, 1960), p. 19.

[45]Faroqhi, "Political Activity," p. 2, explains the procedure of complaint outside the local judicial route in which villagers hired a representative to travel to the Porte and present their grievances. She does not provide a sense of the frequency of this strategy.

[46]The most frequent cases in the court records are disputes regarding inheritance. Following closely are tax cases, complaints by both peasants and various officials, especially tımar holders, who made up 14 percent of the cases.

[47]Obviously, it is easy to make this argument, and yet we do not have any clue about how many villagers chose not to go to court for every villager who chose to go. The Manisa court records, however, give a flavor of the amount and variety of court cases.

[48]Akdağ, *Celali İsyanları*, p. 117.

local feudal lord, the system did not allow the peasant an independent route of complaint. Accordingly, where restricted access to channels of complaint provided peasants with only one route of mitigation—one that was also biased against their interests—the system unwillingly encouraged their collective action. The blocked and static nature of structured inequality led to a dynamic response on the part of those with restricted access. In the Ottoman case, the perception of alternative avenues of redress within the system must have acted as a deterrent to action.

The existence of a court as an intermediate organization between landholder and peasant lowered the incidence of collective engagements while multiplying individual action. As the story of Ibrahim from Alibeyli demonstrates, peasants took their quest into their own hands and sometimes traveled long distances to contact members of the provincial judicial hierarchy. The variety of court cases from the records in Manisa corroborates these points; issues brought to court had to do with individual complaints, either among peasants or between peasants and regional officials, and very few cases involved more than two or three villagers acting together. Often where more peasants were involved it was at the request of the judge, who tried to ascertain the abuse of a tax official by summoning cultivators from the same district. Among the cases under investigation, few involved peasants cooperating within their own village or across villages without first having been accused by a plaintiff and put on the defensive. These were usually tax cases in which one tax official demanded his share of the produce and accused a community or part of a community of not paying.

Whereas court records demonstrate the peasantry's high reliance on the court, other records, especially rescripts issued by the sultans, paint an abusive image of the judge. The small-town judge in these rescripts is depicted as a rapacious, detestable man who abuses his tax-collection duties and makes alliances with unsavory mercenaries and bandits.[49] How can we understand the contradiction in these different sources? Although we have not yet begun to solve the puzzle of Ottoman rural relations, we need to differentiate between the regularity and stability of the institution of the court and the instability and whims of its individual members. While the former established a routine of patronage, the latter ensured that the patronage would remain institutional and not personal. Rural alliances between peasants and local judicial officials did not occur.

---

[49]Inalcık, "Adaletnameler," pp. 75–78; Faroqhi, "Political Activity," pp. 17–19.

Supervision by the state and rotation of office were at the root of erratic kadı performance. After the middle of the sixteenth century, there was a dramatic increase in the number of judges and deputy judges who wanted positions. The result was the reinforcing of the rotation system at the level of judges as well. Inalcık discusses a rotation system that closely resembles that of the tımar holder: "In addition to the bureaucratic concern of finding employment for as many candidates as possible, considerations of a political nature also affected the government's decision to grant a shorter period of tenure (*tasarruf*). In any case, it was a kind of 'constitutional' precept in the Ottoman patrimonial system not to allow government agents to hold a provincial position too long, lest he establish local connections and be integrated into the community."[50] There were too many candidates, too few positions, and many more threatening to overflow the institution, especially young men of peasant origin who crowded the religious schools, which were paths to judgeships.[51] The rewards of a religious education had attracted many men from rural origins to the religious schools, and according to one observer "those who carry turbans . . . together numbered about forty thousand toward the end of the fifteenth century."[52] An attempt was made to remedy the situation in 1597, when a government rescript ordered small-town kadıs to rotate more often, every two years and wait for three years in Istanbul (for schooling) before a new assignment. This period of schooling put intense monetary pressures on the purse of kadıs, who had to perform ceremonial functions in Istanbul.

Under such circumstances of pressure the judges were also prone to abuse the peasantry. To the degree that they needed to ensure their survival on rotation, judges often sought to profit from the peasantry. Evliya Çelebi, the famous traveler, is supposed to have said "that such and such a cadiship brought an annual revenue so much 'in justice' but twice as much 'in injustice.' "[53] There were various mechanisms of enhancing one's livelihood. For example, the kadıs who lived in town farmed out their office to *naibs*, subordinate judges, thereby increasing their own sometimes precarious income.[54] These subordinate judges were poorly trained representatives who ended up going to the villages to conduct legal matters

[50]Inalcık, "The *Ruznamçe* Registers of the *Kadıasker* of Rumeli as Preserved in the Istanbul Müftülük Archives," *Turcica* 20 (1988): 264.

[51]Ibid., p. 257.

[52]Ibid., p. 257, n. 15.

[53]Ibid., p. 266.

[54]Ismail Hakkı Uzunçarşılı, *Osmanlı Devletinin İlmiye Teşkilatı* (Ankara, 1984), p. 117.

and also to make sure that they reimbursed themselves by extracting extra fees from the peasantry. The advice literature, as well as the justice decrees, are replete with cases of abuse by judges and their subordinates against the rural population.[55]

It is difficult to assess the impact of this contradiction whereby judges who were the main source of justice for the peasantry were at the same time exploiting them whenever possible. The only way to reconcile these aspects is to note that the circumstances of peasant abuse started only in the mid-sixteenth century and that there was by then an established collective memory among the peasantry as to the legitimacy of the courts. Even in the seventeenth-century cases the court, despite abuse and exploitation, continued to function on behalf of the peasantry and to solve their problems, especially vis-à-vis the various tax officials. It remained in the interest of the judges to protect the peasantry, especially from its rival elite group, the timar and zeamet holders. Judges became dependent on peasants since they, unlike other elites, lacked arms and armies. But judges never truly became patrons for peasants since they moved around at least as frequently as the timar holders. The peasantry's world of clientship was one where many patrons were temporary and ready to take full advantage of the peasant's resources. Yet the fact that all these patrons were transient should have allowed peasants to plot jacqueries, rebellions, and collective activity to redress all the wrongs done to them. In the next section I demonstrate why that was not the case.

Peasant Rural Organization

The lack of alliances between producers and elites was the result of the structural constraints that separated these groups. At the same time, the structure of patron-client relations and the court institution in the countryside allowed for an alternative form of action that deflected the need for alliances and collective action. But, in the absence of elite allies, the peasantry as a class of exploited rural producers did not organize for rebellion either. The failure of collective action in the villages can be explained by the lack of rural structures conducive to organization.

[55]Inalcık, "Adaletnameler," pp. 75–78. The abuses of the kadıs are recorded by many critics of the period; the anonymous author of *Kitab-i Müstetab*, Selâniki, Akhisari, Koçi Bey, and Mustafa Ali. See also the documents of abuse cited by Faroqhi in "Political Activity," pp. 17–20.

Organization for Production

The mechanics of production set up a routine that reinforced certain relations and ties over others. At the village level, the life of peasants was organized around the basic economic unit of the family farm (çift-hane), which was geared to the production and direct consumption of surplus. The farm unit "consisted of organization of agricultural production on the basis of peasant households, hanes, each of which was given a çift or çiftlik, i.e., a plot of land of sufficient size to sustain one peasant household and pay the "rent" to the land holder (the state). The size of the çiftlik varied with the fertility of the soil from 60 dönüm to 150. This was the basic agricultural unit."[56] Moreover, "since the tımars were indivisible and unalterable units as recorded in the survey books, the çift-hane units too were held indivisible and unalterable in order to protect the fixed tımar income."[57]

The organization of tasks around individual families equipped with the necessary tools and farm animals (two oxen) on their own individual farm remains the most impressive piece of information on peasant self-reliance. The Ottoman rural production unit was focused on the peasant and his family, on his ability to feed his family and pay his dues to the landholder and the state. Families lived in independent, self-sufficient units, very few of which could make up a village. Peasants cultivated the fields and could have gardens around their homes to grow fruits and vegetables. Although they seem to have owned some livestock, they used them for their milk or their labor rather than for meat. Those villagers who owned the most sheep were usually either settled nomads or of nomad descent.[58] Prosperity was measured in ownership of extra oxen, or kitchen and household utensils, and great prosperity in the ownership of vineyards (if the land permitted) and even a couple of slaves. Yet production was organized as an independent, self-reliant process where key decisions were made by the peasant. In this system, which Inalcık differentiates as "title deed land" (tapulu arazi), the head of the household made all production decisions: he had to procure the agricultural implements, the oxen, and the grain. Fairly independent, the Ottoman peasant did not have any added obliga-

---

[56]Inalcık, "The Emergence of Big Farms, Çiftliks: State, Landlords and Tenants," in Contributions à l'histoire économique et sociale de l'empire Ottoman, ed. Jean-Louis Bacqué-Grammont and Paul Dumont (Louvain, 1984), p. 106.

[57]Ibid., p. 107.

[58]Inalcık, "A Case Study of the Village Microeconomy: Villages in the Bursa Sancak, 1520–1593," in The Middle East and the Balkans under the Ottoman Empire: Essays on Economy and Society (Bloomington, 1993).

tions to the landholder other than those stated in the regular law books.[59] The independence of the peasant was reinforced by the mode of collection: the *çift resmi* and other individual incidental taxes were based on individual household production and paid to the landholder or his representative.

The perception that this was the best system of land exploitation was prevalent throughout the Mediterranean and the Middle East, where it was widely replicated. The closest example is the Roman colonate; both systems granted the land to the peasant and allowed him and his family the direct exploitation of its resources. The peasant family had usufructury rights to the state land and owned their house and barn as well as orchards and gardens. The peasant was a life-long tenant on an indivisible unit, and on his death his sons were to continue cultivation together. As a simple and efficient model of land tenure, the state had an interest in maintaining the workings of the system as true to stated rules and as fixed as possible. This meant that the state tried to maintain the family farm unit as the key production unit and forbade its breakup. It also forbade the movement of its peasants short of creating a serf class, and development of these units into larger, less controllable as well as more exploitative units under the control of western-style landlords. Rural classes, on the other hand, reacted to try to modify the system to their advantage, either through the available state channels or through alternative modes of avoidance.

In the attempt to adjust to the changes of the seventeenth century, the state tried to keep the family farm unit intact, while the peasant searched for flexibility that would allow him to adapt. These contradictory spheres of action operated along certain rural institutions. The first feature of importance was the inalienability of the farm unit. The government wished that land units not be broken down, but the data point toward smaller and smaller units, with individuals splitting from the original unit and establishing their own productive unit, even if this latter was smaller.[60]

---

[59]Inalcık, "Köy, Köylü ve Imparatorluk," in *V. Milletlerarası Türkiye Sosyal ve Iktisat Tarihi Kongresi,* pp. 1–11. The land codes are quite specific about the obligations of peasants to their tımar holder; yet these rules do not transform the basic production process into a dependent one. See Barkan, *XV ve XVI Asırlarda Osmanlı Imparatorluğunda Zirai Ekonominin Hukuki ve Mali Esasları,* Vol. 1: *Kanunlar* (Istanbul, 1943).

[60]Inalcık reiterates the argument that the land unit was not to be broken down most recently in his article "Köy, Köylü," p. 2. He first made this argument in "Land Problems in Turkish History," *Muslim World* 45 (1955): 223–24 and developed it in "The Emergence of Big Farms," p. 106. Here, Inalcık insists on this notion of indivisibility, arguing that the state restored units to their original format whenever the integrity of the unit was threatened. The

Therefore, instead of the regular full-size unit, we encounter increasingly smaller units such as the half-size (*nim çift*) or individuals with very little land (*bennak*).[61] This tendency attests to the increased segmentation of peasant family units, which were breaking down under the tension of population pressure or economic distress. This indicates not only a deterioration in the condition of the peasantry but also a change in the social fabric of rural society, where movement out of the family farm unit became an adopted solution.

Closely related was the stratification system, determined originally by the size of the land unit themselves, which also proved to be more flexible than government injunction and regulations suggested. Similarly, mobility and extra income opportunities added flexibility. The stratification system involved more than distinctions based on land size and it differentiated villagers according to wealth, with the poor and landless at the bottom of the hierarchy.[62] Also, the judges' records make it clear that some peasants owned larger houses, more oxen, and more farming and household implements. The state insisted on the distinctions among peasants according to the amount of land they held. Although the system of tenure vis-à-vis the peasantry comes across as quite rigid, some flexibility arose from a variety of alternatives available to the peasant to increase his revenue. For example, a peasant who had a smaller piece of land could also be legally employed by those who had more land. Often richer peasants hired poorer, landless ones. According to the law, peasants could rent and cultivate other plots as long as they planted and sowed their own plots

---

study of the land regulations edited by Barkan attests to the same government requirement; see *Kanunlar,* p. 254. This argument was used by Akdağ, who claimed that since the land unit was not to be broken, the increasing number of extra males in the family would have to leave the land and become vagrants; see *Türk Halkının Dirlik ve Düzenlik Kavgası.* All three have recently been challenged. Cook, *Population Pressure,* pp. 37, 85, shows many more half-size tenures than full-size tenures.

[61]In Cook's data, in 1575 one district of Aydın counts 44 *çifts* and 177 *nim çifts;* see *Population Pressure,* pp. 37, 85. For the *kaza* of Manisa, Emecen shows that overall there were many more half-size tenures (702), compared to 177 full-size tenures in 1575. Furthermore, the comparison of the 1531 survey to the 1575 survey shows dramatic increases in the number of half-size tenures together with comparable decreases in the number of full-size tenures, indicating a breakup of larger tenures. See Emecen, *XVI Asırda Manisa Kazası,* p. 231. Court records provide another account. Manisa records show that often brothers who were not able to manage the farm collectively appeared in court and sold their share to one member of the family. That would explain some of the contention regarding the question of indivisibility, but there are far fewer such cases.

[62]It is difficult here to gauge exact class relations within villages since the records regarding land are state-imposed. The court records provide a glimpse of class relations, but they are biased because a fee was needed to use the court.

first.[63] Obviously, increased cultivation was encouraged by the state, while delinquency was discouraged by the state's threat to take away land left fallow for three years.[64] Extra cultivation seems to have been fairly widespread in the sixteenth century. In Saruhan, 21.35 percent of the villages in the district of Manisa were cultivated by outsiders, that is, by peasants who lived elsewhere and commuted to these lands. These villages seem otherwise deserted; no taxes or other information show on the registers.[65]

The retention of the initial productive unit was beneficial for both the state and the tımar holder. The interests of the tımar holder were best served when he collected his share of the taxes, which allowed him to live, to feed and clothe his retinue, and to attend to war. For this, he received from each family farm unit the combined tax called *çift resmi*, which originally comprised seven particular services equivalent in cash value to 22 akçes. These included a corvée labor of three days, one cartload of hay, one half-cartload of straw, one cartload of firewood, and transport services.[66] Soon after its establishment, the tax was converted into a cash amount of 22 akçes, which the peasant had to pay after selling his produce. Despite this, tımar holders managed to extract services and cash from the peasants on the grounds that these were established by custom. Besides this, the peasant was responsible for the taxes authorized by Islamic law; the tithe (*öşür*) on cereal crops, the poll tax (*cizye*) on non-Muslims, and other taxes. Taxable on tımar, zeamet, and has lands, the tithe was collected by agents of the landholders, who also collected another tax (*salariye*) designed to reimburse them for their expenses during collection. Grain collections took place on the individual fields, sometimes with the judge and the village elders assisting. In the context of these taxes, the peasant was obliged to build a barn and first carry the grain to the storehouse and later to market, the "*akrep bazar*" of the law codes, which was not supposed to be more than one day away.[67]

[63]Barkan, *Kanunlar*. See also Faroqhi, "Rural Society in Anatolia and the Balkans during the Sixteenth Century," pt. 2. *Turcica* 11 (1979): 109.

[64]Lütfi Güçer, *XVI–XVII. Asırlarda Osmanlı İmparatorluğunda Habubat Meselesi ve Hububattan Alınan Vergiler* (Istanbul, 1964). See also Barkan, *Kanunlar*.

[65]This phenomenon was again within the realm of possibilities accepted by the state as long as the integrity of the land unit was maintained. This integrity was maintained by restricting peasant mobility. Although legally free, the peasant was not allowed to move to other lands without the payment of a fine (*çift-bozan akçesi*), and he could be found and recalled by the tımar holder at any time up to 15 years.

[66]Inalcık, "Osmanlılarda Raiyyet Rüsumu," *Belleten* 23 (1959): 580.

[67]Güçer, *XVI–XVII. Asırlarda Hububat Meselesi*, pp. 44–57; Barkan, *Kanunlar*, pp. 6–18.

In general, where taxes were the communal responsibility of a village they tended to increase the level of organization and solidarity of the community, simply because they encouraged communication and organization. Communal organization, however, results only if the villagers are not strictly controlled by the dominant classes. In the Ottoman Empire, although the collection of the *çift resmi* and other individual incidental taxes was not carried out in public or in the community, most of the other taxes required the intervention of other local officials, tax officials, and kadıs. The cohesion of these villagers, however, was not enhanced by their communal responsibilities because collective duties were carried out under strict official monitoring.

Taxes with the potential to bring together a community of cultivators were those the peasant owed directly to the central state: the extraordinary taxes (*avariz-i divaniyye* and *tekalif-i örfiyye*) which were to be collected from special fiscal units comprising three to ten households depending on the income of the unit.[68] Several points about these taxes give us insight into the community of peasants, revealing their villages and organization as quite efficient. Yet the methods of collection also implied rigid control, diminishing the potential for collective action. The *avariz-i divaniyye* comprised four different taxes, the *nüzül, sürsat, kürekçi,* and *avariz akçesi,* the first two related to provisioning the army on campaign, the third to providing the navy with oarsmen and the fourth a cash amount to be used for a variety of extraordinary payments.[69] Every few households were registered according to, yet independent of, the population records. When the time came to pay these taxes, the assessments were sent on to the kadıs, who collected the necessary amounts from the assembled population. At this gathering the villagers divided, according to their ability to pay, into three categories of high, medium, and low (*ala, evsat,* and *edna*) and paid accordingly.[70] This differentiation of the peasant community emerged from registers and was corroborated in the presence of the judge and various intermediary state officials. Situational constraints, and collective responsibility, promoted community-based assistance initiatives.[71] In fact, some of the rare instances of peasant col-

[68]Inalcık, "Military and Fiscal Transformation in the Ottoman Empire, 1600–1700," *Archivum Ottomanicum* 6 (1980): 314. See also Fikret Adanır, "Tradition and Rural Change in Southeastern Europe during Ottoman Rule," in *The Origins of Economic Backwardness in Eastern Europe,* ed. Daniel Chirot (Berkeley, 1989), pp. 9–10.

[69]Inalcık, "Military and Fiscal Transformation," p. 314.

[70]Ömer Lütfi Barkan, "Avariz," *Islam Ansiklopedisi,* 2:13–19.

[71]Güçer, *XVI–XVII Asırlarda Hububat Meselesi,* p. 67.

lective complaint in the Manisa court registers concerned pressuring free-loaders to pay their share.

It is difficult to assess the degree to which taxation procedures organized rural cultivators into a solidary community; some taxes brought communities together (although more in conflict than cooperation), while others remained individually assessed. What taxation did do was to reproduce stability and regularity in the life of a peasantry which, as the next sections show, was more or less fluid and changing.

Temporary Settlements

Both temporary settlements and the nomadic way of life represent fluidity and adaptive change to the environment. Peasants who made use of these alternate arrangements enhanced their subsistence and supplemented their income with other forms of cultivation or husbandry. The first of these categories was the periodic settlement, *mezra'a,* a word used in a variety of ways by scholars; in general, it conveys the sense of an adaptive mechanism on the part of the rural population.[72] The *mezra'a* was quite simple in its administrative formation: when officials conducting surveys identified the existence of a village site, a water supply, a cemetery, and indications of at least periodic if not more permanent life, they registered it as a *mezra'a*—a cultivated but only periodically inhabited area.

The *mezra'a,* together with the more customary renomadization process, provided for many different organizational forms and thus less coordination of the villages. Members of villages moved back and forth in similar yet different modes of production, organizing as necessary for labor, and in the process of movement destabilizing their networks of interaction. What I can show is the movement. The evidence about instability is less clear, since we lack personal or communal narratives that could give this sense. I derive the conclusion of multiorganizational arrangements, instability, and lack of cohesion from court records that illustrate the tension and conflict between peasants and nomads.

Whether a deserted village and its surrounding lands or a periodic settlement for a population, *mezra'as* seem to have fulfilled the functions of a population in flux, demographically as well as politically. Either because

---

[72]Most of the information I have gathered on the *mezra'a* comes from an unpublished article Halil Inalcık was kind enough to let me use as well as from the few court cases referring to these settlements and problems that arose when outsiders tried to acquire these lands; Inalcık, "Mezra'a," unpublished article.

of population pressure or population movement or yet because of banditry, robbery, and disease, villagers used *mezra'as* as extra cultivation territory, as hideouts, as temporary settlements, or as the first lands to evacuate in periods of depopulation. Highland pastures used by nomads and seminomads as refuge areas from the state, bandits, or ecological disasters are organizationally comparable to this type of settlement. The number and the change in *mezra'as* thus ought to reflect the difficulties experienced by the population of an area; numerous *mezra'as* indicate the demographic and economic decline of populations.

The peasantry of the district of Manisa in the late sixteenth and early seventeenth centuries lived in harmony with these periodic settlements and made use of them under pressing conditions. The administrative district of Manisa, according to the 1531 register, contained 150 villages and 11 periodic settlements. Yet, by the end of the sixteenth century, registers showed a decrease in the number of villages to 132 and an increase in the number of periodic settlements to 14. The number of villages and settlements do not really match since the process is not directly correlated. In Manisa during this period, population growth and administrative reorganization occurred at the same time, thus blurring the effects of socioeconomic pressure on the movement of populations. Individual cases demonstrate that villagers left the village after a natural disaster, and that *mezra'as* were cultivated by peasants from surrounding villages, who paid taxes for this extra cultivation.[73] Suraiya Faroqhi argues that, because towns and cities were dependent on the agricultural hinterland for supplies, they traded intensely with closer villages, in the process unintentionally transforming them into *mezra'as* as peasants moved to the towns, attracted by greater opportunities.[74]

Such rural movements had both benefits and drawbacks. An alternative area provided the peasants of the surrounding villages with extra land to cultivate and, more important, with the framework of a village to resettle when conditions in their own villages grew difficult. But the constant movement between villages and periodic settlements disrupted the organization and coordination of the villages. The direct corollary has to be that villagers chose the easy way out: to exit and therefore to pay little attention to mobilizing collective action for a better existence. To the degree that peasants were able to secure extra income and also traveled

---

[73]Emecen, *XVI. Asırda Manisa Kazası*, pp. 111–13.

[74]Suraiya Faroqhi, *Towns and Townsmen of Ottoman Anatolia: Trade, Crafts, and Food Production in an Urban Setting, 1520–1650* (Cambridge, 1984); Inalcık, "Mezra'a."

some distance to these periodic settlement areas to cultivate, they were further removed from their regular organization of production and the site of their social activities.

Nomads, the State, and the Community

Another even more drastic measure of avoidance was renomadization, an extreme form of escape from the state. Nomadic life usually avoids taxation and frequently battles with settled agriculturists. It has a social organization of production entirely different from that of settled communities. In the Ottoman Empire, nomadic organization was the result of struggles with the state. In this section, I make three points. First, nomads in their own communities were at least as organized as peasants. Organization resulted from both their distinct mode of production and the state's attempt to control them and to utilize them in their nomadic and paramilitary formats. Organization within the nomadic communities, however, never became relevant for rural unrest since relationships between the state and the nomads remained at the level of avoidance. The state tried to settle nomads, and nomads tried to escape the state. Second, peasants and nomads did not always ally against state representatives. Rather, they often fought over transhumance rights, roads, gardens, orchards, and fields on the way to pastures, vitiating the potential solidarity of the rural community. Third, the possibility of cooperation was inhibited because of the different organizations and identities created not just by movements back and forth from sedentary to nomadic life styles, but also by all the other alternative labor and paramilitary organizations that were formed. Therefore, I argue that the multiplicity of organizations and identities and the conflict between the two main groups with the most stable identities broke down village-level organization and solidarity further. These conclusions also help account for the lack of rural rebellion.

It is quite different to imagine settled life in the Ottoman villages without taking into consideration the constant symbiosis, in harmony and in conflict, between settled and nomadic populations. The analysis of this symbiosis is all the more important because the Ottoman Empire at its base was established by Turcoman nomads, who over time slowly became sedentary. Also, the ebb and flow from nomad to settled and back to nomadic styles of life continued throughout the centuries as a response to environmental and demographic crises. It is therefore important to consider not only the settled and the nomad populations as distinct entities but also the constant transformation between the two.

The arrival of Turcoman nomads to Anatolia dates to the battle of Manzikerd in 1071; the Anatolian countryside was renomadized following the Mongol invasion (1221–60). Early surveys show that the Turcoman population far outweighed the Greek. During the Turcoman raids the indigenous population either was able to flee or was enslaved by the conquering forces, not necessarily with mass conversions to Islam.[75] Although the destruction of the Byzantine establishment has been associated with the renomadization of Anatolia by the Turcoman forces, it is clear that over time, especially after the rise of the Turcoman principalities in the region, some form of coexistence was reached between the state, the nomads, and the settled people. Over time, as the state tightened its grip, the balance shifted toward the settled population.

According to A. M. Khazanov's description[76] of the nomadic mode of production, the nomads (yürüks)[77] from early Ottoman times did not represent strict nomadic pastoralism but instead a seminomadic pastoralism. A mix of variants of semipastoral nomadism coexisted in Ottoman society; there were groups of nomads who engaged in both agriculture and pastoralism, as well as groups that devoted themselves exclusively to one or the other.[78] In Ottoman society, pastoral nomads existed alongside agriculturists; in addition, some nomadic communities cultivated plots in order both to diversify and to expand their surplus. However, nomads usually cherished the freedom to pick up and leave whenever it was time to find new grazing lands for their herds. Some left permanently; others left the lowlands at the end of the winter (kışlak) for the cool breeze of the high summer pastures (yaylak). Frequent movement correlated highly with flight from tax officials collecting taxes on cultivated land. In addition,

[75]Halil Inalcık, "The Yürüks, Their Origins, Expansion, and Economic Role," in *Medieval Carpets and Textiles: Mediterranean Carpets, 1400–1600*, Vol. 1 (London, 1986), p. 41.

[76]A. M. Khazanov, *Nomads and the Outside World*, trans. Julia Crookenden (Cambridge, 1983), p. 16, describes five characteristics of the nomadic mode of production: "(1) pastoralism is the predominant form of economic activity; (2) its extensive character connected with the maintenance of herds all year round on a system of free-range grazing without stables; (3) periodic mobility in accordance with the demands of the pastoral economy within the boundaries of specific grazing territories, or between these territories (as opposed to migrations); (4) the participation of pastoral mobility of all or the majority of the population; (5) the orientation of production towards the requirements of subsistence."

[77]The appellation "Turcoman" (Türkmen) was changed into yürük by the state administration in order to distinguish the regular pastoralists from those who joined heretical groups under the influence of the shah of Iran. Thus I use the term "yürük" when referring to the nomads and "Türkmen" when referring to heretic Kızılbaş orders. This distinction is clarified in the next section. For further information, see Inalcık, "The Yürüks," pp. 40–42.

[78]Khazanov, *Nomads*, p. 20.

major migratory movements, especially from east to west, were recorded throughout the early history of the empire.[79] These resulted from state interference in the life of nomads who were determined to keep organized control away from their community.

In the classic style of state-nomad struggle, the Ottoman state tried to settle the various nomadic communities and organize them for the purposes of taxation and control.[80] Most early sultans gained the reputation of absolute rulers and imposed forced settlement and relocation on the nomads. Beyazıd I (1389–1402) and Mehmed I (1402–21) were the main centralizing sultans of the Ottoman Empire, and as such earned reputations as enemies of the nomads. Beyazıd I is said to have ordered mass deportations of nomads from Anatolia to Rumelia.[81] Mehmed I and Mehmed II both continued these policies of deportation and forced settlement of nomads in Rumelia in the hope of creating a stronger settled Muslim constituency in Christian regions; they also hoped to repopulate deserted areas from which Christians had fled. Population surveys with entries for Danışmendli, Ak-Keçili, Kızıl-Keçili, and Tahtacı indicate widespread Turcoman settlement in western regions.

The nomadic mode of production forged a distinct lifestyle where the type of organization followed seasonal schedules closely. *Yürüks* in the

---

[79]Inalcık, "The Yürüks," pp. 41, 48–49. Inalcık mentions a document from 1602–5 which records such movement to Saruhan, Chios, and Gemlik.

[80]The Ottoman state represented the success of one group of nomads over various other nomadic contenders. The first sultan of the empire, Osman, appeared in the guise of a bey of a semi-nomadic group of Turcomans in conflict with the *tekfurs* who controlled their summer and winter pastures. Out of the ruins of the Seljuk Empire in the thirteenth century were established a series of small principalities of warriors engaged in Holy War against Byzantium. From among these clans of warriors, one, the Ottoman, became predominant and slowly subjugated others by incorporation, marriage, political bargaining, and settlement. In the words of Inalcık, "in fact, however, the factors which impelled Osman to become a leader of *ghazis* were the same factors as motivated the whole activity in the marches of western Anatolia, in other words the pressure of population and the need for expansion resulting from the movement of immigration from central Anatolia, the decay of the Byzantine frontier-defence system, and religious and social discontent in the Byzantine frontier areas, as well as the desire of Anatolian Turks to escape from Mongol oppression and to start a new life in new territory." Halil Inalcık, "The Emergence of the Ottomans," in *Cambridge History of Islam*, ed. P. M. Holt, Ann K. S. Lambton, and Bernard Lewis (Cambridge, 1970), 1A:267–68. Having established its supremacy over some of the Byzantine *tekfurs* still living in Anatolia and consolidated the support of other Turcoman principalities, the House of Osman went about establishing the nucleus of an agricultural *ghazi* empire, thereby circumventing the dangers encountered by most nomadic empires of receding into the unknown because of an inherent inability to construct long-lasting institutions; Khazanov, *Nomads*, pp. 228–33.

[81]Inalcık, "The *Yürüks*," p. 46.

Ottoman Empire in general engaged in transhumance movements from the summer pastures in the high plateau, where they grazed their animals, to the winter quarters, where they even engaged in small-scale agriculture. During the winter, the *yürüks* of Saruhan exhibited features of the lifestyle of both settled and nomadic populations. *Yürük* community and organization are best understood through their summer pasture activities, especially since the summer was this population's more organized period. The time spent at the summer pasture was when *yürük* life was most active and ordered; on set days during this period, *yürüks* came together for such communal events as the day of separation of animals and the day the animals were shorn. Among the high plateaus of the region, the one in which water was abundant was designated the main summer pasture, and most activities that brought the community together were performed at this central place. Community prayer was held at the central worship area set up for the duration of the summer. Nomads who came to pray on Fridays also shopped at a marketplace next to the praying area.[82] The summer was thus a time when nomad community organization was reinforced and cast in patterns that fostered solidarity. The winter, during which *yürüks* descended to the low-lying pastures and engaged in agriculture, dispersed them and forced them into interaction with the peasantry.

The state also forced other formats on nomad communities. Some communities were settled as agriculturalists, while others were assigned special tasks. The state dealt with these communities as if they were sources of free labor and a military pool. It exempted them from extraordinary taxes in return for military functions, transportation, mining, lumbering, and other similar activities. The state was interested in settling nomads.[83]

---

[82]Enver M. Şerifgil, "Rumeli'de Eşkinci Yürükler," *Türk Dünyası Araştırmaları* 12 (1981): 67.

[83]A state has many reasons to enforce the sedentarization of nomads. First, as good fighters nomads pose a political threat. Second, the settlement of nomadic tribes means a direct increase in the amount of taxable revenue. Not only can a state tax agriculturalists more heavily, it is also easier for tax collectors to find them as opposed to populations who move constantly. Moreover, usually the population growth of settled people is greater than that of nomadic groups. This is not true, of course, during times of famine and especially of plague. Leila Erder, "The Measurement of Preindustrial Population Changes: The Ottoman Empire from the 15th to the 17th Centuries," *Middle Eastern Studies* 11 (1975): 284–301, discusses the fact that movement in sparsely settled borderlands lowers the risks of contact and that nomads are better able to outrun disease, since they move on and abandon their dying members along the way. Another interesting factor seems to be the specific fleas that carry plague, which do not do very well with horse and goat smell and die out. Nomads, the main breeders of goats and horses, are spared from the disease. Reasons of security also direct the state toward settlement issues. It has been argued that nomads represent a threat to settled

Over the long run it forced sedentarization, in the process imposing a different organization and identity on nomads. In the short run, nomads were also reorganized into paramilitary categories with yet again different identities. The multiplicity of group identities that therefore became available to nomads, peasants, and seminomads thus provided various options along which communal association and cooperation could occur.

The military needs of the empire forced organization on nomads. In keeping with the stratified and militarized establishment of the provinces, nomads were organized into quasi-military categories, *eşküncü yürük* (especially in Rumelia), and *yaya* and *müsellem* (especially in Anatolia), as auxiliary forces to be called on by the state during times of war. These auxiliary forces were not exclusively of nomadic origin; they also included peasants willing to join. These were organized in groups (*ocaks*) of 24 nomads at first, with the number slowly rising to 30 by the end of the sixteenth century. Usually, a fifth of each group (usually representing five people) could be called on for military service.[84]

These *yürüks* organized under a military rubric represented an important segment of the nomadic population of the empire. In the Balkans we find 14,435 *yürük* households, 23,000 militarily organized nomad households, and 12,105 reserve military men (*müsellem*) of nomad origin. The total in the Balkans is 49,540 nomads, 71 percent of whom were militarized. In Anatolia a total of 129,416 nomads—77,268 nomads and 52,148 reserve military men (*piyade*, *yaya*, and *müsellem*)—represented the 40 percent that was militarized. These figures should be compared to total population figures. In the Balkans, of a total population of 1,111,799 households, 4.5 percent were of nomad origin, whereas in Anatolia the nomad population was a substantially larger 24.5 percent. Thus, there were many more nomadic settlements in Anatolia than in the Balkans. It is important to note, however, that of those who were of nomad origin, in the Balkans a much higher percentage were organized militarily (71 percent) than in Anatolia (40 percent). This can be explained by the emphasis on militarization and organization in the Balkans, the frontier lands from which holy war against the infidel was waged. More important, though, it

populations, especially during times when resources are restricted. Suraiya Faroqhi, "Rural Society," pt. 2. *Turcica* 11 (1979): 112–13, mentions the transformation of nomads into highway robbers and the frequent "protection costs" to the merchants traveling on roads frequented by nomads. When nomads joined bandits or harbored them in their settlements, they could be asked to pay a fine (*nezir akçesi*) to the state, their guns were confiscated, and they were forbidden to ride on horses; Ahmet Refik, *Anadolu'da Türk Aşiretleri, 966–1200* (Istanbul, 1930).

[84]Şerifgil, "Rumeli'de Eşkinci Yürükler," 72.

should be clear that, especially up to the end of the sixteenth century, the military role of nomads was significant.[85] This is corroborated in the *Mühimme* documents by the frequency of the state's appeals to these auxiliary forces to join wars.

In the Saruhan region, almost all *yürüks* were registered to some separate land (has) belonging to the sultan or a prince; this reflected the state's main way of settling nomads. In the Manisa district of Saruhan, four different types of *yürük* community existed besides those registered to regular tımar lands and pious foundations. The first group, the *Ellici yürüks*, were not sharecroppers (as their name might indicate) but rather belonged to the same military establishment as auxiliary forces. Of each 50, one was enlisted in this group, and unlike the auxiliary forces they worked the (has) lands and paid taxes on the land; married *yürüks* paid 33 akçes and the single paid 6 akçes. Similar taxes were paid by the *Mukataa-hane yürüks* and the *Karaca yürüks*, while the *Urban-i Buğurciyan yürüks* were exempted from extraordinary taxes because they were obliged to raise camels for the state.[86]

The state-nomad relationship was also contested in its military aspects. To the degree that the state tried to remove nomads from their productive activities and enlist them for the army, nomads used a variety of alternative identities to escape mobilization. In many instances *yürüks* registered themselves as cattle dealers (*celep*) or as falconers of the sultan (*doğancı*), or they claimed high rates of casualties in their particular unit, to avoid service at the front.[87] In such cases the state either reordered campaign participation or the payment of a fee (*bedel akçesi*) similar to that paid by tımar holders who did not go to war. When in dire need of soldiers, the state ordered the eligible sons of nomads, their freed slaves, or the sons of their freed female slaves to join the war. Also, regular population surveys were drawn and military groups were replenished when they seemed to have broken down or disintegrated. In such cases the state ordered the secretary of land (*muharrir*) to look for those nomads who wandered aimlessly (*haymana*), to check their status (to avoid registering peasants), and then to enlist them in the military units.[88] These instances all attest to a

---

[85]The figures were presented by Barkan and are reproduced here from Halil Inalcık's work on nomads. Ömer L. Barkan, "Essai sur les données statistiques des régistres de recensement dans l'empire Ottoman aux XVe et XVIe siècles," *Journal of Economic and Social History of the Orient* 1 (1957): 9–36, and Inalcık, "The Yürüks," pp. 44–45.

[86]Emecen, *XVI Asırda Manisa Kazası*, pp. 127–40.

[87]Refik, *Anadolu'da Türk Aşiretleri*, documents 67, 68, 69, 70, 84.

[88]Ibid., documents 89, 81, 63.

constant bargaining between the state and the nomadic population, a process that disguised itself in many varying identities, as nomads tried to escape entering state service or paying their dues. The state was vigilant[89] and the nomads swift at escaping it. Their relationship was complex and exhibited bargaining and incentives on the part of both participant groups. The Ottoman state was not interested in the complete annihilation of the pastoral mode of life, since it would then lose major resources. It therefore controlled and coerced, letting some settle, others engage in transhumance between defined summer and winter pastures. Toward the end of the sixteenth century, the military branch of the *yürüks* began to disintegrate, until the state tried to cancel their organization altogether. The *yürüks* resisted changes in their identity for fear of losing their tax-exempt status. By this time nomads were used to claiming a different identity—as necessary—for the situations they encountered. The constant transformations in their status kept them from organizing along a more stable and specific mode of life.

While state-nomad relations forced different levels of identification and organization, relations between nomads and the settled population ruptured and mended rural communities at different levels. The winter, during which nomads descended to the low-lying pastures and engaged in agriculture, forced them into interaction with the peasantry. Documents emphasize the occurrence of conflict between the two communities. Yet, at the same time, peasants and nomads needed each other and engaged in small-scale trade.

In greater Manisa throughout the sixteenth century, distinctions between nomads and peasants were blurred.[90] In 1531 the *yürüks* represented 44.8 percent of the population and the settled agriculturists 29.92 percent. This percentage changed only very slightly by 1575, to 44.41 and 33.11 percent, respectively. However, when analyzing the distribution of these groups in the area, we find that of the 192 settlements in greater Manisa

[89]For the auxiliary *piyade* and *müsellem* forces who had usufructory right to land, the state paid meticulous attention to its distribution and exploitation. For example, an order sent to the scribe of the imperial divan who also happened to be the secretary of land (*muharrir*) of the *yaya* and *müsellem* shows concern about those *yaya* and *müsellem* who lacked land and resources. At the end of the letter, the sultan urged the *muharrir* to consider a more equal distribution of land. More equal distribution of land and the requisitioning of new land registers (*tahrirs*) represent direct responses to a decrease in the number of the *yürüks* enlisted in these organizations. However, these are also testimony to the care and attention the state paid not to alienate this valuable source of social and military manpower. Ibid., document 62.

[90]These figures were obtained from the raw data provided in Emecen's book, *XVI. Asırda Manisa Kazası*, and complemented by the BBA Tapu Tahrir Registers, 516, 786, 683.

approximately 9 percent were purely peasant villages and 13 percent purely
yürük settlements. In contrast, nearly 50 percent of the settlements were
recorded mixed, with peasants and nomads living together, often with
peasants within the formal bounds of the village and nomads at the edges
and ready to engage in seasonal moves. Noteworthy is that the discussion
is in terms of peasant and nomad settlements, emphasizing the issue of
settlement. Settlement in these records refers to cultivation and payment
of taxes. It is also interesting that 21 percent of the villages were empty and
were cultivated by nomads as well as by peasants who lived outside these
villages. In much of this region, therefore, nomads and peasants were similar in their activities as well as their dependencies. Cooperation between
the distinct groups of villagers and nomads occurred at several levels.
At the level of trade, it is safe to assume that the less-diversified economy
of the *yürüks* forced them to depend on peasants for some agricultural surplus, grain, and seed. Court records also show that these two groups ha-
bitually traded cattle. Also quite frequently villagers sent their grain taxes
to Istanbul with the help of hired nomads who carried the load on their
camels.[91]

Was the possibility of cooperation offset by the conflicts that arose with
interaction? Peasants most often complained about the frequent trespass-
ing of *yürüks,* who let their herds graze either on their fields or in their
gardens and orchards. Beyond the damage to crops, in many areas damage to personal property through robberies was reported. For example,
nomads organized into small bands of 10–15 or larger ones up to 300 to
attack villages, rob and kill the peasants, and move on. These kinds of attacks seem to have been even more frequent to the east, where the Türkmen controlled the nomad population.[92] But other cases demonstrate
that nomads vigorously protected their right to pasture against outsiders
who tried to acquire their land and cultivate it; they would go to their
judge to get a title deed (*hüccet*) confirming their right over pastures. To
the extent that nomad behavior was perceived as a threat to settled agriculture, local and higher-ranking officials from the center attempted to
clarify the rules and regulations for them.[93] Nomads were not the only

---

[91]This series of documents was taken from the kadı records of Saruhan of the late sixteenth and early seventeenth centuries. A selection of these were previously published by
Ibrahim Gökçen, 16. ve 17. Asır Sicillerine göre Saruhan'da Yürük ve Türkmenler (Istanbul,
1946), documents 10, 14, 26, 34, 65. The rest of the examples come from the Manisa court
records, Registers, 11, 12, 102, 104, 106.

[92]See documents 109, 110, 111, 114, 115, 116, 123 in Refik, Anadolu'da Türk Aşiretleri.

[93]Ibid., documents 123, 124.

malefactors in rural society; it is quite common to find reports of abuses of nomads by local state authorities. Most often these authorities charged the nomads both settled and nomad taxes. Under conditions of abuse similar to those suffered by peasants, nomads assembled as a few individuals and protested to the local judge. In places where the nomad population was substantial, separate judges were nominated to handle their affairs.[94]

In western Anatolia settled and nomadic peoples were highly mixed. Nomads and peasants had distinctive modes of production with distinctive settlement patterns. But between these two groups lie numerous intermediate categories: seminomads who moved and settled, nomads who went to war as auxiliary forces and received some exemptions in return, and those who used special assignments as an escape from any sort of societal or state engagement. The resulting array of separate organizations within the nomadic populations provoked continuous transformations from one mode of organization to another, making for good avoidance but not effective collective organization. This fluidity was similarly disruptive in the movement from settled to nomadic and vice versa. More often than not, the result was the numerous transformations of groups from one to another en route to becoming someone else. Furthermore, when considered separately, the two communities, settled and nomadic, were rarely in sufficient harmony to ally in concerted action. And what harmony there was was further disturbed by the religious schism between these communities.

Mosques or *Tekkes?* Religious Affiliation in Rural Communities

Rural Anatolia offered sanctuary to both mosques and dervish lodges (*tekkes*). The countryside was interspersed with these two religious institutions, mosques within the boundaries of the village, but not in every village, and dervish lodges often outside the periphery of the village. There are indications that these institutions corresponded to different segments of the rural populations, especially the settled and the nomadic, respectively. The state manipulated these differences to its advantage, sometimes wreaking havoc with local arrangements. Religious differentiation at the rural level, the actions of the state vis-à-vis the heterodox leadership, and the relative dearth of positions for the excess of dervish leaders

---

[94]For examples, see documents 13, 33, 52, 67, 70, 83 in Gökçen, *Saruhan'da Yürük ve Türkmenler.*

helped to bring about multiple levels of organization and association, as well as competition in the countryside.

The role of religion and religious institutions has long been debated in the literature pertaining to peasant revolt in early modern Europe. There is no doubt as to the role of the parish as one of the central institutions in European villages and the church as the main locus of peasant mobilization. This was so because at a minimum peasants gathered at church on Sundays and were in a relatively spontaneous position to discuss village matters and common grievances after the mass. The parish priest often acted as an active participant in attempts to redress the wrongs in the community and therefore, could assume leadership of disgruntled peasants. Last but not least, religion undoubtedly provided the set of beliefs which most parishioners shared and which brought them together in a common language and set of moral ideas. Religion thus provided the ideas and institutional structure for the cohesion of rural domains in early modern Europe, especially France.

Analysis of Islamic institutions in the Ottoman context is complicated by the existence of two different channels of expression, which sometimes united, but also pitted groups against each other. One was orthodox Islam, represented by the established Sunni hierocracy, the ulema, the learned religious leaders trained at the *medrese* (mosque school). This was the formal, legal, dogmatic religion of the state.[95] Orthodox Islam, "austere in its worship, abstract in its teachings, remote and conformist in its politics,"[96] was closely tied to the state and quite distant from the people. In fact, the only members to have regular dealings with the people were the kadı, at the court, and the imam, at the mosque. Alternatively, most people seem to have found solace in the popular mystical traditions of Sufism, with some of its orders representing a more heterodox form of worship. As Fuad Köprülü notes as he links the Turcoman tribes to these practices, "The Islam of these Türkmen was not exactly the orthodox Islam of the urban Turks. Instead it was a *syncrétisme* resulting from a mixture of the old pagan traditions of the early Turks, a simple and popular form of extremist Shi'ism—with a veneer of Sufism—and certain local customs."[97] It has been argued that people more easily turned to their mystic leader (*şeyh*) than to their imam: "The primary regulators and the directors of the spiritual life of the villagers and the nomads were the

---

[95]Bernard Lewis, *The Emergence of Modern Turkey* (Oxford, 1975), p. 404.

[96]Ibid., p. 405.

[97]M. Fuad Köprülü, *The Origins of the Ottoman Empire,* trans. and ed. Gary Leiser (Albany, 1992), p. 103.

Türkmen shaiks, called babas, who were fully reminiscent of the old Turkish shamans. Their strange clothing, uncanonical practices, and exuberant way of life provoked strong criticism from orthodox sufis."[98] This representative of the mystic orders and leader of the dervish convents resided in rural towns and villages, mixing with the people, appealing to their popular beliefs, providing shelter and companionship to the lost and the poor.

It would be inaccurate to represent Ottoman religious affiliation in a dichotomous way. Reality was far more complex. Yet some generalizations are in order. Inalcık argues that the nomads in the Ottoman countryside were much more closely tied to the dervish convents than their settled counterparts. There were several reasons for this. First and foremost, there was a close connection between the Turcoman nomadic tribes and dervishes (*abdals*) who came to Asia Minor in pre-Ottoman times and later represented a substantial section of the forces that moved westward at the inception of the Ottoman Empire. In return for their participation on the battlefield, these dervishes were given land on which they built their convents.[99] In their role as colonizers, these dervishes were closely tied to the state, which used them as its agents, breaking new territory, settling and forming a nucleus around which peasants gathered. As long as the two, the state and the dervish orders, coincided in their interests, the state allowed their free and unhampered development. The early sultans even founded convents (*zaviyes*) and gave *şeyhs* privileges to facilitate their establishment. Inalcık also argues that, "in the mountainous and high summer pastures in Anatolia, and especially in the frontier regions, it was difficult to compel the semi-nomadic Turcomans to observe the orthodox forms of Muslim life and worship. The abdals and babas inculcated heretical forms of Islam derived from shamanist beliefs and conforming to a tribal social structure."[100]

The settlement of dervishes, similar to that of the nomads, was the product of bargaining and negotiation between various groups and the state. The first sultans supported the settlement and organization of the dervishes because they provided a center around which peasants and nomads could congregate and form villages. Murad I helped found the

---

[98]Ibid.

[99]Ömer L. Barkan, "Osmanlı Imparatorluğunda bir Iskân ve Kolonizasyon Metodu olarak Vakıflar ve Temlikler," *Vakıflar Dergisi* 2 (1942): 281–365. Irène Mélikoff, "Un ordre de derviches colonisateurs: Les Bektachis," in *Mémorial Ömer Lütfi Barkan*, ed. Jean Louis Bacqué-Grammont (Paris, 1980), pp. 149–57, and "Le problème Kızılbaş," *Turcica* 6 (1975): 49–67.

[100]Inalcık, *The Ottoman Empire*, p. 186.

Bektashi order, and Murad II and Beyazıd II channeled funds to provide for it. Part of the process of centralization, the co-optation of Sufi orders would be used as a mechanism to gain control and induce others to join in the realm of the state. The state offered them permanent endowments and made them into allies. Bektashis, for example, became the chaplains of the janissaries.

Not all orders were easily co-opted, however. The Bektashis succumbed to the influence of the more heretical groups and adopted their views. Among these was the extremist Shi'ite sect, the Kızılbaş, known to be under the political domination of the shahs of Iran. Thus, in a sense, the political power struggles between the Ottomans and the Safavids were played out at the societal level between the heretical mystic orders and the state.[101] The infiltration of the Bektashi order by the Kızılbaş divided these orders into two groups, representing a split in mystical religious tradition. Apart from distinctions in religious practice, the major rift was along lines of interaction and acceptance by the state. On the one hand, part of the Bektashi order retained the goals and organization of its inception and therefore belonged to the "established orders" supported by pious foundations, controlled and accepted by the state.[102] Opposite were the secret orders represented by dervishes who "avoided all forms of ostentation, all external organization and symbols," and who "established no link with the state and were more or less opposed to authority," and "were accustomed to live off the fruits of their own labour, accepting no bequest or alms from the state or from individuals."[103] Sultans often tried to establish relations with the wandering dervish types by offering them convents with pious foundations attached to support them. When they succeeded, small-scale convents emerged, often with minor tax exemptions and slight privileges. Success was not all-encompassing, however, since during the fifteenth and early sixteenth centuries some revolts against the authority of the state did gain support from among the Turcoman nomadic and seminomadic population of the empire.

The wandering dervish type was less known and quite effective in his appeal to the disgruntled, so state officials watched him carefully and

[101]The rebellion of Şah Kulu (the name actually means "the Shah's slave") in 1511 around southwestern Anatolia was one such example of the political intervention of Shah Ismail of Iran. This was to no avail, since the defeat of the shah in 1514 by Selim I forced some of these movements underground or across the eastern border; ibid., p. 195.

[102]To the Bektashis we can add the Mevlevis, the Naksbendis, and the Halvetis; ibid., pp. 190–91.

[103]Among these the wandering dervishes, the Kalenderis, the Haydaris, *abdals,* and *babas* are well known; ibid.

subjected him to repression. These dervishes went from town to town, village to village, "almost naked, their heads shaven, and their features scarred."[104] Some of them, the Malamatiya or Qalandariya (Kalenderis), disregarded the Sha'ria and opposed the state.[105] Fuad Köprülü also mentions the Qalandariya, linking them to the Turcoman tribes and describing them in no flattering terms:

> The Qalandars shaved their hair, eyebrows, beards and moustaches and travelled from city to city in rather large groups, carrying their own special banners and beating small drums. Although they had lodges in some cities, they were usually itinerant. It was quite natural that among these groups, which, with few exceptions, were composed of bachelor vagabonds having no understanding of high philosophical concepts or religious experience, the aforesaid principles led to a spiritual nihilism and even to a shocking immorality. It is fairly easy to see how this Qalandriyya order, which also became associated with a poorly understood pantheism and extremist Shi'i tendencies, later played a disruptive role in the social and moral system.[106]

The threat thus perceived kept the state always vigilant, always on the lookout to contain and control these men.

In cities and villages, the central locales of these men were coffeehouses (*kahvehane* and *bozahane*), where they expressed skepticism of authority. Often, during bread shortages, they went to the local coffeehouse, gathered the people, and predicted doomsday. Partly because of wandering dervish patronage, coffeehouses became the center of political information and propaganda: "Public affairs furnished much of the fuel for comment and criticism among coffeehouse patrons. In place of newspapers or public forums, the coffeehouse quickly became the place of exchange of information, where news of the Palace or Porte was spread by word of mouth.... One wishing to hear the latest news—or, more likely, the freshest rumors—needed only to station herself in the coffeehouse for a short time."[107] Ralph Hattox describes the coffeehouse as a primarily Muslim institution in which ethnic groups mixed only rarely, but also as a popular institution that existed in villages and at marketplaces and certainly at the different neighborhoods of the towns. In the marketplace, it

[104]Suraiya Faroqhi, "Seyyid Gazi Revisited: The Foundation as Seen through Sixteenth- and Seventeenth-Century Documents," *Turcica* 13 (1981): 90–122.

[105]Ira M. Lapidus, *A History of Islamic Societies* (Cambridge, 1988), p. 325.

[106]Köprülü, *The Origins*, 104–5.

[107]Ralph Hattox, *Coffee and Coffeehouses: The Origins of a Social Beverage in the Medieval Near East* (Seattle, 1985), pp. 101–2.

is described as a "take-out coffee stall," no doubt a place where people would stop for a few moments on their way to their daily errands. Although it is difficult to imagine this particular coffee stand as a mechanism for the circulation of ideas, there is no doubt that the larger, more stable town coffeehouses must have served this purpose. Otherwise there would have been no reason for state officials to bolt their doors. The threat of these individuals' power for mobilization led the state to restrict the number of coffeehouses in towns and even sometimes to close them down.[108] The court records of Manisa make allusion to one coffeehouse that was shut down by state officials in the late sixteenth century. The degree to which coffeehouses were widespread cannot be assessed with confidence. The court records and the *tahrir* registers I have examined do not mention any coffeehouse in the main market villages or the town.

An interesting paradox develops regarding these wandering dervishes and similar types who opposed the state. The historical record shows that extremists were supported by the shah of Iran[109] and by many Turcoman tribes[110] from all over Anatolia, who provided them with resources and nomadic fighters. Yet it is also true that they accomplished practically nothing in terms of large-scale revolt against the state. Again, therefore, the question arises as to why these potential leaders were unable to mobilize a belligerent population of nomads or others who were, through their constant interaction with the moving segments of the rural population, in contact with and knowledgeable about the possible opposition. The answer, I think, once again lies in the social disorganization of rural life.

---

[108]This information comes from private conversations with Professor Halil Inalcık. For information on coffeehouses, see Hattox, *Coffee and Coffeehouses*, as well as Inalcık, "Bursa XV. Asır Sanayi ve Ticaret Tarihine dair Vesikalar," *Belleten* 24 (1960): 45–102.

[109]Bekir Kütükoğlu, *Osmanlı-Iran Siyâsi Münasebetleri, 1578–1590* (Istanbul, 1962), pp. 7–9. See also Adel Allouche, *The Origins and Development of the Ottoman-Safavid Conflict (906–962/1500–1555)* (Berlin, 1983). According to these authors, the dervishes preached the greatness of the shah of Iran and resources flowed in both directions. And although the Ottoman state fought and deported them (often to Cyprus), their influence did not wane for centuries.

[110]These leaders were connected to and supported by many Türkmen *aşirets* from Anatolia, especially the Ustaclu, Karamanlu, Tekelü, Bayad, and Varsaklar; Kütükoğlu, *Osmanlı-Iran Siyâsi Münasebetleri*, p. 2. Faruk Sümer, *Safevi devletinin kuruluşu ve Gelişmesinde Anadolu Türklerinin Rolü* (Ankara, 1976), adds the Rumlu, Samlu, and Dulkadur tribes to the clans that supported the shahs of Iran. An investigation conducted to find the location of these tribes points to most of Anatolia. We know, however, that especially the tribes Tekelü, Karamanlu, Bayad, Bozulus, and Mamalu were firmly established in western Anatolia. Among these groups there was a strong sympathy between Türkmens and the heterodox leaders. The more established heterodox orders, however, attest to the relations between the peasants and the *şeyhs* as well as between the *yürüks* and the *şeyhs*.

The many representations of Islam were not united. Manisa's villages show relatively little religious organization. Only 27 percent had imams, and three villages were cited as having a mosque: a large number of villages were left without immediate access to religious leadership. *Zaviyes* were scattered at the fringes of villages where nomads lived. In fact, Manisa counted ten well-endowed *zaviyes*. It is impossible to acquire a sense of the more temporary establishments or the wandering dervish types. If the unattached wandering dervishes created trouble for the state, the more established orders reflected the position of the center and lived as alternative islands of conformity—alternative, that is, to the established village-based mosque hierarchy. These orders, once established, developed roots and their descendants stretched across centuries. The Bektashi orders, especially, demonstrate this quite well. The convent of Kızıl Delü, which appears in the tax registers of the eighteenth century, can be traced back to the fifteenth century.[111] But did they constitute a major force in provincial society? What kind of organization did they bring to society?

Many dervish convents served as the nucleus around which villages were formed. As mentioned earlier, dervishes who participated in war at the frontiers received land grants on which they established convents. They turned to cultivation, revived the land, and started small villages. In Manisa, for example, six villages can be easily identified as part of this pattern; they all retained the names of the founding *şeyhs*.[112] There were also ten other villages with convents on their outskirts. Once settled, the dervish convent had to develop its sources of income. Convent members could cultivate the land and live on the produce, especially if they owned

[111]Suraiya Faroqhi traces the history of four *zaviyes* across centuries; see "Agricultural Activities in a Bektashi Center: the tekke of Kızıl Delü 1750–1830," *Südost-Forschungen* 35 (1976): 69–96; "Vakıf Administration in Sixteenth-Century Konya, the *zaviye* of Sadreddin-i Konevi," *Journal of the Economic and Social History of the Orient* 17 (1974): 145–72; "The *tekke* of Hacı Bektaş: Social Position and Economic Activities," *International Journal of Middle Eastern Studies* 7 (1976): 183–208. The four major *tekkes* analyzed by Faroqhi—Seyyid Gazi, Hacı Bektaş, Kızıl Deli, and the zaviye of Sadreddin Konevi—were established convents with well-known *şeyhs*, in touch with the government. In fact, occasionally they collected from the government in the form of contributions and presents. In contrast, the set of documents on Saruhan published by Gökçen in about small, short-lived convents whose minor *şeyhs* were constantly challenged by outsiders. These convents, no doubt, were quite legitimate since their *şeyhs* often obtained the local kadı's help in arbitration. These documents present an issue in the absence of information about sampling. We do not know how Gökçen chose these documents from among many more. Therefore, I exercise caution in their use. See Ibrahim Gökçen, *XVI ve XVII. Asırlarda Saruhan Zaviye ve Yatırları* (Istanbul, 1946).

[112]These are Kürdoğlu Köyü, Karaca Ahmed, Hamza Baba, Kozluca Baba, Sindel Baba, and Gelen Baba; see Emecen, *XVI Asırda Manisa Kazası*, p. 151.

vines and gardens. Obviously, this was much more frequently the case for the smaller convents. Larger convents were forced to rely on the income from pious foundations and state contributions. Most of the time, the income of one or several villages was endowed to a *vakıf* (pious foundation). This meant that peasant taxes (in grain and in cash) were allocated entirely or partially to the pious foundation. In western Anatolia of the late sixteenth century, 17 percent of all dues went to pious foundations.[113]

Organizationally, the dervish convent resembled the tımar. In particular, their dependence on the state for subsidies and contributions made the conventless unable to organize against the state. The convent was usually surrounded by villages or *çiftliks* (or both) the incomes of which went to the pious foundation established to supply it. Some villages were far away; some were nearby. It seems that the smaller dervish convents had taxation rights to villages that were close by, while Faroqhi's documentation indicates a variety of villages, belonging to the larger convents, some of which were farther away than a few hours distance. The larger convents might also have many more villages and *çiftliks* to deal with. They employed several officials to carry out the daily tasks of the establishment.[114] The smaller convents, however, seem to have been engaged more closely in the daily life of the village. It is strongly suspected that they might not have had enough income to hire many administrators; at the most, the data reveal one administrator per convent. Contributions from the state made up an important segment of convent income.[115]

A system of involuntary rotation, the result of scarce positions and close control by the state when such matters were concerned, jeopardized the peace and social organization of the rural community. Many dervishes wandered the provinces with no convent, no place to inhabit, and the in-

---

[113]Faroqhi, "*Vakıf* Administration," pp. 145–46.

[114]For example, Faroqhi published a list of the employees of the *zaviye* of Sadreddin-i Konevi dated 1566–57; see "*Vakıf* Administration," pp. 164–65. The *zaviye* employed two administrators (a *mütevelli* and a *nazır*), a scribe, three collectors of revenue (*cabis*), one imam, one *müezzin,* and six people hired for recitation in the mosque as well as various others of less importance such as the cook, the sweeper, the gatekeeper.

[115]Faroqhi "Seyyid Gazi Revisited," p. 113, finds that a fixed amount of 16,000 akçes annually was contributed to the *zaviye* of Seyyid Gazi by the central administration, and she argues that it was common practice for the state to give money to the *zaviyes* for maintenance and repairs. This was even more the case since "the complex of Seyyid Gazi also fulfilled functions normally associated with *kervansarays* and *derbend* villages, providing a fortified area or at least a safe place in which travellers might spend the night and thereby contributing toward the safety of the road." For the smaller convents analyzed through the Saruhan documents, it seems clear that the state chose to ignore them unless petitioned specifically.

creasing numbers of these dervishes led to intense competition between them. The competition was manifested in ways similar to that of timar holders trying to rob their fellows of their land. In the case of scarce land, complaints were made concerning the failure to go on campaign, and the burden of proof was on the accused to demonstrate his participation. In the case of the dervishes, the charge was often child molestation. Often disadvantaged dervishes complained to the local judge or to the state directly that the current convent holders were incapable good-for-nothings, panderers, and molesters. Dervishes, in their attempt to discredit their confreres, became disruptive; they had nowhere to go and nothing to lose by stirring up trouble.[116] And although these dervishes were not state officials, the scarcity of convents and competition forced them into a system of involuntary rotation. Those out of convents, through appeals to the state, managed to force others out and reap the benefits of office for a while.

The swelling of the ranks of yet another group of idle people roaming around for food and shelter could not have pleased the villagers. Yet, with the established convent leaders, they engaged in a stormy and strong relationship, sometimes based on mutual need, sometimes on conflict. Villagers complained of dervishes not feeding and housing travelers in the hospices—which were often in ruin—and forcing these tired journeyers on to their villages. Villagers who paid their dues to the convent felt cheated.[117] Often the same establishment was also a source of labor, providing peasants with alternative employment. On a more positive note then, especially in larger *zaviyes,* peasants were hired as temporary help, as wagoneers to transport grain to the mill, as laborers to hull the rice, or as "specialists to coat copper kettles with tin or repair them."[118] It seems that larger convents gave out land to sharecroppers, who received at the outset a pair of oxen, a ploughshare, some grain, and sometimes even a place to stay.[119] Rich convents also engaged in the practice of loaning money, and peasants apparently often went to their *şeyhs* to ask for money to make

---

[116]There are numerous examples of these in the court records of Manisa. See especially the last section of Register 102. This insight into the regional situation of Saruhan was confirmed by Halil Inalcık, who argued that there was a vagrant army of such people roaming the countryside. Unfortunately, no data for other areas have been analyzed on this topic to provide fruitful comparisons.

[117]An excellent example is provided in document 56 in Gökçen, *XVI ve XVII. Asırlarda Saruhan Zaviye ve Yatırları.*

[118]Faroqhi, "Seyyid Gazi Revisited," p. 104.

[119]Faroqhi, "Agricultural Activities in a Bektashi Center," p. 83.

ends meet.[120] In general, one must conclude that where the convents existed they engendered strong relationships between their leaders and the
rural population, whether of nomadic or settled type. Faroqhi reaches a
similar conclusion of strong patron-client relations between convent holders and the peasantry. Frequent interaction between the peasants and the
small convent holder was also significant and cast a shadow into *reaya*-
timar holder relations, which, as we have seen, were not close. And, although the dervishes were not always permanent, the institutions were
permanent, and peasants depended on them for communal interaction.

It is not possible to argue that villages were neatly divided along
nomad/settled forms of production and orthodox/heterodox forms of religion. Rather, what we observe are multiple layers of association between
nomads, seminomads, and settled agriculturalists with orthodox figures
(imam) and orthodox Sufis as well as heterodox Sufi orders. Moreover,
while movement unsettled a community, not all dervish sects were actively
involved in moving; some were sedentarized by the state and by the attraction of steady and stable incomes. Those who were engaged in the
pursuit of earthly comforts entered relations with peasants and nomads
that can be characterized as those between patron and client. These were,
however, often disrupted in the seventeenth century by the accusations,
attacks, and competition of their fellows, resulting in low-level havoc in
the provinces.

Village Networks: Trade, Friendship, and Legal Services

Up to this point I have investigated the nature of patron-client relations, the different patrons that peasants acquired through time, and their
impact on the potential for collective action. My arguments thus concentrated on the vertical ties that involved peasants. Along horizontal lines of
association, I also analyzed relations and conflict between the settled and
nomadic populations. A variety of levels of association and divisions between settled and nomad, orthodox and heterodox, and the many varieties
of orders within these spread multiple layers across the countryside. In
many villages, a mosque in the village, a convent tied to a pious foundation outside the village, and a hospice on the road between them was
enough to separate peasants from nomads along different issues and lines
of interaction. These fissures created alternative institutional affiliations

---

[120]In the *zaviye* of Seyyid Gazi, the register of 1599–1600 indicates that 89 of 167 debtors
were peasants from villages where the *zaviye* collected taxes; see Faroqhi, "Seyyid Gazi Revisited," p. 107.

for a population under stress while simultaneously creating conflicts of interests that arose from diversity.

Now I turn to answer whether, left to themselves, without many rotating patrons, villagers interacted enough to be able to organize among themselves. Here, I argue that collective action is easier under conditions of strong internal village communication and solidarity and intense inter-village exchange. To uncover the potential for community organization that is more or less free of macro institutions and vertical relations of control, it is necessary to focus on the networks of interaction within and across village communities. Generally, cross-village communication depends more on markets and trade. Trade of commodities establishes an economic pattern of interaction that can be followed by other more social forms of exchange. For example, after commercial ties are established, brides can be exchanged across villages, establishing a bond. On the other hand, interaction within the villages emerges from relations of exchange and trust. Villages that are closely networked along kinship lines fare less well than those networked along trust. Kinship networks tend to close in on themselves, whereas networks of association based on trust and extra-familial dealings tend to be expansive. In this section, I analyze the court records of Manisa with a view to intervillage and intravillage networks. Although the results are tentative and need to be repeated for many different regions, they point toward patterns of interaction that are conducive to the control rather than to the unity of village populations.

Theoretically, markets and trade relations are part of the larger argument of the factors that link peasants together, induce a relatively high level of interaction among them, and therefore enhance the likelihood of peasant mobilization and collective action. G. William Skinner, who studied marketing and rural structure in China, argued that Chinese marketing systems were equally important as social entities as they were as economic entities. In fact, he called the standard marketing structure a community, implying a set of interactions and connections far more cohesive than the regular impersonal ties of markets.[121] Interesting about the standard market town is that the exchanges that take place are vertical as well as horizontal, while exchanges in smaller minor markets are pri-

---

[121]G. William Skinner, "Marketing and Social Structure in Rural China," pt. 1, *Journal of Asian Studies* 24 (1964):32. To be more precise, we should use Skinner's own definition of the standard market: "that type of rural market which met all the normal trade needs of the peasant household: what the household produced but did not consume was normally sold there, and what it consumed but did not produce was normally bought there" (p. 6).

marily horizontal. Speaking of the marketing community of Kao-tien-tzu, Skinner explains:

> The peasant in Kao-tien-tzu's marketing community, had, by the age of fifty, attended his standard market more than three thousand times. He had, at least, one thousand times on the average, been jammed into a small area along one street with the same male representative of every other house in that community. He made purchases from peasant vendors whose homes lay in all directions from the town, and more to the point, he socialized in the teahouses with fellow peasants from village communities far removed from his own. Nor was the peasant alone in this, for in Kao-tien-tzu there was a teahouse for everyone, and a few persons who went to market failed to spend at least an hour in one or two. Codes of hospitality and sociability operated to bring any community member who entered the door quickly to a table as somebody's guest. Inevitably an hour in the teahouse enlarged a man's circle of acquaintances and deepened his social knowledge of other parts of the community.[122]

The overall result of this kind of interaction is a more homogeneous district within the standard marketing area, fewer cultural and religious distinctions, and interactions of many kinds, including exchanging information on workers, marriage partners, midwives, and craftsmen of various skills. Presumably, all these activities enable communication between villagers of that particular marketing area, ensuring that if collective action becomes necessary the channels of information flow and coordination are already in place. Skinner calls this a community thereby forcing the aspect of commonality and solidarity on the description. At the same time, to the degree that a standard marketing area becomes homogeneous and networks develop to render it internally dependent, it also develops dissimilarities with other marketing areas. Whereas on the one hand the standard marketing area may be a homogeneous unit able to mount collective responses, on the other hand many standard marketing areas do not develop as coherent units.[123]

Given the manner in which the trading network was set up and worked, and given the self-sufficiency of the Ottoman peasant family farm unit, trade did not foster strong bonds across villages. Trade was carried out in relation to the central town and was geared toward the provisioning of the

[122]Ibid., p. 35.
[123]Ibid., pp. 32–42.

town as the hub of a wheel; trade across villages occurred far less often. Ties of dependence seem to have developed along similar lines. Loans were taken from rich members of one's own village or from rich members of the central town. Interestingly, urban women were important among the town dwellers as money lenders to peasants upon high interest. I argue, then, that the lines of communication were directed toward the central town rather than other villages.

An analysis of the Ottoman court records demonstrates that the design of the central town, the village-town relationship, and the needs of the towns generally determined a flow of peasants from the villages to the central town for trade and, at the same time, restricted the flow of trading across villages. To ascertain the nature and level of these relations, we need to look at state requirements, demographic factors, and warlordism as affecting market interaction and behavior. Subsistence agriculture, population pressure, and regional elite demands all worked together to restrict the flow of trade between village and capital. Markets, market activity, prices, and quantities were strictly regulated by the state. According to state requirements, the general understanding for low-level administrative units was that they be self-sufficient and self-contained. This was especially true with regard to the grain trade, which was subject to numerous restrictions across administrative units.[124] To the degree that these units were seen as independent and supervised by local officials interested in maximizing their revenues, movement beyond the administrative unit was not common unless specifically ordered and followed by the central government. On the demographic front, as the need for feeding town populations increased, peasants would be drawn toward central markets, where their goods would be highly valued. The effect of population growth in the sixteenth century would have been increased stress between town and countryside for grains. There would be a greater need to keep the grain produced in the villages themselves, and the towns would necessarily require that more grain find its way to the urban areas to be consumed by nonproducers. The development of powerful warlords with control of the hinterland, and the need to feed their retinues, slowed the transfer of surplus to the capital. Tensions between central and regional forces then manifested themselves at the level of administrative units and their control. The interaction between village and town and in-

---

[124]Faroqhi, *Towns and Townsmen*, p. 191.

teractions across villages should be considered in the context of this tension.[125]

Markets developed in the Ottoman Empire with state permission and in response to local needs. To supply a town was considered as important as feeding armies on the road to war. For both these activities the state made provisions and demanded cooperation from local officials in the maintenance of markets and their function. Markets in small villages, and in summer pastures where peasants and nomads exchanged goods, were also frequent. Finally, in terms of rural administration, the peasant was obliged to carry and sell the grain of the landholder to the nearest market, which according to the regulations should not be farther away than one day's trip. The peasant also had to sell some of his grain to pay taxes in cash and therefore was obliged to go to the market anyway. The markets built in relation to these charges (*akrep pazarı*) were set up once a week and were regional markets that attracted merchants from the surrounding towns.

For the regions under investigation, both Manisa and Tire were the largest town markets, attracting by far the largest number of clients. In the sixteenth century, Manisa court records indicate two other markets for the larger administrative district, each of which set up in villages and functioned as alternative centers where peasants could bring their goods. Both were situated in peripheral areas of their districts, far from the central town of Manisa, and they apparently existed to spare the local peasants from traveling long distances. There is no indication that these villages had larger populations or greater status than other villages in the region; in fact, they were rather small (Konarcalu, 10–12 households; Pazar-ı Yengi/Gökağaç, 20–22 households). In the district of Palamut, the village of Konarcalu was replaced by the village of Palamut in the second half of the sixteenth century as the market village, probably since Palamut became the central administrative unit of the district.[126] For the district of Manisa, then peasants had three main options in addition to a series of small village trading posts that are not reflected in documents: the main town of Manisa and its marketplace, and the two village markets in Konarcalu/Palamut and Pazar-ı Yengi/Gökağaç. Feridun Emecen approximates the number of people interacting in Manisa in 1575 to be 25,000, in

---

[125]Given the scarce information for markets other than the state-regulated market taxes, it is nearly impossible to see whether markets met more often in the sixteenth and seventeenth centuries or whether stationary stores developed instead of markets. It is also impossible to gauge whether markets grew in size or shrank.

[126]Emecen, *XVI Asırda Manisa Kazası*, pp. 268–69.

Palamut 4,000, and in Yengi 10,000. Manisa obviously had the greatest share of market-goers because it served at least four districts.

Given this information regarding the market towns, we need to gauge the impact of this interaction that the centers furthered. That the villagers visited the market in their own region is certainly true, since we know of their obligations to the timar holder. Yet we have to decide further whether this marketing activity affected connections between villages. This brings us back to the question raised by Skinner in his analysis of the Chinese marketing structure as one that fostered collective activity and knowledge. The available data allow speculations that generally agree with the larger picture of separate existences for villages. In my analysis carried out for Manisa in the early seventeenth century, the data show that villages were rather small, with an average of 10–15 households; only a couple of villages reached the size of 100 households. Furthermore, the land registers show that similar crops were grown in all villages, mostly staples with some cash crops like cotton or rice, all of which made it inefficient for peasants to trade across villages. In the late sixteenth century, peasants produced essentially what they needed, from staple to fruits, within the confines of their village and remained self-sufficient in their subsistence. Of course, they used the windmills of villages endowed with better environmental conditions, or bought beeswax from the town. But the trade figures remain unimpressive; villagers traded across villages more often than within their own hamlets. Seventeen percent of court entries refer to trade across villages whereas 3 percent concern intravillage trade. An argument similar to Mark Granovetter's would suggest that loose ties create spanning webs across the boundaries of villages, making potential mobilization easier.[127] This argument is complicated, however, by the fact that much of trade across villages was conflictual. Moreover, the actual load of trade was carried along village–central town routes where the potential for mobilization was low.

Whereas trade relations focus on intervillage networks, interpersonal ties within villages are also needed to assess the extent to which village-level communication can enhance collective action. A village that has developed strong lines of communication and where relationships are not dominated primarily by kin but also reflect work, trade, crafts, and other types of ties will be able to organize and mobilize for collective action faster and more effectively than a village where interaction is limited. The

[127]Mark S. Granovetter, "The Strength of Weak Ties," *American Journal of Sociology* 78 (1973): 1360–80.

amount of interaction can be determined by the number of ties between individuals. These ties could be family ties, trade ties, or relationships of legal representation and guarantorship and more. Not just the number of ties, but also the density and type of ties individuals engage in, indicate the potential for village-level organization. To the degree that villagers engage in relations outside their kin group, to the degree that they rely on friends, neighbors, and other villagers in their daily activities or in outstanding crises, they weave networks that can be used for the dissemination of information, collection of resources, and coordination of activities. These issues have been studied in more or less formalized ways in the context of western European village communities. From among the most successful historical studies, a few have used court rolls as their major source of information about historical village communities. Relationships between members of the community and relations of friendship and trust can best be charted through the study of personal pledging and legal representation (if this latter was not an official function carried out by paid functionaries).[128] To the extent that personal pledging goes on outside the family, it should indicate a close-knit village community, since one would ask a neighbor, friend, or another villager to pledge for him only if he had strong ties with him.

Ottoman villages lend themselves to some of this type of analysis, especially with regard to legal representatives,[129] most of whom were men from the village—either friends or members of the family who would represent the plaintiff or defendant in court in case these could not attend themselves. These legal representatives were not paid functionaries in the village or in court; their names do not repeat frequently across the records. A simple tally of court cases involving legal representatives demonstrates that, in Ottoman villages, peasants relied on their family mem-

---

[128]One such work questions the inordinate amount of solidarity villagers were supposed to have in medieval England and by analyzing data on personal pledging demonstrates otherwise; see Martin Pimsler, "Solidarity in the Medieval Village? The Evidence of Personal Pledging at Elton, Huntingdonshire," *Journal of British Studies* 17 (1977): 1–11. Personal pledging "was a system of providing surety for the fulfillment of a court-incurred obligation—either the payment of a fine or the performance of some specific task (e.g., amending of a trespass, solution of debt)—and the peasant charged with such an obligation was bound to obtain another peasant who would agree to guarantee his future conduct." Personal pledging "itself fulfilled needs for surety within village society. . . . and the choosing of a pledge by a peasant, as well as the agreement of a peasant to serve as a pledge, were, in the last analysis, the result of a personal arrangement between villagers." See Edwin B. De windt, *Land and People in Holywell-cum-Needingworth: Structures of Tenure and Patterns of Social Organization in the East Midlands Village, 1252–1457* (Toronto, 1972), pp. 242–43.

[129]For more information on the use of court records on this matter, see Appendix 2.

bers more than their friends or acquaintances for these temporary legal services. In agreement with this information is the fact that they used legal representatives from their own village, never (in my sample) trusting members of other villages to represent them. In 61 percent of the cases, villagers chose a father or brother to represent them in court. Only 30 percent of the time did they rely on friends. In the early seventeenth century, then, when intravillage conflict rose sharply, peasants often chose to send their kin to court to represent them. These results are by no means conclusive, but they tend to reinforce a pattern of both isolation and dislocation in Ottoman villages.

As we go through the categories of investigation, including peasants, nomads, and religious institutions, recurrent themes combine to confirm the essential point of the social disorganization of the rural mode of life in the Ottoman Empire. Most of the information points toward movement of state or community officials, movement of groups in cooperation and in conflict, fluid and changing identities, and little permanency except for the key actors of our concerns, the peasants. They are the only permanent segment of the rural population, and, as the following chapters depict, portions of this group as well take on the habit of movement.

The central themes around which this chapter is organized—structures and alternatives of control; rotation of officials and potential community leaders; organization of production, labor, and rural life; alternative organizations outside production; and rural networks of trust and trade— each elaborates the lack of bases of organization for the peasantry. Patrimonial structures of control were fashioned under the strict control of a central government with patron-client ties trickling down from state to peasant. The backbone of the system was dependent on one major military-administrative line of command, in which the peasant was the last link. The relationship between the landholder and the peasant, however, was diluted by several other officials. At the same time, the system had a built-in safety device in the court, which was independent of the military-administrative command structure and represented for the peasant an alternative route of action and complaint. It worked effectively because of the direct and independent linkage of the court to the state and because of the rivalry between elites. Therefore, if a peasant was in conflict with one patron, he reached out for another whom he knew not to be tied to his patron. Furthermore, the original patron-client relation was further diluted because of the increasing numbers of state and local officials, tax-farmers, and so on who entered the rural equation and were involved in the taxation of the peasantry. There was no one patron who regulated all activity. There were several patrons, all regulating a segment of rural life and superficially involved in peasant welfare.

The major strength of the state, its diversified structures of control, was reinforced by the rotating nature of these structures. The movement of the military-administrative and legal officials every three or so years reinforced the superficiality of interest in patron-client relations. This situation was strengthened by state ownership of land; there was no private ownership by landholders in the military-administrative channel of command. Thus the threat of strong alliances in the provinces was diffused. Added to the rotation of state officials was the rotation of potential community leaders, religious men, and dervishes, who because of either beliefs or congestion in the ranks were unable to remain in one courthouse or convent long enough to represent the people in their struggle. Although these were potentially the most explosive members of the rural community, they lacked the stability of positions to encourage action.

· When it came to action on the part of the peasantry itself, the organization for production fostered individual production, with little interaction in the collection of taxes and communal affairs. Village organization, administrative divisions among different patrons, and the existence of intermediate categories of cultivation where the peasant could find extra cultivation areas outside the village and therefore not really depend on others nurtured segmentation. Nomads and seminomads simply added more alternatives, more identities, and more ways to evade the state when their plight deteriorated. Alternative organizations in rural areas set up by the state, such as paramilitary formations for the nomads, enriched the number of optional new identities for rural groups.

Finally, it is worth asking whether trust and trade brought peasants together frequently enough for a grassroots network of interaction to emerge. Here, reliance on members of the kin group for key village functions or legal assistance demonstrates that communal ties were not highly developed. Networks of economic interaction were neither numerous nor sophisticated. Furthermore, trade was strictly focused in the direction of central towns and villages.

It is fair to conclude that peasants were members of a weak tenure arrangement in which alliances with other elite members were not easily feasible and organization and resource mobilization opportunities were not furthered by the rural structure. These peasants of western Anatolia, and more generally of all Anatolia, did not engage in rebellion against the state or its officials. Some of them instead moved out of their communities in search of better opportunities. Some became bandits.

5

Celalis: Bandits
without a Cause?

B Y 1600 IN THE OTTOMAN EMPIRE banditry had become a widespread phenomenon, its members drawn from a continuous
supply of vagrant peasants, rebellious religious students, unruly
members of official retinues, and defiant or mutinous soldiers. Each of
these groups turned to banditry in response to state action and resulting
transformations in rural life. The sultan and members of the imperial
council were intimately and consistently involved in shaping these
changes. For all intents and purposes, the state invented and manufactured banditry, and when it was no longer useful the state disposed of it.
This is not to say that the state created banditry per se, ordering shady
individuals to become bandits. Rather, it created disenfranchised groups
with access to weaponry, whom it directed toward actions consistent with
the state's goals of increased coercion and control at the central and regional levels. In the countryside, in response to the economic crisis, the
state invoked, activated, and manipulated structures of control that inhibited class-based movements. At the same time, it sought to centralize by
creating other types of collectivities necessary for military, administrative,
and legitimating goals. And, as is seen in Chapter 6, having created these
groups, the state then actively incorporated them into its strategies of
state centralization. In the process, centralization acquired an alternative
style—that of bargaining and negotiating with the resulting bandits, the
celalis.

The state manufactured banditry in order to channel societal restless-
ness and as a by-product of its own military and politico-administrative
needs. As a result, the new social group it created in many ways remained

its servants. Landlessness, vagrancy, and uneven population movements threatened the countryside with dislocation. Alternative occupations, education, and mobilization into the army became an easy way to divert the masses toward more useful and less threatening pursuits. Then, at least, vagrants were dispersed in a variety of directions, all potentially disruptive, but none as immediately challenging as a movement based on one or more classes. Instead, new social formations such as banditry came to be. Groups who became bandits did not come together of their own will; they were brought together by societal elites for the interests of these elites. Banditry was thus an artificial social construction used as a pseudo-threat or was co-opted into the governing machinery of the state depending on the needs of the ruling class. The identity emerging from banditry was manufactured by these unusual circumstances, and since it was not the product of specific social classes, it was not destined to threaten the state at its core. Proto-rebellion by bandits did not represent collective action in the traditional sense because it did not attempt to destroy the social structure of society; bandits simply wanted to derive as much utility from the system as possible. They found it easier to manipulate the interstices of the system while remaining free of any proclaimed allies or enemies and free of any significant ideology. They could threaten the different arms of the state, slow its functioning, yet never totally abolish it. And, perversely enough, the state used this threat to centralize and increase its control over the scattered regions.

Mobilization of new groups to join the retinues of officials and the armies of the state directly strengthened the state in its centralization schemes. The Ottoman Empire at this time was experiencing a harder time conquering new regions and even holding on to the older regions. The Safavids contested the eastern border, while Europe was intent on at least stopping the Muslim advance. Moreover, the Ottomans had to face improved techniques of warfare and larger armies bearing muskets. Consolidation of territorial control required redirecting vagrants into the military, thereby swelling the ranks of the musket-bearing *sekban* and *sarıca* armies.

The next two chapters are concerned with this phenomenon. In this chapter I redraw the process through which pools of mercenaries became activated in society and later turned to banditry. In the next I trace the history of relations between the state and bandits to demonstrate the manner in which the state was able to use banditry to its own advantage.

Peasant Alternatives

Previous chapters demonstrated that, whether or not one accepts the notion of an economic crisis, the reality of peasant hardships in the early seventeenth century were undeniable. Peasants were affected by population changes, by increased taxation resulting from the efforts of the state to centralize, and by the depredations of various legitimate and illegitimate officials of the government.[1] In fact, both peasants and elites were affected by central and regional disharmony and searched for solutions. Previous chapters also showed that there was practically no way for peasants and elites to engage in rebellious solutions, whether as individual classes or together as a coalition of classes. While both elites and peasants were affected by the new conditions of the empire, the solutions they found did not bring them toward rebellion, alone or together. The reasons for the lack of common destiny can be traced to the structure of disengaged patron-client relations and the control exercised by a state that successfully maintained the existing patterns of rural discontinuity. Compounding this was the inability of each of these classes to perceive political action as possible outside or against the state—the result of effective indoctrination that directed elites and the common men toward the all-powerful state. The outcome of this inability to ally in rebellion turned into the war of all against all where every man fended for himself even at the expense of others. Peasants became the victims par excellence.

It is nearly universally true of agrarian empires that peasants carry the burden of many different nonproductive members of society. This was no different in Ottoman lands, where those with claims on the peasants' bread multiplied daily. Reduced in their ability to pay taxes, peasants often went into debt to make ends meet after the year's harvest was distributed to all who had claims on it.[2] The constant extortion of provincial

---

[1]Many scholars wrote at length about the late sixteenth and seventeenth centuries. Especially those who wrote about the *celalis* spent much time explaining the demographic and economic causes of the decline in the rural population's well-being. For the best examples, see Mustafa Akdağ, *Türk Halkının Dirlik ve Düzenlik Kavgası* (Ankara, 1975); Mustafa Cezar, *Osmanlı Tarihinde Levendler* (Istanbul, 1965); M. A. Cook, *Population Pressure in Rural Anatolia, 1450–1600* (London, 1972); Halil Inalcık "Adaletnameler," *Belgeler* 2 (1965), and "The Ottoman Decline and Its Effects upon the Reaya," in *Aspects of the Balkans, Continuity and Change,* ed. H. Birnbaum and S. Vyronis (The Hague, 1972). The latter two works in particular deal with the abuse the peasantry experienced in this period.

[2]Numerous records exist of peasant quarrels with usurers among the Manisa court records. In one register (no. 102), out of a sample of 85 cases selected from the years 1650–51 ten were about usury. Usurers were overwhelmingly townspeople. It is also interesting that many usurers brought to court were women.

officials aggravated the already precarious condition of the peasantry. Ranging from those considered to be the peasants' closest allies (kadıs) to their fiercest enemies (tax farmers and unexpected company such as janissaries), all provincial officials had invented ways to rob the peasants.[3] Official robbery was compounded by banditry and by rural robbers who plundered even their own people. As a result, the peasant could no longer determine who was a legitimate tax official, a bandit, or a rebel power holder of legitimate origin. In the countryside the distinction between legitimate and illegitimate officers of the state had become quite blurred. The difference between the government tax collector who amassed large, plundering retinues and the illegitimate bandit chief who gave his blessing to pillage was slight. Especially for the peasant, abuse was abuse, whatever its origin.[4] The combination of these factors with the relative ease with which peasants could pay an exit fee (çift bozan akçesi) and leave behind their obligations to landholders produced pockets of free-floating, vagrant individuals in the villages.

For the officials, often much of the loss in official income was compensated for by living off peasants and their land. Documents of the period are replete with cases of governors, bailiffs, commanders, and various local supervisors and members of the janissary robbing the peasantry of their money and grain. Their deeds, which are clearly described in various justice decrees of the period, are worth presenting at length. Here are the words of the Sultan Ahmed I:

> You are not making the rounds of your provinces doing your duties. Instead you are going around taking money from the people unlawfully. And it has been brought to my attention that during these so-called "patrols" which you are making for this purpose accompanied by unnecessary numbers of cavalrymen you are committing the following abuses: If somebody falls out of a tree you make this out to be a murder, you go to a village, settle down, and in order to rout out the supposed killer you harass the people by putting them in irons and beating them. Finally, besides taking hundreds of gold or silver pieces as "blood money," you collect from the villager free of charge as a so-called "requisition" horses, mules, slaves, barley, straw, wood, hay, sheep, lambs, chickens, oil, honey and other things to eat. You lease out your incomes to collectors at excessive rates. They on their part go out to collect with far too many horsemen and instead of satisfying themselves with col-

[3]Probably one of the best reviews of this material can be found in Inalcık "Adaletnameler."

[4]One of the implications of the previous chapter on patron-client relations and the absence of real ties and the number of officials is that anyone who acquired a false diploma (berat) was able to pass as an official and therefore claim a share of the peasants' surplus. See Manisa court records, document 95, Register 102, dating of 1061 (1651).

lecting your incomes according to law and as is prescribed in the record, try to get as much money as they please. And besides the normal villages, they go onto imperial holdings, which are immune, under the pretense of following criminals and demand thirty or forty extra gold or silver pieces per month. And because you, you commanders and bailiffs, have been taking money from brigands and letting them off rather than giving them their just deserts, brigands have been getting hold and have been descending upon the people in groups. This is the sort of tyrannizing that I have been hearing about.[5]

This kind of exploitation by regional officials deeply diminished the resources of the peasants, who saw themselves forced to feed and serve their arch-enemies. In response, the state undertook measures to control corruption and limit widespread abuse.

But the dominant classes were not the only exploiters of the peasants; court records point to the bandits' role as well. Peasants went to court often during the early seventeenth century to complain about the depredations of armed men. This plague, as they viewed banditry, required strong state intervention because a few good Muslim men were incapable of containing assaults. Banditry was increasingly defined as a threat to the economic, social, and moral fabric of society. Hundreds of court documents attest that bandits killed peasants, kidnapped young boys and girls from the villages, raped, trespassed and looted, paraded around with prostitutes, and even violated mosques with insults and disruption.

Often a small band of brigands would cause devastation and misery to many villages, destroying as they wandered. In a typical case brought to the attention of the kadı of Manisa in the year 985, Ferhad B. Abdullah and his companions began a campaign of banditry with an attack on the house of a Christian villager in Horoz, then moved on to a windmill where they pilfered the flour. When villagers from Gökçe, the site of the windmill, chased after the pilferers, a few peasants lost their lives in the encounter. Continuing their way onto Akhisar, the bandits killed more villagers, this action being justified in Ferhad B. Abdullah's view because the victims were unbelievers (*kafirs*). The canyon of Menemen on the way to Bergama witnessed a few more ruthless murders. Ill-fated travelers of the western trade routes, unfortunate inhabitants of the village of Gerü, and unlucky merchants displaying their wares (even a silver water ewer) became prey to this roving band. And just before being apprehended, with the regional authorities breathing down their necks, the bandits one

---

[5]See the *Adaletname* of Ahmet I, BBA Mühimme Register 78, document 4012. The translated text is from Inalcık, "The Ottoman Decline and Its Effect upon the Reaya," p. 344.

last time stopped camel drivers and seized their 4,000 akçes. These actions created vast insecurity among the peasantry in the villages, who knew they had to protect themselves and their families; they also knew they had to arm themselves if any attempt at rebuff was to succeed. This became imperative with time, as some bandits took to kidnapping men and women and selling them to strangers in distant regions.[6]

Peasants generally responded only individually to the socioeconomic and demographic crises in the countryside, acting collectively only on rare occasions. Some of these actions were small-scale, self-help measures that remained local; others broadened to encompass more people and regions and along the way furthered the transformation of the peasantry.

Peasants Respond

When times are hard, there is an increased tendency to bargain and try to make the most of what one has. At the core of individual responses on the part of the peasantry, it is therefore possible to find during periods of decline increased complaint, increased bargaining with local and state officials, some of which is apparent in the registers of the courts. A comparison of the two periods under consideration substantiates this claim. In the first period (approximately 1572–96), early on in the social dislocation, the records deal with cases of disputed inheritance, petty theft, rape, and registration of various items. By the second period (approximately 1650–52), there was a significant increase in the number of cases dealing with tax problems, as well as an increase in the number of cases where peasants or officials claimed to have been cheated out of their income. The cases range from peasants refusing payment of a variety of taxes to officials trying their best to extort money from the living and for the dead. There are cases of peasants and timar holders or other agents coming to court to ask for the remeasurement of a piece of land because a few feet altered the parameters of inheritance, sale, and taxation. All in all, at every level of rural society, court records indicate increased bargaining activity and haggling between patrons and clients, as both were often hurting under the magnitude of the crisis.[7]

---

[6]This case is taken from Manisa court records Register 11, documents 50, 52. Mühimme Register 73 at the Başbakanlık Arşivi also contains many examples of this sort.

[7]Here I compared the information for two periods from the Manisa court records. The first register, no. 11, dated to 1575–90 (983–99). The second set of registers, nos. 102 and 104, dated from 1650–54 (1061–65). Selecting the same number of years, I looked through the types of cases and tried to differentiate between them in terms of cases that would result

Unsatisfied, a peasant could leave the timar holder's plot and offer his services to someone else. And despite the fact that to avoid the excesses of such behavior the law instituted certain disincentives against moving, there are strong indications that peasants considered this option seriously. This is clear from the available documentation on the exit fee (*çift bozan akçesi*) the peasant who left his plot was to pay in return for his desertion.[8] More violent or disruptive responses were also possible. These ranged from suspension of work, escaping tax registration, flight into the mountains at the approach of tax collectors, and outright murder of tax collectors. Among such actions designated as "the weapons of the weak" by James Scott, pilfering, escape, and deceit were all measures peasants took to express their discontent.[9] Finally, within this smaller-scale range of responses, the most frequent and useful (from the point of view of both the state and the peasant) was the court. The availability of such a mechanism of complaint and response from the state led to small-scale and short-lived (for the duration of the case) alliances between peasants. And, as I made the case in the previous chapter, the availability of official channels of complaint and redress of grievances made collective action unlikely and small-scale action very likely.[10]

Different as well as more disruptive of the rural equilibrium were regional movements of population, such as large-scale migration of young peasant men with no land, no job, and no resources. These youths became the source of rural militias, official retinues, religious student organizations (*suhte*), and regional bandit movements. These movements remained only locally threatening before their expansion and their greater strength

---

from socioeconomic ills and cases that were likely to occur under any situation. Inheritance cases, for example, are likely to occur regardless of the socioeconomic problems a society encounters. However, many instances of bargaining over land size, attempts at lowering tax-farming dues, and negotiations over fees for the deceased are all indicators of individuals and groups scrounging for their last penny.

[8]For information on these fees, see Inalcık, "Adaletnameler," and "Osmanlılarda Raiyyet Rüsumu," *Belleten* 23 (1959). It should be noted that after fifteen years of unclaimed residence in another village the migrant peasant was to be entered into the tax registers of the new area.

[9]Some of these measures are discussed in Inalcık, "Adaletnameler," pp. 107–26. I have gotten some of these from private conversations with Halil Inalcık as well as from court records of Manisa or documents published by Ahmet Refik, in *Anadolu'da Türk Aşiretleri, 966–1200* (Istanbul, 1930).

[10]As I stressed in Chapter 4, the cases of negotiation and complaint between peasants and tax officials are one of the main indicators of potential collective action. Yet, for example, in the second period of investigation, from among the isolated 85 cases of Register 102 (Manisa court records), there are 23 cases of straight negotiation between peasant and state official regarding taxation. Only three of these cases involved more than one peasant.

was fabricated by the state's actions. Therefore, what started as population movements, especially of young, landless men, ended up as banditry of the local and larger variety. From the initial population movement to large-scale banditry, the state was responsible for this rural transformation. But before I show how the state was responsible, we need to understand the origins of population movements.

Population Movements

Although no one seems to disagree that the population of the Ottoman Empire grew by roughly 100 percent in the sixteenth century, variation in regional population growth and population pressure as well as the pull and push factors from various communities have been debated. Without doubt population growth was a fairly general phenomenon throughout the empire in the sixteenth century and was manifested primarily in the number of young unattached males. It is also quite well established that this growth was accompanied by isolated instances of population decline, as well as some serious cases of depopulation, after the 1580s and into the early seventeenth century. This decline was regional and depended very much on the makeup of the land, the structure of patron-client relations, and the economic opportunities within the area. Therefore, a region with overall population growth could also register many empty villages. Leila Erder and Suraiya Faroqhi show that for the two regions of Kocaeli (western Anatolia) and Şebinkarahisar (eastern Anatolia) population rose in the sixteenth century up until 1580, after which a slight decline was observed.[11] In central Anatolia, the region of Erciyes Dağı shows a significant growth of rural as well as urban population. Ronald Jennings documents that the population of the three major towns grew 255 percent between 1500 and 1584. The village population growth, 239 percent, was roughly similar.[12] And although there is no indication of this in the registers, peasants fleeing other areas of the empire must have found this region wealthier and more available for settlement. This is partially confirmed by Huri Islamoğlu-Inan's work on the area just to the north of Kayseri, north-central Anatolia. She also finds substantial population growth (100 percent) for the period 1520–75 and relatively greater urban

[11]Leila Erder and Suraiya Faroqhi, "Population Rise and Fall in Anatolia, 1550–1620," *Middle Eastern Studies* 15 (1979): 322–45.

[12]Ronald C. Jennings, "The Population, Society, and Economy of the Region of Erciyeş Dağı in the Sixteenth Century," in *Contributions à l'histoire économique et sociale de l'empire Ottoman,* ed. J.-L. Bacqué-Grammont and P. Dumont (Louvain, 1983), pp. 205–6.

growth. Furthermore, in her explanation of population movements, she argues that when peasants moved away from this area it was not because of increased grain shortages. She finds the economy of this area healthy and the population adapting to the required intensification of agriculture and the resulting changes in crop cultivation.[13]

Overall, present regional studies seem to indicate population growth as well as depopulation across Anatolia. This is especially true for areas west of Konya and east of Sıvas (based much more on speculation because the records for this period and area are rare). For western Anatolia, the area in the north of Kocaeli experienced population growth up to 1580 and then, during the last years of the sixteenth century, many settlements were abandoned. Erder and Faroqhi find thirteen empty villages as well as many others that had lost some of their population. Similarly, the plain of Antalya in the southwest lost much of its population during the seventeenth century. For the region of Konya, W.-D. Hütteroth has found similar depopulation after 1580.[14] On the other hand, looking at data on population growth as well as the extension of arable land, M. A. Cook concludes that there was considerable population pressure on the Anatolian plateau because the population grew faster than the extension of arable land. As another indicator of population pressure, Cook finds that the unity of the peasant holding was not maintained throughout this period: "the peasant holding was never more than half a *çift*, and fell to a third or a quarter by the end of the period."[15]

The regions under study, part of western Anatolia, showed similar patterns of population growth with regional exceptions of depopulation. Among the settled population of the villages of Manisa, there was a 40.14 percent increase in the number of households from 1531 to 1575. From a review of the data on each village, twenty-four villages that had experienced an increase in population from 1531 to 1575 were identified, while sixteen others had lost villagers. On the other hand, 21.35 percent of the villages in Manisa were cultivated by peasants from elsewhere who had deserted their home plots, in a pattern that repeated itself throughout many areas of the Anatolian countryside. There also was an increase of 238

---

[13]Huri Islamoğlu-Inan, "State and Peasants in the Ottoman Empire: A Study of Peasant Economy in North-Central Anatolia during the Sixteenth Century," in *The Ottoman Empire and the World Economy*, ed. Islamoğlu-Inan (Cambridge, 1987), pp. 101–59.

[14]Xavier de Planhol, *De la plaine pamphylienne aux lacs pisidiens, nomadisme et vie paysanne* (Istanbul, 1958), pp. 122–23. See also Erder and Faroqhi, "Population Rise and Fall," p. 324, and Wolf-Dieter Hütteroth and Kamal Abdulfattah, *Historical Geography of Palestine, Transjordan, and Southern Syria in the Late 16th Century* (Erlangen, 1977).

[15]Cook, *Population Pressure in Rural Anatolia*, p. 11.

percent in the number of unmarried men. Similar patterns are observed for the nomadic population of the region. Among these, the nomad households increased by 51.12 percent, while their unmarried male population increased by 266 percent.[16] Also, from 1529 to 1575, the population of the district of Aydın shows a slight decline in the number of households, from 6,334 to 6,181. The number of unmarried males, however, shows a 272.9 percent increase.[17] Population growth and depopulation of certain regions, then, went hand in hand. The depopulation of certain villages is attributed to the regional variation in the fertility of the land, to inflated taxation, and to large-scale population movements where whole villages picked up and left because of bandits and insatiable retinues.[18]

Still, the most important development of this period was the increased number of vagrant youths in the Anatolian countryside: that of the movement of villagers, young men moving away from their fathers' homesteads toward a life of religious education, military service, or banditry. Various explanations and interpretations of this phenomenon range from economic strife and population growth as push factors away from villages to the pull of the life of adventure, military as well as urban. Mustafa Cezar and Mustafa Akdağ reached the conclusion, based on their studies of economic conditions as well as political documents, that population growth and economic strife lay at the root of this push away from villages.[19] Later this push theory was confirmed by Cook, who concluded, based on his study of population pressure, that since there was not enough land brought under cultivation, young men were leaving their villages for opportunities outside. He also found increasing fragmentation of land units to be an indicator of population pressure.[20] His work was challenged by Islamoğlu-Inan, who worked on one of the regions chosen by Cook.

---

[16]Feridun Emecen, *XVI. Asırda Manisa Kazası* (Ankara, 1989), pp. 205–78, and BBA Tapu Tahrir Registers 516, 683, 786.

[17]This has been calculated from the data and tables provided by Cook in *Population Pressure in Rural Anatolia*, pp. 84–85.

[18]After battles with bandits and brigands, the state declared particular zones free of malefactors and urged peasants to return and start cultivation and even appointed inspectors to force them to do so. For example, many villagers migrated during the depredations of the celali Kalenderoğlu (1607–8), and a shuffling of the population of many villages of Saruhan occurred while Yusuf Pasha (1608–9) was plundering and when Cennetoğlu (1625–26), the tımar holder, went on a rampage of the region. M. Ç. Uluçay, *XVII. Asırda Saruhan'da Eşkiyalık ve Halk Hareketleri* (Istanbul, 1944), pp. 15–36. Also see Daniel Goffman, *Izmir and the Levantine World, 1550–1650* (Seattle, 1990), pp. 26–28.

[19]Cezar, *Osmanlı Tarihinde Levendler*, and Akdağ, "Celali Isyanlarının Başlaması," *Ankara Üniversitesi Dil ve Tarih-Coğrafya Fakültesi* 4 (1946): 23–37, and *Türk Halkının Dirlik ve Düzenlik Kavgası*.

[20]Cook, *Population Pressure in Rural Anatolia*.

Islamoğlu-Inan agreed with the population estimates and the increasing numbers of unmarried males in villages. She disagreed, however, with the causes for the movement away from the land, arguing that although wheat and barley production per capita declined the production of other crops, fruits, and vegetables increased, thereby leading to shifts in consumption patterns and not to food shortages and malnutrition.[21]

Why did young peasants leave their homestead if they were well fed? Some scholars have argued that migration was the result of the appeal of adventure outside the village, while others have attributed increased technology and therefore increased opportunities for migration. For example, migration, according to Islamoğlu-Inan, was more of a response to increasing opportunities for employment and the fact that young peasants were drawn to religious schools or armies.[22] There are problems with most of these explanations. For example, explanations that stress the appeal of opportunities in warfare, religious education, and commerce overstate the case for better opportunities outside rural life. But by the middle of the sixteenth century there were clear indications that a religious education was not a guaranteed road to success. Positions in the religious institution had become quite coveted, and since there were not enough positions, rotation became widespread and bribery to avoid rotation followed. What could have been the appeal of such an institution? Also, if no significant challenge existed within the realm of agriculture and cultivation, demobilized mercenaries (ex-peasants) would have returned to their land. As was previously the case during the campaigns of Selim and Süleyman, soldiers of peasant origin would experience a temporary thrill, after which they returned to the homestead and family.

For Halil İnalcık, rather than economic and demographic pushes out of the village, the phenomenon was one of the pull of a new, increasingly available technology. Moreover, this was the result of the expanding "use by the state of mercenary units of *levends* equipped with firearms."[23] In

---

[21]Islamoğlu-Inan, "State and Peasants in the Ottoman Empire," pp. 112–19.

[22]For the "adventure" argument, see ibid. For the technological argument, see, Halil İnalcık, "Military and Fiscal Transformation in the Ottoman Empire, 1600–1700," *Archivum Ottomanicum* 6 (1980).

[23]İnalcık, "Military and Fiscal Transformation," p. 286. In the pre-Kanuni era, the term *levend* was used to designate fighting men, often on horse. During the reign of Kanuni, the meaning of the term changed to a person with no occupation who could do harm, a good-for-nothing. Cezar carefully shows the changes in the terminology through state and other documents. He also cites Hammer, according to whom the origin of the word is found in the word "levée"—which makes sense and provides the understanding of militarism it later acquires (p. 10). In the sixteenth century, the word acquired a variety of closely related mean-

his words, "the landless peasants in Central Anatolia, as well as in Bosnia and Albania, who, . . . had easy access to handguns, welcomed the change as an opportunity for a new livelihood."[24] This new military technology coincided with the needs and responses of the state as well as that of the peasants, thereby altering the seventeenth-century Anatolian countryside. There is no doubt that the state, in need of increasing numbers of soldiers equipped with firearms, would try to recruit from the peasantry. This does not, however, explain the original transformation of the peasantry or their arming themselves locally before leaving their villages. Furthermore, this explanation does not hold in comparative contexts, since the change in technology did not lead to large-scale militarization of the countryside in western Europe. On the contrary, whatever militarization occurred in the French countryside was based on a division of labor and was temporary. Some villagers went to war while others remained to tend to the fields. Furthermore, those peasants who went on campaign returned to their villages after the war.

Inalcık, however, also correctly places the emphasis on the role of the state. Yet he sees militarization as a direct response to the development of firearms and their frequent use by the state's foreign enemies. I think that the response of the state must be placed into a larger framework of state goals. To achieve centralized control, the Ottoman state had to resort to a variety of actions, one of which was to cause the militarization of the countryside. I contend that the attraction of employment outside the village, and the expansion of the bandit movements into full-fledged mercenary armies, can be explained by the centralizing behavior of the state. Centralization occurred through a pattern of interaction between state and society. Accordingly, state policies were the product of regional conditions and actions perceived to be best for control and for the insurance of loyalty among provincial officials.

The Manufacturing of Banditry

Vagrant peasants who had lost their ties to the land either joined the religious schools in the provinces or the military units of local commanders

---

ings: (1) *çift bozan reaya*, peasants who leave their land; (2) those who are ready to be gathered around an important official, retinue men; (3) *korsan*, pirates, and (4) bandits, see *Osmanlı Tarihinde Levendler*, pp. 8–13. Interestingly, the *çift bozan akçesi*, the fee to be paid by peasants leaving their land, was also called *levendiye* or *levendlik*; see Ömer L. Barkan, *XV ve XVIinci Asırlarda Osmanlı Imparatorluğunda Zirai Ekonominin Hukuki ve Mali Esasları:* Vol. 1, *Kanunlar* (Istanbul, 1943), pp. 58–61, n. 1.

[24]Inalcık, "Military and Fiscal Transformation," p. 286.

or the state's armies for the campaigns on the eastern and western borders. Less significant was migration into the cities, which swelled urban populations, leading to further unemployment. While all these movements started out as relatively contained local and regional movements, people's complaints and the state action often inflated their activity and effervescence. The result was the development of large-scale banditry, a new phenomenon that the Ottoman state had to acknowledge as its own creation and absorb or destroy.

Late in the sixteenth century, a wave of unrest broke out in the Anatolian countryside, commanding the attention of the state and many local and foreign observers. Mounted bands of armed men attacked and plundered villages, defying central as well as local authorities. From western Anatolia to northern Anatolia to the southeast and down to northern Syria, armed bandits created havoc, challenging the state and often extracting favorable concessions.

From the late sixteenth to the mid-seventeenth century, the Anatolian countryside experienced the depredations of these bandits, named *celali*, who, taking advantage of the state's preoccupation with wars on two frontiers, attacked villages, small communities, and even large towns. Attacks on itinerant merchants expanded to constant raids on caravan routes, and city sieges intensified to include regular levies from urban populations. Some banditry remained localized (such as that of Yusuf Pasha and Üveys Pasha in Aydın and Saruhan), some spread quickly (such as that under the leadership of Karayazıcı Abdülhalim in Amasya and Çorum and Deli Hasan in Ankara, Kütahya, and Afyonkarahisar), and some (such as the Canbolad family in Kilis and Aleppo) managed to engage Ottoman armies in several provinces. Peace returned to the provinces only after a confrontation between the state and bandits during which Grand Vizier Kuyucu Murad Pasha deployed strong and well-trained armies to slaughter the celalis (1606–7). In only one clash, it is said that 20,000 heads were heaped up in front of the grand vizier's tent.[25] The banditry subsided for a while, to emerge again in 1622 under new leadership (Abaza Mehmet Pasha and later Abaza Hasan Pasha) but a similar constituency. These events were suppressed in 1658 when a new dynasty of grand viziers reestablished strong state control of the provinces.

Disobedience was by no means new in the Ottoman Empire. In fact, beginning with the rebellion of Şeyh Celal in 1519, the government had referred to all rebels, bandits, and simple brigands as celalis[26] and treated

[25] William J. Griswold, *The Great Anatolian Rebellion, 1000–1020/1591–1611* (Berlin, 1983).

[26] Griswold, "Djalali," *The Encyclopedia of Islam* (Leiden, 1981), 2.

them similarly. The label identified all bandits with the legacy of Şeyh Celal, his rebellion, and the major ideological shift in the Ottoman society that threatened state control and established underground linkages to the Shi'ite population of Iran.[27] Celal's rebellion was not long-lived, since the forces sent by the sultan were able to repress the movement and execute its leader. Yet it remained in the collective memory as an incident of great state violence and in the memory of the state as the first internal revolt that threatened the very fabric of society. The image was to be revived by the state on any occasion of dissent, and the threat of anarchy was used to gain popular support. Accordingly, the state used the label to justify its repression of bandits, even where these did not have any of the rebellious content or viability of the original celali.[28] It is within this context and imagery that the banditry of the sixteenth and seventeenth centuries was perceived and dealt with despite the flagrant lack of ideological content in these movements.

Bands of armed men did not spring up overnight; they were the result of a process of low-level militarization that occurred in the countryside during the end of the sixteenth century. The process meant that at least a significant number of peasants, as the main segment of the population in the countryside, either armed themselves or were armed by the state.[29] In

---

[27]The story of Şeyh Celal is important because it combines the antistate revolt element with the ideological component to reinforce the revolt. Şeyh Celal took advantage of the discontent among the Turcoman nomads accustomed to roaming the countryside who were forced to settle by the state. These nomads were also of heterodox Islamic faith and were leaning toward the propaganda of the Safavid state. The opportunity was offered by the state during the campaign of Selim in Egypt. Şeyh Celal capitalizing on the resentment against a centralizing state and, using the imagery of the Mahdi (Islamic messiah), rallied around him what some historians estimate to be a force of around 20,000 men. See Stanford J. Shaw, *History of the Ottoman Empire and Modern Turkey* (Cambridge, 1976), 1:86; Ismail Hami Danışmend, *Izahlı Osmanlı Tarihi Kronolojisi* (Istanbul, 1971), 2:49–50; Mustafa Nuri Pasha, *Netayic-ül-Vukuat*, ed. Neşet Çağatay (Ankara, 1979), 1–2:88.

[28]This is very clear in the writings of many authors who have accepted the Shi'a ideology in the later movements without looking for any actual evidence of it; see Cook, *Population Pressure in Rural Anatolia*; Çetin Yetkin, *Türk Halk Hareketleri ve Devrimler* (Istanbul, 1984); Mehmet Bayrak, *Eşkiyalık ve Eşkiya Türküleri* (Ankara, 1985).

[29]Acquiring arms does not necessarily entail abandonment of cultivation. Peasants can form alternative semimilitary associations and also organize themselves to attend to cultivation. Or they might acquire arms and use this as a means to leave their previous engagements and embark on a new life. Historically, most instances of such agrarian militarization have demonstrated a mix of these alternatives, which seem to coexist pretty easily. Temporary militarization occurred in France, and in China several distinctions were made between the state's rural militias and the independent militias, or local defense associations that kept the farmers on the land while also engaging them in semimilitary organizations of neighborhood patrol. See Philip A. Kuhn, *Rebellion and Its Enemies in Late Imperial China: Mili-*

Vasıtı's description, numerous peasants under stress dispersed their farms, sold their oxen, bought horses, exchanged their plowshares for guns, and decided to use lances instead of ox goads. The rich and the poor, the young and the old, mounted their horses and joined *sekban* armies to build castles and fortresses, to raid faraway frontiers and enemy strongholds. Yet, on their way to glory, they altered their ways, straying from the straight path onto the rebellious one.[30] At the time, contemporary pamphleteers wrote with concern about peasants arming themselves, viewing a peasant who acquired arms as preferring fighting to the daily routine of cultivation.[31] Nevertheless, by the end of the sixteenth century the Ottoman countryside was thoroughly militarized, and peasants who did not leave their villages or join the bandits were falling prey to a variety of militias, brigands, and warlords who used them as their source of provisions.

Militarization of the countryside was the result of actions by the state in response to the crisis of the Ottoman peasants, even as it tried to maintain centralized control. The exact sequence by which militarization was accomplished cannot be clearly determined. Once economic conditions declined, renegade state officials, vagrant peasants, bandits, and brigands all started to plunder and therefore forced the peasants and the state into action. In general, militarization can also be facilitated by the availability of military channels of employment, the access to arms in society, and the development of a certain repertoire of collective action[32] that emphasizes the use of arms. The central source of militarization, however, was the state and its pattern of alternately loosening and reinforcing its social control of the countryside. Therefore, it is this set of state actions that needs to be disentangled and analyzed.

---

tarization and Social Structure, 1796–1864 (Cambridge, Mass., 1980). Elizabeth Perry also supplies examples of peasants who were part-time bandits since the yield of the land was insufficient to maintain their livelihood; see *Rebels and Revolutionaries in North China, 1845–1945* (Stanford, 1980), p. 133.

[30]Vasıtı, *Kuyucu Murad Paşa Vukuatı Tarihi*. Esad Efendi 2236/1, folio 5b. I have translated freely from the author.

[31]Koçi Bey says: "Reaya ki ata binüb kılıç kuşanmağa mutad ola, ol lezzet dimağında caygir olub, tekrar raiyyet ólamaz. Ve askeri dahi olmağa yaramaz. Bilahara güruh-u Eşkiyaya mülhak olub, nice fetna ve fesada bais olur" (When a peasant acquired a gun and a horse, he would like the life of adventure too much and would never return to a life of farming). Koçi Bey refers to the problems related to peasants and their changing status several times in his pamphlet; see Koçi Bey, *Risale*, ed. Zuhuri Danışmend (Istanbul, 1972).

[32]The phrase "repertoires of collective action" was coined by Charles Tilly, who emphasized that in certain historical periods certain types of movements gain prominence; see *As Sociology Meets History* (New York, 1981), and "Social Movements and National Politics," in *State Making and Social Movements: Essays in History and Theory*, ed. Charles Bright and Susan Harding (Ann Arbor, Mich., 1984), pp. 297–318.

Anatolia provided three main opportunities for advancement to the peasantry in the late sixteenth and early seventeenth centuries. They could join religious schools, the retinues of local strongmen, or the Ottoman army. In the first avenue, they acquired a religious education that did not engender immediate positions and success. In the other two, they acquired arms and learned the ways of a new trade that could result in at least temporary upward mobility. Either route, the religious or the military, had the potential of disintegrating, however. And, when it did, banditry and robbery became the preferred response of students and mercenaries.

Whether religious student or mercenary, the state initially treated all rural disruptors in the same manner. It consistently sought to increase the control of the center over the rural areas, bypassing regional state officials feared to have developed an alternative basis of power. To accomplish this goal, the state expanded its military forces, ironically adding to the number of potentially rebellious armed mercenaries. But neither the religious groups nor the mercenaries actually became a threat to the state, because both groups remained devoid of any transformative platform. Neither movement was motivated by any national ideology. Each was motivated by demands for short-term benefits and was easily co-optable into the system. These groups espoused the already available lines of struggle and competition in the countryside; they exploited known conflicts, known rivalries, and therefore attracted more interest than they otherwise would have. For example, the students exploited the conflicts between local judges and other officials in the countryside (*ehl-i örf*) as well as those between villagers and various lower-rung state officials, such as the timar holder, tax collector, and tax farmer. This enhanced their viability, sustaining their existence for as long as twenty years.

Religious Students

The Anatolian countryside in the late sixteenth and early seventeenth centuries was awash with waves of banditry and brigandage unleashed by groups that constantly mixed and separated and reformulated their interests and occupations. Nevertheless, they all stemmed from the same great pool of unemployed, vagrant men who had abandoned their overcrowded ancestral land and taken up various occupations, all temporary in nature. One of these groups were the *suhtes,* religious students, displaced peasants who took the educational route and enrolled to acquire a religious (*medrese*) education. Once these young men received their diplomas, they discovered that jobs were scarce in their new profession. They were therefore unable to enter the system of court employment, which by that time was already congested with large numbers of judges. From about 1575 to 1597, and for a while around 1613, these students rallied together, pillaged peasant households, and looted officials' holdings and merchant caravans.[33] Their preferred activity was to pretend to be itinerant preachers (*cerre çıkmak*), arriving in villages to lead prayers, only to impose heavy taxes on the population. Impersonating such appointed officials as tımar holders, kadıs, deputies, and others was their best trick because it allowed them to collect taxes.[34] Their regions of activity ranged from the Yeşilirmak river basin, encompassing cities such as Amasya, Tokat, and Samsun to the western Anatolian countryside, especially in cities like Aydın, Manisa, and Menteşe as well as the region of Kastamonu and Bolu.[35]

Religious students found themselves outside the employment system for a variety of reasons. First, there was a hierarchy of preference for graduates from certain *medreses,* especially from Istanbul, Edirne, and Bursa, leaving many students from lesser institutes without work. Moreover, government decrees show that favoritism was so rampant that those who acquired degrees from the better institutions were often not qualified, while more meritorious but less-connected youth were excluded from the major centers.[36] Second, since religious education had always been a prestigious and accepted avenue of mobility (although not for peasants), the religious and legal institutions were already experiencing severe overcrowding in the sixteenth century. Waves of semiliterate, vagrant peasants were not a welcome development. The state found a solution to overcrowding in the rotation of judges, thereby forcing more trained individuals into the system.[37] Senior judges also reduced the stress on the system by hiring deputies (*naibs*) and farming out their districts to them. Often these deputies, trained in the less prestigious schools, became very useful

[33]Cezar, *Osmanlı Tarihinde Levendler,* p. 200.

[34]Although I have found cases of impersonation of tımar officials, I have not encountered any about these religious students. Uluçay, *Saruhan'da Eşkiyalık*, pp. 23–24, however, cites at least three *hüküms* to the local kadıs in western Anatolia alerting them to this practice.

[35]Cezar, *Osmanlı Tarihinde Levendler,* p. 200.

[36]There were attempts to remedy this situation. For example, state orders (1575) were circulated to standardize the educational system and accept the best and brightest rather than the well-connected but mediocre; Akdağ, *Türk Halkının Dirlik ve Düzenlik Kavgası*, pp. 256–57; see also Mühimme Register 27.

[37]This argument has been made most clearly by Halil İnalcık in "*The Ruznamçe* Registers of the *Kadıasker* of Rumeli as Preserved in the Istanbul Müftülük Archives," Turcica 20 (1988): 251–75.

to judges who were overextended to too many districts and who were becoming involved in a variety of other societal struggles.

Despite efforts to relieve the burden on religious education, large numbers of youths trained in the *medreses* remained unable to find positions, became bitter, and started roving around the countryside in bands, demanding food, shelter, and subsistence from the peasantry. As they grew from small bands of 15–20 to larger groups, they descended into the villages, destroyed the harvest of peasants' labor, raped, plundered, and even forced peasants to offer them shelter in their homes. What made them a nuisance for the local power holders was that they destroyed crops, attacked villagers, and therefore made it impossible to collect taxes and dues. Furthermore, where they were supported by the local judges they fueled existing tensions between the representatives of the state's military-administrative hierarchy and judicial-administrative order. What made them relatively less threatening to the state was that they usually did not own firearms (they used mostly swords and knives, bows and arrows) and therefore did not constitute quasi-military units representing an alternative militarization. As a result, the state took fleeting action, not always responding by force, and alternated between pardons and force, as well as delegating action to others. This pattern demonstrated the state's willingness to make deals and to contain trouble rather than deal with it directly, as long as it was not a serious threat and did not spill over to border regions or strategically important areas. As long as the suhtes did not claim territory or impose taxes and therefore did not impinge on the authority of the state, they did not get much central attention; they did, however, get deals.

The actions of the state vis-à-vis the suhtes can be categorized. First, there were relatively standard responses to the activities of the suhtes. These were mainly used when the bands were relatively small and complaints were formally lodged with the government for containing their destructive activities. Second, there were nonstandard responses, unexpected by the people or regional power holders who lived in the provinces. They were nonstandard since they reduced the power of the local officials co-opting the disruptive suhtes and empowering them, albeit temporarily. Finally, wartime measures qualified as extraordinary, often polarizing the provincial groups and the state even further.

Standard responses were often the initial responses of the state; as such they were mostly reactive measures, involving regional power holders. Because suhte disturbances were reported to the government by regional officials, *beylerbeyis* and *sancakbeyis,* the first instinct of the state was to invest these officials with the authority to track students down, investigate their crimes, and send them into exile, often to Cyprus. As disorder soared, the state adjusted by establishing information-gathering channels and demanding that the leaders of these movements be sent to Istanbul, where members of the central governing body could obtain fuller reports and devise methods for dealing with the suhtes adequately. Often, suhte leaders' reports informed the sultan of the treachery of his own provincial officials, who, when they apprehended students, confiscated their booty and divided it among themselves. While the state's response was reactive at first (for example, forcing those who stole to return the money, as well as punishing the suhtes), it became proactive as information was gathered and policy was formulated to inhibit similar events in the future.

The nonstandard responses on the part of the state ranged from simple removal of regional officeholders from specific tasks of authority and control, leaving them rather inconsequential administrative chores, to the active militarization of the peasantry against all those proclaimed to be plunderers. The first, more unusual response on the part of the state was to discharge regional officials from authority over disturbances and to establish new leverage over students by having them negotiate among themselves: students with other co-opted students. Here, enlisting the help of the religious students in Istanbul to control and pressure the regional ones to restrict their actions was the first innovation. Shrewd policymakers co-opted certain Istanbul-based religious students and sent them to press regional students to stop their depravity against peasants, merchants, and townspeople. At the same time, not completely trusting these newly co-opted members, the state asked for bonds on their trustworthiness and good behavior. In a sense, then, the center added to its bargaining capabilities by luring some students into its grasp and using them to convince their own kind to withdraw from action.[38] This removed the regional officials from key positions of authority, allowing the state to centralize at their expense. Consolidation of power in the troubled regions proceeded in this manner, thereby empowering certain groups at the expense of others. Militarization of the countryside certainly was among the most unusual responses of the central authorities. Carried out reluctantly, and with extreme caution, it was feared because it raised the specter of armed rebellion in the periphery. In fact, it was often a way for the state to re-

---

[38]Akdağ presents information that shows the state clearly using bonds as an added safety mechanism in Şarkıkarahisar and Amasya; see, *Türk Halkının Dirlik ve Düzenlik Kavgası*, p. 261. Also see Mühimme Register 31, which indicates this same tactic, and Uluçay, *Saruhan'da Eşkiyalık*.

claim a process already under way in regions where peasants initiated organization of militias to protect themselves from bandits, plunderers, and rapacious officials.[39]

Sultanic edicts demonstrate both state thinking and regional developments in the process of negotiation. Kanuni (1520–66) and Murad III (1574–95) claim to have discovered the real perpetrators behind the scenes in the provincial disturbances. Their edicts reflect these discoveries. An edict of Kanuni in 1565 identified "the retainers of the local commanders, deputies of judges, timar holders, small-time commanders (voyvodas), and the powerful among the reaya," that is, the lower-level officials, as oppressors and therefore asked the judges and local commanders to appease the students.[40] But, since in his edict of 1579 Murad III claimed that it was also the higher-level commanders and judges who engaged in swindle and thievery, he asked the people to arm and to protect themselves.[41] This was a measure of last resort. Before that he had tried the co-optation of the leadership of the suhtes. Representatives of the suhtes were brought from different regions to Istanbul, measures to end the struggle were discussed, and incentives to cooperate with the demands of the center were provided. Consequently, a commission of twelve student representatives was appointed to help prevent the crimes by students. Conciliatory, the state ordered that crimes committed before the decree be forgiven. As a further incentive, successful students were to be allocated 1,000 akçes, taken into higher-level schools, and assigned positions as aides to the state.[42]

When co-optation failed, the state tried militarization of the peasantry. This last resort was tricky, because it was sometimes activated by societal forces and at other times by the state. It was, however, always negotiated by the state and fully appropriated by it. Murad III's edict was promulgated while the Ottoman Empire was at war with Iran (1577–89) and before it went to war with Austria in 1593. Even before hostilities with Iran, realizing that regional forces would be mobilized, peasants and community leaders asked the state for permission to militarize on their own, elect a leader (yiğitbaşı), and have semimilitary forces (ileri) under his command protect the villages in the absence of regular troops. This peasant initiative

---

[39]There are documents in the court records which refer to these militia in the villages yet mostly refer to them as a group of good Muslims rather than armed men. The story, however, often clarifies who these men are.

[40]Kanuni's adaletname has been published by Akdağ in Türk Halkının Dirlik ve Düzenlik Kavgası, p. 503, and by Inalcık in "Adaletnameler," p. 99.

[41]Akdağ, Türk Halkının Dirlik ve Düzenlik Kavgası, p. 286.

[42]Ibid., pp. 262–63. Documents in Mühimme Register 36 attest to this.

had the potential to create alternative centers of power able to resist state intervention, and therefore it had very low priority on the agenda of state makers in Istanbul. In fact, it was resisted, and the state responded by leaving 40–50 low-salaried tımar holders in each provincial subdivision and ordering them to collect all arms in the villages. But as regional unrest continued, the state agreed willy-nilly to have villagers form their own alternative quasi-military organizations, and militarization of the countryside took on added significance. Both peasants and regional officials of the state took advantage of central decisions to arm at the local level. As peasants armed themselves, power holders started hiring free-floating, unemployed, unattached ex-peasant mercenaries (*levends* and *sekbans*),[43] thereby increasing the size of their retinues to fight against the students. In fact, they used the student threat as the justification to enlarge their regional military power.

The ad hoc nature of state action can best be understood in the context of the conflicting decisions that were made. Just as the state was asking its people to take up arms and protect themselves against the students, it sent conciliatory communiqués to the students. The general amnesty offered the students was accompanied by parallel orders to the villages: peasants were not to allow these students into their villages, were to alert government officials, and were to organize their own local militias seriously. The orders regarding rural militias instructed peasants to form groups of ten, each with a leader. These groups were to be organized for the protection of the provinces and had orders to execute suhtes on sight.[44]

In the long run, co-optation emerged as the most frequent route to consolidation in the seventeenth century. Murad III's imperial order of 1584 solidified the prior agreements between the government and representatives of the suhtes. The *kemerbaşlar,* who became permanent representatives of the students, represented the institutionalization of this co-optation. Eleven of them were selected in Istanbul, each as representative of a province, and were to remain there permanently to deal with matters of suhtes. This provided these religious troublemakers with allies at the center and thus a false sense of security and acceptance. But more impor-

---

[43]Cezar comes to the conclusion that the terms *sekban* and *doğancı* both came from a tax obligation such as *avariz-i divaniyye* or *tekalif-i örfiyye*, developing as service in return for exemption from these taxes. He also says that as early as the times of Fatih Sultan Mehmed these were troops that could be added to the janissary forces but were not as trained as the janissaries. After the mid-sixteenth century, *sekban* meant all kinds of soldiers and was used frequently in relation to celalis; see Cezar, *Osmanlı Tarihinde Levendler,* pp. 28–29.

[44]Akdağ, *Türk Halkının Dirlik ve Düzenlik Kavgası,* p. 273; Mühimme Register 48.

tant, the co-optation of the religious leaders was meant to decrease the power of regional provincial officials. The institutionalization of the state-suhte relations and their regulation from the center would remove one of the reasons offered by local provincial officials for increasing the size of their retinues. At the end of a process whereby suhtes were co-opted, peasants were militarized, and regional officials were harnessed, central authorities clamped down on the provinces.

How important were the suhtes? Not very. As the state reacted to a network of forces and dealt with various levels of struggle in the provinces, state makers viewed the suhtes as a symptom of general provincial malaise. The religious students were not important in their own right; they could easily be annihilated by a strong army. Still, this was never done. Why? On the one hand, suhtes became important because of the unintended consequences of their activities. State action triggered by the suhtes enabled villagers to buy arms more easily, allowing the countryside to become militarized and new social formations to emerge. Peasants saw the benefits of acquiring arms to protect themselves and their farms. State officials stationed in the countryside started defining their position as separate from the state; they had used the suhtes and bandits to increase the size of their own armies, and when the state responded by co-opting religious students, their perception of the state's interests and ties to them were altered. This change was to steadily make its way into the seventeenth century. The result was increased competition in the provinces for retinues and for state preference. The actions of the state alienated many of its officials, all the while keeping the image of state office as ever more rewarding.

On the other hand, suhtes did not seem to command serious interest. Throughout the crisis, little was done to acknowledge their misfortunes or to accommodate them. State officials felt forced to take new action only when suhtes moved closer to Istanbul, when Bursa, Balıkesir, in fact, all of western Anatolia seemed terrorized by the threat of suhtes and Afyonkarahisar became the feared center of the students. The suhte problem became acute when the military's attention was diverted to the war with Iran in 1581–82. At this time, new edicts, pardons, and solutions of various kinds were promulgated. When the state finally acknowledged the lack of proper jobs for those who had a *medrese* education as the cause of these events, authorities promised those who repented their misconduct a leasehold (land) or a suitable occupation. But those who had been educated wanted jobs consistent with their education and refused to return to the land.

Early in the seventeenth century, religious students were engulfed in a wave of banditry. Attitudes toward the suhtes changed when banditry and mercenary armies became common in the countryside and further rivalries and battles were ignited. For the first time a concerted effort was made to deal with the student group as such, with its symbolic strength and its interests; that effort was deployed to destroy them as an independent unit, separate from other struggles in the provinces. For example, in 1613 an order was issued banning the students' distinctive dress everywhere outside Istanbul, Edirne, and Bursa—a direct attack on a group that defined its identity by its education and therefore by its costume.[45] Although most historians believe this action followed reports that the students had swelled in their ranks and were in fact giving government commanders a fierce fight, I disagree.[46] I think that by this time banditry had become so widespread that curbing the actions of one group was perceived as a logical start. Suhtes were relatively less important and had distinctive features (especially their clothing), making them easier targets. History books report that after 1613 the suhtes tended to disappear. Historical narratives imply that suhtes mixed in with the other groups slowly forming and organizing around plunder and ravage of the countryside. Religious students lost their distinctiveness, but they gained in numerical and organizational strength as they allied with other potential bandits, brigands, and mercenaries.

Bandits and Mercenaries

Militarization of the countryside in the form of pools of mercenaries available for hire was the result of momentous dealings between the state and vagrant peasants who chose to arm themselves and earn their livelihood by attacking peasants and other rural dwellers. As I discussed earlier, these vagrants were peasants who themselves had given up rural life for the world outside the confines of agriculture. The phenomenon of peasants leaving their land and livelihood was not new in the Ottoman Empire; on a smaller scale, it had happened throughout the fifteenth century. Those who left their villages were easily absorbed into the army as salaried soldiers (*yevmlü*) and returned to their land after wars. At that time, the land must have absorbed them on their return, since no large-

---

[45]Cezar, *Osmanlı Tarihinde Levendler,* p. 206.

[46]Naima reports that, when the governor-general of Karaman was on campaign, there were more than 3,000 *suhtes* in the town of Larende; ibid., p. 207.

scale disturbance occurred.[47] Also, during the reign of Süleyman, peasants—when needed—were recruited into the imperial army and given military status. The fifteenth and early sixteenth centuries, then, had provided an example for peasant mobility into military (*askeri*) status. Koçi Bey, the famous pamphleteer of the seventeenth century, warned against this kind of mobility, arguing that once the peasant left his village he would never return because he would fancy his gun and horse too much. Moreover, since the peasant was not worthy of military status, he would turn to banditry. The magnitude of this movement from land to army was beyond the wildest imagination of most pamphleteers.

In the seventeenth century militarization became the most significant transformation in the countryside. It was triggered and maintained by the centralization needs of the state, which affected both central and regional armies. Peasants were enticed by official grandees to join their retinues or were directly enlisted into the sultan's army. The availability of firearms in the countryside facilitated the move away from the land to military pursuits. Two routes are therefore worth analyzing in detail: that of retinues of local power holders and that of state armies.

Militarization was in large part the result of growth in the retinues of regional power holders. In the early seventeenth century retinues gained importance as competition among elites increased and retinues became economic and political assets. As local officials ranging from *beylerbeyi* and *sancakbeyi*, to bailiffs and their police forces, to such low-level officials as stewards and wardens competed for state privileges, they focused on their own welfare and became less reliable members of the rural community.[48] Their behavior was significant on two levels regarding both peasants and the state. Although these officials, especially the high-ranking ones, always maintained large households mirrored after the sultan's, the competition created by the state forced them to enlarge these retinues for increased prestige and power. The larger their retinues, the more powerful they were and the more important was their military contribution to wars; and the favors they gathered from the state grew accordingly.[49] Having a retinue (*kapu halkı*) became a matter of prestige and honor and

[47]Akdağ, Türk Halkının Dirlik ve Düzenlik Kavgası, p. 98. Also see Inalcık, "Military and Fiscal Transformation," p. 292, n. 22.

[48]Akdağ, *Türk Halkının Dirlik ve Düzenlik Kavgası*, p. 242.

[49]I. Metin Kunt, *The Sultan's Servants: The Transformation of Ottoman Provincial Government, 1550–1650* (New York, 1983), p. 89.

an indicator of local power.[50] The need for more and more men drove power holders to enlist peasants, shifting the source of retinues from traditional slaves to peasants.

Expanding one's household was both economically and politically lucrative. The greater the retinues, the greater the need for revenues to feed, clothe, arm, and maintain these men as a regular little army. Ironically, the need to feed vagrant peasants hired as soldiers became a reason to further exploit the peasantry.[51] Also, the larger retinues were better able to terrorize peasants into surrendering their grain, fowl, and savings. Vagrant peasants (*levends*) easily attached themselves to the service of some official and served him until he fell out of favor with the government: "Since they had no official status, a change in governors left these men unemployed: those that did not take to brigandry were easily persuaded to back their leader's attempt to capture office by rebellion."[52] Once they left their villages and entered the service of various governors, then, these men became part of semimilitary forces with no regular relationship to the land. In fact, in many of their actions they hindered rural development and even pillaged and ransacked the houses in their own villages. Thus the indirect effect of the competition created by the state was to further the flow into governors' households and start a process whereby mercenaries were hired and fired according to the gain or loss of fortune of individual state officials, destroying once and for all the standardized and centrally controlled manner in which the sultan commanded his men and governed over his people.[53]

The retinues of these regional officials gained such significance that they became indicative of a regional leader's intentions to conspire against the government. State officials were in a quandry; on the one hand, larger retinues for *beylerbeyis* and *sancakbeyis* and other miscellaneous pashas

[50]The *kapu halkı*, the household, was composed of vagrant peasants (*levends*) first and foremost, irregular soldiers (*sekbans*), as well as all kinds of other temporarily employed musketeers (*tüfenkçi*) and volunteers; see Cezar, *Osmanlı Tarihinde Levendler,* pp. 265–76.

[51]Uluçay, *Saruhan'da Eşkiyalık,* uses mainly court documents that specifically describe the abuse these men who belonged to the governors and other regional officials inflicted on the peasantry.

[52]Suraiya Faroqhi, "Rural Society in Anatolia and the Balkans during the Sixteenth Century," pt. 2, Turcica II (1979): 134. Cezar, *Osmanlı Tarihinde Levendler,* p. 264.

[53]Again, this is not an entirely new development, since Mustafa Selâniki, *Tarih-i Selâniki (1003–1008/1595–1600),* ed. Mehmed Ipşirli (Istanbul, 1989), p. 37, mentions these men at the service of the governors and other officials for the last combat of the Sultan Kanuni, the siege of Szigetvar in 1566.

meant better ability to fight increasingly difficult wars. On the other hand, too many of these semitrained vagrants made for an unruly, not always trustworthy army. Even more alarming was the competition which ensued for the highest bidder, where local beys sometimes outbid the state in making an army. For example, a certain Mehmet Pasha was famous for bidding more than the state in his attempt to put together an army against the bandit chief Karayazıcı.[54] During the vezirate of Kuyucu Murad Pasha, these matters were foremost under discussion. Kuyucu Murad Pasha, the astute grand vizier of the time, often convinced the powerful regional pashas to leave their retinues behind when he was about to engage them in internal wars.[55] This grand vizier is also known to have reprimanded Nasuh Pasha, the *beylerbeyi* of Diyarbekir, for gathering a few thousand men and bringing them to join the army under the command of Kuyucu at Bayburt (1609).[56]

The trouble with these retinues was that once the practice of keeping them was established it was difficult to alter it in any way. Threats, loss of tenure, displacement, and relocation were only temporary aggravations which these regional officials tried to resolve quickly. Moreover, these officials felt practically no obligation to a group of mercenaries whom they hired for specific duties. These were not slaves they had bought, nor were they in-house trained men in the style of the tımar holders' *cebelüs*. There was no long-term investment in these men; they were easily discarded and easily replaced.[57] And, as they were relocated, the officials moved somewhere else and tried to hire new men and establish themselves in a new area. Although the 1700s were to become the century of negotiations between the state and emboldened regional officials, some local leaders al-

---

[54] Akdağ, *Türk Halkının Dirlik ve Düzenlik Kavgası,* p. 385.

[55] Kuyucu Murad Pasha told the rebel Yusuf Pasha to come join the army and to leave a large segment of his retinue in Manisa to keep law and order there. This was a ruse used by Kuyucu to keep the large retinue away and therefore enable his own men to defeat the rebel; Mustafa Naima, *Tarih-i Naima* (Istanbul, 1283/1866–67), 2:63–64.

[56] The men are carefully described: "Bin nefer tüfenk-endaz safi kızıl çuha giyer, ve beş yüz nefer sekbanı sarı giyer, beş yüz neferi dahi siyah takyeli ve beş bin kadar atlısı alay gösterdiler." Naima, *Tarih-i Naima,* 2:37. Charles Fraser translates the passage: "One thousand musketeers wearing fine scarlet robes; five hundred foot-guards wearing yellow regimentals; and five hundred more wearing black caps; and five thousand cavalry, was the display which Nasuh made on this occasion"; *Annals of the Turkish Empire from 1591 to 1659 of the Christian Era* (London, 1832), p. 364. Many other references can be found regarding the large *kapu halkı* of pashas, *beylerbeyis,* and *sancakbeyis* in the histories of the period.

[57] These mercenaries were hired precisely because the regular retinues and members of the great official households had declined quite drastically during the late sixteenth and early seventeenth centuries.

ready used their retinues to pressure central officials into surrendering increased control over land and taxation.[58]

Ottoman leaders were obliged to confront the ramifications of the activities carried on by local power holders. They did so because almost daily reports described the abuse of those officials with larger retinues.[59] Between regional officials, their retinues, and religious students, the peasants found the countryside demolished, their surplus taken away from them, their houses and farms ransacked, their women and children raped and abused. Where villages sponsored small-scale local protective measures against such devastations, they were quickly provided with the central government stamp of approval. In response to complaints from the provinces and demands for protection, the state let the peasants arm themselves and form protective organizations such as low-level militias, thereby making it more difficult for the provincial power holders to plunder.[60] The new village organization encouraged by the central government was a militia (*ileri*) organization, which most villagers would not join since it entailed danger and severed their ties to the land, even if temporarily. When the ranks of the *ileri* organization filled, they did so with the poor, the landless, the *levends*.[61] In the process, the *ileri* organization lost its civic guise, becoming more of a quasi-military organization than a militia. It is possible that the model central officials pursued was more like the semimilitarized nomads, who formed true militias in that both

[58]The case of Ilyas Pasha is indicative. Ilyas Pasha was considered a loyal official of the government and was often assigned to the provinces of Anatolia or Rumelia. He had gained his reputation by his courageous defense of the state against Kalenderoğlu and various smaller rebellious companies. When in financial trouble, he had been bailed out by the state and had been assigned *sancaks* as *arpalık* many times. Despite this, around 1620 Ilyas Pasha started to gather a large retinue in the region of Balıkesir. Threatened, state officials tried to interfere and accorded him the title of vizier. Emboldened, Ilyas Pasha enlarged his realm of activities and attacked the city of Manisa and its surrounding villages. Records indicate that peasants took flight into the mountains. But Ilyas Pasha's strength was temporary. We discover from documents that, as long as Ilyas Pasha had allies in the government, he acted to increase his power, using his allies as well as his retinue. When his allies were murdered, he was quickly defeated by opposing forces. Uluçay, *Saruhan'da Eşkiyalık*, pp. 37–42.

[59]See the quotation from the justice decree of Ahmed I at the beginning of this chapter.

[60]The court records of Manisa document cases in which villagers on horses chase bandits after they have attacked their village and try to apprehend them and bring them to court. In one instance two women described in court how their husbands joined a group of villagers pursuing bandits before they were killed by musket fire. None of these documents mention, however, the *ileri* militia by name. Manisa court records, Registers 11, 12. In Register 11, cases 50 and 51 are typical examples.

[61]Akdağ, *Türk Halkının Dirlik ve Düzenlik Kavgası*, p. 291.

the military and the civic character of the organization were maintained.[62] But in the seventeenth century vagrancy was widespread, and men in search of employment were willing members of local militias. In the absence of ties to the land, these vagrants became permanent militias. This rural transformation was facilitated by the widening availability of firearms in the countryside.

Beginning with the rebellion of Prince Beyazıd in 1559, firearms had become common in the countryside, and peasants found the means to acquire firearms cheaply from artisans manufacturing a surplus. The prince was able to persuade many vagrants to bear arms and fight for him by promising them timar holdings when he became sultan.[63] The promise never materialized because Beyazıd was eliminated; yet the practice of hiring vagrant peasants and letting them acquire arms became common.[64] The availability of firearms facilitated the process of militia formation, adding to the unruly element. In those days, "an ordinary musket could soon be purchased for three to five gold ducats—that is, for a half or even a third of the price of a horse."[65] This prompted the state to issue numerous edicts threatening the manufacturers of firearms and enjoining local officials to inspect and collect firearms in the villages.[66]

Retinues, local militias, and a peasantry under siege prompted two directly opposed state policies: arming peasants for purposes of local village-level defense, and prohibiting carrying arms and engaging in the service of officials, bandits, and others. The threat of religious students, as discussed in the previous section, also added a great deal to the central government's decision to ask peasants to form their own militias. On the one hand, the state was encouraging low-level militarization of the

---

[62]Kuhn, *Rebellion and Its Enemies*, p. 13. The concepts of militia and militarization of the countryside come from Kuhn. He shows that in China militias are not entirely military organizations. They remain tied to the community and share the values and norms of the community.

[63]Halil Inalcık, "The Socio-Political Effects of the Diffusion of Fire-arms in the Middle East," in *War, Technology, and Society in the Middle East*, ed. V. J. Parry and M. E. Yapp (Oxford, 1975), p. 196. See also Mücteba Ilgürel, "Osmanlı Imparatorluğunda Ateşli Silahların Yayılışı," *Istanbul Üniversitesi Edebiyat Fakültesi Tarih Dergisi* 32 (1979): 303–4.

[64]A document dated 1578 discusses a *sancakbeyi* of Aydın who was able to collect 1,500 firearms from the peasants in his district which he loaded onto a boat journeying from Izmir to Istanbul and sent to the Porte; see Ilgürel, "Ateşli Silahların Yayılışı," p. 307, n. 19.

[65]Inalcık, "Military and Fiscal Transformation," p. 294. See also Ronald C. Jennings, "Firearms, Bandits, and Gun-Control: Some Evidence on Ottoman Policy towards Firearms in the Possession of Reaya, from Judicial Records of Kayseri, 1600–1627," *Archivum Ottomanicum* 6 (1980): 339–58.

[66]Inalcık, "The Socio-political Effects of Fire-arms," and "Military and Fiscal Transformation," p. 294. See also Ilgürel, "Ateşli Silahların Yayılışı," pp. 304–7.

countryside, and on the other hand, it was trying to control the degree and effect of this militarization. Both were policies of centralization, despite the fact that they were contradictory. By taking over control of the militias, the state was appropriating societal forms of self-defense as a make-belief of its own control. And, by trying to control the flow of arms, the state was extending its policing arm into the countryside.

The central grip of the state was felt through another typical centralization policy: the reestablishment of local control through central officials. The attempt to create an alternative protective organization at the village level lost its original purpose when the central government assigned officials to lead the militia. Whether to head the militia or to maneuver local cleavages, the central government found it in its best interest to assign centrally trusted men to the provinces. The recruitment of central or local officials to the leadership position of such militia extended central control for a while. Mustafa Cezar argues that the conditions set on these leaders—whether they were timar holders on rotation or other officials such as *çavuş* or *serdar*—did not encourage them to act honestly. The men who assumed the leadership of the *ileri* used their position and their newly acquired vagrant army to hit the peasantry for various dues.[67] Furthermore, when evidence of disruption continued, state officials sent yet more central officials, this time inspectors who also took the opportunity to seize food and demand service from the peasants. M. Ç. Uluçay's documents describe the exactions of these men together with the gifts they received. The state at this time was involved in a war to defend Sakız and Çeşme, and two pashas had been assigned to protect these areas. On their way to their assigned posts, they sojourned in Manisa, exacting from the people food, shelter, and provisions for themselves and their retinues. During the same year, the tax collector (*muhassıl*) of Aydın and Saruhan, Mustafa Pasha, departed the district after three days and left behind a five-page list of goods and provisions he and his men had consumed.[68] In the year 1659, the inspector (*müfettiş*) Ismail Pasha came to Manisa and stayed about five days, during which the peasants spent 511,641 akçes on him and his retinue. To keep the inspector in good spirits, they also showered him with gifts in the amount of 144,000 akçes.[69] The list of officials who visited, whether billeting or tax collecting or inspecting, and at the same time lived off the peasantry and the townspeople can-

[67]Cezar, *Osmanlı Tarihinde Levendler*, p. 328.
[68]Uluçay, *Saruhan'da Eşkiyalık*, pp. 323–29, document 136.
[69]Ibid., pp. 106–7.

not be overestimated. It is thus fair to conclude that each of the measures of centralization and control had adverse effects on the peasantry.

The two state reactions, formation of local militias and assignment of officials from the center, alternated in an ad hoc fashion over the late sixteenth and early seventeenth centuries. After the first few decrees, the central government chose to overlook official plunder and instead focused its attention on vagrant, bandit, and religious student plunder. Responding to complaints from the periphery, Murad III (1574–95) frequently sent orders for the general inspection of vagrants, calling them a threat to village security and pointing to their illegal activities. A decree, for example, dated 10 October 1576 to the *sancaks* of Aydın, Saruhan, and Hamid ordered the inspection of vagrants and asked the beys of the region to control the influx of vagrancy in their lands. A similar order was dispatched eight days later to the beys of a neighboring region requesting similar contributions from the leadership.[70] A few years later, after the obvious failure of regional official involvement in centralization and control, Murad III sent out a justice decree (*adaletname*) to various regions of the empire mandating low-level militarization of the countryside. This time peasants were to arm to stop the treacherous beys from entering their villages, thereby helping themselves as well as hindering officials in their regular tax-collecting functions.[71] This policy did not remain in effect for long, since this time officials' complaints were considered and decrees contradicting the original *adaletname* were promulgated enabling officials to enter villages in the capacity of tax collectors and to keep order.[72] A few years later, the new sultan, Mehmed III, returning from battle at Eğri, issued a new order demanding the reinstitution of the *ileri* in the villages and specifying how this should be accomplished. The decree also specified that the peasants themselves should choose a leader from among them to head these militia. As a response, the peasantry started organizing again.[73]

These contradictory policies resulted from trying to control and appease many provincial groups at the same time. The state was attempting to play the elites against each other and also to control other class ani-

---

[70]Cezar, *Osmanlı Tarihinde Levendler,* p. 136.

[71]Akdağ, *Türk Halkının Dirlik ve Düzenlik Kavgası,* pp. 330–33. This is the same decree mentioned in the section on religious students. It therefore attests to the same fear of the provincial officials' inability to control the chaos of the countryside and to their ability to profit from this chaos.

[72]Ibid., p. 355.

[73]Ibid., p. 370.

mosities in the provinces. On the one hand, it wanted to alleviate the plight of the peasantry; on the other hand, it depended on the officials and their retinues for war. It had to maintain their loyalty and ensure their livelihood as large combat units. Therefore, it had little option but to seem to be furthering the goals of both sides. Ottoman state officials throughout the early seventeenth century continued to suffer from this situation. They tried new measures, some of which worked while others failed. For example, to keep order during the war, Mehmed III's government resorted to an unusual measure. *Beylerbeyis* who were out on rotation were appointed as provisional officials to areas that needed the most control and regulation.[74] In the seventeenth century, the attempt was also made to institutionalize the keeping and feeding of large retinues by instituting a new series of taxes for just that purpose. There were several of these taxes (*kapı harcı, imdad-i hazariye,* and *mübaşiriye*), collected three times a year,[75] and designed to relieve tensions among officials. But these were just more ad hoc measures with mixed results.

Different outcomes of these state policies can be observed at the village level, but the single most important was the militarization of the countryside. The availability of alternative avenues of livelihood (even though sometimes temporary) for vagrants seemed to have facilitated the choice to leave the land. More peasants became vagrants and left their villages in search of a more exciting life. And, although what state officials had in mind was a limited form of militarization, the outcome of their policy was to provide arms and the skeleton of organization to those very men who were poor and had nothing else to do. The fluctuation observed in the policies of the state, especially shifts from pro-peasant to pro-official, in the long run had dramatic unintended consequences. In particular, the orders by Murad III and Mehmed III to restrict the marauding activities of local officials eventually left them unable to feed their retinues. Unhappy, hungry soldiers quit the service of these men and went into business on their own, as bandits.

The problem, then, was more serious for men who entered the service of these officials, since their tenure with an official was never guaranteed and they often found themselves with nowhere to go. When they were let go en masse, or their patron was out of grace, they resumed the life of

---

[74]The *beylerbeyi* of Rumeli, Hasan Pasha, was assigned to Anatolia. Similarly, the *beylerbeyi* of Trablus-şam, Nuh Pasha, was assigned to Karaman, and *beylerbeyi* Ahmet Pasha to Rum. Akdağ argues that this measure did not work; *Türk Halkının Dirlik ve Düzenlik Kavgası,* p. 341.

[75]Cezar, *Osmanlı Tarihinde Levendler,* pp. 286–87.

vagrancy and reverted to banditry. They also made themselves available to the next governor who needed to establish himself in the province, increase his share of the revenue, and keep his enemies in line. Ultimately, they formed pools of roving mercenaries ready for hire by any strongman with a desire to control a region. The strongest among these contenders was the state, and it entered into negotiations for mercenaries in a similar fashion.

The interests of the central and rural actors coincided in this period of heightened war. The state needed musket-bearing armies. The manner of combat had been drastically altered in the preceding century, and the Ottoman state felt the need to use an increasing number of musketeers. Governors and other regional officials already brought these men to the campaigns as their own men. It was now a matter of the state appropriating the practice for purposes of its own expansion and centralization and altering it to fit its needs.[76] At the same time, vagrants and men who belonged to pasha retinues needed better employment opportunities. The state became an important client for the mercenaries. At the same time, it remained a strong client imposing its needs and formats on the organization of mercenaries. It even instituted a system similar to rotation with mercenaries. State needs soared by periods of war. Peacetime became a rotation of sorts, which like all other rotations in the empire imposed hardships on the affected population.

The organization of the units and the bargains arranged reflected the needs of the state. The policy of the state vis-à-vis these troops became one of using the captains and head captains as condottiere-style leaders with their own military unit, ready to be bargained with for specific campaigns. The sources for these fighting units were regular-yet-unattached vagrant peasants, rural militiamen, retinues discharged by governors, or a mix of all these categories—that is, men who turned to banditry and highway robbery for lack of employment. The vagrant peasants were easily drawn into the army; army service afforded them exemption from taxation, and the state organized them into squadrons and gave them arms, organization, and a livelihood. The village-based militiamen, organized under the watchful eye of the state, formed categories of defense and acquired arms to protect their own domain. Despite the fact that these ret-

---

[76]In Chapter 3 I describe in detail the changes that every unit of the Ottoman army underwent in the sixteenth century. It should be noted that the need for firearms also altered the janissary army, which gained in strength, legitimacy, and prominence in state affairs. The events of the next century bear this out; see Inalcık, "Military and Fiscal Transformation," p. 289, n. 14.

inues were often provisional and volatile, they still organized around some known military principles. They congregated around different categories of leadership that emulated those of the central *kapıkulu* organization, the army of the sultan. Two major ranks of leadership—captain (*bölükbaşı*) and head captain (*başbölükbaşı*)—were taken from the janissaries and indicated similar organizational and military roles. The captain managed a unit of fifty men, and the head captain commanded a few of these units.[77] When they were not in the service of a provincial official, these vagrant-soldiers kept their units intact under a designated captain and looked for alternative employment as a whole squadron (*bölük*). Further, all those who were in and out of these organizations engaged in banditry on the side when their resources were depleted.

Rural Anatolians were ready to offer their services to the state as long as they were paid and fed. As Inalcık sums up:

> Janissary officers, *cawushes*, were sent from Istanbul to each *kadılık* (county) with a decree of the sultan authorizing the enrolling of *re'aya* (toward the end of the century members of the *a'yan* replaced the *cawushes* in this job). The newly enrolled men were provided with an advance payment, *bakhshish*, amounting to 12 grush in 1698, to enable them to prepare for the expedition. A given sum representing the salary *ulufe,* also was paid out in advance. This was reckoned by multiplying the daily fee by the number of the days in service which could extend over two, three, four, or six months. In addition, the men received some *ta'yinat* or *dhakhire-baha*, a cash equivalent of their own food ration and the fodder for their animals. The *ulufe* amounted to two and a half *grush* per month, and the *ta'yinat* to one-eight of a *grush*.[78]

Organizational formats impacted the bargaining power of both the state and unit leaders. Maintaining intact militia or retinue organizations made it easier for the state to negotiate with the leadership and hire squadrons rather than individual men. This facilitated the formation of large-scale armies but provided several middle-ranging squadron officers leverage over the state, because they understood the state's needs and manipulated these to their own advantage. The central government avoided this by appointing head captains and ordering their organization to report to a more senior central official (*serçeşme*), again chosen for the regulation of this new army only. The government wanted to incorporate this new army into the military system. After all, its organization emulated

[77]Ibid., pp. 292–93, n. 23.
[78]Ibid.

central *kapıkulu* army format. And the new army seemed to be an important and loyal segment of the Ottoman military, which responded to challenges and demonstrated its prowess in the battlefield.

Nevertheless, the state encountered difficulties in the process. First, the
sekbans were not loyal only to the Ottoman state; they could become loyal
to any other entity that paid a salary deemed sufficient. The key to the
sekban units was their internal organization and esprit de corps. Their
leadership could be captured by anyone.[79]

Second, their integration into the military raised many bureaucrats'
eyebrows and angered the traditional state army. Although these soldiers
were never trained in the style of the Ottoman central army and always
seemed to return to the life of vagrancy, they developed expectations
about their treatment and demanded the prestige accorded to janissary
units. Whether at the service of a local official or at the service of the
state, these units insisted on gaining status as members of the janissary
corps' *sekban* units. The cold shoulder they received increased their discontent, as they were accorded neither job security nor prestige. The fact
that the different armies were formed from different segments of the population and that no mixing was allowed only accentuated the tension between them. Clearly, the janissary army drawn from the *devşirme* was the
sultan's army, had more prestige, and was deemed superior.[80] Resistance
to the idea of inferiority on the part of the Anatolian *sekban* forces, which
were clearly underprivileged, became the rallying idea for the demobilized units.

Third, demobilization used to contain state expenditure, a sort of
group rotation, had deleterious effects on state and society. Competition
with permanent armies and rotation in and out of service based on war
rendered the demobilized units vicious in their activities. The practice of
rotation addicted them to plunder as a way of surviving when out of
work. This mode was not limited to the mercenaries; it was condoned by
their leaders. There was a constant flow from legitimate to illegitimate
forms of organization, at higher levels—beys and pashas who turned to
rebellion and looting—as well as at lower levels—*bölükbaşıs* who left the

---

[79]Inalcık says, "Sekban esprit de corps made bölüks join forces at moments of common
danger and unite under the command of a single leader, as it happened, for instance, in the
case of Karayazıdjı"; ibid.

[80]Selim and Murad both took *levends* into the janissary army. Yet there was opposition to
this practice on the part of the janissaries, and therefore the practice was stopped. Akdağ
argues that it would have been a good policy.

retinues to form their own bandit groups. However, by Osman's reign, the idea of a permanent *sekban* army was fully formed in the minds of some state bureaucrats.

To sum up, state actions and provincial reactions interacted to alter rural social structure permanently. During the late sixteenth and early seventeenth centuries, alternative modes of organization developed at the provincial level. On the one hand, these were the result of the inability of the peasantry to organize along more conventional lines. Some of the factors involved in this lack of peasant organization were divisions created by orthodox and heterodox religious practice, the varying relations of conflict and harmony between peasants and nomads, the multiplicity of local officials with varying ties to the state, strong state involvement in community crisis organization, and the corruption of local officials. On the other hand, local militarization and banditry developed as alternative modes of organization. Some of these originated independently of any other societal form and developed to espouse the basic military and political formats of Ottoman society. Others did not. As most of the argument makes clear, the state was instrumental in the creation of the alternative mode of organization. And when developments occurred independently of the state, it quickly moved in to appropriate them and use them for the benefit of centralization and administrative control.

Philip A. Kuhn discusses the ways local militarization in the eighteenth- and nineteenth-century Chinese countryside developed as an alternative mode of organization, and especially how it managed to do so along existing lines of political and social organization. Chinese society, he argues, by the late 1820s had developed local networks of collaboration protecting peasants from excessive taxation through a variety of means. In the Chinese case, official systems of militarization were developed through the observation of local practice.[81] Key to an understanding of Ottoman society is the lack of institutional forms to espouse in Ottoman society; the state developed them for the society as the process evolved. Therefore local militarization took on state format. Even if small-scale transformation into vagrancy occurred on its own and local militarization started on peasant initiative, the central government was quick to claim the development, adopting it to its own format. These alternative organizations then grew under the state's aegis.

---

[81]Kuhn, *Rebellion and Its Enemies.*

Banditry as a Social Type

Whether through direct employment in state armies or indirect employment by local power holders, vagrants turned into mercenaries and became organized along state military lines. It is difficult under these conditions to see the bandit as a rural product; instead, it is necessary to accept the role of the state in the production of this new social type.

It is clear that banditry was the result of a pooling that occurred when societal institutions such as the military and officials' retinues (and, less so, religious schools) recruited the landless, the vagrant, and the destitute into their midst, training them, providing them with organization, using them during campaigns, and demobilizing them en masse at the end of war. These demobilized soldiers formed pools of mercenaries available for hire but also engaged in banditry, pillage, rape, and destruction along the way. It is therefore not useful to think of these men as peasants, or vagrants, or students. Rather, it is important to rethink them under a new category and to delineate their characteristics and the implications of these characteristics.

Two basic characteristics of this group are immediately visible. First, these individuals acquired multiple, fluid identities. From being simple peasants they moved to being landless vagrants, soldiers, mercenaries, and bandits. From vagrancy to militia to mercenary armies the bandit emerged as a social type, a type clearly separate from his original birthplace in peasant society, fighting for some privilege and permanency in his own world. Second, the process by which bandits became part of the collectivity was different from other group-formation practices. Here, horizontal ties were formed because the linkages of each individual to his own reference group were cut. Bandits did not come together of their own will; they were brought together by societal elites for the interests of these elites. Banditry was thus an artificial social construction that became a threat, was used as a pseudo-threat, or was co-opted into the governing machinery of the state depending on the needs of the ruling class. Its rebellion did not represent collective action in the traditional sense since it did not attempt to destroy the social structure of society; it simply wanted to derive as much utility from society as possible. It manipulated the interstices of the system, having no proclaimed ally or enemy and no significant ideology.

The state was the most significant actor in the transformation of vagrants and mercenaries into bandits. It created this phenomenon as a by-product of its attempt at shaping structures of coercion and control at the central and regional levels. The Ottoman state created, activated, and manipulated structures of control that inhibited class-based movements; yet, again, state institutions created collectivities necessary for its military, administrative, and legitimating goals. And, as we see in the next chapter, the state that created this movement actively incorporated it into its strategies of state centralization. In the process, centralization acquired an alternative style—that of bargaining and negotiating with an artificially created group, the celalis.

The bandit no doubt was a vagrant peasant at the outset. However, in response to the policies of centralization and control of the Ottoman state, the peasant was transformed into a bandit who separated himself from the rest of peasant society and established a world of his own in which there was no place for his origins. In fact, the transformation produced a new threat to rural society; once more, then, through a different channel, villagers became the victims of state policy. And bandits became the agents of this new kind of exploitation. It is therefore impossible to agree with the romantic characterization of the phenomenon of banditry as often seen in the literature.

Most studies on banditry have worked with the underlying assumption that peasants and bandits were the same "social type" and were members of the same rural community. In the work on China, for example, the peasant has not been set apart from the bandit. According to Elizabeth Perry, although the bandit abandoned the community in many cases to join the army, and engaged in banditry against the peasantry, he still was considered a member of peasant society. Perry works from the premise that when there is scarcity "violence against fellow competitors" is to be expected; therefore, the two strategies she observes in China, predatory and protective, have their inherent rationalization in the peasant community itself. Although these bandits grew to organize and became a serious challenge to the state, they were accepted as one of the many organizational forms through which peasants expressed their discontent. As they left the village, these peasants who became bandits did not alter their mode of collective behavior or their demands. In this case, as Perry reminds us, "a rabbit never eats the grass around its own hole"—bandits did not plunder their own communities. "Apparently," she concludes, "some bandit groups thus did evidence a redistributive ethos."[82]

[82]Perry, *Rebels and Revolutionaries*, pp. 73–74.

Eric Hobsbawm conceptually collapses the two categories of peasant and bandit.[83] His analysis presents one particular form of banditry he claims to be the essential one: social banditry. The social bandit acts in basic social protest against poverty and oppression, and social banditry is manifested in theft, highway robbery, and various other kinds of activities richly detailed in his case studies. Through these activities bandits voice popular discontent; they steal from the rich to distribute to the poor and they claim to represent the "moral good" in rural community.

> The point about social bandits is that they are peasant outlaws whom the lord and state regard as criminals, but who remain within peasant society, and are considered by their people as heroes, as champions, avengers, fighters for justice, perhaps leaders of liberation, and in any case as men to be admired, helped and supported. This relation between the ordinary peasant and the rebel, outlaw and robber is what makes social banditry interesting and significant. It also distinguishes it from two other kinds of rural crime: from the activity of gangs drawn from the professional "underworld" or of mere freebooters ("common robbers"), and from communities for whom raiding is part of the normal way of life, such as for instance the Bedouin.[84]

Accordingly, despite the fact that bandits live on the margins of peasant society, they are accorded the same symbolic space because they share the values of this community; peasants thus share the political and social ideology of bandits, often allying with them.[85] The village community further sees the bandit as a hero fighting against central state and local oppression. The similarity of the goals makes the bandit social because he is perceived as working for the community. Furthermore, social banditry is a general phenomenon, universally found wherever societies are based on agriculture.[86]

[83]Eric J. Hobsbawm, *Primitive Rebels* (New York, 1959), and *Bandits* (New York, 1981).

[84]Hobsbawm, *Bandits*, pp. 17–18.

[85]Many studies have already listed the implications of Hobsbawm's definitions. Among them is Nathan Brown, "Brigands and State Building: The Invention of Banditry in Modern Egypt," *Comparative Studies in Society and History* 32 (1990): 258–81, and Pat O'Malley, "Social Bandits, Modern Capitalism, and the Traditional Peasantry: A Critique of Hobsbawm," *Journal of Peasant Studies* 6 (1979): 489–501. Some of these themes also appear in the writings of the most eminent critic of Hobsbawm, Anton Blok. See, for example, Blok, "The Peasant and the Brigand: Social Banditry Reconsidered," *Comparative Studies in Society and History* 14 (1972): 494–503, and *The Mafia of a Sicilian Village, 1860–1960: A Study of Violent Peasant Entrepreneurs* (Prospect Heights, Ill., 1974).

[86]Hobsbawm, *Bandits*, pp. 19–20.

The element of social protest has become appealing to many historians and social scientists who have gone on to interpret many historical records of banditry as social protest, thereby awarding the phenomenon legitimacy. I argue that the historical record has to be carefully examined before such judgments can be made. I further contend that under scrutiny the records tend to present a few cases of social banditry embedded in the widespread exploitation of the peasantry by typical brigands and thiefs. Most countries that have experienced banditry have a few redistributive cases for multitudes of more regular villains. The Ottoman seventeenth century is one such example.

The question of whether the majority of rural bandits are redistributors or simply opportunistic highway robbers with little ideology or social and political commitment remains operative. There is no doubt that Robin Hoods existed in rural society. Peasants have produced many folk stories and songs as homage to those who remained part of the community of peasants and helped them by stealing from the rich to distribute to the poor. These unique individuals originally helped create the myths we read in most popular writings. For Hobsbawm, these were simply outstanding social beings with a developed sense of justice who were able to carry out the work necessary to restore equality. Often, however, among those who captured the imagination of the peasantry were those whose initial acts of charity were carefully orchestrated to ensure the complicity of the rural population.[87] Mythologized versions of these characters then traveled through the lands and became part of the repertoires of village life.

The existence of these repertoires and the stress on mythical characterizations bring about methodological issues. Differences in historical records become difficult to reconcile. On the one hand, it is often hard to match the historical record with the stories, poems, and mythological explanations of events that flourish in the imagination of many individuals. The historical record often refers to these bandits as dangerous rebels because it is in the interest of the state to rally the population against these men. And the popular stories vary too often, amplify the deeds of these men to the level of the superhuman, and therefore lose their credibility.

---

[87]Pierre Bettez Gravel, for example, clarifying some of Hobsbawm's thoughts, argues that "in times of social discontent, there are always individuals who, for reasons that may be selfish and personal, break away from the main body of the peasantry to become outlaws and leaders of bands. These events often co-exist with broader insurrectional movements, and although the bandit may not be aware of them, he soon becomes identified with them in the minds of the populace"; "Of Bandits and Pirates: An Essay on the Vicarious Insurgency of Peasants," *Journal of Political and Military Sociology* 13 (1985): 209–17.

Richard Slatta reflects this well when he says, "Owing to their great notoriety and popular fascination, bandits exist in a netherworld between fact and fiction."[88]

A tradition of folk heroes was widespread in Ottoman lands. A vast oral and written repertoire of myths cherished by common folk for centuries survived into the twentieth century. This literature experienced a revival, especially when Marxist scholars who studied the exploitation of the peasantry by a large agrarian state discussed social banditry as a type of peasant rebellion. Peasants were responding to their exploitation by leaving their land, becoming outlaws who raided government officials, military and judicial, and escaped to the mountains. Among these authors we can find Kemal Tahir; Yaşar Kemal, famous for his novel *Ince Mehmed;* the Czech historian Xenia Ceinarova; and the Russian historian A. S. Tveritinova.[89] Among the well-known social bandits, Pir Sultan Abdal, Köroğlu, and Dadaloğlu opposed the policies of the state and struggled against local leaderships that were oppressing the peasants. Their status as social bandits remains unchallenged despite state accusations of attacks on the peasantry.

A discrepancy between state documents and popular production exists for the Ottoman Empire as well. Government officials in state documents referred to well-known social bandits as celalis and ordered regional leaders to annihilate them. The popular literature transformed them into heroes who inspired every male child in rural Anatolia. It is safe to assume that reality lay somewhere in between. The central government no doubt pressed for an identification with ordinary celalis to account for more regional control. But, within the popular literature also, conflicting points emerge, making an accurate assessment of social banditry difficult. First, there are just a few heroes, each associated with a multitude of epics. The *dramatis personae* behind these epics are often unknown. It is also unclear

[88]See Richard W. Slatta, ed., *Bandidos: The Varieties of Latin American Banditry* (New York, 1987), p. 1. This book tries to point out the concrete reality of bandits. There is no doubt that about some of these men there exists a popular myth that prevails at another level, that of the collective consciousness of the people. In this volume by Slatta, only two articles deal with this issue carefully, those of Chandler and Lewin, which attempt to distinguish between the myth and the reality of social banditry.

[89]The works by these authors are discussed at length in Bayrak, *Eşkiyalık ve Eşkiya Türküleri*. See also Yetkin, *Türk Halk Hareketleri*. Bayrak, especially, agrees with their perspective and in fact presents cases of social banditry through the epic poems manufactured by folk society. The cases, however, are interspersed through centuries, and the actual number of cases is the product of four centuries from the sixteenth to the twentieth, amounting to not many more than three or four folk heroes per century. It is therefore safe to say that those about whom legends were created were quite rare.

whether these few names had become generic names used by minstrels, troubadours, and balladeers all over. To determine an answer to these questions is beyond the scope of this book. Yet these are sufficient indications that it is difficult to take much of the popular production at face value.

Some preliminary methods for determining whether bandits were credible social bandits exist. Most often, court records confirm or fail to corroborate claims by the state because these records are produced outside the state's domain. These documents constitute accurate reproductions of peasant complaints and reflect rural reality better than either state or popular evidence in their direct representation of peasants' issues and concerns. For western Anatolia, court records present evidence of overwhelming bandit activity: 20 percent of the cases are related to banditry.[90] Interaction of bandits with the state is also important for determining whether they were social bandits. For, although the state was clearly against them, it dealt with them in different ways. One was to bargain over acceptance of government positions. Given the description of social bandits as "primitive rebels," it is difficult to perceive them as actors willing to enter the state and become part of it. Köroğlu, for example, never negotiated with the government for an administrative position.

Köroğlu comes closest to the characterization of a social bandit rebelling against local oppression (in the region of Bolu) and thereby gaining prominence among the peasants. He is known for his famous call to arms:

> I am Köroğlu; I shatter the rocks,
> I am the people's sword; I search for justice,
> I hold the Sultan responsible,
> Those who wake up join me![91]

His appeal to the peasants to join his struggle against the ruling elite did not succeed. Köroğlu rebelled around 1580–81 and at the time was branded celali by the state. He (as the captain) and his troops (a squadron of demilitarized mercenaries and vagrant peasants, approximately 200 men with their horses) set up quarters in the mountains and periodically descended to attack local officials.[92] Some documents of the period show that Köroğlu attacked both judges and other local officials with reputa-

---

[90]This is just for the second period under investigation, Registers 102, 104, and 106.
[91]I have translated this verse from Bayrak, *Eşkiyalık ve Eşkiya Türküleri*, p. 37.
[92]Ibid., pp. 36–38.

tions for tyranny and innocent villagers;[93] other documents testify to his social consciousness, indicating that unlike other bandits he and his men never trampled village fields, even at the cost of their own security.[94] Evliya Çelebi, the great traveling chronicler of the time, says that Köroğlu was both a celali (obviously a label adopted from state discourse, since he was at the time traveling with Sultan Mehmed IV) and a minstrel.[95]

Still others argue that he was part bandit, part social bandit. But in the hearts and minds of those who repeated Köroğlu epics, he was a hero. Finally, state reports and orders to local officials regarding Köroğlu are exactly the same as those for any other small-scale bandit leader, suggesting that the state afforded blanket treatment to all rebels. An Armenian source offers hints as to how celalis and social bandits could be mistakenly placed in the same category. Tebrizli Arakel discloses that Köroğlu and his friends Köse Sefer, Mustafa Bey Giziroğlu, and Koca Bey roamed the countryside accompanied by ill-reputed and shady members of celali bands.[96] The association between celalis and Köroğlu—even if temporary—was manipulated. It helped the Ottoman state officials to label Köroğlu as a celali. And, more recently, it has been appropriated by historians and folklorists who attribute Köroğlu's character and deeds to all the celalis. Both interpretations are distortions that served the interests of particular perspectives.

In the case of most bandits, central state records, local judicial records, and contemporary chroniclers, poets, and minstrels all reveal that peasants suffered a great deal from these bandits and repeatedly asked the government for help. The legends about Karayazıcı and Canboladoğlu are legends of fear, not of pride. The stories and folk songs are about giving advice to those bandits who have forsaken their lives for evil and oppression. For example, in one folk song the western Anatolian bandit leader Haydaroğlu is warned that if he continues his evils he and his troops will

---

[93] Akdağ, *Türk Halkının Dirlik ve Düzenlik Kavgası*, pp. 298–99, has published some of the *mühimme* documents relating to the case of Köroğlu, and they clearly indicate attacks on both local officials and the people. For attacks on the people, we rely only on state documents, which may exaggerate the damage to convince peasants to collaborate with the authorities. Apart from Akdağ, both Pertev Naili Boratav and Faruk Sümer use historical documents as well as folklore to analyze the origins and the degree to which reality and myths are intertwined in the history of Köroğlu. There seems to be consensus for this folk hero especially that documents and myth refer to the same person and that Köroğlu is a historical figure of some importance.

[94] Pertev Naili Boratav, *Folklor ve Edebiyat* (1982) (Istanbul, 1983), 2:232.

[95] Quoted in Bayrak, *Eşkiyalık ve Eşkiya Türküleri*, p. 120.

[96] Boratav, *Folklor ve Edebiyat*, 2:239–40.

be lined on hooks.[97] Haydaroğlu is also known because he was romanticized by modern authors despite the violence of his actions. Not only did he bring about pain and disarray to his own people, he also sought government positions several times.[98]

In another type of historical source, especially important for eastern Anatolia, Armenian priests and chroniclers narrated the stories of the bandits they encountered. It is quite hard to imagine these characters, with nicknames like "Kesekes ('Strike and Kill'); Kör Ghaya ('Blind Rock'), Abu Hancher ('Dagger Father'), Topuzi Böyük ('Big Mace'), Siki-Böyük ('Big-Bodied'), and Ghara Sahat ('Last Judgment'),"[99] as benevolent Robin Hoods putting their lives on the line for the benefit of some peasants. The tales the Armenian chroniclers tell are ferocious: "They resorted to inhuman torture, hanging the peasants by their feet to force them to reveal where they had hidden the remainder of their victuals. An old sick monk in the Cloister Hovhannavank was tortured to death in an effort to make him disclose the hiding-place of the church treasures and vestments."[100] There is no doubt that we are here dealing with a phenomenon far from that imagined by Hobsbawm.

I argue that an analytical distinction has to be made between the peasant and the brigand. Even if the brigand was originally from the same village, the transformations I have described refashioned him to benefit from new conditions and new alternatives. In the process, he developed a new persona, disloyal to his origins and even helping to repress members of his village. Either through the devastation they caused when unem-

---

[97]These folk songs, ballads, and stories have equally survived to modern times. Some of them were composed by government sympathizers such as Katip Ali, a seventeenth-century poet; see M. Çağatay Uluçay, "Üç Eşkiya Türküsü," *Türkiyat Mecmuası* 13 (1958): 89–90. Others were local poets, wandering minstrels who gave voice to the pain and suffering of the people and praised local commanders who were able to alter the conditions of human misery, even for a short while. Such is the ballad of Birri Mehmed Dede, a local Manisa poet who wrote a poem in praise of Nasuh Pasha, an ex-rebel who had been appointed tax collector (*muhassıl*) of Manisa after his brief encounter with Grand Vizier Kuyucu Murad Pasha. And it is true that the poet exaggerates by according Nasuh Pasha heroic status; yet he was successful at eliminating most of the region's bandits—in fact, his potential rivals in tax collecting; ibid., pp. 92–93.

[98]Halil İnalcık, "Haydar-oğlu Mehmed," *Encyclopedia of Islam* (Leiden, 1969), pp. 317–18.

[99]I use the transliteration and translation from the text despite the fact that both are incorrect. For example, "Siki-Böyük" refers to the nickname of a bandit rebel with a large penis; see Edmond Schütz, "An Armeno-Kipchak Document of 1640 from Lvov and Its Background in Armenia and in the Diaspora," in *Between the Danube and the Caucasus: A Collection of Papers Concerning Oriental Sources on the History of the Peoples of Central and South-Eastern Europe*, ed. Györg Kara (Budapest, 1987), p. 252.

[100]Ibid.

ployed and in search of food and shelter or through the service they rendered the patrons who hired them as members of their retinues, bandits committed crimes and atrocities and demonstrated that their first loyalty was not to the peasant—that in fact they could often act against the peasant. Interestingly enough, Anton Blok makes the same observation about alternative paths of employment: "When bandits assume retainership (either part time or full time) they serve to prevent and suppress peasant mobilization in at least two ways: first, by putting down collective peasant action through terror; second, by carving out avenues of upward mobility which, like many other vertical bonds in peasant societies, tend to weaken class tensions."[101] This remained accurate for the seventeenth century across Anatolia.

Bandits and peasants were different social types who no longer shared the same community, did not engage in the same type of activities, and whose organization and demands in collective action did not coincide. Through adaptation to local ecological and political conditions, a segment of peasant society was transformed, and over time this new group lost the ties and relations to land and labor that characterize the peasantry. They formed a new group whose relations to the means of production were entirely different from that of peasants. They related more closely to the noncultivating classes in rural society, although their origins and their means of subsistence were different. But the fact that they hired out their services to other classes did not make them loyal allies either. They were opportunistic and took advantage of their position to commandeer resources from the weak, from whichever walk of life.[102] It is thus not suitable to think of rural society as bipolar, with peasant and landlords as the sole actors. As much as the constant movement from retinues to banditry blurred the distinctions between classes, the introduction of this new group in rural society also altered the relationships between these two classes by offering each another focus of discontent. Moreover, the relationship of the peasants to the new groups and the new cleavages in society become even more important when evaluating collective action.

The movements, the organization, and the demands of peasants differ from those of bandits. Even if the two groups can ally in a cause against the state, their different lives make it impossible for them to collectively

---

[101]Blok, "The Peasant and the Brigand," pp. 499–500.

[102]The *mühimme* as well as court records provide instances of banditry against the timar holders, especially those small landholders who were increasingly more destitute because of state policies. The timar holders also used the court to report incidents of theft, cases of abuse against them. See Manisa court records, Registers 11, 12, 102, 104, 106.

join forces with ease.[103] Most important are each group's relationships to the land. For peasants, land is the main factor of agricultural production; they are tied to it for their livelihood. Bandits, on the other hand, have given up their right to the land; either they have been forced out by ecological conditions or they have left willingly. Their attachment to the land is practically nonexistent or, at best, temporary.

Peasants who earn their livelihood from the land pay taxes to landholders and to the state based on their yearly income. Their relationship to the noncultivating classes is based on the exploitation of their labor. Bandits do not pay taxes. They do not engage in any productive activity to be taxed on. Bandits engage, in one form or another, in violent taxation of the peasantry; in that sense, they are closer to the noncultivating classes. Both are engaged in the extraction of surplus; they are therefore in competition. This was certainly the case in the Ottoman Empire, where bandit leaders and landholder/officials usually competed and tried to enlarge their retinues in the hope of more wealth and control. And to the degree that a landholder or powerful local pasha was able to recruit many of these bandit bands, he could ensure that part of the loot was his. Therefore, a constantly changing cycle of alliance and competition between bandits and officials bewildered the peasantry, keeping the community suspicious and vigilant.

Bandit and peasant also differ in terms of their organizational capabilities. Whereas peasants need already existing village institutions to bring them together and assure interaction, bandits seem to espouse any institutional form quite easily. In fact, though Hobsbawm would have us think of bandits more as extrainstitutional, with no form or concrete organization, banditry has the potential of being both quite adaptable and quite rigid.[104] In the Ottoman case, it was clear that peasants needed to be mobilized into collective action, whereas bandits were already mobilized by another institutional force outside their objective. And once organized by

[103]Eric R. Wolf, *Peasant Wars of the Twentieth Century* (New York, 1973), pp. 34–35, explains the geographic and organizational parcelization of the Mexican Revolution by differentiating between the peasant-based segment (Zapatistas in the South) and the bandit-based segment (Villistas in the North). Part of his explanation depends on the differences between these two movements: one being more regional and less mobile, and the other getting its support from a mobile cavalry drawn from a large pool of bandits and cowboys.

[104]This argument is also at variance with that of Hobsbawm, who sees banditry more or less as "spontaneous bands"; see *Primitive Rebels*, p. 26. Hobsbawm does not take into consideration somewhat permanent forms of organization and mobilization which bandits acquire either through incorporation into another institution or emulation of the formats of other institutions.

state officials into military units, they were able to maintain the military formations despite the fact that they were demobilized. It is interesting that bandits did not scatter but rather chose to keep the institutional format of the system that rejected them. The peasant's dependence on the land and on the various village institutions made his collective action much less daring and more localized. This is true since peasants had more to lose from collective action than did bandits. Also, bandits were not tied to the land and were therefore mobile and able to launch large-scale collective movements in which various regional bands formed united troops.

The Ottoman peasant who chose a life of vagrancy and was drawn into banditry as well as part-time mercenary activities was in the long run transformed into an individual quite different from his original self. This is clearly seen when we analyze the differences in the demands of the various rural groups involved. Peasant demands ranged from requests for less taxation by state and local officials to requests for being removed from one district and entered into the jurisdiction of another.[105] The demands of the bandits varied according to their strength, their leadership, and the positions of their leaders. In most cases, it is clear that the celalis were not interested in the overthrow of the Ottoman dynasty. The only celali rebel leader who could be seen as a potential state maker was Canboladoğlu Ali Pasha of northern Syria (see Chapter 6). In general, bandits did not represent any particular group in society. They did not represent or espouse any of the class cleavages in society.

Some leaders were interested in loot, just loot, as much as possible and as quickly as possible. Edmond Schütz explains, for example, that the vice-chiefs of Deli Hasan refused the military administrative positions offered to them. They had been encouraged by the amount of loot they had gathered in Sıvas and Tokat and were more interested in continuing such piratical expeditions.[106] Others were interested in the security and permanence of their loot. They therefore attempted to acquire a domain and the right to tax the peasants on this domain. Their troops, however, often did not know how to refrain from plundering, so misery and destitution continued. Furthermore, analysis of the pamphlets of the period shows that the original mercenary soldiers (yevmlü) as well as the later ones (sekban/sarıca) were mainly interested in being included in the prestigious

---

[105]This was one of the methods the peasants employed to lower their exploitation. If the kadı of another nearby administrative unit was regarded as more lenient toward peasants, they would want to be reentered in the records under his jurisdiction. Such documents were found among peasant complaints. See, for example, *Topkapı Arşivleri*, document 2387.

[106]Edmond Schütz, "An Armeno-Kipcak Document," p. 253.

kapıkulu army, with permanent status and salary. The author of *Kitab-i Müstatab,* an anonymous advice book written in the early seventeenth century, claimed that "Turks, Kurds, Gypsies, and many from among the *reaya* now found ways to intrude into the military class which up to then was strictly reserved—under the fundamental laws of the Ottoman state—to *kuls*."[107] In fact, Inalcık argues that the rebellion of Abaza Mehmed must be seen in light of the rivalry between the *kapıkulu* and the mercenary segments of the Ottoman military establishment.[108]

Finally, the very introduction of banditry as an alternative path in rural society affected the prospects of collective action. As was argued by Blok, banditry represented a response to destitution and oppression as well as to the extractive apparatus of the state. Banditry became an alternative for destitute, vagrant peasants with no other opportunity. And while it opened a channel of alternative employment, it also closed many other alternatives that could have been more valuable to the peasant. In terms of collective action, there were several ways banditry was liable to alter existing class tensions and to obstruct group formation. It drew on the poorest and yet the youngest and most able element of society. Older men, married heads of families, or women do not usually constitute the fighting force of a rebellion. Once the young men were off engaged in coercion and control for local officials, or warfare for the state, or looting on their own account, the peasantry was left with a demographic segment of society less likely to rise up in revolt.[109] Second, banditry in general depletes the economic resources of an area. Bandits either add to the violent extraction of surplus or aid in it. It has been argued that the more destitute a group, the less they are able to rebel, having to focus more exclusively on subsistence. By participating in the exploitation of the peasantry, bandits ensured that peasants who were not able to secure their surplus for the year would be very unwilling to engage in collective action. A report of 1604 emphasized the pain and suffering:

Several hundred horsemen and musketmen [*sekban*] including [the names of twenty-four such as Arslan Gazioğlu, Ali and Mehmed Çavuş, and Sarı Mehmed and Köroğlu] who, like brigands [*emsali eşkiya ile*] came to the province, pillaged the goods of the poor, burnt their houses, killed more than 200

[107]Text quoted in Inalcık, "Military and Fiscal Transformation," p. 287, n. 11.
[108]Ibid., p. 298.
[109]This is corroborated by the information we have on western European rebellions. As one studies closely the stories of French rural rebellion, one hears of younger folk, men and women, as the peasant producers engaged in rebellion.

men, ran off with young boys and virgin girls, and stole more than 50,000 sheep, goats, horses, and good camels, and took the stores of barley, wheat, oil, honey, and other commodities; then they captured more than 300 men, torturing them night and day.[110]

The tortures intensified as peasants were unable to pay the troops the amounts they wanted. Also, many of these bandits/soldiers would invade an area and go through it village by village, demanding taxes (*sekban akçesi*).[111] The retinues of Ottoman officials also served to change the rural scene. These men, who were hired as personal retinues, often acted to help their retainer in the collection of taxes and in the various exactions and to serve as personal bodyguards.[112] One can assume that these bodyguards made sure the taxes were paid and the extras pocketed. Legal and illegal, such men made it impossible for the peasantry to resist. Even when the leadership tried to control their retinues, especially after rebel leaders obtained legitimate positions, it was difficult to restrain men who were accustomed to looting. The rise of banditry should definitely be added to the reasons peasants were unable to engage in collective action.

[110]I have used the translation provided by Griswold, *The Great Anatolian Rebellion*, p. 49.
[111]Ibid.
[112]Faroqhi, "Rural Society," pt. 2, p. 134.

6

State-Bandit Relations: A Blueprint for State Centralization

A Political Invitation: May 1606

A List of Matters Concerning the Slave Canboladoğlu Ali Pasha:

This slave petitions that if he is appointed to the position of the beylerbey of Aleppo he will undertake to go with 5,000 men to the campaign called for the coming spring Likewise, if by the favor of the sultan he is given, with the aforementioned province, a vezirate, then he promises to take 10,000 men to the campaign

Beyond this, if he is bestowed with [several words missing] and some of his adherents [words missing] and to some of his men the offices of *müteferrika* and *çavuş* and division chief is proffered then he promises to bring twenty [thousand?] courageous men to the imperial campaign and will sacrifice heart and soul to whatever duty he is entrusted

Like his father and grandfather, if he is assigned as administrator of the Turkoman tribes of Aleppo, he undertakes to send 200 camel units [He requests] the office of beylerbey in Maraş [be given] to Haydar Bey, the former bey of Aintab on the condition of participating in the campaign with 2,000 men

[He requests] the *sancak* of Hama [be given] to Ebu Zeyd Bey on the condition of participating with 500 men in the campaign [He requests] the *sancak* of Maarra [be given] to his [Canboladoğlu's] uncle's son Mehmed Bey,

189

along with the rights of tax farming on the condition of participating with
500 men in the campaign

He requests the *sancak* of Uzeyir [be given] to Hüseyn Paşaoğlu Ali Bey on
the condition of participating with 500 men in the campaign [He requests]
the *sancak* of Malatya [be given] to Derviş Paşa, the former bey of Samsad,
on the condition of participating in the campaign with 1,500 men . . .

On the delivery of 120 camel units and the promised possession [cattle?] the
chieftainship of the Turkomans of Aleppo should be given to the *müteferrika*
Derviş And he [Canboladoğlu] requests that of the great fiefholders, six be
made *müteferrikas,* fourteen be made *çavuşes* and 500 be given the basic rank
of division officer[1]

By the end of his letter, Canboladoğlu Ali Pasha had promised more than
16,000 men to fight the upcoming wars on the eastern front and demanded fourteen high-level administrative positions in the east for himself and a variety of his regional officials. The fulfillment of these demands
would have been tantamount to handing over control of the eastern flank
of the empire.

This letter warrants special attention because it did not propose a simple military deal between a state leader and his general. Rather, this was
a deal between odd partners: the sultan of the Ottoman Empire and one
of the most infamous bandits of the period. The letter was written by
Canboladoğlu Ali Pasha and sent to Sultan Ahmed I, who inscribed in his
own hand on the upper left-hand corner of the letter: "This goes too far,
is it possible to give this much?"[2] Clearly, the question was posed at the
imperial council, where the various ministers and dignitaries discussed the
appropriateness of the deal. Thereafter, the orders of the period indicate
the demands that were fulfilled by the state. Most important, history
demonstrated that Canboladoğlu Ali Pasha, at least for a while, was successful at becoming the legitimate representative of the Ottoman government in Aleppo, having negotiated for himself the title of governor-
general in September 1606. Yet by December 1607 Canbolad was defeated
in battle by the sly grand vizier Kuyucu Murad Pasha and lost his position, his army, and his wealth. What is most remarkable about this epi-

---

[1]Letter from Ali Emiri Tasnifi document 616, Istanbul Archives; translation from
William J. Griswold, *The Great Anatolian Rebellion, 1000–1020/1591–1611* (Berlin, 1983),
pp. 240–43.
[2]Ibid., p. 268. We know from Ali Emiri Tasnifi documents 456, 457, and 459 that some of
these demands were granted.

sode is not this reversal of fortune but that the sultan should have resorted to deal making with a declared bandit rebel in the first place.

Deal making between the sultan and bandits suggests a process of consolidation for the state that is not immediately apparent. It might in fact be interpreted incorrectly: the inscription by Ahmed I indicated at least a moment of weakness, a hesitancy over how much of a price could be paid to a criminal. Yet, given war on the western frontiers and the campaign being prepared for the eastern frontier, some type of arrangement was necessary. Bandits had to be prevented from sabotaging war efforts and instead encouraged to guarantee and provide extra soldiers at the front. A consideration of the final outcome reveals even more subterfuge on the part of the state; the arrangement with Canboladoğlu Ali Pasha became part of a policy by which the grand vizier accorded himself more time in preparation for war against the bandit. Contrary to apparent weakness, the state actively bargained, co-opted when necessary, and annihilated potential contenders as swiftly as it could.

A patrimonial regime that ensured undivided control by either eliminating potential rivals or securing loyalty by incorporation into the household had to develop a strong tendency for deal making and brokerage. Both the elimination of rivals and the incorporation of potential rivals were important political activities of the Ottoman state. But when the tradition of sending young princes away for study and training (often as provincial governors) was ended, and the practice of fratricide was stopped at least for a time, it became more important to adopt co-optation as a mechanism of control. The head of the patrimonial household and his immediate entourage would then benefit by co-opting dissent into the system, as well as by increasing their power by gaining new allies. Rhoads Murphey clearly links the need of the administration in the seventeenth century to these changes in Ottoman traditions. He argues that another important way to increase state allies was through marriages. In his words, "the malleability of these top-level bureaucrats was guaranteed by the bonds of filial obligation imposed through marriage to princesses of the royal line."[3] The practice was extended to regional officials and prominent families who were co-opted through marriages. Even more daring was the proposed marriage alliance between a rebel governor, Ipşir Mustafa Pasha, and the daughter of Sultan Ibrahim I. As Evliya Çelebi asserted when he told the story of these marriages, they were not

[3]This type of marriage alliance was regularized by the reign of Süleyman the Magnificent (1520–66), Rhoads Murphey, "The Historical Setting," in *The Intimate Life of an Ottoman Statesman, Melek Ahmed Pasha (1588–1622)*, trans. R. Dankoff (New York, 1991), p. 32.

really for financial resources. They were political, enhancing the power and control of the state in a particular region and launching significant careers in Ottoman administration.[4]

Political motives were reinforced by cultural representations. State incorporation came with a wealth of symbolism; the state offered its clients appropriate ceremonial accoutrements. The symbols of belonging to the state circle were flaunted as rewards for those inside and as messages to outsiders that being on the inside was preferable. Even those once labeled the worst enemies of the state could later be treated to the best of Ottoman panache. Both Canboladoğlu Ali and Abaza Mehmed ended their days at the Sublime Porte and as guests of the sultan were treated on par with his closest advisers. Symbolic incorporation came with material largesse, both available as extremes of reward only from the state's authority and coffers.

In this chapter, I deal with one of the most important forms of political bargaining in the seventeenth-century Ottoman Empire: the practice of bargaining with bandit chiefs. During the seventeenth century the Ottoman state made ample use of political deal making and co-optation as a way to incorporate the claims of bandit chiefs at the helm of large bands of mercenary troops. I argue here that these concessions to bandits were not signs of great weakness. These deals were instead calculated to balance international and internal pressures so that the Ottomans did not have to simultaneously confront warfare on three fronts. Geopolitical considerations were among the most important reasons for consolidation through bargains and incorporation. This interpretation goes against the grain of many historical narratives as well as the more traditional sociological view of primitive rebels. Historians of the Ottoman seventeenth century have emphasized the decline banditry signaled, focusing on periods of relatively weak state leadership and largely ignoring the periods of consolidation that followed state-bandit confrontations.[5] As a result, analysts have described the state as weak and in decline, experiencing frequent

---

[4]Ibid., p. 34.

[5]Narratives by contemporaries and later scholars, Selâniki, Topçular Kâtibi, Naima, and Peçevi, stressed the dangers of the rebels and the weakness of the state. Joseph von Hammer, *Histoire de l'empire Ottoman*, trans. M. Dochez (Paris, 1844), who bases a lot of his material on these contemporary authors, presents a similar view. There is also a set of foreign historians and consular and diplomatic personnel who described the imminent end of the empire by aggrandizing the bandit problem. Certainly it was in the interest of these foreign dignitaries to exaggerate the doom of an empire that was once dreaded by Europeans. See, for example, Orhan Burian, *The Report of Lello, Third English Ambassador to the Sublime Porte* (Ankara, 1952).

breakdowns, and the bandits as authentic threats to the survival of the state. At the same time, arguments made in the "primitive rebel" literature, as well as in broader writings on peasant-bandit relations, have described banditry as a form of rebellion against the state in response to exploitation, poverty, and state control. On this reading, primitive rebels did not confront the state in search of benefits within the established structure but instead presumably fought as a form of social protest.[6] Scholars of both the Ottoman Empire and primitive rebellion describe bandits as threats to the state. In my view, these bandits were more often used as part of a process of state consolidation. Where others see state weakness, I see state strength.

The nearly hundred years under investigation provides a variety of stories of bandits, all of whom exhibit a roughly similar life cycle closely determined by state manipulation. In general, banditry, which was a by-product of a process of centralization and control in the provinces, acquired dimensions that became threatening to society until it was absorbed into the process of consolidation. The state then claimed victory in the subordination of its former clients. This is not to say that bandits were not at times dangerous to the state; they could become so because they controlled large numbers of mercenaries. The reason they did not become a truly serious threat was that the state never broke down and bandits made no serious attempt to destroy it. There were no real opportunities for these bandits to direct their action into an effective campaign against the state,[7] a state that was relatively strong and capable of deflecting any threat to its existence. Instead, the bandits were incorporated into the state. At the same time, the fear of banditry was also used to rationalize more control and more consolidation of territory. There were few bandit leaders whose actions could constitute a threat of serious consequences to the Ottoman government. More often than not, the rhetoric of fear and lawlessness was used to legitimize increased state interference.

In terms of state centralization, the single most important phenomenon of the time was the existence of vast pools of mercenary armies ready for

[6]The interpretation of rebellion as social protest against poverty and oppression is best made by Hobsbawm in *Primitive Rebels* (New York, 1959) and in *Bandits* (New York, 1969).

[7]This argument is in line with Theda Skocpol's in *States and Social Revolutions: A Comparative Analysis of France, Russia, and China* (Cambridge, 1979), where she identifies the breakdown of the state as the initial structural change that opens opportunities for revolutionary action. Revolutions do not happen in strong states. Similarly, many others in the literature have pointed this out for almost all major revolutionary upheavals. See Eric R. Wolf's *Peasant Wars of the Twentieth Century* (New York, 1973) as an excellent example of this argument.

hire by local or national power holders. Control of these mercenary armies gave the local power holders the bargaining chips with which they could request positions from the state. Since the ability to conduct war at international frontiers depended on the control of pools of mercenaries, gaining armies from bandits either through political bargaining or internal warfare was an essential task of the state in its efforts to consolidate territory and thereby strengthen its geopolitical position. Both the recruitment and the annihilation of bandit armies depended on the nature and region of international conflict. When there was international warfare, the state mostly chose to recruit armies, and when peace was established the state chose to contain banditry. The events recounted in this chapter were not similar to the peasant rebellions encountered by European states, and the bargains were not similar to those between European state makers and merchants and bankers. The main transactions in this period of Ottoman history were between the state and a set of mercenary/ bandit armies whose leaders achieved occasional legitimacy. Therefore, Ottoman state centralization proceeded along different lines. A strong and centralized state emerged out of negotiation and battle with internal mercenaries, a process in part shaped by international pressures.

Although much of the political bargaining and warfare for consolidation remains quite similar, there were three different formats of state-bandit relations in the period under consideration. This period can further be divided into two major pockets of bandit activity, 1590–1611 and 1623–48, periods that were preceded by important battles on the eastern or western fronts and succeeded by periods of renewed state control in all aspects of state rule. Each of these twenty-year intervals saw more or less constant small-scale rural banditry of the sort that remained in kadı reports and a few large-scale—Anatolian in scope—bandit movements by organized groups that attracted direct state intervention. This distinction is important because the presence of constant bandit activity by small-time bandits in localities constituted the fuel for the rhetoric of the state and convinced local communities that preemptive and protective action on the part of their government was necessary. Yet large-scale state actions and consolidation were a response to the larger, more destructive, but also more isolated and unusual bandit activities. It should also be said that there is little comparison between the damage caused by the local and the Anatolian rebels. I deal mostly with the larger rebel groups while providing some contrast with the local groups.

The process of interaction with rebels on the Ottoman scene from 1590 to 1611 represents the archetypal form of state consolidation via deal making with bandits. In this category, rebels were co-opted or crushed according to state needs; they were co-opted to be sent away from battle when perceived to be a liability to the Ottoman armies or co-opted when their manpower became necessary for prolonged military campaigns. Each of the bandit leaders demanded state positions and incorporation into the Ottoman bureaucracy. As was the case with the Ottoman elites, bandit leaders perceived success as high-ranking positions in the Ottoman provincial administration and strove for incorporation. Their "rebellions" were therefore maneuvers for mobility within the system, not opposition to the system. Accordingly, the Ottoman state made use of these bandits for consolidation, reinforcing its hold over its servitors, eliminating potential contenders, and appointing trusted and powerful men to positions of importance in the provinces.

Not all bandits, however, fit this model. Although the process of interaction with another type of bandit rebel was quite similar to the first group in terms of bargaining and warfare, the aims of this second type were closer to secession from the empire. Only one bandit leader, in northern Syria, Canboladoğlu Ali Pasha, used his control of a relatively well-defined and wealthy territory to attempt a rebellion. Even his aspirations to secession, however, were ambivalent, since they were also mixed with demands for high office in the Ottoman system and, more important, seem to have been instigated by foreign powers. The suppression of this particular rebel meant the reincorporation of northern Syria and the reassertion of Ottoman control and administration over the lands. Finally, a third type of bandit activity under consideration spans the period 1623 to 1648 and shows essentially no significant difference from the first except for the politicization of bandits' rhetoric. Neither bandit organizational format nor leadership was much altered. Again, no significant politicization of banditry occurred; what did occur was that the bandit leaders learned to capitalize on internal state problems and used them as rebellious rhetoric. Yet, when state officials offered the rebels state positions, they took them. In each of these cases, then, with slight variation, the same process of consolidation through bargaining and warfare with bandit/mercenary rebels occurred.

Consolidation through Deal Making with Bandits

The period 1550–1650 in Ottoman history is infamous in classic studies as one in which the empire was plagued by internal strife and bandit vio-

lence. A by-product of Ottoman actions, banditry hurt most the populations of villages and towns and forced the state to reconsider some of its
international aspirations, weighing these against internal civil disorder to
reconcile the competing demands of internal and external consolidation.
Two periods of bandit activity, 1590–1611 and 1623–48, bear a remarkable
resemblance to each other. Throughout the century, there was a nearly
stable pool of vagrants and mercenaries available for hire. Leaders and followers emerged from these pools, demonstrating striking similarities in
both constituency and goals. Those who continued on to pillage and rape
were branded celali.[8]

For most bandits there was no reason to confront the state other than
the fact that it represented "the most promising power domain,"[9] the
most obvious center to which claims had to be directed. Most bandit leaders, it is important to note, had no real claim *against* the state; they had
been officials of the state in one capacity or another, either in the service
of a governor or as a steward (*kethüda*) or deputy lieutenant-governor (*mütesellim*), and they wanted new and better positions. This is corroborated
by the fact that, once these rebels acquired positions as governor or
governor-general, they did not go about declaring independence, coining
their own money, sending ambassadors to other countries, or engaging in
other activities that would indicate the formation of a new state. All the
narratives of the period make this clear.[10] It was instead the possibility
they perceived of gaining more and carving out a greater domain that
made banditry and opposition to the state appealing. To receive lucrative
and powerful positions in the state administration, most of these rebels
used ties to their own patrons in the government. In acquiring larger domains, their goal was not independence from the Ottoman state; rather,
they were interested in domains to tax, as functionaries of the state. The
privilege to tax was not, however, essential; when these celalis did not
have a territorial base, they just plundered. Either way, the bandit leaders

---

[8]There was great variety in the size and importance of groups who acquired the label
"celali." The smallest groups ranged from 10–15 to 50–100 men. The larger groups included
at least 2,000 *sekban/sarıca* troops involved at any point in time. Topçular Kâtibi Abdülkadir,
Vekayii Tarihiye, Süleymaniye Esad Efendi no. 2151, folio 73, tells us that Karayazıcı, one of the
first important rebels, gathered at least 20,000 men.

[9]Elizabeth J. Perry, *Rebels and Revolutionaries in North China, 1845–1945* (Stanford, 1980),
p. 72.

[10]See Mustafa Akdağ, "Kara-yazıcı," *Islam Ansiklopedisi,* (Istanbul, 1955): 339–43; William
Griswold, "Djalali," *Encyclopedia of Islam* (Leiden, 1981); and Griswold, *The Great Anatolian
Rebellion.*

needed to provide resources for their mercenaries as their basis for claims to power. Furthermore, these leaders, often commanders of mercenary units (*bölük-başı*), were men caught up in the competition for the pool of mercenaries; the larger their share, the greater their potential revenue and the stronger their bargaining position vis-à-vis the state. Often, then, at the leadership level banditry was motivated by personal greed, aspirations of power, and the ability to forge alliances that would enhance personal domination over larger retinues. In this sense, in fact, they differed little from the court-appointed governors and other officials who engaged in the same competition to enhance their personal armies.[11] In fact, the Porte treated them as such and applied a variant of the rotation policy to them.

In most cases these mercenary leaders never became a serious threat to the state because of their inability to ally; they were scattered, and they betrayed each other for temporary benefits. In fact, William Griswold asserts that "no *celali* ever united with another for more than a short time and then only as a matter of convenience."[12] While the leaders of smaller bands tended to look for friends with whom to associate and share the loot, the larger bands were strictly hierarchically organized, not allowing for much alliance between chieftains.[13] Griswold and others also add that there was no unifying ideology to the celali rebellions.[14] The correspondence between chieftains never indicates any urgency to act in concert for some described insurrectionary objective. As I have argued in previous chapters, this lack of ideology and common political goal is the result of the peculiar nature of the mercenary units, which assembled a variety of groups and peoples in one major institution, albeit temporarily.

Although banditry evokes images of impetuous and reckless violence rather than careful planning and organization, celalis managed to exhibit both characteristics, largely because they organized in response to being hired by the state. These mercenary troops were arranged in companies with a company leader to supervise and direct their participation and were often mobilized and demobilized by the army after a war or dis-

[11]See Chapters 3 and 5.

[12]Griswold, *The Great Anatolian Rebellion*, p. 57.

[13]Vasıtı, *Kuyucu Murad Paşa Vukuatı Tarihi*, Süleymaniye, Esad Efendi no. 2236, folio 8b, for example, describes the alliances between relatively less dangerous chiefs such as Deli Pürsün, Sevilmiş-oğlu, and Köse Mahmud. Deli Pürsün and Köse Mahmud acted together in the pillage of an important *hassa çiftlik* in Ine-önü.

[14]Griswold, *The Great Anatolian Rebellion*, p. 57. See also Mustafa Akdağ, *Türk Halkının Dirlik ve Düzenlik Kavgası* (Ankara, 1975).

persed after the death of a governor.[15] Halil Inalcık describes the procedure for their enrollment into the army:

> The sultan sent an order to the local authorities and a special commissioner was appointed to supervise the whole operation and to lead the assembled troops to their destination. The sultan also sent standards, as many as the number of the companies to be formed. Under each standard a *bölük*, i.e., a company of fifty or sometimes of one hundred *sekban*, would be assembled. The moment a standard was taken back the *bölük* under it was considered to be legally dissolved and, from then on, their activities as a group were held to be illegal. Before the enrollment started, the local authorities chose the *bölük-başı*, the heads of the *bölüks* to be set up, and then a *baş bölük-başı*, a commander over them.... Each *sekban* received a "bonus" (*bakhşiş*) to prepare himself for the expedition and also his salary in advance for the months he was going to serve. All this was to be distributed through the *baş bölük-başı*, and the *bölük-başı*. They were real masters and organizers of these soldiers, comparable to the *condottieri* of medieval Europe.[16]

When the companies dissolved, they remained organized around their *bölük-başı* and therefore kept their units intact. Observant contemporaries of the bandit campaigns tell us very little about the larger organization of many units, since they assume correctly that bandits emulated the state armies in their modus operandi. This is only to be expected, since the training and assembling was carried out by high-ranking military commanders. Therefore, the encounters between the state armies and bandit armies were between known entities, with similar organizational and tactical knowledge.

Each period of banditry began with local incidents (for example, in western Anatolia) and then continued with the rebellion of much larger, more threatening bands which engaged the state in armed battle. Moreover, throughout the period, the smaller bands and the local banditry of officeholders coexisted with the larger bandit companies. The larger bands were not regional; they covered vast territory. One bandit army, that of Deli Hasan, for example, moved from Sepedlü north to Sivas, Tokat, Amasya, Çorum, and west to Ankara, then Kütahya in western Anatolia and just south to Afyonkarahisar, defeating Ottoman armies sent

---

[15]See Halil Inalcık, "Military and Fiscal Transformation in the Ottoman Empire, 1600–1700," *Archivum Ottomanicum* 6 (1980): 283–337.

[16]Halil Inalcık, "The Socio-Political Effects of the Diffusion of Fire-arms in the Middle East," in *War, Technology, and Society in the Middle East,* ed. V. J. Parry and M. E. Yapp (London, 1975), p. 200.

to crush them. Many of these bandits extorted money from the cities they stopped at. Some city dwellers chose to bargain with rebels and offer them large amounts of money to save their city from ransacking.[17] There is a rather typical chronicle of state-bandit interaction that fits most of the cases from the first to the second period. I present the more general features of this history and then the individual cases with their variations.

To tell the story of state centralization in relation to banditry is not simple. The process is often blurred by the fluidity of the boundaries between legitimate and illegitimate positions in the provinces. From high-ranking officials such as governors to lower-ranking agents and tax collectors, many state officials oscillated between legitimate taxation and unlawful exactions, breaking the law several times during their tenure. They were, as a result, removed from their posts and reinstated several times, making it difficult to separate the legitimate state officials from the illegitimate. Throughout this period of Ottoman history, all sorts of local and regional officials resorted to illegal exactions and excessive oppression of the peasantry with the help of the *sekban/sarıca* armies they assembled. Government officials therefore often confronted in petitions parallel complaints regarding legitimate and illegitimate officers.[18] We should analyze banditry and its centralizing consequences in this light of general provincial confusion, where the declining landholding classes, vagrant peasants, bandits, and local power holders were all struggling to hold on to what they had and often evolved into rapacious and dangerous groups.

Many famous bandits first emerged as relatively unimportant leaders when violence erupted after looting by their mercenary troops. Usually, they were leaders of companies in the service of a provincial official or demobilized by an army. Once a group acquired some shape as a celali band, new leaders emerged from among the ranks to replace older, defeated, or co-opted ones. As the plunder of villages and towns continued,

---

[17]Griswold uses a document published by Akdağ attesting to the fact that the troops of Deli Hasan extorted 80,000 kuruş from the people of Ankara. Griswold also gives us an idea of the amount this extortion represents: 9,600,000 akçe as compared to 202,973,744 akçe, the total expenditure for the Ottoman state in the first half of 1607. See Griswold, *The Great Anatolian Rebellion* p. 251, n. 69.

[18]Akdağ gives perhaps the best examples of high-level officials' plunderings. In the spring of 1600, the governor-general of Sivas sent a letter to the government arguing that the vizier Mehmet Pasha, who had been dispatched to fight the celali Karayazıcı, was more a bandit than his supposed enemy. As Akdağ explains, there was little difference between these two commanders, since they both led armies of mercenaries who were often fed through looting; see *Türk Halkının Dirlik ve Düzenlik Kavgası*, pp. 390–95. Other examples abound of governors, kadıs, and other officials demanding the tax payments of their predecessors and inflicting much larger sums than called for.

the bad fortune of the region was reported by local governors or kadıs to the authorities, and the state responded by ordering relatively less important military commanders (*Celali serdarı*) to undertake police action. These first attempts at suppression were rarely successful at eradicating banditry in Anatolia. Another measure simultaneously undertaken by the state was the appointment of viziers to unruly regions. Mustafa Naima writes of the eastern provinces: "Indeed, it was considered of the utmost importance, by the government of Constantinople, that a vezir should be appointed to each of the eastern provinces, in order to check and subdue any spirit of rebellion which might arise, and which, in fact, seems to have been very generally the case with them all."[19] When lower-ranking officials or special viziers failed, divide-and-conquer tactics were also tried: the mercenaries were provoked to act against rebellious religious students in the hope that each would subdue or exhaust the other. Uncharacteristically, the suhtes were even ordered to arm themselves to fight the bandits,[20] a mistake the state surely came to regret. Later in the process, the state dispatched larger armies or offered bandit leaders positions in the provincial government, thereby co-opting them into the Ottoman system. The result of these bargains was to establish the leadership of the mercenaries in legitimate positions, where they could administer provinces, tax the population, and respond as loyal members of the Ottoman administration to calls to battle. Many a bandit was lured into the privilege of Ottoman administration, especially when the position was offered with a robe of honor thrown in to impress. Co-optation eventually became the mechanism of pacification par excellence, especially favored by grand viziers on campaign with few military resources to squander. On the other hand, celali troops were less susceptible to the temptations afforded by legitimate roles and often returned to a life of depredation after one infraction; looting rather than collecting taxes proved to be a difficult habit to break.

When these depredations were accompanied by an unwillingness to participate in Ottoman campaigns, the fate of the now-legitimate governors was sealed. During the reign of Ahmed I in particular, state policy aimed to disempower all former bandits who had acquired positions without disciplining their unruly followers; by war or by conciliation, or by a combination of the two, all-out war was declared on the recalcitrant ban-

---

[19]Quotation from Charles Fraser's translation in *The Annals of the Turkish Empire from 1591 to 1659 of the Christian Era* (London, 1832), 1:307.

[20]Akdağ, *Türk Halkının Dirlik ve Düzenlik Kavgası*, p. 403.

dits, leading to their ultimate annihilation. After the defeat of the celalis, the state claimed supremacy and undertook to control its provinces and its people, even those from faraway villages, towns, and cities. To buttress this image further, after each victory the grand viziers usually reordered refugees back to their homesteads and vouched for their safety. They also redesigned central administrative tasks, increased provincial controls, and consolidated the hold of the state across center and periphery. After all, most celali unrest centered in Anatolia, the heartland of the empire, and recuperation required not so much territorial consolidation of a periphery as reestablishment of administration. This was accomplished by appointing new officials, trusted men who would remain loyal to the state. The same general episode can be followed with slight variations for each celali.

Although the basic pattern of state-bandit relations was repeated again and again, the sites of confrontation between the Ottomans and European neighbors in the west and Persian neighbors in the east changed frequently. More so than internal problems, battles on the frontiers, and occasionally successful attempts by foreign neighbors to reconquer territory, occupied the sultans' and grand viziers' attention. The reign of Süleyman the Magnificent had set a standard of grandeur and prestige that was not repeated. After his reign some major conquests were accomplished, and the rest of the sixteenth century and a large part of the seventeenth were spent battling on the two major fronts, often with great logistical difficulty and meager success. Still, despite the shorter reigns of the later sultans, their youth, and their numerous grand viziers, the state actively engaged in the consolidation of its territories.[21]

The many Iranian wars—waged during the period 1590–1611—were nothing but wars of consolidation in which each power challenged one major buffer zone, ranging from the Caucasus to Kurdistan to Azarbaijan (1579–90 and 1588–1612). At the other end of the empire, after the defeat of the Ottomans at Lepanto (1571), Christian powers at the western borders were emboldened and looking for ways to exercise their superiority. It was only at the conclusion of the Persian war of 1579–90 that the Ottomans were able to engage in a 13-year war (1593–1606) that continued into the

---

[21]I refer here to the numerous grand viziers who were appointed during these two periods. Some were even appointed, dismissed, and reappointed within the same year. For example, the period 1590–1611 was directed by three sultans, Murad III, Mehmed III, and Ahmed I, but experienced twenty changes of grand vizier. Although the period 1623–48 was directed by only two sultans, Murad IV and Ibrahim, numerous *valide* sultans, *şeyh-ül islams,* and janissary *ağas* interfered and often allied in complicity to rule the state. During this 21-year period, changes of grand vizier occurred fourteen times.

reigns of two new sultans.[22] When peace was signed between Austria and the Ottomans in 1606 (Treaty of Sitva Torok), the Ottoman forces had to regroup quickly to prepare for the eastern front as well as face various pockets of rebellion by bandit chiefs. Although it is impossible to argue that the Ottoman state was still entertaining imperialist dreams, it was forcefully defending its territories and conducting wars to maintain and consolidate the territorial gains of earlier sultans. Warfare, then, was an inevitable aspect of the state's consolidation functions.

Despite the numerous changes and the young age of sultans in the period 1623–48, warfare at the two borders continued. Osman II confronted the Polish forces only to ensure that the old borders were maintained before turning to the internal reforms he had planned for his administration. The incompetence of Mustafa at internal as well as international affairs brought the members of the government together in their resolve to bring Murad IV to the throne. Murad's tenure began with the fall of Baghdad, orchestrated by the cunning Shah Abbas, who took advantage of the internal disorders in the Ottoman lands to seize territory. Numerous attempts at the reconquest of Baghdad were muddled by the activities of bandits until, nearly single-handedly, Murad IV consolidated his power, reestablished order, and tried to push at the eastern frontiers once again. Ultimately the strength of the eastern campaign prevailed: territory was reincluded into the Ottoman realms, a new treaty was signed confirming the Ottoman borders, and the destructive border raids and incursions were contained (1638–39).[23]

Consolidation through war and the further development of administration were accomplished during the tenure of three sultans and their grand viziers. Despite the general notion that this was a time of decline when intrigues were many and various untrained favorites meddled in the affairs of government, the overall result of these activities was far from grim for the state. On the contrary, this was a time of strong administrative reform, with decisive modifications in such legal areas as the review of the old Ottoman legislative code and the development of a new and more comprehensive code that accommodated changing times. This was also a time when the state forcefully tapped into the empire's resources and peoples so as to include them in military and administrative functions. This inclusion and penetration was a crucial component of further state consolidation. Ahmed I and his grand vizier Nasuh Pasha have been

[22]Stanford J. Shaw, *History of the Ottoman Empire and Modern Turkey* (Cambridge, 1976), 1:183–84.
[23]Ibid.

credited with the most innovative use of mercenaries, the creation of *sek-ban* and *sarıca* units, by which regular state troops were strengthened. While these new armies were composed of Turks, Kurds, and other people from Anatolia, other troops were drawn by enslaving people from Abkhazia, Circassia, and other regions in the Caucasus.[24] This increased heterogeneity of the military and regional administration brought together groups that would have otherwise remained isolated. Common service provided the new glue of the Ottoman state in this period.

Bargains and Force, 1590–1611

Mehmed III and Ahmed I both had strong grand viziers who were often able to conduct warfare at the borders and return to the capital to put down the uprisings of troops. That the men of the imperial council took part in intrigues did not hinder government officials from making appropriate decisions. Most coups against the key decision makers and warriors in the government remained unsuccessful and control was quickly reclaimed, as for example was the experience of Grand Vizier Yemişçi Hasan Pasha in 1602–3. Other coups were more successful, such as that organized by Derviş Pasha against Lala Mehmed Pasha in 1605–6. But it remains fair to say that most of the grand viziers who came to power during this time were consolidators, like Yemişçi Hasan Pasha, Yavuz Ali Pasha, Lala Mehmed Pasha, Derviş Pasha, and finally in 1606 the famously shrewd grand vizier, Kuyucu Murad Pasha, who received his nickname Kuyucu from his practice of stacking the bodies of rebels into wells. The famous rebels Karayazıcı Abdülhalim, Deli Hasan, Tavil Halil, Kalenderoğlu, Yusuf Pasha, and Musli Çavuş were all active during the tenure of these grand viziers. The grand viziers made decisions on their own, under the sultans' orders, or within the imperial council, to pursue, co-opt, or ignore the rebels. The following is their story.

Almost every account of the celalis starts with a description of the battle at Mezö-Keresztes and Grand Vizier Çağalazade Sinan Pasha's move to dismiss those tımar holders who were either missing or had fled during the war.[25] Several historians have argued that the deserters were the main constituents of the major bandit revolts that followed, attributing origin

---

[24]Murphey, "The Historical Setting," p. 33.

[25]His order was to apprehend and execute all those sipahis who were not present at the roll call. For more details, see Chapter 3.

and cause to the rebellions. The deserters were expelled from the army and took their revenge by fighting the empire, its people, and its government. The deserters of the battle of Mezö-Keresztes are not important for this particular reason, but rather because their desertion signals a new period of state consolidation in Ottoman history. They are important because they provoked an important policy decision on the part of the state to start recovering the land grants of some older tımar holders who had accumulated large estates through regular additions. At the same time, some deserters were also soldiers of different ranks (janissaries, cavalrymen, paid halberdiers, police officers, frontier soldiers) who earned larger salaries.[26] Their dismissal provided state officials the possibility of saving resources to reward new and fresh blood better able to fight wars. There is no doubt that this event set loose many discontented cavalrymen, who took to roaming the Anatolian plains. Scholars have suggested that Karayazıcı Abdülhalim drew his manpower from these deserters, but this turns out to be only partially correct.[27] Mostly, however, the deserters of Mezö-Keresztes were zeamet holders with large incomes and may have been leaders close to Karayazıcı, while his troops were musket-bearing soldiers who formed bandit companies in the provinces.[28]

Karayazıcı himself was a musketeer who had risen through the ranks to become a company leader (bölük-başı).[29] During the three years from 1599 to 1602, Karayazıcı's armies lived off the peasantry of Anatolia and were organized in military units, while their leaders behaved like European condottieri. When engaged in war on the western front, the Ottomans sent a commander to halt Karayazıcı's actions. In a dramatic move, the Ottoman commander joined the rebel forces—unfortunately for him, since he

[26]Whereas Akdağ gives an excellent analysis of the action of the grand vizier, Griswold dismisses it by saying that it was a quick and premature decision. See Akdağ, *Türk Halkının Dirlik ve Düzenlik Kavgası*, pp. 375–76, and Griswold, *The Great Anatolian Rebellion*, p. 20.

[27]One can see this in the standard histories of the period as well as in the specialized accounts of the celalis. For a few examples, see M. A. Cook, ed., *A History of the Ottoman Empire to 1730* (Cambridge, 1976), pp. 129–30, and Shaw, *History of the Ottoman Empire*, 1:185–86. SEE ALSO GRISWOLD, *The Great Anatolian Rebellion*, pp. 20–21. Akdağ, however, is the only one (*Türk Halkının Dirlik ve Düzenlik Kavgası*, p. 381) to investigate this claim, and he finds that some of the *leaders* Karayazıcı relied on were sipahis.

[28]A further confusion here might come from the fact that during the celali period bandits claiming to be sipahis descended on villages and demanded taxes. Court cases of complaining peasants tell us about these impostors. See also Akdağ, *Türk Halkının Dirlik ve Düzenlik Kavgası*, p. 406.

[29]Topçular Kâtibi Abdülkadir, *Vekayii Tarihiye*, folio 73. Naima, *Tarih-i Naima* (Istanbul, 1283/1866–67), 1:232.

was soon double-crossed by Karayazıcı.[30] When the Ottoman statesmen, after great deliberation, determined that the rebel leader would cost them too much in time and soldiers, especially when the western campaign was full-blown, they decided to bargain with him. Karayazıcı was offered the *beylik* of Ayintab, and later the *sancakbeyliği* of Amasya, in the hope that he would settle into a peaceful position (1600).[31] He was later transferred to Çorum. In both cases, the state actively tried to secure Karayazıcı an official position, giving him and his men an area to tax and to live off. But the rank-and-file mercenaries under Karayazıcı continued their regular looting, also extracting numerous illegal taxes in addition to legal ones. After the Ottoman army had won several victories in Europe and the threat of the Wallachian rebellion of Prince Michael the Brave had been suppressed, the decision was made to launch an army against the celalis of north-central Anatolia.[32] The new commander of the Ottoman army chased the rebels south and east, decimating them in an ambush. The result of the defeat was the splintering of the remaining celali forces into many groups and the flight of Karayazıcı north to the Canik mountains, where he died a short while later. Throughout his career as a bandit chief, Karayazıcı remained apolitical, despite rumors to the contrary.[33]

Selâniki, a contemporaneous chronicler of Karayazıcı and the only celali leader he wrote about in his treatise, *Tarih-i Selâniki,* alleges that Karayazıcı declared himself to be a descendant of the shah and sent around decrees bearing his *tuğra* (imperial signature). None of the other contemporaries of Selâniki repeat this information. Naima, writing later, provides a short text of what he calls an order (*hükm*) by Karayazıcı that declares victory over the Ottomans in the region and tells of his control over the region. He also claims to have sent out an imperial order, thus likening himself to a sultan.[34] Since it is most likely that Naima took his information from Selâniki, we need to question the original source. Akdağ doubts Selâniki's claims on the basis that all the orders and correspondence written by Karayazıcı simply bear his signature. Also, none of the accounts of the men involved with Karayazıcı make a similar claim re-

---

[30]Mustafa Efendi Selâniki, *Tarih-i Selâniki,* ed. Mehmet Ipşirli (Istanbul, 1989), 2:827, and 836–37. See also Griswold, *The Great Anatolian Rebellion,* pp. 28–30.

[31]Akdağ, "Karayazıcı," p. 341; Mustafa Nuri Pasha, *Netayic ül-Vukuat,* ed. N. Çağatay (Ankara, 1979), 1–2:184.

[32]Griswold, *The Great Anatolian Rebellion,* p. 36. For the depredations of the celalis in Amasya and Çorum, see Akdağ, *Türk Halkının Dirlik ve Düzenlik Kavgası,* pp. 387–88.

[33]Selâniki, *Tarih-i Selâniki,* p. 837; Akdağ, "Karayazıcı," p. 342.

[34]Naima, *Tarih-i Naima,* 1:246–47.

garding the political ambitions of this bandit chief. Also, William J. Griswold, who has surveyed all the foreign sources and the diplomatic correspondence of the period, does not report such intentions regarding Karayazıcı. This is quite telling, since as was the case with Canboladoğlu, Europeans would have been the first to notice such secessionist plans and would have tried to use them to their advantage. I tend to agree with the latter interpretations, since the actions of Karayazıcı, unlike those of the more political rebel Canboladoğlu, do not suggest any political ambition. Karayazıcı's words remained the expression of a proud rebel and were never translated into deeds.

Deli Hasan, Karayazıcı's brother, allegedly rebelled to avenge his brother's loss to the Ottoman army, but he was willing to come forward to demand a deal with the state, drawing on his connections within the state apparatus. Deli Hasan's rebellion came at a time when Grand Vizier Yemişçi Hasan Pasha was at the Austrian front with most of the effective army, but also at a time when the state was undergoing elite struggles, with different military factions pulling different key state officials into conflict. Among the issues displeasing the members of the Six Cavalry Divisions was the fact that janissaries were able to establish themselves in the provinces and increase their power and income, while inadequate outsiders were running the palace affairs and the sultan refused to go to war. Moreover, another important complaint was that celalis were acquiring positions of importance in the provincial government. These central state cavalrymen declared most governors and provincial dignitaries to be similarly corrupt; they named the rebels Deli Hasan, Tavil Halil, and Kara Said and equated them to the governors of Erzurum, Gusah Nefer Pasha, and Sıvas, Ahmed Pasha, who engaged in similar pillage of the countryside.[35] When the claims culminated in the vilifying of the grand vizier, he returned from the front to take matters into his own hands, calmed the various military factions, made deals with the celalis, and then proceeded to dispose of the unruly sipahis.

It was at this moment of internal struggles that Deli Hasan sent his deputy Şahverdi to Istanbul to solicit a pardon and request a provincial post. Being the right moment, his contact at the palace was able to cut a deal for him for the governorship of Bosnia and, according to Naima, the government sent this bandit "a drum, a flag, and a robe of honor." After Deli Hasan managed to get 400 of his men admitted into the Six Cavalry

---

[35]Griswold, *The Great Anatolian Rebellion*, p. 43.

Divisions, he gathered his troops and went to Bosnia.[36] Joseph von Hammer-Purgstall, who described this army as a curious bunch of soldiers with long hair, amulets, talismans, and other strange effects, believed that the Ottomans were interested in sending Deli Hasan to fight the infidels at the western front.[37] Like his brother, Deli Hasan was also not interested in any position that would lead to autonomy from the empire. He wanted a legitimate post in the Ottoman establishment. His trusted allies and vice-chiefs were not even interested in that; all they were interested in was loot, gathered in the old-fashioned way, as they had practiced it in eastern Anatolia, especially Sıvas and Tokat.[38]

The mercenaries of Deli Hasan fought in Eszek and in Pest against the Christians. Despite their participation in war, celali troops simultaneously distinguished themselves in the plundering of Ottoman territory. While his troops were plundering, it is said that Deli Hasan was corresponding with Venice and the pope, offering to sell territory for gold.[39] When this was discovered, Deli Hasan fled to Belgrade and was later killed in 1604. Deli Hasan's demise was also connected with events of 1603–4, whereby the new sultan, Ahmed I, was confronted with the revival of the eastern campaign just as he ascended the throne. Battles were raging in both east and west, while Deli Hasan's usefulness in the western frontier had outlived itself and the Ottoman armies had to confront Shah Abbas's violations of his agreements with the Ottoman Empire. All this greatly diminished the usefulness of this bandit-governor; orders followed to execute him.

The arrogance with which Tavil Halil, a third bandit leader, rejected the offer of the provinces of Aleppo, Anatolia, and Sıvas—nearly all of Anatolia—leaves no doubt that these rebels lacked political motives. Given a chance to control such a large territory, Tavil Halil showed no interest and later was assigned to the *beylerbeyliği* of Baghdad, with twelve of his key men receiving different *sancakbeyliğis*.[40] Feeling besieged from

[36]Hammer, *Histoire de l'empire Ottoman*, 2:307.

[37]Ibid.

[38]I refer here to the fact that some of the vice-chiefs of Deli Hasan refused the military administrative posts offered by the state in order to continue looting; see Edmund Schütz, "An Armeno-Kipchak Document of 1640 from Lvov and Its Background in Armenia and the Diaspora," in *Between the Danube and the Caucasus: A Collection of Papers Concerning Oriental Sources on the History of the Peoples of Central and Southern-Eastern Europe,* ed. György Kara (Budapest, 1987), p. 253.

[39]I. H. Uzunçarşılı, *Osmanlı Tarihi* (Ankara, 1983), 3-1:102. See also Griswold, *The Great Anatolian Rebellion,* pp. 44–45.

[40]Griswold, *The Great Anatolian Rebellion,* p. 55.

all sides at his accession, Ahmed I had decided with his imperial council on a conciliatory policy with the bandits. After the defeat of the Ottoman forces against Tavil, Ahmed I decided to go on campaign against the cela-lis himself but retraced his steps back to the capital quickly. The deal that Sofu Sinan Pasha (the temporary governor in Istanbul) had arranged dur-ing Ahmed's absence for Tavil, which he had luckily refused, was far too generous and Ahmed promptly dismissed the governor from office.[41] Af-ter this incident, Ahmed resolved to pursue his policy of incorporation and conciliation with the celalis, hoping to induce them to become loyal Ottoman governors and incorporate their armies into his. In fact, he had himself made deals with bandits during his campaign; several hundred of these bandit-musketeers received pardons and were quickly formed into Ottoman army units. As more celalis joined the Ottoman system, Gris-wold argues, "*celali* leaders moved both socially and politically from Mus-lim Turkish peasants to loyal Ottoman *askeri,* their followers filling the ranks of the sultan, manning the siege machines to fight against the Per-sian and the Habsburg enemies, and partaking of the perquisites of the ruling Ottomans."[42]

Kalenderoğlu, probably one of the most organized bandits of the early period, is famous for having sent a letter to his fellow bandit, Musli Ça-vuş, coaxing him into join his forces: "If we win over Kuyucu [the grand vizier], then we will have the Ottomans give up everything east of Scutari [i.e., Anatolia]; if we do not win we will be content being the heroes of folk songs!"[43] Although the content of this letter seems to show an in-terest in secession, Kalenderoğlu never took action in that direction. He had one of the longest histories of negotiations with the Ottoman state; by the time he became important, Kuyucu Murad Pasha, having made peace with the Habsburgs (Sitva Torok, 1606), had declared a secret, all-out war against the celalis.

---

[41]Ibid., p. 54. There seems to be some disagreement in the literature regarding the de-mand for these three regions. While Griswold asserts that it was Sofu Sinan Pasha who ar-ranged the deal for Tavil, Peçevi argues that Tavil first asked for these regions and then, when Sofu came up with the deal, he did not answer the overtures by the state. Naima says that Tavil wrote a letter to the government (probably inquiring about a position), but that Sofu Sinan Pasha arranged the deal including these regions. What is certain is that when Ahmed I found out the details of the deal he dismissed the pro-tem governor. See Peçevi, *Tarih-i Peçevi* (Istanbul, 1980), 2:314. See also Naima, *Tarih-i Naima,* 1:432–33.

[42]Griswold, *The Great Anatolian Rebellion,* p. 56.

[43]M. Ç. Uluçay, *XVII. Asırda Saruhan'da Eşkiyalık ve Halk Hareketleri* (Istanbul, 1944), p. 17. I have translated rather freely from his text. Naima provides a slightly different text for the letter.

Around this time, Grand Vizier Derviş Pasha had begun a period of consolidation; he aimed to direct all forces to the east (although the grand vizier himself was not willing to go to war) to fight the Persians and continued the sultan's policy of conciliating the celalis in order to acquire mercenaries for the front.[44] One of his first actions in power was to send troops to the Persian front to recover Azerbaijan, which had recently been lost to Shah Abbas. The troops departed willy-nilly, they were unprepared, and their appointed commander, Ferhad Pasha, who knew this well, expected the failure that was to befall them. There were also plans to send armies against the rebels after the wars, especially after a successful conclusion at the western front. While plotting war with external enemies, during his few months of tenure as grand vizier Derviş Pasha took the necessary steps to apply pressure on his internal enemies, those groups and individuals potentially threatening to the state. Derviş Pasha identified the vital problems of the empire: fiscal imbalance, administrative inefficiency, and the inordinate power of certain central and regional officials. He vowed to go after each of these. He secured new sources of funds for the state, altered the corrupt administrative practices of the bureaucracy, and tightened the control over the various political and mercantile elites whose power and wealth were crucial to the renewed strength of the state.[45] For example, he instituted a new tax, the balcony tax, aimed at taxing the rich who could afford balconies on their houses.[46] After Derviş Pasha was executed on charges of lèse-majesté, the new grand vizier, Kuyucu Murad Pasha, continued centralization and control in the center while also taking advantage of continued preparations for the eastern campaign. More than anything, he used these preparations to trick the bandits, draw them into the supposed war effort, and destroy them as they integrated themselves into the army. Conciliation had become a ruse, not a policy. And Kuyucu went on an unprecedented effort to eradicate banditry. Convinced that these mercenary troops should not

[44]As is seen in the next section, this is when Canbolad Ali Pasha sent the famous List of Matters cited at the beginning of the chapter.

[45]I am aware of the controversy that exists regarding the actions of this grand vizier. It is clear that Naima, for example, who liked the grand vizier Lala Mehmed Pasha, was not about to accept any of Derviş's actions; see *Tarih-i Naima*, 1:441–49. Peçevi, *Tarih-i Peçevi*, 2:324–25, similarly described Derviş Pasha as a man who like a snake could bite anyone in his path and saw no good in his actions. However, Hammer and Griswold, who gather their information from a variety of sources, present a more balanced account and present some of the centralization policies of this grand vizier in a positive light. See Hammer, *Histoire de l'empire Ottoman*, 2:324–25; Griswold, *The Great Anatolian Rebellion*, pp. 160–61. See also Burian, *The Report of Lello*, pp. 25–27.

[46]Griswold, *The Great Anatolian Rebellion*, p. 159.

even be incorporated into the Ottoman army, he proceeded to wipe them out. By the end of the decade, just before Kuyucu died, the Ottoman state had managed to control its internal troublemakers, established peace in its provinces, and demonstrated forcefully that dissent was an unacceptable gamble.

After a preliminary battle between the Ottoman forces and Kalendero-ğlu, Ottoman armies were ordered toward the more important bandit, Canbolad Ali Pasha, whose activities were deemed more serious than those of Kalenderoğlu. Yet, to keep the latter occupied and unable to join other rebels, especially Canbolad, Kuyucu Murad Pasha resolved to offer him a post and proposed a governorship in January 1607. By March he had offered Kalenderoğlu a second governorship, but since the celali continued his rampage, the grand vizier retracted his offer soon afterward. When the grand vizier was ready to attack Canbolad, he wrote to different bandits and offered them appointments.[47] Among these was Kalendero-ğlu, who was presented with a new position for the third time—the province of Ankara, which he had trouble taking control of because the kadı and residents opposed him vehemently and asked for Ottoman military help to keep him away. His mercenaries' reputation for looting was such that the inhabitants of Ankara gave 200,000 ducats to buy them off. While other celalis joined Kalenderoğlu to fight Ankara's feisty residents, Ottoman squadrons arrived to help but were quickly defeated by these mercenaries. Kalenderoğlu was to spread more fear as he continued on to Bursa, the ancient capital, and then toward Istanbul.[48]

This was the first time the government felt threatened from so nearby. With Kuyucu still engaged in battle in the east against the bandit Can-bolad, state officials took special measures. Kalenderoğlu, on the other hand, must not have had much more in mind than intimidating the capital and pushing Ahmed I into offering him another position in the Ottoman administration. In Istanbul, however, the provincial militia (il erleri), 40,000 urban citizens, and small numbers of troops were called in to protect Bursa, Istanbul, and the surroundings.[49] These efforts produced little success, as only 6,000 men returned, but Kalenderoğlu changed his itin-

[47]The account of this correspondence varies. Some say that bandits wrote to him offering to join his campaign. See Vasıtı, *Kuyucu Murad Pasha Vukuatı Tarihi*, folio 7b. For a detailed exposition of Kalenderoğlu's exploits, see Topçular Kâtibi Abdülkadir, *Vekayii Tarihiye*, folios 221b–227a.

[48]Peçevi, *Tarih-i Peçevi*, 2:332–34; Hammer, *Histoire de l'empire Ottoman*, 2:329; Naima, *Tarih-i Naima*, 2:10–12.

[49]Griswold, *The Great Anatolian Rebellion*, pp. 180–83.

erary and shifted to the south to set up his winter camp. As he was leaving, he did not neglect to ask for a position from Ahmed I—just in case the government wanted to reward him! Before the final showdown, when the grand vizier was finally able to overtake Kalenderoğlu, he eliminated all the rebel's potential allies; each received a post and was sent away. Tavil Halil received the *sancak* of Bodrum, Muslu Çavuş became governor of Içel, and others were dispatched to various positions. Kalenderoğlu joined the shah of Persia after his defeat, setting off a diplomatic tangle between the two countries.

With Canbolad Ali Pasha and Kalenderoğlu defeated, Kuyucu Murad Pasha proceeded to the business of retracting the offices he had so generously offered: Tavil Halil simplified matters by being murdered by one of his own men. Kuyucu ordered his trusted officer, Zülfikar Pasha, to entice the bandit Muslu Çavuş to his camp and have him murdered. He himself wrote a letter to the bandit Yusuf Pasha, inviting him to his side to help in the preparations for the eastern campaign. He called him "my son," made him the tax collector (*muhassıl*) of the *sancak* of Saruhan, and captured the rebel's imagination: "My son, I have heard of some of your virtues and high talents, which I esteem very much. Although you have such a considerable number of men under you, yet no rumor of any injustice practiced by you is any where heard. The reverse of injustice in you must be the case."[50] Yusuf was convinced to join, only to be beheaded in Kuyucu's tent. And so it went for most of Anatolia's celali leaders; they were able to bargain with the government when they pushed the limits of a state engaged in wars on two fronts, or when they had to be kept away from the battleground, or when the state employed a ruse only to confront them later.

It is difficult to characterize any one of these celalis as major contenders for the Ottoman throne. They were able military men strongly supported by crucial *sekban/sarıca* groups and some factions in the Ottoman state. Their actions were most successful when they were able to mobilize great numbers of *sekbans* (which they could do only with the promise of loot, since it is doubtful they could ever pay them), and when the Ottoman state was unable or unwilling to direct its resources and its army against the rebels. On the other hand, as this analysis shows, they were at the mercy of the Ottoman state, which was able to control, contain, and co-opt these men through its power and patronage. The practical determi-

---

[50]Naima provides the text of the letter that attests to the ruse of the grand vizier, see Fraser, *Annals of the Turkish Empire*, p. 381. See also Hammer, *Histoire de l'empire Ottoman*, 2:340; Griswold, *The Great Anatolian Rebellion*, p. 206.

nant of state action was the perceived balance between the international concerns and the internal issues that propelled the decision-making apparatus of the state to attack or to bargain with these rebels. In each case, the policy of small-scale warfare with an imperial army was tried. When this policy failed, or when the external pressures were deemed more consequential, the state endeavored to co-opt the celali leaders into the system: for Karayazıcı, the positions at Amasya and Çorum, for Deli Hasan, Bosnia and Temeşvar, for Tavil Halil, Baghdad, and for Kalenderoğlu, the region of Ankara were all temporary prizes en route to later defeat through tougher state action.

That these deals were part of a larger plan to control, take advantage of, and later discard the rebels was apparent in the choices of destination of the celalis. Governorships were handed out not only to reduce the danger to the state but also to benefit from such temporary deals. In the fourteenth century, insofar as possible, the state sent captured rebels to the border regions—in the belief that the harsh conditions obtaining in areas of expansion and constant warfare would constitute enough punishment for any rebel. In the seventeenth century, the practice of sending bandits to the frontier regions continued, especially when these were battlegrounds with the Austrians or Persians. The state clearly wanted to benefit from extra armies in this region. Deli Hasan, for example, brought with him 10,000 troops to the western front.[51] The engineers of this policy did not seem to think about the long-term consequences of such policies—and there were probably none—since they believed that after international conflicts they would return to settle scores with the bandits.

Institutionalization of this policy occurred at different levels. Making deals with rebels to bolster the army became standard practice. Both central state officials and battlefield commanders of the Ottoman army struck their own deals to increase their forces. This was especially true when the pool of mercenaries became extremely valuable to an imperial army faced with two war zones. When Çağalazade Sinan Pasha was appointed to the eastern front, he managed to gather an army of 40,000 men. His ability to muster such an army while many forces were engaged in the west was partially due to his ability to incorporate the troops of the celali Karakaş Ahmed Pasha in return for the *beylerbeylik* of Çıldır.[52]

Viewed from the provincial towns and villages, state action was essential for the continued welfare of the empire. Throughout these bandit

---

[51]Griswold, *The Great Anatolian Rebellion*, p. 44.
[52]Ibid., pp. 101–2.

skirmishes, emboldened local officials had taken the law into their own hands and themselves begun to plunder and loot. At the local level, then, the larger cases of banditry had encouraged increased lawlessness.[53] Therefore, to the depredations caused by the larger armies of rebels in each region had to be added the smaller local events that brought peasants to the brink of disaster. Heaps of local reports were amassing at the doors of the imperial palace demanding the sultan's response. Without a strenuous campaign of local control, great dislocations would threaten the land, agriculture, the people, and therefore the state as well. It was in the interest of the government to impress the locals with the vigor of the action it was capable of undertaking. At the local level, this attempt to establish calm and security was partly instituted by annihilating notorious bandits and immediately controlling and collecting arms following internal wars. Since the state had often armed local militia to defend themselves, the collection seemed contradictory. Yet it had two purposes: to eliminate potential violence and to provide the public with the sense that the state was back in control and therefore in no need of local help.

The celali who represented some variation from the more common form, Canboladoğlu Ali Pasha, did confront the state head on with what seemed to be close to the makings of a contending state apparatus. His appearance, however, coincided with one of the decisive moments of the Ahmed I administration, where a collection of powerful viziers and commanders were well on their way to integrating their power. These men constituted a faction in the Ottoman administration, yet it was the winning one. And they had resolved to eliminate potential threats to internal security. Although Grand Vizier Derviş Pasha was at the head of this faction, it was Kuyucu Murad Pasha, the famous enemy of the rebels, who annihilated a large part of the celali troops. Ahmed I had especially appointed this latter to become the grand vizier, asking him personally to concentrate his efforts first in Anatolia to defeat Canboladoğlu, then the other rebels Tavil, Kalenderoğlu, and Kara Said. Finally, after the destruction of rebel forces, Kuyucu Murad was to continue on to the Persian

[53]Many documents attest to this in the registers of those years. For example, in one region of western Anatolia (Hamid), Ömer Bey and his steward, roaming the countryside with 600 mounted soldiers, were exacting illegal taxes (*salma*) from the peasantry, rich and poor. In the region of Antalya, Arslan Bey and his 400 men were collecting between 800 and 900 kuruş from the villagers, stealing and killing along the way. Akdağ, *Türk Halkının Dirlik ve Düzenlik Kavgası*, pp. 392–93, mentions similar cases. Uluçay, *Saruhan'da Eşkiyalık*, p. 100, presents numerous documents that attest to the greed and destruction engendered by all levels of officials taking advantage of the confusion precipitated by the celalis.

front, fight the principal enemy of the Ottomans, the shah of Iran, and regain the territory lost in previous battles.[54] This vizier, who had been appointed specifically to the task of subjugating rebels, operated by means of ruse, lies, and subterfuge.

There is no doubt that the Ottoman state took the case of Canboladoğlu Ali Pasha more seriously than it did other celali depredations. Canboladoğlu was located in northern Syria, a geopolitically, ethnically, and economically separate and potentially secessionist area. What made these regional advantages more critical was that not only the Ottomans but also Europeans kept close watch over northern Syria. In fact, in this case a reading of the foreign interests in the region reveals how much of the struggle of the celali leader was tied to the provocation of the Europeans, especially Grand Duke Ferdinand, who coveted Cyprus and northern Syria as stepping stones to an alliance with the shah of Persia and the final destruction of Ottoman forces.[55] European aspirations to control northern Syria and its vicinity led them to send many intermediaries in search of alliances with key local power holders who would be willing to antagonize the Ottomans. The economic wealth and importance of the area as an entrepôt made these political ambitions even more compelling. Despite this regional potential, the movement of Canbolad never became fully separationist. From all indications, in 1606 it looked as if Canboladoğlu Ali Pasha was ready for the implementation of what would be the first major secession from the empire. A few years later, the dream and its major initiator were dead.

The Canbolad family had control of the region from Kilis to Aleppo for at least a generation and had the opportunity to construct strong local patronage ties. This area was far from Ottoman central control. In fact, it lay more than 30 days' march from Istanbul. As a result, from its conquest in the early sixteenth century this region had presented special problems, which the state had decided to deal with by delegating authority. Control was divided between multiple power holders and different classes in society, making it difficult for any one group to emerge. The Ottomans encouraged groups such as tribal chiefs, janissaries, and local notables to participate in the rule of northern Syria.[56] Short tenure in office for centrally appointed regional officials was also employed as a useful mecha-

---

[54]Topçular Kâtibi Abdülkadir, *Vekayii Tarihiye*, folios 230a, b.
[55]Griswold, *The Great Anatolian Rebellion*, pp. 84–85.
[56]Ibid., p. 60.

nism of control.[57] During the long wars with Persia, a nearby border region, the Ottoman state diverted its attentioin away from northern Syria and allowed one major family, the Canbolads, to take control.

Northern Syria represented the intersection of many diverse ethnic groups, including Kurds, Arabs, and Turcoman tribesmen. In this diversity there was always an element of disdain for the *devşirme* process (the Balkan levy of children) that had established "infidels" in leadership positions within the state.[58] Aleppo and its surroundings were also quite wealthy. Access to the control of the provinces of northern Syria meant a rich tax base from agriculture as well as from trade. It was situated on several trade routes, and local merchants benefited handsomely from this privileged position.[59]

Canboladoğlu Ali assumed the leadership of the region after the death of his uncle Canboladoğlu Hüseyin and his foreign interests were increasingly becoming prominent after the battle of Lepanto.[60] He consolidated his position by allying with power holders to the south of Syria as well as with celali leaders to the immediate north.[61] He further took action to obstruct the roads to Mecca and Medina, holy sites of prime importance to the sultan's political prestige.[62] The potential for contention between Canboladoğlu and the Ottoman state became a reality when, in May 1606, the Syrian leader decided to use all available means for bargaining to secure his position. In a letter to Ahmed I, he requested the *beylerbeylik* of

[57]Griswold, *The Great Anatolian Rebellion*, p. 256, n. 1, quotes Withers, "Through peradventure they be maazold [from *ma'zul olmak*, to be dismissed] again, before they be scarce warm in their places."

[58]It is not easy to discuss the ethnic factor. Although we know that ethnic differences existed, we can only speculate about their influence. Perhaps further research into Arab sources might indicate more.

[59]The tax returns of this area indicate its wealth. In the early seventeenth century, the tax returns of Kilis were estimated to be three-quarter million akçes and of Aleppo 2.8 million akçes. These figures are quite significant when compared to most of Anatolia. See Ayn-i Ali Efendi, *Kavanin-i Al-i Osman der Hülasa-yi Mezamin-i Defter-i Divan* (Istanbul, 1979).

[60]Canboladoğlu Hüseyin had been executed by Çağalazade, the commander of the army at the eastern front, for a delayed arrival at the scene of battle. Çağalazade's words were fatal: "You were given the vilayet of Aleppo on condition that you would reach and unite with the army punctually. How is it that you arrived like this *after* we returned? Why did you not reach us when the enemy attacked us?" Griswold, *The Great Anatolian Rebellion*, p. 108. The interest of Europeans was aroused after Lepanto, since the Ottoman navy's defeat heightened Europe's hopes of success against the Turkish enemy.

[61]He is said to have allied with Tavil from Baghdad and Ma'anoğlu Fahreddin from southern Syria. He also tried to ally with Kalenderoğlu, Kara Said, and Cemşid from western and central Anatolia.

[62]Vasıtı, *Kuyucu Murad Paşa Vukuatı Tarihi*, folio 7b.

Aleppo in return for much needed military reinforcements for the Persian front. In this letter (presented at the opening of this chapter) Canboladoğlu offered 10,000 soldiers in return for this position, which would transform him immediately into the most powerful man in the region. Furthermore, to consolidate his power around the periphery of northern Syria, Canbolad made further demands, including *sancaks* for his commanders and police and gendarme positions for his other men, each time offering more soldiers for the imperial army. In the process, he committed nearly 60,000 men to the Ottoman army.[63] By securing offices for commanders and other officials loyal to him, Canbolad was obviously trying to guarantee his own security by establishing a protective zone around himself and creating his own patronage ties. Despite Ahmed I's reaction that Canbolad was demanding a little too much, the Ottoman state certified him as the governor-general of Aleppo in September 1606.[64] The new governor then proceeded to engage in deliberations with the shah of Persia and the grand duke of Tuscany.

To the Ottoman administration, the indicators of potential regional dissent with political implications were clear in northern Syria. Not only was this a remote and distinct territory with Canbolad in the highest official position, there were also strong indications of maneuvers toward organized administrative and military authority. Organization in the administration districts and in the governor-general's jurisdiction was not new in the Ottoman Empire. In fact, every governor-general held his own council and developed his own administrative structure, which usually imitated that of the imperial council. But contemporaries of Canboladoğlu describe more than a regular administration; they argue that he coined his own money, had prayers read in his name, and called himself "The Prince and Protector of the Kingdom of Syria," all the while building his army.[65] Griswold, who had surveyed the European sources and consular reports, argues that despite their keen interest and their previous involvement Europeans at this stage stayed put and refrained from interference, choosing not to jeopardize their relationship with the Ottomans. Nevertheless, they were all eager to control this territory, although the Tuscans were the only

---

[63]Griswold, *The Great Anatolian Rebellion,* pp. 240–42.

[64]Ibid., pp. 118–20.

[65]Ibid., p. 123. See also Hammer, *Histoire de l'empire Ottoman,* 2:328–29. Hammer also argued that the army of Canboladoğlu was assembled from men from varied and dispersed regions, but that when they gathered under his command they were given training quite similar to that of the Ottoman army.

ones to openly support Canboladoğlu's claims.[66] There was, then, by the end of 1606 every indication that Canbolad was looking for the first opportunity to rebel and secede from the empire.

This realization motivated Grand Vizier Kuyucu Murad Pasha, who mobilized for a campaign to the east with the declared aim of fighting Shah Abbas but the disguised one of securing northern Syria. Peace with the Habsburgs had been signed (November 1606), and there was no reason to wait. He dispatched his best men to positions of priority in the regional and central administration of the empire, thereby ensuring the security and effective administration of all functions of the Ottoman lands in his absence from the center.[67] It was also important to strike fast, since Canboladoğlu had not yet had time to benefit from all his alliances and to cash in on the deals he had made. Kuyucu Murad Pasha marched toward northern Syria, eliminating celalis on the way with a variety of tricks: driving away Kalenderoğlu by offering him a good deal with the *sancak* of Ankara,[68] entrapping another bandit, Serradcızade Ahmed Bey, with offers of Konya, while discarding the heads of Ahmed Bey's men into wells prepared for this grisly use.[69] After many more subterfuges, Murad Pasha's and Canbolad's armies met at Oruç Ovası to the north of Aleppo, where the mercenary army was decimated. It is said that Kuyucu Murad Pasha had 20,000 heads of mercenaries piled in front of his tent.[70] With Canboladoğlu defeated, Kuyucu continued to fight the rest of the mercenary armies and supposedly had up to 100,000 men beheaded. Among these were at least forty-eight bandit chiefs whose heads were sent to Istanbul.[71]

This battle ended a major era in the history of the Ottoman Empire, since the violence of Kuyucu Murad showed the state's capacity for repression. Political bargaining and co-optation were used to stop territories from becoming the domains of strong, independent, and militarily alert men. This had always been the policy of the Ottoman Empire; yet,

[66]Griswold, *The Great Anatolian Rebellion*, p. 123.

[67]For example, Tiryaki Hasan Pasha was nominated *beylerbeyi* of Rumelia, Maryol Hüseyin *beylerbeyi* of Anatolia, Çakırcıbaşı Halil *ağa* of janissaries, and Baki Pasha *defterdar*; see Hammer, *Histoire de l'empire Ottoman*, 2:329.

[68]It seems that Kalenderoğlu and Kara Said had offered to join the Ottoman armies, but since the grand vizier was suspicious of their allegiance he decided that it was better to remove them from the potential battle zones; Griswold, *The Great Anatolian Rebellion*, p. 137. See also Vasıtı, *Kuyucu Murad Paşa Vukuatı Tarihi*, folio 7b.

[69]Hammer, *Histoire de l'empire Ottoman*, 2:329.

[70]Griswold, *The Great Anatolian Rebellion*, pp. 145–46.

[71]Hammer, *Histoire de l'empire Ottoman*, 2:336; Naima, *Tarih-i Naima*, 2:45.

when rotation was not sufficient, the state resorted to force to maintain its traditional goal. How important this was to the state is reiterated by the story of Kuyucu, who summoned a perfectly legitimate but increasingly powerful commander and vizier, Nasuh Pasha, and scolded him on the ever-increasing size of his personal retinue.[72] When the state mustered enough military strength, it moved to consolidate by eradicating rebel leadership.

For all its increasing reliance on force, the state's harshest measures were reserved for use only against Canboladoğlu. This was precisely because the rebellion of the Syrian governor was considered a direct threat to the consolidation of the state. The relative magnitude of this threat becomes obvious when compared to the activities of other bandits: while most bandits criss-crossed Anatolia in search of booty, Canboladoğlu remained in his region, deliberately manning his districts with troops and, more important, enjoying the backing of European powers. Yet like the first set of movements building a power base very much depended on the ability to mobilize mercenary companies and direct them into contentious action.

The more ceremonial and theatrical aspect of state consolidation kicked in with Canbolad's defeat. The rebel was brought to the palace where he stayed with the young Sultan Ahmed I, consulting as well as repenting. His sons were placed in the harem school, provided with an allowance, and thereby given the chance to become the sultan's servants in the future. Canbolad was treated as part of the state. It is said that he explained to the sultan that his earlier actions were the result of bad advice and that he would prove worthy of the sultan's trust. He was subsequently sent to Temeşvar as governor, only to be strangled later at the orders of Kuyucu Murad Paşa. His ultimate fate should not blind us to the significance of his rehabilitation. The willingness of Sultan Ahmed to consult and accept Canbolad, by far the most threatening of the celalis, is indicative of the message the state intended for potential lawbreakers: the government route was always open. The early 1600s set this pattern, which was to be emulated throughout the century. The second period of uprisings differed only slightly. Here political rhetoric was added to the scenario. The bandits of the second period presented political reasons for their rebellion; they learned to use political events for their goals, which remained the same loot or taxes.

[72]Hammer, *Histoire de l'empire Ottoman*, 2:333–34; Cezar, *Osmanlı Tarihinde Levendler*, p. 299.

Immediately after Kuyucu's success, the challenge of further centralization was confronted. As this internal war was considered a major victory
against bandits, the natural progression was the establishment of order
and peace in the provinces. Because the population of the provinces had
either migrated to the major walled cities, especially to Istanbul, or had
escaped to mountain hideouts, one of the first orders of business was to
command the people to return to their villages and revive cultivation of
the land. Kuyucu convinced the sultan to issue a decree ordering people
to leave Istanbul. In the imperial orders requiring the repopulation of
Anatolia, threats were used to guarantee compliance.[73] Once the population of Anatolia, the real victims of this era, were dealt with, Kuyucu
turned his attention to the regional bureaucracy, replaced many governors
and lower-level bureaucratic officials, and continued to eliminate bandits
as they were detected. At the same time, he required a complete evaluation of empire's administrative apparatus: detailed studies of its institutions, legal, financial, and military.[74] Thorough and conservative, Kuyucu
was able to resettle the Anatolians, reshuffle provincial governors and
governor-generals, and conduct two short campaigns against Persia in an
attempt to reclaim some of the territory lost in prior years. He was still at
war when he died in 1611 and was replaced by Nasuh Pasha, the man who
was to make peace with the Persians.

Unfortunately, although a page in the celali horrors had been turned
with Kuyucu, the local pillage continued, since it was practically impossible to exhaust the sources of celalis and potential celalis in every locality.
The process by which mercenaries emerged and were drawn into armies
continued to feed more men into the system. And as long as a complete

---

[73]Hrand D. Andreasyan recounts the difficulties encountered by his Armenian compa-
triots when they attempted to journey home. He also attests to the fact that the grand vizier
who had instigated this action was willing to negotiate some tax exemptions for those returning since he knew they would face hardships; "Celalilerden Kaçan Anadolu Halkının
Geri Gönderilmesi," in *Ismail Hakkı Uzunçarşılı'ya Armağan* (Ankara, 1976), pp. 45–53.

[74]As to be expected, many works came out of this evaluation. I used, for example, the
surveys of Ayn-i Ali *Kavanin-i Al-i Osman der Hülasa-yi Mezamin-i Defter-i Divan* (Essay on
the Duties and Ranks of the Servants of the House of Osman), concerned with the government and the army, salaries and wage systems; *Risale-i Asakir-i Osman* (Essay on the Soldiers
of Osman), describing the organization and condition of the janissary guards; *Kanun-u Os-
maniye* (Ottoman Law), explaining the traditional criminal law, the status, and the taxes of
the people of the empire; and *Kanun-u Malı-ı Mısır* (The Financial Law of Egypt), with the
explanation of Egypt's financial system. These were all commissioned during Kuyucu's tenure as grand vizier. See Shaw, *History of the Ottoman Empire*, 1:290–91; Griswold, *The Great
Anatolian Rebellion*, pp. 209–10.

reorganization of the empire failed to occur, the celalis would remain significant at the local level, if not at a larger scale.

The Politicized Rhetoric of Bargaining, 1623–1648

The second period of political movements came about after a few years of interruption in the ability of the state to respond to crises of Anatolian origin. This interruption was the result of different political factions having come head to head to the extent that, for the first time in the history of the empire, they were able to determine which sultan was to rule. At the death of Ahmed I in 1617, his brother, Mustafa I, came to power supported by Kösem Sultan, the wife of Ahmed I, and her allies. But a year later another faction, that of chief eunuch Mustafa Ağa, brought Osman II to the throne on the claim that Mustafa I was insane. So Osman came to power not too long after the death of Ahmed I, the sultan who together with Grand Vizier Kuyucu Murad had demonstrated strength and the ability to deal with internal Anatolian disturbances, banditry, and chaos. Kuyucu had first incorporated the bandit chiefs into the army, asking them to participate in the upcoming wars, and then had their heads cut off. Partly as a result of his capable and effective entourage, Ahmed I had become a strong leader who practiced centralized control and had stable achievements to show for it. Osman II promised to be even more successful than his father, but he did not last long. In 1622 he was removed from office by the janissaries and sipahis and was later murdered. And although this was the first time in Ottoman history that a sultan was removed from office and assassinated, this event did not signify the breakdown of the state that some scholars have attached to it.[75] It was a simple coup, where internal factions of the state and the state army, in apprehension of this sultan's policies, cooperated in an attempt to persuade him to alter his plans; when the gathering turned into a mob, mutinous soldiers took liberties they had never taken before. The sultan was murdered, and the fool Mustafa I was restored to the throne for another year.

The policies of Osman II, who was quite young (14–18 during his reign), distinguish themselves as methods of strong central control; they were policies of consolidation at the center effected to purge elements that

---

[75]The only real threat to the House of Osman was in 1687–88, when there was a bid to bring in a sultan from outside the line of Osman.

might oppose the throne—potential disrupters, and especially the army. The janissaries as well as the central cavalry units had already demonstrated their aptitude for palace intrigue. For Osman II, the campaign in Poland confirmed the degree to which the janissaries had departed from their original ideals, and he understood well that given their emergence as a local force they would help bring about the decentralization of the empire. The importance of the janissaries was undeniable; they had grown from 12,000 in the 1420s to 40,000 in the 1620s. They were active in the trade and administration of cities and towns all across the empire and were intermarrying into the local notable class.[76] Trying to control them, Osman II developed poor relations with this central army, which, according to the traditional blueprint, was *his* army. It should be remembered that sultans were careful to keep the janissaries happy; they gave them initial gifts, the "accession tax," and were careful not to introduce debased coins at their accession. Osman II crossed the army, circulating rumors that he was going to disband it to replace it with a Türkmen army of Anatolian origin rather than that of slave origin. The military was only one of the elite groups Osman II planned to handle harshly. Another important group he intended to tackle was the bureaucracy. Starting with the restricted powers of the *şeyh-ül-islam,* the ulema suffered political and economic losses. Osman II cut off their benefices (*arpalık*), forcing the ulema class into dependence on the crown; he restricted their privileges and tried to control the activities in the palace. Within a few months, the entire military and bureaucratic apparatus felt that a shrinkage of their power was imminent.

When rumors spread that the sultan was embarking on a pilgrimage as a subterfuge to go to Anatolia and form a new army based on Turkish peasants, the janissaries lost their calm. With the support of the bureaucracy, they assembled to protest against the sultan and his supporters, but soon enough, through the machinations of their leadership, they forced the sultan to forgo his plans, and execute his closest allies; finally, still not satisfied, they deposed the young sultan, killing him a short time later.[77] A survey of the contemporary sources shows no indication of a premeditated revolt against Osman II, especially not one with the intent to depose him. The rally of the army started as a routine event. In fact, as

---

[76]Inalcık, "Military and Fiscal Transformation," p. 299.

[77]Peçevi, *Tarih-i Peçevi,* 2:379–80; Naima, *Tarih-i Naima,* 2:225–31; Hammer, *Histoire de l'empire Ottoman,* 2:374–79; Uzunçarşılı, *Osmanlı Tarihi,* 3-1:137–43. See also Inalcık, "Fiscal and Military Transformation," p. 297.

Hammer also seems to indicate, when Mustafa I was found and liberated from his captivity, it became clear to the janissaries that they could claim him as their leader and depose the sultan. As a result, Osman II, a sultan with high potential, was silenced forever. A few years later, Murad IV attempted the same kind of centralization policies, assembled an emergency imperial council meeting to alter the course of Ottoman history, and yet earned the respect of the household.

During the transition that followed the coup against Osman II, a new wave of rebellion shook Anatolia. Internal squabbles had no doubt debilitated the state; Mustafa was unable to rule and the state was losing legitimacy. The transition to Murad IV was a shift to a very young sultan who still needed strong allies in the imperial council to rule effectively. Yet the state had not disintegrated during the coup against Osman. Anatolian bandits, however, had embarked on a similar campaign of disrupting state and local governance. Again, there were two waves of these celali activities; the more trivial, smaller-scale banditry that remained localized, causing damage essentially to a rural population, and the larger and more significant movements that blazed across Anatolia, causing desolation and challenging the state for better placement in the Ottoman system.

The assassination of Osman II provided the unique opportunity to politicize these rebel demands and couch them in terms that could be perceived as threatening to the state. The rebels' actions had demonstrated no serious intentions against the Ottoman state, but this time the rebels had acquired a more sophisticated rhetoric that evoked sociopolitical inequalities and issues of contention. For example, they focused on the differences between armies—the central army of the janissaries and the central cavalry units and the regional army composed of *sekban* and *sarıca* groups. These two groups had been at odds with each other since the earlier struggles for the throne and yet, during the reigns of Selim II and Murad III, peasants had been asked to join the janissaries. This was the natural outcome of the changes in the timar system and the new requirements for war on the part of the Europeans. The rift between the two parties increased when *sekban* leaders came to occupy comfortable positions in the state administration. The positive aspects of this policy—increasing numbers of musket-bearing soldiers in the army and decreasing numbers of vagrant peasants in Anatolia—were offset by the blurring of boundaries between different types of armies and the opening up of a channel of advancement from regional to central positions which led to increased competition. Abaza Mehmed Pasha was a celali who used this struggle between armies to his advantage.

Abaza Mehmed Pasha, who had been a loyal officer of the Ottoman state protected by his patron, the two-time grand vizier Halil Pasha, declared his opposition to the state for allowing the janissaries to dictate Osman II's murder.[78] His stated political aims, however, do not appear to be entirely his. There is some evidence that Kösem Sultan privately invited Abaza Mehmed to fight those who murdered Osman II. Rumors also circulated to the effect that Abaza was persuaded to revolt by some *şeyh* claiming to have had visions of Abaza in high office. Abaza was of mixed background. Although he had been the treasurer of Canboladoğlu Ali Pasha,[79] the protection of Halil Pasha had turned him into a loyal official. First the sword bearer of Halil Pasha, then admiral, later provincial governor of Maraş, and finally the governor-general of Erzurum,[80] he had proved not only loyal but also competent at serving the state and the people. His ability to mobilize *sekban* and *sarıca* depended on his ability to exploit the rivalry between janissary and *sekban*, as well as on traditional looting, which no doubt was one of the main goals of these mercenary troops. Abaza Mehmed made his reputation fighting against and often murdering janissary officials who plundered villages and exacted high taxes and fees.[81]

Abaza Mehmed was declared a celali when infighting in the fortress of Erzurum between his men and the janissaries led to violence between the two groups.[82] When Abaza threw the janissaries out of Erzurum, he was considered a celali and was ordered to Sivas, where he went, taking with him 15,000 men ready to fight.[83] The chaos at the center did no doubt motivate certain local governors to join Abaza when he appealed to them to join his fight. Others might have been forced into joining through vi-

---

[78]He claimed to have corresponded with Osman II about the plans regarding the janissaries. At least some sources corroborate this: see Hammer, *Histoire de l'empire Ottoman,* 2:384.; Çetin Yetkin, *Türk Halk Hareketleri ve Devrimler* (Istanbul, 1984), p. 203.

[79]Naima, *Tarih-i Naima,* 2:240–41.

[80]Ibid., 2:208; Hammer, *Histoire de l'empire Ottoman,* 2:384.

[81]Hrand D. Andreasyan, "Abaza Mehmed Pasha," *Istanbul Universitesi Edebiyat Fakültesi Tarih Dergisi* 22 (1968): 131–34.

[82]Abaza is supposed to have been quite cruel to janissaries whom he had executed. Naima, *Tarih-i Naima,* 2:410–11, recounts that when a man denied that he was a janissary, Abaza would have him lower his trousers so that he could see whether his shins and calves had the characteristic signs of wearing the janissary trousers.

[83]Many of these men were reassembled from the troops of the previous set of celali leaders, recently defeated by the Ottoman state armies. They were therefore the men of Karayazıcı, Canboladoğlu, Kalenderoğlu, Tavil Halil, and so forth. They were ready to congregate under a new commander and avenge the massacre of their leaders and their fellow fighters by Grand Vizier Kuyucu Murad Pasha; see Hammer, *Histoire de l'empire Ottoman,* 2:389.

olence. Three campaigns were directed against Abaza Mehmed, after which he was temporarily reinstated in Erzurum. Each campaign was more substantial than its predecessor, with men of reputation appointed to fight and several attempts at deal making. The second campaign, for example, in April 1624, was directed by the grand vizier Çerkez Mehmed Pasha, the janissary Ağa, and the governor-generals of Anatolia and Karaman. After a defeat the bandit leader was ready to deal. More important, it took a short time for him to spring back on his feet, since his patron in the palace quickly came to the rescue and offered him a compromise: fighting against the Persians in return for a pardon. After the failure of these measures, finally, the new grand vizier Hüsrev Pasha was able to conduct a successful campaign against him and Abaza surrendered.[84]

It is interesting that, despite Abaza's defeat, the grand vizier chose to confer upon him robes of honor in order to transform him into a loyal Ottoman servant. Furthermore, the grand vizier enlisted 600 of Abaza's men into the order of armorers (cebeci).[85] These actions demonstrate the zeal with which the state officers wanted to get rid of the celali issue. Again, promoting these bandits, incorporating them, making sure that they felt honored was worth the effort since incorporation meant peace and armies. Abaza was then assigned to Bosnia, where he again skirmished with janissaries.[86] Later on, after fighting campaigns in the west, Abaza became close to Sultan Murad IV and stayed in Istanbul. Yet he was executed when the sultan finally started to conduct his own consolidation policies. It is again an interesting fact that Abaza, the bandit chief, was buried with ceremony and pomp next to Kuyucu Murad Pasha, the grand vizier who had spent his last years purging celalis from Anatolia.[87] These actions were largely ceremonial; but they emphasized to the potential contenders that the route within government service was more lucrative in power and prestige. It also reminded them that contention was never rewarding, even though in the short term some state policies of political bargaining may have inspired some to become bandits.

Probably Abaza Mehmed's greatest achievement was to turn his personal leadership and rebellion into a political program for the sekban and sarıca who followed him. By capitalizing on the rivalry within the Ottoman military, he was able to gather large armies and threaten the state. Abaza can be likened to the celali leaders of the early seventeenth century

[84]Ibid., 2:426.
[85]Ibid.
[86]Ibid., 2:427; Naima, Tarih-i Naima, 3:196.
[87]Naima, Tarih-i Naima, 3:196–205, 225–32.

in trying to earn a better position through the system rather than through secession. Again, there was no attempt at secession from the empire; rather, there were numerous bids to create better and better positions for the bandit chief himself. The attention Abaza received from the palace set the pattern for a series of movements in the later seventeenth century, all of which capitalized on the janissary-mercenary rivalry in the Ottoman military. The political rhetoric had become successful, despite the failure of its initiator, Abaza Mehmed Pasha.

During this second period of activities, any low-level officials who could formulate an issue that was related to internal developments in the empire did so. With the new ability to politicize the rhetoric of banditry, banditry itself became more widespread among petty officials. In the western Anatolian peninsula, many such bandits sprang up, declaring some kind of issue with the state while spending their time and energies looting. Cennetoğlu declared himself to be tımar holder fighting for the rights of the class of tımar holders. The tımar holders were in decline and state policies had been geared toward the elimination of small land tenures in favor of larger ones. Cennetoğlu chose this specific issue, hoping that he would appeal to the large numbers of dispossessed cavalrymen and thereby acquire the power to make demands on the state. Yet from Bursa to Saruhan to Izmir, numerous tımar holders wrote the state complaining about the depredations caused by this bandit; for, despite his rhetoric for the tımar holders, he was highly successful at robbing them.[88] Ilyas Pasha, another low-level official in western Anatolia, raised his *sekban* army before even developing a cause to fight for. He later provided a misunderstanding with the grand vizier Hüsrev Pasha as the grounds for bandit activities. Karahaydaroğlu, wanted to avenge the death of his father—killed by state officials—when he joined other celalis in the mountains. Gürcü Abdünnebi, yet another bandit, used a tax issue to gather about 15,000 *sekban* and *sarıca* mercenaries and march toward Istanbul.[89]

The small-scale banditry of these local officials remains interesting in the nature of their interaction with the Ottoman Porte. The activities of these bandit chiefs help confirm two hypotheses of the general argument. On the one hand, the fact that they emulated the political rhetoric of their predecessors attests to the learning and the imitation effect of banditry, stripping it further from interpretations such as primitive rebels fighting injustice and deprivation. As befit the times in which they operated as

[88]Uluçay, *Saruhan'da Eşkiyalık,* pp. 35–36. See also Goffman, *Izmir and the Levantine World, 1550–1650* (Seattle, 1990), pp. 26–30.

[89]Uluçay, *Saruhan'da Eşkiyalık,* pp. 54–55.

bandit chiefs, these local brigands declared relevant political issues that they claimed to resolve by their banditry. Each one of these men politicized these issues in their negotiations with the state. Yet mostly they operated through patrons in the state administration who they hoped would broker deals for them. Over time, they remained loyal to their primary objective of loot and positions within the state. On the other hand, their specific dealings with the state attest to the importance accorded to deal making by state makers. These considerably less consequential bandits, located far from the significant frontiers, were not offered state positions. Karahaydaroğlu, for example, considered himself important enough to ask for appointment as *sancakbeyi* twice during his career as a rebel bandit chief, only to be firmly rebuked by the grand vizier.[90] As temporary and deceptive as these state deals were, they were made sparingly as part of a careful strategy of state consolidation.

By the time Abaza had become close to Sultan Murad IV, and looked as if he would give up banditry altogether, the central corps of sipahis were again in revolt, asking for the heads of all the prime leaders of the state: the grand vizier Hafız Pasha, the religious leader, the minister of finance, the *ağa* of the janissaries, and many others (1632). Although the sultan first gave in to the demands of these rebellious masses, causing the death of his grand vizier and other trusted men, he quickly changed his course of action and had the main instigator arrested and beheaded. In the aftermath of this movement from among the central troops of the army, Murad IV resolved to undertake a strong campaign of consolidation and control of the empire. With that aim, he rather hastily convened a meeting of the imperial divan under an emergency regulation.

The *ayak divanı* was the first herculean effort at consolidation since Süleyman the Magnificent. Murad IV convened his grand vizier, the *şeyh-ül-islam,* the high judges of Anatolia and Rumelia, the ulema, the *ağa* the of janissaries, and other important dignitaries in May 1632, just a few months after the revolt of the sipahis. After having assured himself of the loyalty of these men, he addressed each of the segments of the military and bureaucracy of the empire, confronting them with their crimes, accusing them of unruliness and corruption, and giving them little time to defend themselves. Many were executed. Janissaries were followed by sipahis, who were followed by corrupt judges, and every group was urged to purge its ranks of the rebellious and dishonest. What the state could not accomplish, especially in the provinces, the people were asked to do on

---

[90]Halil Inalcik, "Haydar-oğlu Mehmed," *Encyclopedia of Islam* (Leiden, 1969).

their own. Therefore, as was true of his predecessors, Murad IV ordered the people's justice to prevail for the last part of the cleanup; popular mass action occurred as the state proclaimed a general call to arms (*nefir-i 'am*). Malefactors, sipahi, janissary, and mercenary were eliminated.[91] All this activity was followed by an internal campaign of consolidation and reform. Relying on the surveys and reports of the previous decades, Murad IV undertook an inspection of existing institutions. In the reform that ensued, some institutions were abolished, while others were revived only after their makeup and constituencies were massively altered. For example, as was previously discussed in relation to the timar system, this tenure institution was maintained yet was reorganized by the governors in charge of regional consolidation. In this particular case, reorganization and consolidation meant that officials with no clear and direct benefit to the state were replaced by new men, often referred to as upstarts. Finally, all kinds of restrictions were formulated in order to keep the moral values of the country on the right track. Murad IV believed that safety and order could be maintained only if the people upheld strong moral values, refraining from alcohol, smoking, and other vices. He therefore proclaimed these to be prohibited and sent spies to inspect towns and cities.[92]

Both the victories of Ahmed I's grand vizier Kuyucu Murad Pasha and of Murad IV brought about periods of lull in celali activity. Both the grand vizier and later the sultan had succeeded at destroying celali leaders and numerous mercenaries. Yet the conditions that led to the emergence of these movements were never eliminated. The system by which governors and governor-generals yearned for large armies to increase their power and prestige did not change; as we saw with Murad IV as well, sultans still issued decrees ordering the people to arm themselves; state officials still recruited from mercenary pools and contracted with their leadership for campaigns, and at every level the state still encouraged low-level militarization of the countryside. As it battled the mercenaries, it also created more. This is not to say that state makers were not aware of the dangers of militarization; they experienced its consequences daily. Yet, as long as mercenaries were of utility to the state's most significant function of warfare, the process was to be tolerated. And reform and reorganization were to be attempted to alleviate structural tensions for a while.

---

[91]Inalcık, "Military and Fiscal Transformation," pp. 304–7; Shaw, *History of the Ottoman Empire*, 1:197.

[92]Naima, *Tarih-i Naima*, 3:168; Howard, "The Ottoman *Timar* System," pp. 204–6; Hammer, *Histoire de l'empire Ottoman*, 2:448–53.

We can therefore see Murad's attempt at the reorganization of the timar as a band-aid rather than a real cure.

Another reason for the continuation of these policies, which inevitably ended up in mercenary pools, was that they were not that threatening after all. The mercenaries and other vagrant armed men up to this time entered the services of provincial officials who were officers of the state. However large their retinues became, they remained in the service of the state and searched for upward mobility through the state. The seventeenth century proved that the state was able to consolidate its power quite rapidly through negotiation and war with these governors, be they legitimate or illegitimate. They remained part of the state apparatus. And when they ventured outside, they were quickly co-opted back inside. The danger to the state was to come only when local notables (*ayans*) with no direct allegiance to the state started accumulating armies and men. They did not belong to the state and were not easily drawn into it. Therefore, when they gained control of local militias and transformed them into their retinues, they became more dangerous. They were locally rooted. Unlike state officials they did not rotate positions, and they established local allegiances and strong patron-client ties. They became the real agents of decentralization. For most of the seventeenth century, however, the Ottoman state achieved central domination and remained in control of its officers. It was only a deviant by-product of the system that some of those men that were incorporated through negotiation happened to be bandits.

7

Conclusion

ALTHOUGH EXPLANATIONS OF STATE FORMATION vary according to discipline and theoretical outlook, they all tend to emphasize one master process derived from the western experience. Sociologists, anthropologists, historians, and political scientists generally perceive the western trajectory as *the* course of action through which states centralize, allowing for little variation. They have taken the western model of state development and enshrined it into a perspective of the world. In this view, state formation was carried out through struggle between state and society, with the state increasingly achieving control over a contentious, rebellious society. In the process, the state increased its strength—building its military and bureaucratic-administrative capacities and penetrating society to dominate it. This process originated from the state's need for territorial consolidation, achieved through war with the necessary resources drawn from the population. Where resources were drawn from the rural sector, populations rebelled, especially in the form of interclass alliances. Where cities were predominant, deals were made with urban capital holders.

This explanation is based on and does characterize the western patterns of state formation in the early modern period. Yet preoccupation with the western model of state formation does not allow for adequate study of the divergence offered by non-western societies. History demonstrates that the non-western processes of state formation had different trajectories with varied results. These states did not uniformly undergo rebellions, and they certainly did not always become strong states with dominant control over their societies. Given the inability to explain this variation with the predominant model of state formation, how can we better account for the different paths we uncover? And how do we find the underlying causes of the differences between western and non-western processes, thereby helping to theorize more freely about a larger process?

I have tried to answer this question in a specific context, introducing a non-western case of state consolidation in order to highlight the differences between processes and to draw out the relevant components of state formation. I have brought the non-West, and more specifically the Ottoman Empire, into a fresh historical as well as a new comparative sociological perspective. The aim was twofold: to examine Ottoman history of the seventeenth century in order to expand on the theoretical setting of state centralization, and to develop a new theoretical perspective to make better sense of historical events of the seventeenth century. I therefore used history to expand on theory, and then theory to elucidate history. This process has enabled me to build a more inclusive explanation of state formation and a better explanation of the intricacies of Ottoman state-society relations. Obviously, a single case is not sufficient; further studies are necessary for theoretical refinements. Still, the case of the Ottoman Empire does show that the study of state formation requires additional focus on non-western state-society relations. It provides a significant case of the state as bargainer, negotiating and embracing individuals, social classes, and especially groups such as bandits, in order to control them and to establish its centralized rule over vast territory. I argue that the combination of patrimonial rule with a brokerage style of centralization emphasized flexibility in political rule applied to achieve state goals.

More specifically, the comparison of European, especially French, and Ottoman histories of the seventeenth century demonstrates that state formation does not proceed in the same way in all societies. I have identified at least two different processes. Whereas the French state centralized by subjugating societal classes that collaborated in rebellion against its increased penetration, the Ottoman state centralized mostly through negotiation and incorporation of bandit armies that were largely the product of state consolidation in the first place. The French state engendered a strong center-periphery dislocation, followed by the rebellions of peasants and landlords, with both disaffected groups losing income or autonomy. The Ottoman state, on the other hand, was able to manipulate most classes in society and divert them from rebellion. The price was the rise of banditry, which the state eventually had to control, although under less threatening circumstances. There are a few direct conclusions to draw from this comparative analysis: that the process of state centralization was far from uniform, or even unidirectional; that class-based revolts do not always result from the process of state formation; that the nature of state-society relations would bear out the most crucial differences in the two processes.

In the West, state makers who were ultimately successful at building centralized, differentiated organizations with a monopoly of coercion over a defined territory were those who manipulated the structure of society according to their own agendas. In the process, they encountered resistance from the various segments of the population they attempted to subjugate and tax, as well as from existing alternative organizations. Yet western states were increasingly better at taxing, and controlling, and became more powerful than any other contending power holder in society. I have suggested that such state consolidation processes are not necessarily unidirectional; that states experience temporary setbacks, yet without total breakdown of the governmental apparatus. State development can occur in states that start out as more centralized units and attempt to maintain their centralized control. In such cases, development does not necessarily follow from increased state control. A different combination has emerged from my study, of strong control function interspersed with more relaxed forms of domination. The case of the Ottoman Empire demonstrates that a variety of mechanisms of control can be successful, if these are devised to maintain a close check over potentially separatist elements. The history of the seventeenth century presents such various methods of control, ranging from low levels of militarization in the countryside to internal warfare with large-scale bandits. In all these methods of control the state succeeded at maintaining order because it made political decisions to respond to and alter societal forms. And centralization occurred despite periods when local forms of militarization and banditry seemed to threaten stability.

I have also suggested that revolts against the state are not always part of the process of state formation. The literature has assumed that, given state exploitation and control of these groups, they will singly or in alliance revolt. I have argued for the importance of state-society relations in precipitating or hindering revolts. State-society relations are a combination of the social structure of society and the centralization policies of the state. The social structure makes for determinate action and reaction between state and society. In that sense social structure and state action are part of a process of development whereby the state selects a course of action that weighs the structure of society against state goals, and society is shaped and reshaped through action and reaction. The key to this approach is the study of the dynamic between the state and societal forces, with a close eye to the structural changes this very dynamic engenders.

These two variables, social structure and state action, make up the core of state-society relations and account for both rebellions and lack of rebellions in the West and the non-West. These contrasting outcomes are typified in the comparison of France and the Ottoman Empire. The central difference is that in France strong peasant-noble alliances against the absolutist state were formed throughout the seventeenth century, whereas in the provinces of the Ottoman Empire interdependence and collaboration were not the norm. Peasant rebellions occurred in France when state policies were aimed at the long-term subordination of all regional power holders, thus creating common local interests with peasants, with the existing provincial social structure already encouraging dependence and communal interaction between landlords and peasants. French peasants chose to remain in their villages and protest through the existing provincial structure, which included alliance with an equally disgruntled nobility. Centralization pushed the sword nobility and state makers into intense conflict over regional autonomy and set peasants and state makers into conflict over increasing taxes. The peasants found natural allies in the nobility, who also opposed the state. Conversely, peasant revolts were unlikely in the Ottoman Empire, where state policies were aimed at the short-term division and control of regional power holders and where the provincial social structure did not promote strong patron-client or communal alliances. The relative lack of rebellion was the result of the state's ability to subdue each social class, and of the relative barrenness of a social structure that inhibited easy communication and organization within the rural framework.

In emphasizing the interaction of state action and social structure, I have focused on two important variables in the sociological literature while discarding many other arguments based on the individual characteristics or mentalities of particular groups. By emphasizing social structure as well as state action, I have demonstrated that, despite the fact that classes have mutual interests, they may not perceive such mutuality or be able to put together a viable movement. Peasants and other classes have grievances and interests; yet they may not be able to translate these into concerted political action, especially of the revolutionary type. The route from material interest to political action may be even more tortuous and arduous than suggested by models based on western experience. The lack of rebellions was not culturally determined but the result of structural barriers that had to be toppled before collective action could occur.

The cultural context can act as a facilitator or an obstacle to a movement, yet it cannot on its own account for the transformative action. I do not argue that there was no culture of dissent in the Ottoman Empire. Instead, I see the state-society compact as embedded in the circle of justice and in the state-centered reward structure to be the major cultural context within which actors and groups make their demands and act on them. Adapting from William H. Sewell, I see culture as informing the structure of institutions and the nature of social relations in a society.[1] In this sense, it is embedded in the structure of society, providing the more general understandings and guidelines for action. Thus, an understanding of the state as the center of rewards and privileges dominated the Classical Age of the Ottoman Empire, lasting well into the seventeenth century and shaping the parameters within which certain action was acceptable. The belief in the circle of justice and its implications for the dominance and protection of the people certainly affected the worldview of peasants. Yet, again, on the more practical level, this worldview was mediated by the existence of kadı justice and the court as the alternative channel of grievances that provided the peasantry a voice in rural matters. A larger repertoire of ideas regarding justice was negotiated at the level of the courts as the institutional embodiment of the cultural format.

One of the strongest themes to emerge from this book is that of the ability of the Ottoman state to manipulate societal classes to maintain the kind of order that inhibited rebellions. This was possible essentially because of the nature of state-society relations in the Ottoman Empire. For each class, I have demonstrated the manner in which the social structure of the empire, and the specific actions of the state, made control possible. Contrary to historical arguments that maintain that the Ottoman state had lost control of the provinces and its different classes by the late sixteenth century, I have compared the Classical Age to the seventeenth century to demonstrate that the state was quite able to coordinate and control its various constituencies.

By the Classical period, the command over various classes based on the differentiation and functioning of the patrimonial household was well developed. The state ensured the loyalty of its servants as it rewarded them through incorporation, and it rotated them to keep them from developing alternative allegiances. This slave-servant system ensured that the ruling class could not develop an autonomous identity and institution outside

---

[1] William H. Sewell, Jr., "Ideologies and Social Revolutions: Reflections on the French Case," *Journal of Modern History* 57 (1985): 61.

the state itself. Individuals were sustained as servants of the state through state policies and acquired their status through the state. Having no independent basis of power or wealth of their own, they remained subservient to the state. Thus we have to imagine a class of elite members of the state whose social position in life was strikingly different from their European counterparts in medieval and early modern times. The system then manifested itself in the difficulties in acquiring power, wealth, and status independently from the state and in the numerous checks and counterchecks on each official's discretionary power.

Control of rural populations started in Ottoman history with a concerted attempt at the subjugation and forced settlement of the nomadic element in society. To the degree that the state was able to transform nomads into settled agriculturists, it succeeded at their administrative and military control. The subsequent establishment of the rivalry between the timar system of land tenure and the judicial system of direct incorporation ensured that the peasantry was not only locked into a strict structure of authority but also provided with an alternative channel of grievance release. Rural populations, then, were not only controlled by a series of patrons but also made to believe that they had legitimate channels of complaint that would elicit state response. At the level of the rural social order, minimal communal organization, intracommunity interaction, and intercommunity contact in the market made it more difficult for peasants to prepare for collective action.

State intervention in both the European and the Ottoman contexts undoubtedly led to greater state domination that resulted from more bureaucratic forms of control. Most arguments in the literature on the role of the state in generating revolt acknowledge this possibility. What is more important, however, is the manner in which state officials in the Ottoman case—as opposed to that of Europe—turned this intervention to the state's advantage and were able to enhance the state's ability to bargain and control societal classes. The Ottoman state was quite successful at the manipulation of classes in order to ensure continued support for itself. There would be no rebellion of a single class or of a class alliance. Given a combination of control and rotation, state provincial officials of all stations were not to develop patron-client ties with the cultivators, making a potential alliance between the two difficult.

To make matters worse for social classes, in the seventeenth century state responses to the changing international world system ushered in a period of intraelite struggles, with the state carefully dampening the possibility of elite uprisings. Dispersing groups of elites to provincial positions where they competed with the existing notables and power holders for a livelihood, as well as for authority and control, the state introduced new layers of intraelite conflict. Especially through the mechanism of handing out provincial and central state positions, the state was able to draw into its ranks the personnel of its provincial administration while discarding others. Furthermore, the careful mixing of central and provincial officials created antagonisms across levels of administration. The various forms of disruption and co-optation in the early seventeenth century contributed a great deal to a general sense of chaos among elite ranks, and to intraelite conflict. Where possible the state strengthened old forms of exploitation between patrons and clients, and where impossible it furthered new forms of exploitation of the rural population. Already suffering from the seventeenth-century crisis and manipulated by state action, peasants and elites were unable to unite in rebellious action.

Theorists of state formation are correct to assume that state consolidation did not occur smoothly. What they do not account for is the diversity of conflict that can occur during processes of state development. This diversity, as I have suggested, is dependent on the type of state-society relations that develop. As we have discovered in the case of the Ottoman Empire, the process of consolidation itself produced a different group for the state to bargain with. Peasants who did not or could not gain their livelihood from the land chose to pursue a career off the land. The opportunity for this career path was offered by the state itself. To fight wars with its European and Persian enemies, the Ottoman state enlisted these peasants, turning them into soldiers. Through a process of militarization and demilitarization, these soldiers found that their fortunes fluctuated, and over time they organized themselves into pools of mercenaries available to any power holder. These men were to tip the balance of rural social relations for an extended period.

Though bandit/mercenaries were of rural origin, I have argued that they were transformed by low-level militarization resulting from state consolidation. Their rural identity changed from peasant to bandit/ mercenary. In the absence of clear-cut class distinctions among the peasants, it is impossible to describe their identity further. I do not argue here that the unequal distribution of resources was unimportant. I simply alert the reader to the fact that the data are unavailable to substantiate an assumption of class formation. What was substantiated, however, is that the level of rural stratification and mobility resulted in bandits being a mixed blessing. They were hired by local power holders and therefore intensified the class struggles in rural society. At the same time, banditry demonstrated a channel of mobility for the destitute and the vagrant, providing them with employment opportunities other than agriculture and thereby relieving rural tensions.

Traditional historians of the Ottoman Empire have tended to focus on the purported inability of the state to absorb mercenaries into its ranks. It is, however, essential to understand that the state never endeavored to absorb these thousands of men permanently. The cost of any such absorption would have been prohibitive. The state instead instituted a policy of rotation to absorb them temporarily, either by hiring their services or later on by attracting their leaders to powerful positions. This state policy should not be perceived as an inability to carry out state goals; it was part of its goals. What might have appeared to be weakness was instead shrewd political behavior: disposable, bargain recruitment.

This interaction with bandits can be better understood by comparison with the attempts of the Chinese state to regularize the regional militia forces that had developed in late Imperial China. It is interesting to contrast these two state policies, since at first sight the local militarization in the provinces bore a close resemblance. The Ottoman state had itself taken part in the creation of these militia, whereas in the Chinese case the local militia originated out of societal necessity: the Chinese people organized both to meet communal needs and to form tax resistance units. As Philip A. Kuhn argues so eloquently, the Chinese state was threatened by the rise of these alternative rural organizations and tried to control and regularize them by fitting them into state-made societal formats. The goal was to force these irregular militia into predictable relations with the state.[2] The Ottoman state, however, had created its own alternative militia; it was not threatened by it. Instead, it used the militia to bring more control into rural society. Furthermore, when militia units escaped control by becoming bandits, the state used bargaining tactics to lure them back into the state realm. In this comparison, we can detect with more subtlety the different efforts at consolidation when intermediate-level organizations form within a social structure. Both societies ended up with alternative modes of organization in rural areas; yet their governing elites perceived these alternative modes differently because of their different degree of involvement in their creation. A comparison of Chinese and Ottoman techniques of local militarization would be a further useful way to plumb the intricate nature of state-society relations.

[2]Philip A. Kuhn, *Rebellion and Its Enemies in Late Imperial China: Militarization and Social Structure, 1796–1864* (Cambridge, Mass., 1980).

The astute political action of the Ottoman leadership was a form of state consolidation. The state used the bandits to consolidate territory and centralize further control. Banditry, of course, engendered a certain level of chaos in society, and the state had to respond on occasion to appeals by its people to subdue these unruly mercenaries. Yet the most important function of banditry was its contribution to a consolidation campaign. Here the differences with the West are more important than just the different societal groups that were engaged in the struggle against the state. Whereas the European states had to fend off serious rival contenders who were intent on challenging the monarchy and its centralized practices, the Ottoman bandits were not intent on altering the system. The French state, for example, was threatened by those who engaged in intrigue and rebellion to undermine the monarchy. The Ottoman bandits were instead intent on benefiting from the existing system; they perceived success as incorporation into the Ottoman regional or central administration. Moreover, the Ottoman state succeeded, at least up to the middle of the seventeenth century, in convincing bandits that their best bet was incorporation into the Ottoman administration. State officials demonstrated the merit of this practice; they incorporated legitimate officials as well as illegitimate ones into the system in order to keep them under supervision. To the degree that they were successful at distributing positions for the political purposes of the state only, rather than for administrative reasons, they remained successful at keeping consolidated rule within their territorial boundaries.

Another important finding in this book is the degree to which the rigidity of the original state-society structure was tampered with as the need arose. The French state, for example, was building toward an increasingly more rigid style of state control, through the penetration and administration of the provinces by an established group of central officers. Most traditional explanations of the transformation from the multitude of medieval kingdoms to the modern state have emphasized this very rigidity in the European processes. It reminds us of Max Weber's explanation of the evolution of a rational bureaucracy as central to the understanding of European transformations. The Ottoman state pokes holes into this picture, demonstrating some of the shortcomings of this approach. The Ottoman state frequently changed the positions, levels of administration, and norms of legitimacy in order to adapt to new circumstances and to consolidate at the same time. The Ottoman state developed by a series of fits and starts, while using a combination of rational-legal and traditional aspects of rule. The state did not develop in a unilinear evolution from traditional to more formal and legalistic forms. The process was instead a mixed mode that reverted to traditional features, or to pure bargaining, or to purely administrative dogma, when necessary.

Scholars who have focused on the more traditional aspects of state rule have overemphasized the sultanistic aspects of rule and have therefore spent many pages analyzing the state's strength and weakness according to whether the sultan or the grand vizier ruled supreme. Arguments raged as to whether the *palace* really governed the provinces or was unable to rule. When vizier households gained prominence, this was interpreted as indicating a loss of power of the sultan and therefore the state. I disagree. I assess the state in its more institutional format as distinct from the person of the sultan or the grand vizier. I have analyzed decision-making processes that were the outcome of imperial council negotiation or correspondence between sultan and grand vizier and have looked for the more composite aspects of state action. During the sixteenth century the Ottoman state thereby moved from "being the sultan" to being an institution. The state as an institution is much easier to gauge in terms of strength and capacity. It was not the sultan or the grand vizier who fought the wars; it was rather the state's army under the supervision and direction of these leaders. Therefore, my interpretation of army mutinies and riots to obtain more pay or even to depose a sultan or unseat a grand vizier are also distinct from traditional interpretations. These mutinies were not threats that could destroy the state; they were coups that were dealt with by state officials. In fact, there was no attempt to overthrow the House of Osman until 1687–88, when a radical movement to bring an outsider to the throne emerged briefly.

The viability of revolt casts light on the sociological interpretations of the Ottoman seventeenth century that have sprung up recently. Unlike Jack Goldstone's interpretation that the Ottoman state experienced a few severe cases of state breakdown, I find no evidence of setbacks of this magnitude. As I have demonstrated, there is no evidence of the elements necessary for state breakdown as Goldstone defines it: no elite revolts and no popular uprisings. And, as I have repeatedly shown, the third necessary component of state breakdown, intraelite struggle, actually worked to consolidate state strength, because it was mostly produced by state actions and diverted attention away from the state. The Ottoman state was able to avoid severe breakdowns by simultaneously creating conflict among elites and absorbing some elites into the state bureaucracy. It managed crises; it did not fold under them. As such, the Ottoman case is different from the European states Goldstone analyses, France and England (although these two remain very different from each other). Therefore, the Ottoman case cannot be stretched to fit Goldstone's western model of state breakdown.[3] The specific historical events Goldstone presents as markers of state breakdown actually resulted in state-society bargains that consolidated state power.

As a result of such complex and unpredictable consolidation strategies, and with the rise of banditry and the development of a state policy of incorporation through negotiation, the western distinctions between legitimacy and illegitimacy became blurred. In fact, as the sole source of legitimacy, the state used its legitimacy as a powerful weapon in its consolidation. The genius of Ottoman state policy was to define the bandits as outside the realm of legitimacy by calling them celalis (a reference to a dangerous sixteenth-century rebel) and then incorporating them selectively. There is nothing new about the state holding the keys to legitimacy in the empire. Rather, what is new and interesting is that the state did not follow strict rules as to the handing out of legitimate positions; instead, it distributed positions creatively for its political purposes. It should be added that this process did not jeopardize the state as long as the distribution of rewards to illegitimate officials was temporary, calculated, and reversable. For all its flexibility, the state remained the arbiter of legitimacy, bolstering its position even by incorporating its potential challengers.

Traditional historians who do not see the calculated aspect of state policies at this time argue that the Ottoman state was weak. Accordingly, the deals the Ottoman state made with bandit leaders are described as originating from a position of weakness rather than of strength. Ottoman rulers had no other choice, say historians, because they had to fight their foreign enemies. The position I take differs: where many historians see weakness, I see strength. The Ottoman state combined military strength with cultural legitimation. In the crucial period of the seventeenth century, the state was able to manipulate both these strengths to increase its bargaining power vis-à-vis most societal groups, old and new. Most vivid

[3]For example, I dwell on 1589 as the movement of soldiers in Istanbul, attempting to reestablish more firmly the control of the sultan. This brief interlude did not represent a breakdown of the state; the state did not stop functioning; elites were not rebelling against the state. Elite troops were demanding more intervention from the sultan; see Chapter 2. For Goldstone's breakdown dates, see *Revolution and Rebellion in the Early Modern World* (Berkeley, 1991), p. 350.

were the examples of bargaining with bandits. The Ottoman policies of incorporation of bandits were policies of strength. They originated from a need to incorporate more armies into the war effort against the Habsburgs or the Persians, as well as from the need to undermine the regional strength these bandits could acquire if left to their own devices. The state in the Ottoman Empire was strong since it was able to preempt potentially disruptive action by the bandits as well as exploit it when it became important.

It is interesting that those traditional historians who see rebellion in the actions of the celalis never stop to consider the question of whether these rebellions were crushed or not. They never ask this question because the answer in history would contradict their description of these events as rebellions. If a state experiences revolts against itself, it is natural that it will try to destroy all rebels as well as potential contenders. Ottoman history demonstrates that state officials were far more interested in containing chaos in using bandit/mercenaries for military purposes. Only when they were not entirely useful did the state engage in the destruction of these groups. Otherwise, it maintained the practice that fed more soldiers into its warring armies. Not only was there rarely annihilation of so-called rebels, but there was also no larger-scale attempt at altering the structural conditions that gave rise to banditry. Some Ottoman institutions were restructured at periods of consolidation; yet none of the practices that led to banditry were altered. In fact, continuing my analysis where we left off would demonstrate many other cases of similar origin.

Most historians argue that the seventeenth century established the institutions that led to the decentralization of the eighteenth century. The state practices of the seventeenth century are described as sowing the seeds of decentralization. Again, I disagree. None of the deals of the seventeenth century led to decentralization in the later periods. First, the deals that were made were broken. Second, the deals that were made were either with bandits or with governors and governor-generals, all state personnel who were regularly rotated. As long as an official was rotated, he ensured himself of a good deal for a while and did not threaten the state with decentralization. Similarly, although careful attention was paid to the issue of households, that a vizier assembled a large household did not threaten the state with decentralization. Decentralization only occurred when the men who made deals or gathered armies became permanent inhabitants of a region and used their deals and their armies to acquire regional benefits and autonomy from the state. The eighteenth century clearly experienced this phenomenon, since those who became power holders were notables; a mixed group consisting of janissaries with local occupations, local notables, and even judges who were no longer rotated. They were all members of regional society and had an interest in the maintenance of the region and even in the acquisition of autonomy. This was not the case in the seventeenth century, when the Ottoman state consolidated territory and authority over groups. The "rebellions" of the seventeenth century are the fictions of historians.

Finally, to return to the comparative perspective, the results of this study are in a sense counterintuitive. Throughout the seventeenth century the Ottoman state appeared weaker than the French, which was steadily and carefully moving toward a centralized administration. The Ottoman state, in contrast, was moving toward a similar goal by leaps and halts, erratically and at times giving false impression of weakness. Yet the Ottoman state was strong and outlasted the French ancien régime, having benefited from being more creative and less constrained by strict rules regarding centralized administration.

The Ottoman state proved to be more flexible than brittle. At each stage it paid attention to the socioeconomic structures of the empire and took steps that enhanced its own goals in the context of the societal forces. In part this attention to the regional structures of control, to the economic and societal forces at play, came from the sheer size of the empire. It is possible to argue that the greater size of the Ottoman Empire forced the state to bend more and to devise strategy by adaptation to the latest regional developments. Creative strategizing, a clear by-product of the size of the empire then, was of benefit to the state. And the best way the Ottoman state devised to do just that was to become the state as bargainer par excellence—bargaining to co-opt and to incorporate, embodying within itself potential forces of contention. This strategy whereby inclusion into the state became the singly desirable reward worked to enhance the state's control over its vast territory.

The Ottoman strategy of incorporation was a far cry from the European state makers' agenda. In France, the state first worked to exclude from the realm of the state all the regional power holders, and only much later did it develop the policy and ideology of inclusion. By then the French state had been toppled and replaced through a bloody revolution. The western states therefore could have benefited from the Ottoman example, but they (and many analysts) did not see it for what it was, as strength rather than weakness. And even if correctly understood, the Ottoman route would likely have seemed below the rigid dignity of European monarchs. It is quite difficult to imagine Louis XIII or Louis XIV sitting at his desk scribbling, "This goes too far; is it possible to give this much?" on the letter from a bandit leader, or any rebel for that matter. It is probable that a letter of this kind would have never reached the French monarch in the first place. But Ahmed I was willing to listen and, if necessary, to bargain openly with those he declared to be celalis, bandits.

Appendix 1

The Study Area

Two western Anatolian communities, the provinces of Aydın and Saruhan, represent the areas under investigation. These were relatively wealthy regions of the empire, with sections reserved as the crown lands assigned to the princes of the empire. These regions are interesting for a variety of reasons. First of all, both Aydın and Saruhan were central regions under the control of the Ottoman Empire for the period under investigation. In fact, they remained under Ottoman control until the end of World War I and were reintegrated after the War of Independence. In that sense, they are core Ottoman provinces, with many other advantages for study.

I chose to focus on Aydın and Saruhan after careful investigation aimed at identifying two relatively similar regions about which there were primary and secondary sources of evidence that could be brought to bear on my substantive questions. The selected areas therefore had to have sources of evidence on the nature and mechanics of the provincial administration, the transformation of this administration, the agricultural mode of production, village- and town-level social organization, administration and networks of interaction, trade, cooperation, and intermarriage, as well as state-level and popular information and documentation on banditry, social movements, and military and paramilitary activities. Along all these dimensions, Aydın and Saruhan were the areas with the richest amount of information. These provinces were largely agricultural and were areas where the importance of the traditional system of provincial administration (the tımar system) and the micro level agricultural unit of production (the *çifthane* system) cannot be underestimated. Therefore, most of the regulations vis-à-vis provincial administration, assessments of land tenure, and the changes in agriculture and its techniques applied to these regions. Situated not far from the center of power and yet within good traveling distance to warrant some organization from the state as well as from the regional authorities, Aydın and Saruhan seem to be ideal for investigation in geopolitical terms. Furthermore, these are two regions with no peasant rebellions (I claim the absence of peasant rebellion for all the Ottoman Empire) which were instead severely affected by small-scale banditry. Movements of banditry originated in many districts of Saruhan, and travelers' reports as well as official texts document this quite vividly. Banditry in these regions remained regional, however, and did not diffuse to other areas of the empire. Occasionally, the region underwent the infiltration of more powerful and organized bandits from the east, who overwhelmed the Anatolian countryside and inflicted much damage on the area of our concern.

Aydın and Saruhan were two relatively wealthy, productive regions of the empire, with medium-sized towns, Tire and Manisa, into which flowed grains and other agricultural products from villages. The regions thereby provided an opportunity to study networks of communication between villages and between villages and towns. I paid particular attention to this fact, since choosing the most isolated of provinces with no central towns would bias the investigation in favor of my hypothesis that rural communities were not very well connected. These provinces were, then, carefully selected regions where the economic self-sufficiency of the villages and the lack of a larger town to supply did not lead to social and political isolation.

Last, Aydın and Saruhan are provinces with comparable amounts of data on provincial structure and land transfers, with the town of Manisa in Saruhan having particularly rich court records. The land registers are of more erratic nature, but land registers in the seventeenth century were quickly becoming a luxury. Added to the variety of documentation is the fact that, especially on Saruhan, there were a variety of written texts from travelers providing descriptions of banditry.

The Province of Saruhan

The province of Saruhan in the sixteenth century contained thirteen administrative districts (*kaza*): Manisa, Menemen, Marmara, Gordos, Nif, Ilıca, Adala, Mendehorya (Tarhaniyet), Demirci, Kayacık, Akhisar, Gör-

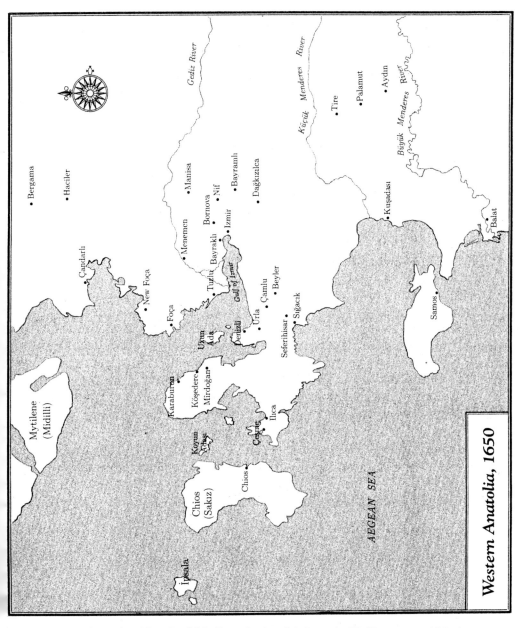

Map 2. Reproduced from Daniel Goffman, *Izmir and the Levantine World, 1550–1650*, published by the University of Washington Press, copyright © 1990 by the University of Washington Press and used by permission.

dük, and Güzelhisar. Data on land and land transfers were recorded for these administrative districts.

The administrative district of Manisa, for which most of the data were collected, comprised five smaller administrative districts (*nahiye*): Manisa, Doğanhisarı, Canşa, Palamut, and Yengi, according to the 1531 register. These in turn comprised 150 villages and eleven periodic settlements (*mezra'*as). After some population growth and internal administrative reorganization, the district of Manisa in *1575* comprised *132* villages and fourteen periodic settlements. These were to be found within the boundaries of six small administrative districts, the *nahiyes* of Manisa, Belen, Emlak, Palamud, Yengi, and Yundağı. A district such as Palamud which experienced a dramatic rise in the number of villages did not do so just because of population growth but rather as a result of the redrawing of administrative districts.[1]

The district of Manisa, located in the lower Gediz valley, embraces several fertile valleys and rich river basins, particularly the Bakırçayı and Kumçayı basins. Settlements stretch from these rich river basins to the slopes of three mountains, Manisa Dağı (Sipil Dağı), Çaldağı, and Yund dağı. The three mountains encircle the plain of Manisa, providing room for a variety of villages scattered on the plain and others strewn over the hillsides, looking out over the plateau. From this hub of the province, settlements stretched out in different directions along river basins, making the most of nature's gifts, yet periodically relocating after floods and forcing tax collectors to draw and redraw administrative boundaries. As villages grew to develop into important regional market areas, they imposed their name onto administrative districts, therefore alerting us to regional socioeconomic transformations of import. Feridun Emecen points to one such administrative change for Turgutlu, which earned administrative district status as it developed a major market.[2]

Overall, the province of Saruhan was able to handle the production of key grains and produce and to intensify production during the sixteenth century (as demonstrated by the comparison of the 1531 and 1575 registers) in response to population growth. The area produced wheat, barley, millet, rye, oats, lentils, and chickpeas, especially in the regions around Manisa, with wheat produced foremost in the Yengi and Palamud regions. Cotton (especially in Palamut and Yengi), rice, tobacco, and grapes, pri-

---

[1] Feridun Emecen, *XVI. Asırda Manisa Kazası* (Ankara, 1989), pp. 111–13.

[2] Ibid., pp. 113–14. See also Çağatay Uluçay, "Manisa," *Islam Ansiklopedisi*, (Istanbul 1945), p. 288.

marily marketable goods, were produced in this region.[3] Among the 132 villages, 70 of them engaged in rice cultivation and therefore were dependent on capital investment in waterways and irrigation as well as a steady and ample supply of water. As registers of the region indicate, this was not always a simple process; often, rather wide fluctuations in ecological conditions, the cold and arid winters, droughts, and locust infestations, caused variation in the level of production. Emecen calculates that the annual wheat and barley subsistence per person dropped in the sixteenth century, no doubt due to population growth outstripping increased production.[4]

The Saruhan registers also demonstrate that the entire population of the villages was not sedentary; there was a large nomadic and seminomadic element engaged in animal husbandry. Therefore, a mixed peasant-nomad economy predominated. By the end of the sixteenth century, parts of this population, especially in the region to the southeast of Manisa, were settling and becoming sedentary.

The central town of the Saruhan province, Manisa, to the south of the Gediz river on the lower slopes of Manisa Dağı (Sipil), counted 1995 taxpayers, with a total population of at least 7,000 people.[5] Manisa was known for its cotton markets and the type of leather named after it (indicating that some tanneries or some sort of leather production must have existed). The importance of this town in the late sixteenth and early seventeenth centuries can be attested from the number of pious foundation (vakıf) shops (according to Suraiya Faroqhi between two and three hundred) and the caravans that came from Iran with merchants, referred to as *acem tüccarı*. According to Faroqhi, in Manisa these people were prominent enough to get protection from the state vis-à-vis the local governor.[6]

As can be seen in the sixteenth-century registers, the market dues (*bac-ı pazar*) of Manisa formed part of the crown lands (has) assigned to princes of the empire. Yuzo Nagata, looking at the taxes in the 1531 registers, concludes that Manisa was not very developed and that its development was geared toward the agricultural hinterlands. He makes this point because *bac-ı pazar* taxes were not very high and only an oil mill, a *boza* beverage

---

[3]Yuzo Nagata, "16. Yüzyılda Manisa Köyleri," *Istanbul Üniversitesi Edebiyat Fakültesi Tarih Dergisi* 32 (1979): 751.

[4]Emecen, *XVI Asırda Manisa*, p. 243.

[5]Suraiya Faroqhi, *Towns and Townsmen of Ottoman Anatolia* (Cambridge, 1984), p. 303.

[6]Ibid., pp. 32–55. Information on the *acem tüccarı* was also retrieved from the Manisa court records, Registers 102, 104.

shop, and a candle store appear in relation to this tax.[7] Faroqhi's interpretation is different. She argues that during the late sixteenth and early seventeenth centuries the productive potential of this area and the coastlands was directed toward internal and even international trade. Cotton, wool, and leather became the major valuable exports of this area. In Manisa, cultivation of cotton increased, and the town was developing a reputation for woolens and other cloths such as broadcloth (çuha).[8] Faroqhi also cites an observer who visited Manisa in the very early eighteenth century and declared that the only activity of commercial import was the cotton trade.[9]

The Province of Aydın

Much less documentation has come down through the centuries related to Aydın, partly because of major fires in the central towns of this province. Especially the absence of court records from Tire or Izmir makes it rather difficult to piece together the life in the towns and villages of this province. Historians have assembled part of the history of this area from land records and taxation records; there is, however, a lifelessness to this information. The province of Aydın comprised eleven administrative districts in the sixteenth century: Köşk, Tire, Sart, Alaşehir, Birgi, Kozhisar, Beyşehir, Bozdoğan, Arpaz, Sultanhisarı, and Yenişehir. Before Izmir developed at the end of the century to eclipse other towns in the region, Tire was the most important center of the province. The town of Tire counted a tax-paying population of 2,374 in the late sixteenth century.[10]

The province of Aydın is naturally divided into two large river basins, those of Küçük Menderes to the north and Büyük Menderes to the south, creating two very rich alluvial plains naturally circumscribed by mountain ranges. The town of Tire is situated on the plain fed by Küçük Menderes, in between the Boz Dağları range (especially the mountain of Çalıbaba) to the north and Aydın Dağları to the south. Along the river banks of Büyük Menderes, small towns such as Aydın and Sultanhisarı developed slightly. These are not dealt with in the literature because they do not seem to have had marketplaces of their own. Faroqhi derives much of the agricultural and productive activity of this region from what appeared in the markets

---

[7]Nagata, "16. Yüzyılda Manisa," p. 734.

[8]Faroqhi, *Towns and Townsmen*, p. 137.

[9]The observer is Pitton de Tournefort, ibid., p. 120.

[10]Ibid., p. 303.

of Tire and other towns. She argues that cotton production and rice cultivation must have been important given their recurrent mention in regulations regarding sales to the merchants and weavers of Tire. The
neighboring towns of Akçeşehir and Aydın-Güzelhisar were the main areas where yarns were spun. There was then a road between Aydın-
Güzelhisar and Tire much traveled by caravans carrying goods. Moreover,
chestnuts, apples, grapes, and many other fruits made their way to the
market in Tire.[11]

In the western Anatolian hinterland, in a well-defined area to the south
of the plain created by Küçük Menderes and north of the Aydın mountains, Tire became a central town with large markets, *hans* and *kervansarays,* attracting trade and merchants from beyond the empire. Apart from
the productive gardens and orchards around the town itself, the surrounding fields produced cotton, tobacco, sesame, and a variety of fruits. The
town was quite developed according to many travelers who reported on
its conditions, size, and livelihood.[12] According to Faroqhi, Tire in this
century could count between 500 and 599 *vakıf* shops. She writes that
"Halil Yahşi Bey b. Abdullah, one of Sultan Murad II's commanders, constructed a mosque in Tire which is still extant . . . Yet with more than 120
stores it surpassed most other foundations of western and central Anatolia
with respect to the number of business properties associated with it."[13] To
demonstrate further the importance of cotton thread in Tire, she cites a
petition from Tire in which local weavers maintained that cotton thread
produced in this region found its way to Venice and to Spain and could be
found in markets there.[14]

[11]Ibid., pp. 29–32.
[12]Hrand D. Andreasyan, "Ermeni Seyyahı Polonyalı Simeon'un Seyyahatnamesi (1608–
1619)," *Türkiyat Mecmuası* 10 (1953). Evliya Çelebi also mentions this town.
[13]Faroqhi, *Towns and Townsmen*, p. 35.
[14]Ibid., p. 136.

Appendix 2

Primary Sources from the Ottoman Archives

I PRESENT INFORMATION FOR TWO SIGNIFICANT PERIODS, collecting data on land tenure, timar and other provincial appointments, and court affairs for the periods 1572–82 and 1654–55. I chose these two periods because between them, in 1632–34, Sultan Murad IV ordered a reorganization and revamping of the provincial system.

Tapu Tahrir Registers

These are the population surveys carried out after the conquest of an area by the Ottomans. They were regularly checked by state officials assigned to bring them up to date and became the basis of the information Ottoman historians acquired on population, taxation, administration, and agriculture in specific areas. They are of two kinds, detailed registers (*mufassal*) and summary registers (*icmal*), according to the detail of the information provided. The detailed registers "list by town quarter and by village the names of the adult males, the different taxes levied, the estimated income from each, and whether the revenues calculated from each source were destined for the sultan's treasury, for the salaries of his cavalry officers and provincial governors, or for the upkeep of a particular pious foundation."[1]

These are not totally accurate sources of information. They have a variety of problems, many of which have been aptly presented by Amy

[1] Amy Singer, "Tapu Tahrir Defterleri and Kadı Sicilleri: A Happy Marriage of Sources," *Tarih* 1 (1990):97.

Singer in her article on these sources.[2] One is of particular significance for this study. The registration process relied on the tımar holder to bring the peasants under his jurisdiction to the officials in charge of recording. Yet, as many have warned, this led to a degree of underreporting. Furthermore, in this book I provide information that questions whether the tımar holder even knew his peasants. We must therefore seriously wonder about the population figures in these registers.

I have used a few of these registers for Aydın and Saruhan for both periods under investigation. Although I was not interested in general population figures, I used these registers to identify settled and nomadic communities, the movements from nomadic to settled, and the movements from villages to temporary settlements (*mezra'a*). Furthermore, these registers helped provide a general overview of the communities under investigation. Although I did not use the taxation, production, or population figures formally, I assessed them to describe and understand the communities. I used military registers to cross-check tımar and zeamet holders with other sources of information. Register 516 is the summary register for Aydın in 1572. Arranged by individual has, zeamet, and tımar holders, the register provides their income, briefly describing the settled or nomadic community and the type of income (from trade, agriculture, etc.) Register 683 (1582) provides the lists of tımar and zeamet holders in Saruhan. Finally, Register 786 (1655), also of military nature, provides the information for both provinces on land distribution.

Ruznamçe Registers

These were by far the most important registers for the study of regional elites and especially state-elite interaction. Whereas the *tapu tahrir* registers have been widely used, the *ruznamçe* have not been exploited with the same attention. Data were collected on tımar bestowals from 1550 to 1650 from the *ruznamçe* registers in the Archives of the Prime Ministry in Istanbul. Douglas Howard describes these registers: "*Ruznamçe* means 'daybook'; these registers contain the daily records of the *Defter-i haqani*, the Ottoman Imperial Registry. They are a chronological record of certificates (*tezkeres*) for *tımars, ziamets,* and *hasses* issued by the *beglerbegi* or by the central administration, and received at the *Defter-i haqani*."[3] These

---

[2]Ibid., pp. 95–125.
[3]Douglas Howard, "The Ottoman *Tımar* System and Its Transformation, 1563–1656," Ph.D. diss., Indiana University, 1987, p. 42.

registers turn out to be a mine of information on the timar system and have been used only sparsely.[4]

The format of these registers and of each entry is quite clear. First, both the date of entry into the register and the bestowal date are entered, making it easier to check for sampling biases. Preceding the date of entry is information about the location of the timar, the new possessor (with his name and rank, position, and sometimes father's name), and sometimes the name of the previous possessor, if there is one and if he is known. The next section in the entry is a listing of the revenues of the timar, by village or any other source, with a final total of the timar holder's share. Finally, this information is brought to life by a paragraph explaining the circumstances of the bestowal, the process of bestowal, and the date of bestowal.

For the first period under consideration, I used three registers: BBA Ruznamçe 37 (980/1572), 46 (984/1576), and 59 (990/1582).[5] Dates were recorded for each entry, and one of every ten entries was fully recorded. For each entry, then, the date of transfer as well as the date of entry into the register was recorded. This method was used to check for eventual underrepresentation or overrepresentation of the sample. No adjustments were deemed necessary. From the three registers examined, 42 cases (10 percent) for Aydın and 45 cases (10 percent) for Saruhan were fully recorded and used in the analysis.

For the second period, sampling was different. In these registers, since the handwriting was very bad, sampling was not carried out by choice. All entries I was able to read completely (with no missing data) were included; the others were not used. Furthermore, no procedure was used to check for the representativeness of the sample. I assumed that there was no particular reason for the exceptionally bad handwriting but the scribe himself or concerns related to space. It should also be noted that in this second period the date of entry into the register was either missing or unreadable. Again I examined three registers, and 23 cases (39 percent) for Aydın and 31 cases (43 percent) for Saruhan were fully recorded and used

---

[4]The following are the only publications I am aware of: Lajos Fekete, *Die Siyaqat Schrift in der Turkischen Finanzverwaltung* (Budapest 1955); Bistra Cvetkova, ed., *Turski Izvorni za Bulgarskata Istoriia*, Vol. 3 (Sofia, 1968), pp. 145–86; I. Beldiceanu-Steinherr, M. Berendei, and G. Veinstein, "Attribution du timar dans le province de Trébizonde (fin du XVᵉ siècle)," *Turcica* 8 (1976): 279–90; I. Metin Kunt, *The Sultan's Servants: The Transformation of Ottoman Provincial Government, 1550–1650* (New York, 1983); Douglas Howard, "The BBA Ruznamçe Tasnifi: A New Resource for the Study of the Ottoman Timar System," *Turkish Studies Association Bulletin* 10 (1986): 12–19, and "The Ottoman Timar System."

[5]These were selected because they were close to each other in time and because they contained enough data for each area.

in the analysis. The following three registers were used: BBA Ruznamçe 676 (1064/1655), 681 (1065/1655), and 685 (1065/1655).[6] In the comparison of the two periods it should also be mentioned that the 10-year study (1572–82) versus 1-year study (1654–55) is not intentional. There simply were no other registers for the second period that were legible.

Kadı Sicilleri

The *kadı sicils* are the court records from all the transactions a judge carried out during his tenure. They range from family (marriage, dowry agreements, divorce settlements, inheritance) to land (copies of imperial land registers, land disputes) to commerce (issues of credit and loans, prices, weights, measures) to tax collection (land taxes, market, pious foundation taxes) to personal and criminal issues. The office of the local judge was organized according to regional jurisdictions of somewhere between 100 and 150 villages. These 100 villages were further subdivided into ten smaller jurisdictions to which the judge sent deputies to handle routine matters. The judge held his court in the central town, with villagers coming to him from everywhere under his jurisdiction.

I put these records to various uses. Reading through the cases, I developed a sense of what the struggles were in rural communities. I gathered many stories of conflict, cooperation, and exchange from these records, some of which I used as vignettes to illustrate definite points. The court records were my main source of information on commercial ties and on conflict and cooperation within and across villages. The court records for part of Saruhan are available at the Manisa Museum (Manisa Etnografya Müzesi), but those for the region of Aydın are not available. Therefore, for the analysis of social interaction in rural communities I restricted myself to the city of Manisa and the villages under the jurisdiction of the kadı of Manisa. I used five registers, two from the first period, Registers 11 and 12, and three from the second, Registers 102, 104 and 106. Since these registers contain at least as much if not more information on internal city affairs, I had to weed out those cases and concentrate on cases across Manisa and villages, and within villages. I discarded cases if damage to the paper or a particularly difficult script made it impossible to understand the context.

The *kadı sicils* are a biased source. First, only those cases that are conflictual or require court registration appear overwhelmingly in the

---

[6]There were no registers for 1650. These three were the closest to my cut-off date.

records. Therefore, conflict is overrepresented in this sort of data. Also, cases that were resolved at the village level by family members or friends do not appear, introducing a sampling bias into the data. Furthermore, since court appearance required a fee, only those who could afford to pay this fee took their matter to court. Presumably, others tried to resolve their conflict within the villages, by asking the village elders to adjudicate. This was certainly true for some matters, since they came to court despite their original reliance on village elders; here the plaintiff or defendant explained that the more trusted members of the village were unable to solve their differences and therefore they had to appeal to the court. Distance from the court must have had an impact on the number of cases that reached it.[7] This is not to limit the role of the court. On the contrary, I think that the Ottoman courts were regularly and repeatedly used by the people. This is corroborated by the fact even Christian peasants who had their own internal justice system—according to the *millet* system of minority administration—consulted the Islamic judge and delivered their claims to the authority of the religious Islamic law, the *Shari'a*.

Mühimme Registers

These represent the sultan's orders in response to conflicts, problems, or questions that arose in the provinces. They are interesting sources since they summarize the problem and then provide the order of the state. But since they are summaries of state versions of the provincial situation, their reliability must be questioned. The best way to check for such problems of reliability is to compare the issues with those mentioned in the histories of the time. I use a selection of *mühimmes* from the Başbakanlık Archives as well as from published works in order to assess state responses to certain known regional conflicts. I also use them to assess the state's language in referring to different types of regional actors: religious students, bandits, and provincial officials.[8]

---

[7]For more information on the *kadı sicils*, see Singer, "Tapu Tahrir Defterleri and Kadı Sicilleri."

[8]For more information on *mühimme* registers, see Uriel Heyd, *Ottoman Documents on Palestine, 1552–1615: A Study of the Firman According to the Mühimme Defteri* (Oxford, 1960).

Bibliography

Primary Sources, Archival

National Archives

Başbakanlık Arşivi, Istanbul.
  Ali Emiri Tasnifi 456, 457, 459, 616
  Cevdet Dahiliye 516
  Kamil Kepeci 262, 266
  Maliyeden Müdevver 563
  Mühimme 31, 36, 48, 71, 73, 78, 79
  Tımar Ruznamçe 37, 46, 59, 676, 681, 685
  Tapu Tahrir 516, 683, 786
Topkapı Sarayı Arşivi, Istanbul. Documents E 721/83, E 721/84, E 721/96, E 2387, E 2459, E 4642, E 4732, E 5795, E 8400/47, E 8806, E 10758/1, E 11845/12

Regional Archives

Manisa Etnografya Müzesi, Manisa. Kadı Sicilleri 11, 12, 102, 104, 106

Miscellaneous

Kanun-name-i Osmani bera-yi Tımar Daden, Bibliothèque Nationale, Paris, A. F. Turc 41.
The Turkish Letters of Ogier Ghiselin de Busbecq. Trans. E. S. Forster. Oxford 1927.

Primary Sources, Narratives, and Advice Literature

Ayn-i Ali Efendi. *Kavanin i Al-i Osman der Hülasa-yi Mezamin-i Defter-i Divan.* Ed. Tayyib Gökbilgin. Istanbul: Kalem Yayınları Matbaası, 1979.

Aziz Efendi. *Kanun-name-i Sultani li Aziz Efendi, Aziz Efendi's Book of Sultanic Laws and Regulations: An Agenda for Reform by a Seventeenth-Century Ottoman Statesman.* Ed. and trans. Rhoads Murphey. Sources of Oriental Languages and Literature no. 9. Cambridge: Harvard University Press, 1985.

Kitab-i Müstetab. Ed. Yaşar Yücel. Ankara: n.p., 1974.

Koçi Bey. *Risale.* Ed. Zuhuri Danışman. Istanbul: Milli Eğitim Basımevi, 1972.

Naima, Mustafa. *Tarih-i Naima.* 6 vols. Istanbul, 1283/1866–67.

Peçevi, Ibrahim. *Tarih-i Peçevi.* 6 vols. Istanbul, 1283/1866–67. Reprint, Istanbul: Enderun Kitabevi, 1980.

Selâniki, Mustafa Efendi. *Tarih-i-Selâniki* (1003–1008/1595–1600). Ed. Mehmed Ipşirli. 2 vols. Istanbul: Edebiyat Fakültesi Basımevi, 1989.

Topçular Kâtibi Abdülkadir. *Vekayii Tarihiye,* Süleymaniye Esad Efendi no. 2151.

Vasıtı. *Kuyucu Murad Paşa Vukuatı Tarihi.* Süleymaniye Esad Efendi no. 2236/1.

Secondary Sources, General

Adas, Michael. "From Avoidance to Confrontation: Peasant Protest in Precolonial and Colonial Southeast Asia." *Comparative Study of Society and History* 23 (1981):217–47.

Anderson, Perry. *Lineages of the Absolutist State.* London: Verso, 1979.

———. *Passages from Antiquity to Feudalism.* London: Verso, 1978.

Armstrong, John A. "Old Regime Governors: Bureaucratic and Patrimonial Attributes." *Comparative Studies in Society and History* 14 (1972): 2–29.

Aston, Trevor, ed. *Crisis in Europe, 1560–1660.* New York: Basic Books, 1965.

Avrich, Paul. *Russian Rebels, 1600–1800.* New York: W. W. Norton, 1972.

Barkey, Karen. "Rebellious Alliances: The State and Peasant Unrest in Early 17th-Century France and the Ottoman Empire." *American Sociological Review,* 56 (1991):699–715.

———. "The Uses of Court Records in the Reconstruction of Village Networks: A Comparative Perspective." *International Journal of Comparative Sociology* 32 (1991):196–216.

Bendix, Reinhard. *Nation-Building and Citizenship.* Berkeley: University of California Press, 1977.

Bercé, Yves-Marie. *Revolt and Revolution in Early Modern Europe.* New York: St. Martin's Press, 1987.

———. *Révoltes et révolutions dans l'Europe moderne (XVIe–XVIIIe siècles).* Paris: Presses Universitaires de France, 1980.

Bettez Gravel, Pierre. "Of Bandits and Pirates: An Essay on the Vicarious Insurgency of Peasants." *Journal of Political and Military Sociology* 13 (1985):209–17.

Bloch, Marc. *Feudal Society,* Vol. 1: *The Growth of Ties of Dependence;* Vol. 2: *Social Classes and Political Organization.* Trans. L. A. Manyon. Chicago: University of Chicago Press, 1961.

———. *The Historian's Craft.* New York: Vintage Books, 1953.

Blok, Anton. *The Mafia of a Sicilian Village, 1860–1960: A Study of Violent Peasant Entrepreneurs*. Prospect Heights, Ill.: Waveland Press, 1974.

——. "The Peasant and the Brigand: Social Banditry Reconsidered." *Comparative Studies in Society and History* 14 (1972):494–504.

Braudel, Fernand. *The Mediterranean and the Mediterranean World in the Age of Philip II*. 2 vols. New York: Harper and Row, 1972.

Brenner, Robert. "Agrarian Class Structure and Economic Development in Pre-Industrial Europe. *Past and Present* 70 (1976):30–75.

Bright, Charles, and Susan Harding, eds. *Statemaking and Social Movements: Essays on History and Theory*. Ann Arbor: University of Michigan Press, 1984.

Brown, Nathan. "Brigands and State Building: The Invention of Banditry in Modern Egypt." *Comparative Studies in Society and History* 32 (1990):258–81.

Brustein, William. "Class Conflict and Class Collaboration in Regional Rebellions, 1500–1700." *Theory and Society* 14 (1985):445–68.

Brustein, William, and Margaret Levi. "The Geography of Rebellion: Rulers, Rebels, and Regions, 1500 to 1700." *Theory and Society* 16(1987):467–95.

Childs, John. *Armies and Warfare in Europe, 1648–1789*. New York: Holmes and Meier, 1982.

Chirot, Daniel. "The Rise of the West." *American Sociological Review* 50 (1984):181–95.

Coveney, P. J., ed. *France in Crisis, 1620–1675*. Totowa, N.J.: Rowman and Littlefield, 1977.

Davies, C. S. L. "Peasant Revolt in France and England: A Comparison." *Agricultural History Review* 21 (1973):122–34.

——. "Les révoltes populaires en Angleterre (1500–1700)." *Annales: Economies, sociétés, civilisations* 24 (1969):24–60.

De windt, Edwin B. *Land and People in Holywell-cum-Needingworth: Structures of Tenure and Patterns of Social Organization in the East Midlands Village, 1252–1457*. Toronto: Pontifical Institute of Mediaeval Studies, 1972.

Duara, Prasenjit. *Culture, Power, and the State: Rural North China, 1900–1942*. Stanford: Stanford University Press, 1988.

Dunn, Richard S. *The Age of Religious Wars, 1559–1715*. New York: W. W. Norton, 1979.

Eisenstadt, S. N. "Bureaucracy, Bureaucratization, and Debureaucratization." *Administrative Science Quarterly* 4 (1959):302–20.

——, ed. *The Decline of Empires*. Englewood Cliffs, N.J.: Prentice Hall, 1967.

Evans, Peter, Dietrich Rueschemeyer, and Theda Skocpol, eds. *Bringing the State Back In*. Cambridge: Cambridge University Press, 1985.

Foster, Robert, and Jack P. Greene, eds. *Preconditions of Revolution in Early Modern Europe*. Baltimore: Johns Hopkins University Press, 1970.

Fulbrook, Mary. *Piety and Politics: Religion and the Rise of Absolutism in England, Württemberg, and Prussia*. Cambridge: Cambridge University Press, 1983.

Goldstone, Jack A. *Revolution and Rebellion in the Early Modern World*. Berkeley: University of California Press, 1991.

Goubert, Pierre. *L'ancien régime*, Vol. 1: *La société*. Paris: Armand Colin, 1969.

——. *The French Peasantry in the Seventeenth Century.* Cambridge: Cambridge University Press, 1986.

——. *Louis XIV and Twenty Million Frenchmen.* New York: Vintage Books, 1970.

Granovetter, Mark S. "The Strength of Weak Ties." *American Journal of Sociology* 78 (1973):1360–80.

Hintze, Otto. *The Historical Essays.* In Vol. 4, *The Formation of States and Constitutional Development: A Study in History and Politics,* ed. Felix Gilbert. New York: Oxford University Press, 1975.

Hobsbawm, Eric J. *Bandits.* New York: Pantheon Books, 1981.

——. "The Crisis of the Seventeenth Century." *Past and Present,* nos. 5–6 (1954):33–53, 44–65.

——. "The General Crisis of the European Economy in the Seventeenth Century." *Past and Present,* no. 5 (1954):33–63.

——. "Peasants and Politics." *Journal of Peasant Studies* 1 (1973):1–15.

——. *Primitive Rebels.* New York: W. W. Norton, 1959.

Hobsbawm, Eric J., and George Rudé. *Captain Swing: A Social History of the Great English Agricultural Uprising of 1830.* New York: W. W. Norton, 1968.

Jones, A. H. M. "The Roman Colonate." *Past and Present,* no. 13 (1958):1–13.

Kautsky, John H. *Aristocratic Empires.* Chapel Hill: University of North Carolina Press, 1982.

Khazanov, A. M. *Nomads and the Outside World.* Trans. Julia Crookenden. Cambridge: Cambridge University Press, 1983.

Kuhn, Philip A. *Rebellion and Its Enemies in Late Imperial China: Militarization and Social Structure, 1796–1864.* Cambridge: Harvard University Press, 1980.

Lachmann, Richard. "Elite Conflict and State Formation in 16th and 17th Century England and France," *American Sociological Review* 54 (1989):141–62.

——. "Feudal Elite Conflict and the Origins of English Capitalism." *Politics and Society* 20 (1985):350–77.

——. *From Manor to Market: Structural Change in England, 1536–1640.* Madison: University of Wisconsin Press, 1987.

Ladurie, Emmanuel LeRoy. *The Peasants of Languedoc.* Chicago: University of Illinois Press, 1980.

Laitin, David D., Roger Petersen, and John W. Slocum, "Language and the State: Russia and the Soviet Union in Comparative Perspective." In *Thinking Theoretically about Soviet Nationalities: History and Comparison in the Study of the USSR,* ed. Alexander J. Motyl. New York: Columbia University Press, 1992.

Mann, Michael. *The Sources of Social Power,* Vol. 1: *A History of Power from the Beginning to A.D. 1760.* Cambridge: Cambridge University Press, 1986.

Markoff, John. "Governmental Bureaucratization: General Processes and an Anomalous Case." *Comparative Studies in Society and History* 17 (1975):479–503.

Menning, Bruce W. "The Emergence of a Military-Administrative Elite in the Don Cossack Land, 1708–1836." In *Russian Officialdom: The Bureaucratization of Russian Society from the Seventeenth to the Twentieth Century,* ed. Walter McKenzie Pintner and Don Karl Rowney. Chapel Hill: University of North Carolina Press, 1980.

Méthivier, H. "A Century of Conflict: The Economic and Social Disorders of the 'Grand Siècle.'" In *France in Crisis, 1620–1675,* ed. P. J. Coveney. Totowa, N.J.: Rowman & Littlefield, 1977.

Migdal, Joel S. *Peasants, Politics, and Revolution: Pressures toward Political and Social Change in the Third World.* Princeton: Princeton University Press, 1974.

———. *Strong Societies and Weak States.* Princeton: Princeton University Press, 1988.

Moore, Barrington, Jr. *Social Origins of Dictatorship and Democracy: Lord and Peasant in the Making of the Modern World.* Boston: Beacon Press, 1966.

Mousnier, Roland. "The Fronde." In *Preconditions of Revolution in Early Modern Europe,* ed. R. Forster and J. P. Greene. Baltimore: Johns Hopkins University Press, 1970.

———. *The Institutions of France under the Absolute Monarchy: 1598–1789.* 2 vols. Chicago: University of Chicago Press, 1979, 1984.

———. *Peasant Uprisings in the Seventeenth Century: France, Russia, and China,* trans. Brian Pearce. New York: Harper Torchbooks, 1970.

———. "Recherches sur les soulèvements populaires en France avant la Fronde." *Revue d'histoire moderne et contemporaine* 5 (1958):81–113.

O'Malley, Pat. "Social Bandits, Modern Capitalism, and the Traditional Peasantry: A Critique of Hobsbawm." *Journal of Peasant Studies* 6 (1979):489–501.

Paige, Jeffery M. *Agrarian Revolution.* New York: Free Press, 1975.

Parker, Geoffrey. *The Army of Flanders and the Spanish Road, 1567–1659: the Logistics of Spanish Victory and Defeat in the Low Countries' Wars.* Cambridge: Cambridge University Press, 1972.

———. *Europe in Crisis, 1598–1648.* Brighton: Harvester Press, 1980.

Parker, Geoffrey, and Lesley M. Smith. eds. *The General Crisis of the Seventeenth Century.* London: Rutledge & Kegan Paul, 1985.

Perry, Elizabeth J. *Rebels and Revolutionaries in North China, 1845–1945.* Stanford: Stanford University Press, 1980.

Pimsler, Martin. "Solidarity in the Medieval Village? The Evidence of Personal Pledging at Elton, Huntingdonshire." *Journal of British Studies* (1977) 17:1–11.

Popkin, Samuel L. *The Rational Peasant: The Political Economy of Rural Society in Vietnam.* Berkeley: University of California Press, 1979.

Porchnev, Boris. *Les soulèvements populaires en France au XVIIᵉ siècle.* Paris: Flammarion, 1972.

Raeff, Marc. "Patterns of Russian Imperial Policy toward the Nationalities." In *Soviet Nationality Problems,* ed. Edward Allworth. New York: Columbia University Press, 1971.

Root, Hilton L. *Peasants and King in Burgundy: Agrarian Foundations of French Absolutism.* Berkeley: University of California Press, 1987.

Rudolph, Susanne Hoeber. "Presidential Address: State Formation in Asia—Prolegomenon to a Comparative Study." *Journal of Asian Studies* 46 (1987):731–46.

Salmon, J. H. M. "Venality of Office and Popular Sedition in Seventeenth-Century France: A Review of a Controversy." *Past and Present* 37 (1967): 21–43.

Scott, James C. *Domination and the Arts of Resistance: Hidden Transcripts*. New Haven: Yale University Press, 1990.

——. *The Moral Economy of the Peasant*. New Haven: Yale University Press, 1976.

——. *Weapons of the Weak: Everyday Forms of Peasant Resistance*. New Haven: Yale University Press, 1985.

Sewell, William H., Jr. "Ideologies and Social Revolutions: Reflections on the French Case." *Journal of Modern History* 57 (1985):57–96.

——. "Marc Bloch and the Logic of Comparative History." *History and Theory* 6 (1967):208–18.

Skinner, G. William. "Marketing and Social Structure in Rural China.'" *Journal of Asian Studies* 24 (1964):3–43.

Skocpol, Theda. *States and Social Revolutions: A Comparative Analysis of France, Russia, and China*. Cambridge: Cambridge University Press, 1979.

Slatta, Richard W., ed. *Bandidos: The Varieties of Latin American Banditry*. New York: Greenwood Press, 1987.

Stinchcombe, Arthur L. *Constructing Social Theories*. New York: Harcourt, Brace, 1968.

——. *Theoretical Methods in Social History*. New York: Academic Press, 1978.

Tilly, Charles. *As Sociology Meets History*. New York: Academic Press, 1981.

——. *Coercion, Capital, and European States, AD 990–1990*. Oxford: Basil Blackwell, 1990.

——. *The Contentious French*. Cambridge: Belknap, 1986.

——. *From Mobilization to Revolution*. Reading, Mass.: Addison-Wesley, 1978.

——. "Social Movements and National Politics." In *State Making and Social Movements: Essays in History and Theory*, ed. Charles Bright and Susan Harding. Ann Arbor: University of Michigan Press, 1984.

——. "War Making and State Making as Organized Crime." In *Bringing the State Back In*, ed. Peter B. Evans, Dietrich Rueschemeyer, and Theda Skocpol. Cambridge: Cambridge University Press, 1985.

——, ed. *The Formation of National States in Western Europe*. Princeton: Princeton University Press, 1975.

Walton, John. *Reluctant Rebels: Comparative Studies of Revolution and Underdevelopment*. New York: Columbia University Press, 1984.

Weber, Max. *Economy and Society: An Outline of Interpretive Sociology*, ed. Guenther Roth and Claus Wittich. 2 vols. Berkeley: University of California Press, 1978.

White, Harrison C. *Identity and Control: A Structural Theory of Action*. Princeton: Princeton University Press, 1992.

Wolf, Eric R. *Peasant Wars of the Twentieth Century*. New York: Harper and Row, 1973.

Zagorin, Perez. *Rebels and Rulers, 1500–1660*. 2 vols. Cambridge: Cambridge University Press, 1982.

Zunz, Olivier. *Reliving the Past: The Worlds of Social History*. Chapel Hill: University of North Carolina, 1985.

Secondary Sources, Ottoman Empire

Abdul Rahim, Abu-Husayn. *Provincial Leaderships in Syria, 1575–1650.* Beirut: American University in Beirut, 1985.

Abdul Rahim, Abdul Rahman, and Yuzo Nagata. "The Iltizam System in Egypt and Turkey: A Comparative Study." *Journal of Asian and African Studies* 14 (1977): 169–94.

Abou-el-Haj, Rifaat A. "The Ottoman Vezir and Paşa Households, 1683–1703: A Preliminary Report." *Journal of the American Oriental Society* 94 (1974): 438–47.

Adanır, Fikret. "Tradition and Rural Change in Southeastern Europe during Ottoman Rule." In *The Origins of Economic Backwardness in Eastern Europe,* ed. Daniel Chirot. Berkeley: University of California Press, 1989.

Akalın, Şehabeddin. "Nasuh Paşa'nın Hayatına ve Servetine dair." *Istanbul Üniversitesi Edebiyat Fakültesi Tarih Dergisi* 8 (1955):11–12.

Akdağ, Mustafa. *Büyük Celâlî Karışıklıklarının Başlaması.* Ankara: Ankara Üniversitesi Basımevi, 1963.

——. *Celali Isyanları (1550–1603).* Ankara: Ankara Üniversitesi Basımevi, 1963.

——. "Celâli Isyanlarının Başlaması." *Ankara Üniversitesi Dil ve Tarih-Coğrafya Fakültesi Dergisi* 4 (1946):23–37.

——. "Celâli Isyanlarından Büyük Kaçgunluk, 1603–1606." *Tarih Araştırmaları Dergisi* 2 (1964):1–49.

——. "Genel Çizgileriyle XVII. Yüzyıl Türkiye Tarihi." *Tarih Araştırmaları Dergisi* 4 (1966):203–47.

——. "Kara-yazıcı." *Islam Ansiklopedisi.* Istanbul: Millî Eğitim Basımevi, 1955.

——. "Osmanlı Tarihinde Âyanlık Düzeni Devri 1730–1839." *Tarih Araştırmaları Dergisi* 8–12 (1970–74):51–61.

——. "Tımar Rejiminin Bozuluşu." *Ankara Üniversitesi Dil ve Tarih-Coğrafya Fakültesi Dergisi* 3 (1945):419–31.

——. *Türk Halkının Dirlik ve Düzenlik Kavgası.* Ankara: Bilgi Yayınevi, 1975.

——. *Türkiye'nin Iktisadî ve Içtimaî Tarihi.* 2 vols. Ankara: Tekin Yayınevi, 1979.

——. "Yeniçeri Ocak Nizamının Bozuluşu." *Ankara Üniversitesi Dil ve Tarih-Coğrafya Fakültesi Dergisi* 5 (1947):291–309.

Allouche, Adel. *The Origins and Development of the Ottoman-Safavid Conflict (906–962/1500–1555).* Berlin: Klaus Schwarz, 1983.

Andreasyan, Hrand D. "Abaza Mehmed Paşa." *Istanbul Üniversitesi Edebiyat Fakültesi Tarih Dergisi* 22 (1968):131–34.

——. "Celalilerden Kaçan Anadolu Halkının Geri Gönderilmesi." In *Ismail H. Uzunçarşılı'ya Armağan. Ankara: Türk Tarih Kurumu, 1976.*

——. "Ermeni Seyyahı Polonyalı Simeon'un Seyyahatnamesi (1608–1619)." *Türkiyat Mecmuası* 10 (1953):269–76.

Arnakis, G. G. "Futuwwa Traditions in the Ottoman Empire: Akhis, Bektashi Dervishes and Craftsmen." *Journal of Near Eastern Studies* 12 (1953): 232–47.

Aymard, Maurice. *Venise, Raguse et le commerce du blé pendant la seconde moitié du XVIe siècle.* Paris: École Pratique des Hautes Études, 1966.

Bacqué-Grammont, Jean-Louis. "Études turco-safavides, III, notes et documents sur la révolte de Şâh Veli b. Şeyh Celal." *Archivum Ottomanicum* 7 (1982):5–69.

——. "Sur deux affaires mineures dans les 'registres d'affaires importantes.'" In *Mémorial Ömer Lütfi Barkan*, ed. Jean-Louis Bacqué-Grammont. Bibliothèque de l'institut français d'études anatoliennes d'Istanbul Series. Paris: Librairie d'Amérique et d'Orient, Adrien Maisonneuve, 1980.

Baer, Gabriel. "The Administrative, Economic, and Social Functions of Turkish Guilds." *International Journal of Middle East Studies* 1 (1970):28–50.

——. "Ottoman Guilds: A Reassessment." In *Türkiye Sosyal ve Ekonomik Tarihi (1071–1920)*, ed. O. Okyar and H. Inalcık. Ankara: Hacettepe Üniversitesi 1980.

Barkan, Ömer Lütfi. "Avariz." *Islam Ansiklopedisi*. Istanbul: Millî Eğitim Basımevi, 1945.

——. "Çiftlik." *Islam Ansiklopedisi*. Istanbul: Millî Eğitim Basımevi, 1945.

——. "Defter-i Hâkâni." *Encyclopedia of Islam*. Leiden: E. J. Brill, 1981.

——. "Essai sur les données statistiques des régistres de recensements dans l'empire Ottoman au XVᶜ et XVIᶜ siècles." *Journal of the Economic and Social History of the Orient* 1 (1957):9–36.

——. *XV ve XVIıncı asırlarda Osmanlı Imparatorluğunda Ziraî Ekonominin Hukuki ve Mali Esasları:* Vol. 1, *Kanunlar*. Istanbul: Bürhaneddin Matbaası, 1943.

——. "Mülk Topraklar ve Sultanların Temlîk Hakkı." *Istanbul Hukuk Fakültesi Mecmuası* 7 (1941):157–76.

——. "Osmanlı Imparatorluğu Bütçelerine Dair Notlar." *Istanbul Üniversitesi Iktisat Fakültesi Mecmuası* 17 (1955–56):193–224.

——. "Osmanlı imparatorluğunda bir iskân ve kolonizasyon metodu olarak vakıflar ve temlikler." *Vakıflar Dergisi* 2 (1942):281–365.

——. "The Price Revolution of the Sixteenth Century: A Turning Point in the Economic History of the Near East." *International Journal of Middle Eastern Studies* 6 (1975):3–28.

——. "Tahrir Defterlerinin Istatistik Verimleri hakkında bir Araştırma." IV. Türk Tarih Kongresi, Ankara, 10–14 Kasım: 1940, 290–294. Ankara: [n.p.], 1952.

——. "Tımar." *Islam Ansiklopedisi*. Istanbul: Millî Eğitim Basımevi, 1945.

——. *Türkiyede Toprak Meselesi*. Istanbul: Gözlem Yayınları, 1980.

Bayrak, Mehmet. *Eşkiyalık ve Eşkiya Türküleri*. Ankara: Yorum Yayıncılık, 1985.

Beldiceanu, Nicoarà. *Les actes des premiers sultans conservés dans les manuscrits turcs de la Bibliothèque Nationale à Paris*. 2 vols. Paris: Mouton, 1964.

——. *Le tımar dans l'état Ottoman (début XIVᶜ–début XVIᶜ siècle)*. Wiesbaden: Otto Harrassowitz, 1980.

——. "Le tımar de Muslih ed-Din, précepteur de Selim Şah." *Turcica* 8 (1976): 91–109.

Beldiceanu, Nicoarà, and Irène Beldiceanu. "Riziculture dans l'empire Ottoman XIVᶜ–XVᶜ siècle." *Turcica* 9 (1978):2–4.

Beldiceanu-Steinherr, Irène. "Les laboureurs associés en Anatolie (XV^c et XVI^c siècles)." In *Contributions à l'histoire economique et sociale de l'empire Ottoman,* ed. Jean-Louis Bacqué-Grammont and Paul Dumont. Louvain: Editions Peeters, 1983.

———. "Loi sur la transmission du timar (1536)." *Turcica* 11 (1979):78–102.

———. "Le règne de Selim Ier: Tournant dans la vie politique et religieuse de l'empire Ottoman." *Turcica* 6 (1975):34–48.

Beldiceanu-Steinherr, Irène, and Jean-Louis Bacqué-Grammont. "A propos des quelques causes de malaises sociaux en Anatolie centrale aux XVI^c et XVII^c siècles." *Archivum Ottomanicum* 7 (1982):71–115.

Beldiceanu-Steinherr, Irène, Mihnea Berindei, and Gilles Veinstein. "Attribution de timar dans la province de Trébizonde (fin du XV^c siècle)." *Turcica* 8 (1976):279–90.

Berktay, Halil. "The Search for the Peasant in Western and Turkish History/Historiography." *Journal of Peasant Studies* 18 (1991):109–85.

Birge, John Kingsley. *The Bektashi Order of Dervishes.* London: Luzac, 1965.

Boratav, Pertev Naili. *Folklor ve Edebiyat (1982).* 2 vols. Istanbul: Adam Yayıncılık, 1983.

Braude, Benjamin. "International Competition and Domestic Cloth in the Ottoman Empire, 1500–1650: A Study in Underdevelopment." *Review* 2 (1979):437–51.

Braude, Benjamin, and Bernard Lewis. eds. *Christians and Jews of the Ottoman Empire.* 2 vols. New York: Holmes & Meier, 1982.

Braudel, Fernand. *Civilisation and Capitalism, 15th–18th Century,* Vol. 3: *The Perspective of the World.* Trans. Siân Reynolds. New York: Harper and Row, 1982.

Bruyn, C. *Voyage au Levant.* Paris: [n.p.], 1714.

Burian, Orhan. *The Report of Lello, Third English Ambassador to the Sublime Porte.* Ankara: Türk Tarih Kurumu, 1952.

Cahen, Claude. "Iktâ." *Encyclopedia of Islam.* Leiden: E. J. Brill, 1981.

Cezar, Mustafa. *Osmanlı Tarihinde Levendler.* Istanbul: Çelikcilt Matbaası, 1965.

Çizakça, Murat. "Incorporation of the Middle East into the European World-Economy." *Review* 8 (1985):353–77.

———. "Price History and the Bursa Silk Industry: A Study in Ottoman Industrial Decline, 1550–1650." *Journal of Economic History* 40 (1980): 533–50.

Cook, M. A. *Population Pressure on Rural Anatolia, 1450–1600.* London: Oxford University Press, 1972.

———, ed. *A History of the Ottoman Empire to 1730.* Cambridge: Cambridge University Press, 1980.

Cvetkova, Bistra A. "Documents turcs concernant le statut de certaines localités dans la région de Veliko-Tărnovo au XVII^c siècle." In *Mémorial Ömer Lütfi Barkan,* ed. Jean-Louis Bacqué-Grammont. Bibliothèque de l'institut français d'études anatoliennes d'Istanbul Series. Paris: Librairie d'Amérique et d'Orient, Adrien Maisonneuve, 1980.

———. "Early Ottoman Tahrir Defters as a Source for Studies of the History of Bulgaria and the Balkans." *Archivum Ottomanicum* 8 (1983):133–213.

——. "L'évolution du régime féodal turc de la fin du XVIe jusqu'au milieu du XVIIe siècle." *Etudes historiques à l'occasion du XIIe congrès international des sciences historiques Vienne*, Vol. 2. Sofia, August-September 1965. Sofia: [n.p.], 1965.

——. "Mouvements antiféodaux dans les terres bulgares sous domination Ottomane du XVIe au XVIIIe siècle." *Etudes historiques à l'occasion du XIIe congrès international des sciences historiques Vienne*, Vol. 2. Sofia, August-September 1965. Sofia: [n.p.], 1965.

——. "Les sources Ottomanes concernant le mouvement des Haïdouks aux XVe et XVIIIe siècles." In *Between the Danube and the Caucasus: A Collection of Papers Concerning the Oriental Sources on the History of the Peoples of Central and South-Eastern Europe*, ed. György Kara. Budapest: Akadémiai Kiadó, 1987.

——, ed. *Turski Izvorni za Bulgarskata Istoriia, Vol 3. Sofia: n.p., 1968.*

Danışmend, Ismail Hami. *Izahlı Osmanlı Tarihi Kronolojisi.* 6 vols. Istanbul: Türkiye Yayınevi, 1971.

Dankoff, Robert, trans. and comm. *The Intimate Life of an Ottoman Statesman, Melek Ahmed Pasha (1588–1662).* Albany: State University of New York Press, 1991.

Darling, Linda T. "Adaptations in Administration: The Ottoman Fiscal System." In *Political Economies of the Ottoman, Safavid, and Mughal Empires,* ed. Tosun Arıcanlı, Ashraf Ghani, and David Ludden. Forthcoming.

Elker, Salâhaddın. *Divan Rakamları.* Türk Tarih Kurumu Yayınlarından Series. Ankara: Türk Tarih Kurumu Basımevi, 1953.

Emecen, Feridun. *XVI Asırda Manisa Kazası.* Ankara: Türk Tarih Kurumu Basımevi, 1989.

Erder, Leila. "The Measurement of Preindustrial Population Changes: The Ottoman Empire from the 15th to the 17th Centures." *Middle East Studies* 11 (1975):284–301.

Erder, Leila, and Suraiya Faroqhi. "The Development of the Anatolian Urban Network during the Sixteenth Century." *Journal of the Economic and Social History of the Orient* 23 (1980): 265–303.

——. "Population Rise and Fall in Anatolia, 1550–1620." *Middle Eastern Studies* 15 (1979):322–45.

Ergenç, Özer. "Osmanlı Klasik Dönemindeki 'Eşraf ve A'yan' üzerine Bazı Bilgiler." *Osmanlı Araştırmaları* 3 (1982):105–18.

Faroqhi, Suraiya. "Agricultural Activities in a Bektashi Center: the tekke of Kızıl Deli, 1750–1830." *Südost-Forschungen* 35 (1976):69–96.

——. "Agricultural and Rural Life in the Ottoman Empire (ca. 1500–1878)." *New Perspectives on Turkey* 1 (1987):1–108.

——. "Camels, Wagons, and the Ottoman State in the Sixteenth and Seventeenth Centuries." *International Journal of Middle Eastern Studies* 14 (1982):523–29.

——. "Land Transfer, Land Disputes, and Askeri Holdings in Ankara (1592–1600)." In *Mémorial Ömer Lütfi Barkan,* ed. Jean-Louis Bacqué-Grammont. Bibliothèque de l'institut français d'études anatoliennes d'Istanbul Series. Paris: Librairie d'Amérique et d'Orient, Adrien Maisonneuve, 1980.

——. "The Peasants of Saideli in the Late Sixteenth Century." *Archivum Ottomanicum* 8 (1983):215–49.

——. "Political Activity among Ottoman Taxpayers and the Problem of Sultanic Legitimation (1570–1650)." *Journal of the Economic and Social History of the Orient* 35 (1992):1-39.

——. "Political Initiatives 'From the Bottom Up' in the Sixteenth- and Seventeenth-Century Ottoman Empire: Some Evidence for Their Existence." In *Osmanistische Studien zur Wirtschafts- und Sozialgeschichte: In Memoriam Vančo Boškov,* ed. Hans Georg Majer. Wiesbaden: Otto Harrasowitz, 1986.

——. "Political Tensions in the Anatolian Countryside around 1600: An Attempt at Interpretation." *Varia Turcica,* Vol. 9: *Festschrift for Robert Anhegger,* ed. Jean-Louis Bacqué-Grammont et al. Istanbul: Editions Divit Press, 1987.

——. "Rural Society in Anatolia and the Balkans during the Sixteenth Century." Part 1. *Turcica* 9 (1977):161–95.

——. "Rural Society in Anatolia and the Balkans during the Sixteenth Century." Part 2. *Turcica* 11 (1979):103–53.

——. "Seyyid Gazi Revisited: The Foundation as Seen through Sixteenth- and Seventeenth-Century Documents." *Turcica* 13 (1981):90–122.

——. "Sixteenth-Century Periodic Markets in Various Anatolia Sancaks, Içel, Hamid, Karahisar-ı Sahib, Kütahya, Aydın, and Menteşe." *Journal of the Economic and Social History of the Orient* 22 (1979):32–80.

——. "XVI.–XVIII. Yüzyıllarda Orta Anadolu'da Şeyh Aileleri." In *Türkiye Iktisat Tarihi Semineri Metinler/Tartışmalar,* ed. Osman Okyar. Ankara: Hacettepe Universitesi Yayınları, 1975.

——. "Social Mobility among the Ottoman 'Ulema in the Late Sixteenth Century." *International Journal of Middle Eastern Studies* 1 (1973):204–18.

——. "The *tekke* of Hacı Bektaş: Social Position and Economic Activities." *International Journal of Middle East Studies* 7 (1976):183–208.

——. "Textile Production in Rumeli and the Arab Provinces: Geographical Distribution and Internal Trade (1560–1650)." *Osmanlı Araştırmaları* 1 (1980): 61–83.

——. "Town Officials, Tımar-Holders, and Taxation: The Late Sixteenth-Century Crisis as Seen from Çorum." *Turcica* 18 (1986):53–92.

——. *Towns and Townsmen of Ottoman Anatolia: Trade, Crafts, and Food Production in an Urban Setting, 1520–1650.* Cambridge: Cambridge University Press, 1984.

——. "*Vakıf* Administration in Sixteenth-Century Konya, the *zaviye* of Sadreddin-i Konevi." *Journal of the Economic and Social History of the Orient* 17 (1974): 145–72.

Fekete, Lajos. *Die Siyaqat Schrift in der Turkischen Finanzverwaltung.* Budapest: n.p., 1955.

——. "Türk Vergi Tahrirleri." *Belleten* 11 (1947): 299–328.

Filipoviç, Nedim. "Bosna-Hersekte tımar sisteminin inkişafinda bazı hususiyetler." *Istanbul Üniversitesi Iktisat Fakültesi Mecmuası* 15 (1953–54):154–88.

Findley, Carter. *Bureaucratic Reform in the Ottoman Empire: The Sublime Porte, 1789–1922.* Princeton: Princeton University Press, 1980.

——. "Patrimonial Household Organization and Factional Activity in the Ottoman Ruling Class." In *Türkiye'nin Sosyal ve Economik Tarihi (1071–1920)* [Social and economic history of Turkey.]. Proceedings of the First International Congress on the Social and Economic History of Turkey, Ankara, 11–13 July 1977, ed. Osman Okyar and Halil Inalcık. Ankara: Hacettepe Üniversitesi, 1980.

Fleischer, Cornell. *Bureaucrat and Intellectual in the Ottoman Empire: The Historian Mustafa Âli (1541–1600)*. Princeton: Princeton University Press, 1986.

——. "Royal Authority, Dynastic Cyclism, and 'Ibn Khaldunism' in Sixteenth-Century Ottoman Letters." *Journal of Asian and African Studies* 18, nos. 3–4 (1983):198–220.

Fraser, Charles. *Annals of the Turkish Empire from 1591 to 1659 of the Christian Era*. London: J. L. Cox & Son, 1832.

Genç, Mehmet. "A Comparative Study of the Lifeterm Tax Farming Data and the Volume of Commercial and Industrial Activities in the Ottoman Empire during the Second Half of the 18th Century." In *La révolution industrielle dans le sud-est européen*, ed. Nikolay Todorov. Sofia: [n.p.], 1954.

——. "Osmanlı Maliyesinde Malikane Sistemi." In *Türkiye Iktisat Tarihi Semineri, Metinler/Tartışmalar*, ed. Osman Okyar. Ankara: Hacettepe Üniversitesi Yayınları, 1975.

Gerber, Haim. "The Monetary System of the Ottoman Empire." *Journal of the Economic and Social History of the Orient* 25 (1982):308–24.

Gibb, H. A. R. B., and Harold Bowen. *Islamic Society and the West*. 2 vols. Oxford: Oxford University Press, 1957.

Goffman, Daniel. "A European Commercial Network in Seventeenth-Century Western Anatolia." Paper presented at the Annual Meeting of the American Historical Society, Chicago, Ill., 20 November 1986.

——. *Izmir and the Levantine World, 1550–1650*. Seattle: University of Washington Press, 1990.

Gökbilgin, Tayyib. "Kanuni Sultan Süleyman'ın Tımar ve Zeamet Tevcihi ile ilgili Fermanları." *Tarih Dergisi* 22 (1968):35–48.

——. 'Nasuh Paşa." *Islam Ansiklopedisi*. Istanbul: Millî Eğitim Basımevi, 1945.

Gökçen, Ibrahim. *XVI ve XVII. Asırlarda Saruhan Zaviye ve Yatırları*. Istanbul: Marifet Basımevi, 1946.

——. *16 ve 17. Asır Sicillerine göre Saruhan'da Yürük ve Türkmenler*. Istanbul: Marifet Basımevi, 1946.

——. *Tarihte Saruhan Köyleri*. Istanbul: Berksoy Basımevi, 1950.

Göyünç, Nejat. "Hâne deyimi hakkında." *Istanbul Üniversitesi Edebiyat Fakültesi Tarih Dergisi* 32 (1979):331–48.

Griswold, William J. "Djalâlî." *Encyclopedia of Islam*. Leiden: E. J. Brill, 1981.

——. *The Great Anatolian Rebellion, 1000–1020/1591–1611*. Berlin: Klaus Schwarz, 1983.

Güçer, Lütfi. *XVI.–XVII. Asırlarda Osmanlı Imparatorluğunda Hububat Meselesi ve Hububattan Alınan Vergiler*. Istanbul: Sermet Matbaası, 1964.

Hammer-Purgstall, Joseph von, *Histoire de l'empire Ottoman*. Trans. M. Dochez. 3 volumes. Paris: Imprimerie de Bethune et Plon, 1844.

Hattox, Ralph S. *Coffee and Coffeehouses: The Origins of a Social Beverage in the Medieval Near East*. Near Eastern Studies Series. Seattle: University of Washington, 1985.

Heyd, Uriel. *Ottoman Documents on Palestine, 1552–1615: A Study of the Firman According to the Mühimme Defteri.* Oxford: Clarendon Press, 1960.

Howard, Douglas. "The BBA Ruznamçe Tasnifi: A New Resource for the Study of the Ottoman Tımar System." *Turkish Studies Association Bulletin* 10 (1986):12-9.

———. "The Ottoman *Tımar* System and Its Transformation, 1563–1656." Ph.D. diss., Indiana University, 1987.

Hütteroth, Wolf-Dieter, and Kamal Abdulfattah. *Historical Geography of Palestine, Transjordan and Southern Syria in the Late 16th Century.* Erlanger Geographische Arbeiten Series. Erlangen: Erlanger, 1977.

Ilgürel, Mücteba. "Abaza Hasan Paşa Isyanı." Doçentlik Tezi, *Istanbul Üniversitesi Edebiyat Fakültesi Tarih Bölümü*, 1976.

———. "Osmanlı Imparatorluğunda Ateşli Silahların Yayılışı." *Istanbul Üniversitesi Edebiyat Fakültesi Tarih Dergisi* 32 (1979):301–18.

Imber, Colin. "The Status of Orchards and Fruit-Trees in Ottoman Law." *Tarih Enstitüsü Dergisi* 12 (1981–82):763–74.

Inalcık, Halil. "Adaletnameler." *Belgeler* 2 (1965):49–145.

———. "The Appointment Procedure of a Guild Warden (*Ketkhüdâ*)." *Wiener Zeitschrift für die Kunde des Morgenlandes* 76 (1986): 135–42.

———. " 'Arab' Camel Drivers in Western Anatolia in the Fifteenth Century." *Revue d'Histoire Maghrebine* 10 (1983):256–70.

———. "Bursa and the Commerce of the Levant." In *The Ottoman Empire: Conquest, Organization, and Economy.* London: Variorum Reprints, 1978.

———. "Bursa XV. Asır Sanayi ve Ticaret Tarihine dair Vesikalar." *Belleten* 24 (1960):45–102.

———. "Capital Formation in the Ottoman Empire." *Journal of Economic History* 29 (1969):97–140.

———. "A Case Study of the Village Microeconomy: Villages in the Bursa *Sancak*, 1520–1593." In *The Middle East and the Balkans under the Ottoman Empire: Essays on Economy and Society.* Bloomington: Indiana University Press, 1993.

———. "Centralization and Decentralization in Ottoman Administration." In *Studies in Eighteenth-Century Islamic History*, ed. Thomas Naff and Roger Owen. Carbondale: Southern Illinois University Press, 1977.

———. "Çiftlik." *Encyclopedia of Islam.* Leiden: E. J. Brill, 1965.

———. "Comments on 'Sultanism': Max Weber's Typification of the Ottoman Polity." *Princeton Papers in Near Eastern Studies* 1 (1992):49–72.

———. "Documents on the Economic and Social History of Turkey in the 15th Century: I. The Terekes, Official Lists of Effects of Deceased Persons (Summary)." *Revue de la faculté des sciences économiques de l'Université d'Istanbul* 15–16 (1953–53):44–48.

———. "The Emergence of Big Farms, *Çiftliks:* State, Landlords and Tenants." In *Contributions à l'histoire économique et sociale de l'empire Ottoman*, ed. Jean-Louis Bacqué-Grammont and Paul Dumont. Louvain: Editions Peeters, 1984.

———. "The Emergence of the Ottomans." In *The Cambridge History of Islam*, ed. P. M. Holt, Ann K. S. Lambton, and Bernard Lewis. Vol 1A. Cambridge: Cambridge University Press, 1970.

——. "L'empire Ottoman." Actes du Premier Congrès International des Études Balkaniques et Sud-Est Européennes, Sofia, 26 Août–1 Septembre, 1969. Sofia: [n.p.], 1969.

——. "Haydar-oğlu, Mehmed. Encyclopedia of Islam. Leiden: E. J. Brill, 1969.

——. Hicrî 835 Tarihli Sûret-i Defter-i Sancak-ı Arvanid. Ankara: Türk Tarih Kurumu, 1954.

——. "Impact of the Annales School on Ottoman Studies and New Findings." Review 1 (1978):71–99.

——. "Imtiyâzât." Encyclopedia of Islam. Leiden: E. J. Brill, 1981.

——. Islam Arazi ve Vergi Sisteminin Teşekkülü ve Osmanlı Devrindeki Şekillerle Mukayesesi. Islam Ilimleri Enstitüsü Yayınları Series. Ankara: Ankara Üniversitesi İlâhiyat Fakültesi, 1959.

——. "Jews in the Ottoman Economy and Finances (1450–1500)." Manuscript, Chicago, Ill.

——. "The Köprülü Family." New Encyclopedia Britannica. 1975.

——. "Köy, Köylü ve Imparatorluk." V. Milletlerarası Türkiye Sosyal ve Iktisat Tarihi Kongresi, Tebliğler. Ankara: Türk Tarih Kurumu Basımevi, 1990.

——. "Land Problems in Turkish History." Muslim World 45 (1955):221–28.

——. "Mahkama." Encyclopedia of Islam. Leiden: E. J. Brill, 1981.

——. "Mezra'a." Unpublished manuscript.

——. "Military and Fiscal Transformation in the Ottoman Empire, 1600–1700." Archivum Ottomanicum 6 (1980):283–337.

——. "The Nature of Traditional Society: Turkey." In Political Modernization in Japan and Turkey, ed. Robert Ward and Dankwart Rostow. Princeton: Princeton University Press, 1964.

——. "The Origin and Description of the Circle of Justice." Paper presented at the University of Chicago, 1985.

——. "Osmanlı Bürokrasisinde Aklâm ve Muâmelât." Osmanlı Araştırmaları 1 (1980): 1–14.

——. "Osmanlı Hukukuna Giriş: Örfî-Sultanî Hukuk ve Fatih'in Kanunları." In Osmanlı İmparatorluğu: Toplum ve Ekonomi. Istanbul: Eren Yayıncılık ve Kitapçılık, 1993.

——. "Osmanlılarda Raiyyet Rüsumu." Belleten 23 (1959):575–610.

——. "The Ottoman Decline and Its Effects upon the Reaya." In Aspects of the Balkans, Continuity and Change, : Contributions to the International Balkan Conference, UCLA, 1969, ed. H. Birnbaum and S. Vyronis. The Hague: Mouton, 1972.

——. "The Ottoman Economic Mind and Aspects of the Ottoman Economy." In Studies in the Economic History of the Middle East, ed. M. A. Cook. Oxford: Oxford University Press, 1970.

——. The Ottoman Empire: The Classical Age, 1300–1600. New York: Weidenfeld and Nicolson, 1973.

——. "Ottoman Methods of Conquest." Studia Islamica 3 (1954):103–29.

——. "The Question of the Emergence of the Ottoman State." International Journal of Turkish Studies 4 (1983):71–79.

——. "Rice Cultivation and the *Çeltükci Re'aya* System in the Ottoman Empire." *Turcica* 14 (1982):69–141.

——. "The *Ruznamçe* Registers of the *Kadıasker* of Rumeli as Preserved in the Istanbul Müftülük Archives." *Turcica* 20 (1988):251–75.

——. "Servile Labor in the Ottoman Empire." In *The Mutual Effects of the Islamic and Judeo-Christian Worlds: The East European Pattern*, ed. Abraham Ascher, Tibor Halasi-Kun, and Bela K. Kiraly. New York: Brooklyn College Press, 1979.

——. "Social and Economic History of Turkey (1071–1920)." In *Türkiye'nin Sosyal ve Economik Tarihi (1071–1920)* [Social and economic history of Turkey]. Proceedings of the First International Congress on the Social and Economic History of Turkey, Ankara, 11–13 July 1977, ed. Osman Okyar and Halil Inalcık. Ankara: Hacettepe Üniversitesi, 1980.

——. "The Socio-Political Effects of the Diffusion of Fire-arms in the Middle East." In *War, Technology, and Society in the Middle East*, ed. V. J. Parry and M. E. Yapp. Oxford: Oxford University Press 1975.

——. "State and Ideology under Sultan Süleyman I." In *The Middle East and the Balkans under the Ottoman Empire: Essays on Economy and Society*. Bloomington: Indiana University Press, 1993.

——. "Süleyman the Lawgiver and Ottoman Law." *Archivum Ottomanicum* 1 (1969):105–38.

——. "The Yürüks: Their Origins, Expansion, and Economic Role." In *Medieval Carpets and Textiles: Mediterranean Carpets, 1400–1600*, Vol. 1. London: Halı, 1986.

Islamoğlu, Huri, and Suraiya Faroqhi. "Crop Patterns and Agricultural Production: Trends in Sixteenth-Century Anatolia." *Review* 2 (1979):401–36.

Islamoğlu, Huri, and Çağlar Keyder. "Agenda for Ottoman History." *Review* 1 (1977): 31–55.

Islamoğlu-Inan, Huri. "State and Peasants in the Ottoman Empire: A Study of Peasant Economy in North-Central Anatolia during the Sixteenth Century." In *The Ottoman Empire and the World Economy*, ed. Huri Islamoğlu-Inan. Cambridge: Cambridge University Press, 1987.

Issawi, Charles. "The Decline of Middle Eastern Trade, 1100–1859." *Papers on Islamic History*, ed. D. S. Richards. Philadelphia: University of Pennsylvania Press, 1970.

Jennings, Ronald C. "Firearms, Bandits, and Gun-Control: Some Evidence on Ottoman Policy towards Firearms in the Possession of Reaya, from Judicial Records of Kayseri, 1600–1627." *Archivum Ottomanicum* 6 (1980):339–58.

——. "Loans and Credit in Early 17th Century Ottoman Judicial Records: The Sharia Court of Anatolian Kayseri." *Journal of the Economic and Social History of the Orient* 16 (1973):168–216.

——. "The Population, Society, and Economy of the Region of Erciyeş Dağı in the Sixteenth Century." In *Contributions à l'histoire économique et sociale de l'empire Ottoman*, ed. Jean-Louis Bacqué-Grammont, and Paul Dumont. Louvain: Editions Peeters, 1983.

———. "Urban Population in Anatolia in the Sixteenth Century: A Study of Kayseri, Karaman, Amasya, Trabzon, and Erzurum." *International Journal of Middle Eastern Studies* 7 (1976):21–57.

Kafadar, Cemal. "Les troubles monétaires de la fin du XVIe siècle et la prise de conscience ottomane du declin." *Annales: Economies, sociétés, civilisations* 2 (1991):381–400.

———. "When Coins Turned into Drops of Dew and Bankers Became Robbers of Shadows: The Boundaries of Ottoman Economic Imagination at the End of the Sixteenth Century." Ph.D. diss., Institute of Islamic Studies, McGill University, Montreal, 1986.

Kàldy-Nagy, Gyorg. "XVI. Yüzyılda Osmanlı Imparatorluğunda Merkezi Yönetimin Başlıca Sorunları." *Tarih Araştırmaları Dergisi* 7 (1969):49–55.

Kàldy-Nagy, Julius. "The 'Strangers' (*Ecnebiler*) in the Sixteenth Century Ottoman Military Organization." In *Between the Danube and the Caucasus: A Collection of Papers Concerning Oriental Sources on the History of the Peoples of Central and South-Eastern Europe*, ed. György Kara. Budapest: Akadémiai Kiadó, 1987.

Karpat, Kemal. "Millets and Nationality: The Roots of the Incongruity of Nation and State in the Post-Ottoman Era." In *Christians and Jews in the Ottoman Empire*, ed. Benjamin Braude and Bernard Lewis. New York: Holmes & Meier, 1982.

Keyder, Çağlar. "The Cycle of Sharecropping and the Consolidation of Small Peasant Ownership in Turkey." *Journal of Political Science* 10 (1983):130–45.

———. "The Dissolution of the Asiatic Mode of Production." *Economy and Society* 5 (1976):179–96.

Kissling, H. J. "The Sociological and Educational Role of the Dervish Orders in the Ottoman Empire." In *Studies in Islamic Cultural History*, ed. G. E. von Grünebaum. Published in *American Anthropologist* 22 (1954).

Köprülü, Mehmed Fuad. *Les origines de l'empire Ottoman*. Philadelphia: Porcupine Press, 1978.

———. *The Origins of the Ottoman Empire*. Trans. and ed. Gary Leiser. Albany: State University of New York Press, 1992.

Kunt, Ibrahim Metin. "Derviş Mehmet Paşa, Vezir and Entrepreneur: A Study in Ottoman Political-Economic Theory and Practice." *Turcica* 9 (1977):197–214.

———. "Ethnic-Regional (*Cins*) Solidarity in the Seventeenth-Century Ottoman Establishment." *International Journal of Middle Eastern Studies* 5 (1974):233–39.

———. "Kulların Kulları." *Boğaziçi Üniversitesi Hümaniter Bilimler* 3 (1975): 27–42.

———. *The Sultan's Servants: The Transformation of Ottoman Provincial Government, 1550–1650*. New York: Columbia University Press, 1983.

Kütükoğlu, Bekir. *Osmanlı-Iran siyâsi münasebetleri, 1578–1590*. Istanbul: Istanbul Edebiyat Fakültesi Matbaası, 1962.

Lapidus, Ira M. *A History of Islamic Societies*. Cambridge: Cambridge University Press, 1988.

Lewis, Bernard. "Defter." *Encyclopedia of Islam*. Leiden: E. J. Brill, 1965.

———. *The Emergence of Modern Turkey.* Oxford: Oxford University Press, 1975.

———. "Ottoman Observers of Ottoman Decline." *Islamic Studies* 1 (1962):71–87.

Lowry, Heath W. "The Ottoman Tahrir Defters as a Source for Urban Demographic History: The Case Study of Trabzon (1486–1583)." Ph.D. diss., University of California at Los Angeles, 1977.

Lyber, Albert Howe. *The Government of the Ottoman Empire in the Time of Suleiman the Magnificent.* Cambridge: Harvard University Press, 1913.

McGowan, Bruce. *Economic Life in Ottoman Europe: Taxation, Trade, and the Struggle for Land, 1600–1800.* Cambridge: Cambridge University Press, 1981.

———. "Food Supply and Taxation on the Middle Danube (1568–1579)." *Archivum Ottomanicum* 1 (1969):139–96.

Mardin, Şerif, "Power, Civil Society and Culture in the Ottoman Empire," *Comparative Studies in Society and History* 11 (1969):258–81.

Masters, Bruce. *The Origins of Western Economic Dominance in the Middle East: Mercantilism and the Islamic Economy in Aleppo, 1600–1750.* New York University Studies in Near Eastern Civilization Series. New York: New York University Press, 1988.

Mehmed, Mustafa A. "La crise ottomane dans la vision de Hasan Kiafi Akhisari (1544–1616)." *Revue des études sud-est européennes* 12 (1975):385–402.

Mélikoff, Irène. "L'Islam hétérodoxe en Anatolie." *Turcica* 14 (1982):142–54.

———. "Une ordre de derviches colonisateurs: Les Bektachis." In *Mémorial Ömer Lütfi Barkan,* ed. Jean-Louis Bacqué-Grammont. Bibliothèque de l'institut français d'études anatoliennes d'Istanbul Series. Paris: Librairie d'Amérique et d'Orient, Adrien Maisonneuve, 1980.

———. "Le problème Kızılbaş." *Turcica* 6 (1975):49–67.

Murphey, Rhoads. "The Functioning of the Ottoman Army under Murad IV (1623–1639/1032–1049): Key to the Understanding of the Relationship between Center and Periphery in Seventeenth-Century Turkey." 2 vols. Ph.D. diss., University of Chicago, 1979.

———. "The Historical Setting." In *The Intimate Life of an Ottoman Statesman, Melek Ahmed Pasha (1588–1662).* Trans. and comm. Robert Dankoff. New York: State University of New York Press, 1991.

———. *Regional Structure in the Ottoman Economy.* Wiesbaden: Otto Harrassowitz, 1987.

———. "The Veliyyuddin *Telhis:* Notes on the Sources and Interrelations between Koçi Bey and Contemporary Writers of Advice to Kings." *Belleten* 43 (1979):547–71.

Mustafa Nuri Pasha. *Netayic-ül-Vukuat.* 2 vols. ed. Neşet Çağatay. Ankara: Türk Tarih Kurumu, 1979.

Nagata, Yuzo. "16. Yüzyılda Manisa Köyleri: 1531 Tarihli Saruhan Sancağına Ait bu Tahrir Defterini İnceleme Denemesi." *İstanbul Üniversitesi Edebiyat Fakültesi Tarih Dergisi* 32 (1979):731–58.

———. "Some Documents on the Big Farms (*çiftliks*) of the Notables in Western Anatolia." *Studia Culturae Islamicae* 4 (1976):37–67.

Ocak, Ahmet Yaşar. "Un Cheik Yesevi et Babai dans la première moité du XIIIᶜ siècle en Anatolie: Emirci Sultan (Şerefü'd-Din Ismail b. Muhammed)." *Turcica* 12 (1980);114–24.

——. "Quelques remarques sur le rôle des derviches kalenderis dans les mouvements populaires et les activités anarchiques aux XVᶜ et XVIᶜ siècles dans l'empire Ottoman." *Osmanlı Araştırmaları* 3 (1982):69–80.

Okyar, Osman, ed. *Türkiye Iktisat Tarihi Semineri Metinler/Tartışmalar.* Ankara: Hacettepe Üniversitesi Yayınları, 1975.

Okyar, Osman, and Halil Inalcık, ed. *Turkiye'nin Sosyal ve Economik Tarihi (1071–1920)* [Social and economic history of Turkey]. Proceedings of the First International Congress on the Social and Economic History of Turkey, Ankara, 11–13 July 1977. Ankara: Hacettepe Üniversitesi, 1980.

Orhonlu, Cengiz. "Murad Paşa." *Islâm Ansiklopedisi.* Istanbul: Millî Eğitim Basımevi, 1945.

——. *Osmanlı Tarihine Aid Belgeler: Telhisler (1597–1607).* Istanbul Üniversitesi Edebiyat Fakültesi Yayınları Series. Istanbul: Istanbul Üniversitesi Edebiyat Fakültesi Basımevi, 1970.

——. "Osmanlı Teşkilâtına Aid Küçük bir Risâle 'Risâle-î Terceme'." *Türk Tarih Belgeleri Dergisi* 4 (1967):39–49.

Özkaya, Yücel. "XVIII. Yüzyılın Sonlarında Tımar ve Zeâmetlerin Düzeni Konusunda Alınan Tebdirler ve Sonuçları." *Istanbul Üniversitesi Edebiyat Fakültesi Tarih Dergisi* 32 (1979):219–54.

Parmaksızoğlu, Ismet. "Kuyucu Murad Paşa'nın Iran'a Gönderdiği bir Mektup." *Türkiyat Mecmuası* 13 (1958):419–29.

de Planhol, Xavier. *De la plaine pamphylienne aux lacs pisidiens, nomadisme et vie paysanne.* Istanbul: Bibliothèque archéologique et historique de l'institut français d'archéologie à Istanbul, 1958.

——. "Geography, Politics and Nomadism in Anatolia." *International Sociological Journal* 2 (1959):525–31.

Refik, Ahmet. *Anadolu'da Türk Aşiretleri, 966–1200.* Istanbul: Devlet Matbaası, 1930.

Reychnan, Jan, and Ananiaz Zajaczkowski. *Handbook of Ottoman-Turkish Diplomatics.* Paris: Mouton, 1968.

Rodrigue, Aron. *French Jews, Turkish Jews: The Alliance Israélite Universelle and the Politics of Jewish Schooling in Turkey, 1860–1925.* Bloomington: Indiana University Press, 1990.

Sahillioğlu, Halil. "Années sivis et crises monétaires dans l'empire Ottoman." *Annales: Economies, sociétés, civilisations* 5 (1969):1070–91.

Schütz, Edmond. "An Armeno-Kipchak Document of 1640 from Lvov and Its Background in Armenia and in The Diaspora." In *Between the Danube and the Caucasus: A Collection of Papers, Concerning Oriental Sources on the History of the Peoples of Central and South-Eastern Europe,* ed. György Kara. Budapest: Akadémiai Kiadó, 1987.

Şerifgil, Enver M. "Rumeli'de Eşkinci Yürükler." *Türk Dünyası Araştırmaları* 12 (1981):64–79.

Shaw, Stanford J. *History of the Ottoman Empire and Modern Turkey.* Vol. 1. *Empire of the Gazis: The Rise and Decline of the Ottoman Empire.* Cambridge: Cambridge University Press, 1976.

Shaw, Stanford J., and Ezel Kural Shaw. *History of the Ottoman Empire and Modern Turkey.* Vol. 2. *Reform, Revolution, and Republic: The Rise of Modern Turkey, 1808–1975.* Cambridge: Cambridge University Press, 1977.

Shinder, Joel. "Early Ottoman Administration in the Wilderness: Some Limits on Comparison." *International Journal of Middle Eastern Studies* 9 (1978): 497–517.

Singer, Amy. "Tapu Tahrir Defterleri and Kadı Sicilleri: A Happy Marriage of Sources." *Tarih* 1 (1990):95–125.

Stoianovich, Traian. "Balkan Peasants and Landlords and the Ottoman State: Familial Economy, Market Economy, and Modernization." In *La révolution industrielle dans le sud-est européen,* ed. Nikolay Todorov. Sofia: [n.p.], 1954.

——. "Land Tenure and Related Sectors of the Balkan Economy, 1600–1800." *Journal of Economic History* 13 (1953):398–411.

Sugar, Peter F. *Southeastern Europe under Ottoman Rule, 1354–1804.* Seattle: University of Washington Press, 1977.

Sümer, Faruk. "Karaman-oğulları." *Encyclopedia of Islam.* Leiden: E. J. Brill, 1981.

——. *Oğuzlar (Türkmenler): Tarihleri-Boy Teşkilâtı Destanları.* Ankara: Ankara Üniversitesi Basımevi, 1972.

——. *Safevi Devletinin Kuruluşu ve Gelişmesinde Anadolu Türklerinin Rolü.* Ankara: Ankara Üniversitesi Basımevi, 1976.

Tekindağ, M. C. Şahabeddin. "Canbulat." *İslâm Ansiklopedisi.* Istanbul: Millî Eğitim Basımevi, 1945.

Türkay, Cevdet. *Başbakanlık Arşivi Belgelerine göre Osmanlı İmparatorluğunda Oymak, Aşiret ve Cemaatlar.* Tercüman Kaynak Eserler Series. Istanbul: Tercüman Yayınevi, 1979.

Uluçay, M. Çağatay. *XVIInci Yüzyılda Manisa'da Ziraat, Ticaret ve Esnaf Teşkilâtı.* Istanbul: Resimli Ay Matbaası 1942.

——. *XVII. Asırda Saruhan'da Eşkiyalık ve Halk Hareketleri.* Istanbul: [n.p.], 1944.

——. "Manisa." *İslâm Ansiklopedisi.* Istanbul: Millî Eğitim Basımevi, 1945.

——. "Üç Eşkiya Türküsü." *Türkiyat Mecmuası* 13 (1958):85–100.

Uzunçarşılı, Ismail Hakkı., *Osmanlı Devletinin İlmiye Teşkilatı* Ankara: Türk Tarih Kurumu Basımevi, 1984.

——. *Osmanlı Tarihi.* 15 vols. *Tarihi.* Ankara: Türk Tarih Kurumu Basımevi, 1983.

Veinstein, Gilles. "Ayán de la región d'Izmir et commerce du Levant (Deuxième moitié du XVIII⁰ siècle)." *Etudes balkaniques* 3 (1976):71–83.

——. "L'hivernage en campagne: Talon d'achille du système militaire Ottoman classique." *Studia Islamica* 58 (1983): 109–48.

——. "Trésor public et fortunes privées dans l'empire Ottoman (milieu XVI⁰–début XIX⁰ siècles)." *Actes des journées d'études Bendor* 3–4 (1979): 121–34.

Yetkin, Çetin. *Türk Halk Hareketleri ve Devrimler.* Istanbul: Say Kitap Pazarlama, 1984.

Wallerstein, Immanuel. "The Ottoman Empire and the Capitalist World Economy: Some Questions for Research." *Review* 2 (1979):389–98.

Wallerstein, Immanuel, and Reşat Kasaba. "Incorporation into the World-Economy: Change in the Structure of the Ottoman Empire, 1750–1839." In *Économie et sociétés dans l'empire Ottoman (fin du XVIIIe–début du XXe siècle)*. Paris: Éditions du Centre National de la Recherche Scientifique, 1983.

Zahir, Ilhan. "Tımar Sistemi Hakkında bir Risâle." *Istanbul Üniversitesi Edebiyat Fakültesi Tarih Dergisi* 32 (1979):905–35.

Zilfi, Madeline. *The Politics of Piety: The Ottoman Ulema in the Postclassical Age (1600–1800)*. Studies in Middle Eastern History 8 Minneapolis: Bibliotheca Islamica, 1988.

Index

Abaza Mehmed Pasha, 71, 192, 222–25, 226
Abou-el-Haj, Rifaat A., 59
Absolute authority, of sultan, 28, 30–31
Administrative units (*sancaks*), 37–38, 77
Advice literature. *See* Pamphleteers
Agriculture, 87, 93; in Aydın and Saruhan, 243–44, 246–47, 248, 249; intensification of, 149, 151; and nomadic pastoralism, 116, 118, 122; production organizations for, 108–13
Ahmed I, 220; bargaining with bandits by, 190, 207–8, 210, 211, 242; and Canboladoğlu, x, 189–91, 213, 218; on exploitation of peasants, 144–45; use of mercenaries by, 202–3; war on bandits by, 200–201
Aristocracy. *See* Elites
Army: *kapıkulu* (central officials), 29, 34, 35, 79, 173–74, 186–87; provincial, 35, 37, 74, 75, 76. *See also* Cavalry army; Janissary army; Mercenaries
Arpalık (fodder money), 80, 81, 82–83
Askeri (military) class, 30–31, 32, 33, 164
Autonomy: lack of, in slave-servant system, 32–33; of minorities, 43; of regional officials, 26, 241
Ayak divanı (emergency council), 226
Aydın, province of, 243, 248–49

Baghdad, fall of, 202
Balkan levy of children (*devşirme*), 31, 32, 174, 215
Bandit leaders: Abaza Mehmed Pasha, 71, 192, 222–25, 226; Şeyh Celal, 153–54; Deli Hasan, 186, 198–99, 206–7, 212; emer-

gence of, 199–200; Kalenderoğlu, 167n.58, 208, 210–11, 217; Karayazıcı, 166, 182, 199n.18, 203, 204–6; Köroğlu, 180, 181–82; motivations of, 196–97; state co-optation of, 192–93, 200, 210, 211, 212; Tavil Halil, 206, 207–8, 211. *See also* Canboladoğlu Ali Pasha
Bandit rebellions, 50, 142, 153, 203, 240
Banditry: army organization of, 197; in Aydın and Saruhan, 244; in China, 15–16, 177; development of, 152–53, 154, 230; in Europe, 5; as peasant organization, 175; politicized rhetoric of, 225; social, 178–83
Bandits (*celalis*), x, 230; character of, 22, 176, 177; as detriments to rural society, 20–21; as exploiters of peasants, 145–46, 182, 183, 187–88; as instruments of state, 8, 11–12, 177; Kuyucu Murad Pasha's war on, 153, 203, 208, 209–11, 213–14, 217–18, 220; and peasants compared, 183–85; and population movements, 147–48; role in centralization, 141, 142, 177, 231, 237; state bargaining with, 2, 3, 9, 12–13, 17, 192; state co-optation of, 22, 194–95, 205, 206–7, 208, 217, 218; state incorporation of, 237, 239–40, 241–42; as tax collectors, 100; vagrant peasants as, 156, 176, 177, 187
Bandits (Hobsbawm), 178n.84
Bargaining, state, 9; with bandit leaders, 203–8; with bandits, 2, 3, 9, 12–13, 17, 181, 192; brokerage style of, 10, 11, 14, 191, 230; and incorporation of bandits, 237, 239–40, 241–42; with nomads, 121; with religious students, 158–62. *See also* Co-optation

Battle of Lepanto, 46, 201, 215n.60
Battle of Mezö-Keresztes, 70, 203, 204
Bektashi orders, 125–26, 129
Beyazid, Prince, 168
Beyazid I (1389–1402), 117
Beyazid II, 35, 42
Beylerbeyis. See Governor-generals
Beys (state officials), 71, 156, 199, 234
Blok, Anton, 184
Bölük-başıs (company leaders), 197, 198, 204
Bowen, Harold, 31n.17, 42
Braude, Benjamin, 53
Brokerage, 10, 11, 14, 191. *See also* Bargaining; Co-optation
Bureaucrats (*ehl-i kalem*), 29, 46, 53; checks on power of, 32–34; and Murad IV's consolidation, 226; Osman II's restrictions of, 221; and patrimonial system, 25, 26, 27. *See also* State: officials; *Ulema* (religious) class
Busbecq, Ogier Ghiselin de, 68–69

Çağalazade Sinan Pasha (grand vizier), 70, 203, 212, 215n.60
Canboladoğlu Ali Pasha, 182, 192, 210, 211; deal making with Ahmed I, x, 189–91, 218; secessionist plans of, 186, 195, 206, 213, 214–17
Capital-coercion continuum, of state formation, 6–8
Cavalry army (*sipahis*), 51, 63, 66, 98; appropriation of wealth of, 70, 225; decline of, 68; revolt by, 35, 206, 226; role in assassination of Osman II, 220–21. *See also* Land (*tımar*) holders
Celalis. See Bandits
Cennetoğlu, 225
Centralization, ix, x-xi, 17, 43–44; brokerage style of, 10, 11, 14, 191, 230; and capital-coercion continuum, 6–8; in China, 15–16; in Classical Age, 28; and codification of laws, 29; dealmaking with Abaza Mehmed Pasha, 224–25; by Derviş Pasha, 209; in European states, 1–4, 6, 230, 232, 237, 241; flexibility in, 18–19; mercenaries as tool of, 235–36; and militarization of peasants, 152, 169–70; patrimonial system of, 10, 11, 32, 230; and recovery of *tımar* holdings, 204; role of bandits in, 141, 142, 177, 231, 237; in Russian Empire, 13–15; threats to, 218; types of, 5–6, 10
Centralizing decree of 1531, 63
Central officials, 34, 35, 79; as leaders of peasant militias, 169–70; organization

of, 173–74; rivalry with mercenaries, 186–87; state officials, 71, 80–81, 156, 199, 234
Çerkez Mehmed Pasha (grand vizier), 224
Cezar, Mustafa, 169
China: bandit-peasant relationship in, 177; centralization in, 15–16; market systems in, 133–34; militarization in, 15–16, 175, 236
Christians: arquebusiers (musketeers), 68; assimilation of, 31; as mercenaries, 207
Çift-hane (family farm unit), 93, 108–11; self-sufficiency of, 134, 135; taxation of, 111–13
Circle of justice, 27–28, 85, 233
Civil society, absence of, 40–41
Çızakça, Murat, 52–53
Class alliances: in France and Ottoman state compared, 22–23, 232; for rebellion, 7, 21, 91, 234, 235
Classical Age, 24–25, 28, 233
Coffeehouses, 127–28
Collective action, 17, 88n.9, 142; barriers to, 89, 187–88, 232; class alliance for, 21, 22–23; and court patronage, 104–5; peasant mobilization for, 184, 185, 186, 234; and public transcripts, 85n.1; and rural organization, 107, 137; state actions as cause of, 86–88. *See also* Peasant rebellion; Rebellions
Company leader (*bölük-başı*), 197, 198, 204
Competition: among elites, 39, 40, 54, 56–57, 238; in *tımar* system, 66, 76
Condottieri, 5n.8, 172, 198, 204
Confiscation by state (*musadara*), 33
Consolidation: by Murad IV, 226–28; policies of Osman II, 220–21; warfare as means to, 201, 202. *See also* Centralization
Convents (*zaviyes*), 125, 129–32
Cook, M. A., 149, 150
Co-optation: of bandit leaders, 192–93, 200, 210, 211, 212; of bandits, 194–95, 205, 206–7, 208, 212, 217, 218; brokerage style of, 10, 11, 14, 191; through marriage, 191–92; of religious students, 158–62; state incorporation strategy, 237, 239–40, 241–42. *See also* Bargaining
Cossacks, 14–15
Court cases: about banditry, 144–45, 184n.102; patron-client bargaining in, 146; peasant complaints in, 91, 92, 105, 167n.60, 181; and peasant kinship ties, 138–39; about usury, 143n.2
Court-peasant relations, 102–7. *See also* Judges; Peasants

Court records (*kadı sicils*), 253–54
Crisis in 17th century, 48–54; monetary fluctuations as, 49–50; price revolution as, 51–52; reaction to, 53–54; state policy and elites, 57–58, 59
Cultivator-noncultivator relations, 89, 91. *See also* Patron-client relations; State: and peasants
Currency (*akçe*) debasement, 34, 49–50

Decentralization, in 18th century, 240–41
Decision making, by imperial council, 33–34
Decrees, 29; centralization, 63; to control vagrants, 170, 171; *mühimme* registers, 120, 254; ordering peasants to leave Istanbul, 219; regarding religious students, 160, 161
Deli Hasan, 186, 206–7, 212; bandit army of, 198–99
Demilitarization of nobility, 4
Demographic changes, 48, 135, 250–51; population growth, 49, 51, 52; population movement, 90, 147–49, 150–51, 219; temporary settlements, 113–14
Dervishes (*abdals*), 125; convents of, 125, 129–32; lodges of, 123; wandering, 126–31
Derviş Mehmed Pasha (grand vizier), 32, 82, 209, 213
Deserters, 203–4
Devaluation of currency (*akçe*), 34, 49–50
Devşirme (Balkan levy of children), 31, 32, 174, 215
District governor. *See* Governors
Districts (*sancaks*), 37–38, 77
Duara, Prasenjit, 15, 16

Economic activity, state control of, 41–42, 52
Ehl-i kalem. See Bureaucrats
Elites, 11, 41, 135; and banditry, 142, 176, 185; checks on power of, 32–34, 209, 221; competition among, 39, 40, 54, 56–57, 238; conflict among, 78–79, 234–35, 238; Cossacks, 14–15; effect of tax reform on, 72–73; and European state formation, 3–4, 55; *kapıkulu* army, 29, 34, 35, 79, 173–74, 186–87; lack of opposition to state, 55–56; and militarization, 164–67; and peasant alliance, 11, 91, 143, 235; power struggles of, 60; and slave-servant system, 30–33, 233–34; and state decline, 19–20; *ulema* (religious) class, 30, 38–39, 60, 124, 221. *See also* Governor-generals; Land (*tımar*) holders
Emecen, Feridun, 246, 247

England: centralization of, 3–4, 6, 7; demilitarization of nobility in, 4
European states: alliance with Canboladoğlu, 214; banditry in, 5; centralization of, 1–3, 6, 7–8, 237–38; introduction of firearms in, 152; rebellions against, 4–5, 124, 194
Exit fee, paid by peasants, 144, 147

Family farm unit (*çift-hane*), 93, 108–11; self-sufficiency of, 134, 135; taxation of, 111–13
Farmers, coexistence with nomads, 116, 118, 122
Faroqhi, Suraiya, 247, 248–49
Ferdinand, Grand Duke, 214
Ferhad B. Abdullah, 145
Firearms, 142, 168; and changing nature of warfare, 51; and decline of cavalrymen, 68–70, 75; and militarization of peasants, 151–52, 164
Fodder money (*arpalık*), 80, 81, 82–83
Folk heroes, social bandits as, 180–81, 182n.93
France: centralization in, 3, 6, 7, 230, 237, 241; demilitarization of nobility in, 4; incorporation of regional powerholders in, 241–42; rebellion in, 11, 232
Fratricide, 28, 191

Gaza (holy war), 27
Genç, Mehmet, 52, 53
Gerber, Haim, 50
Gibb, H. A. R. B., 31n.17, 42
Goldstone, Jack A., 19, 50, 238–39
Governor-generals (*beylerbeyis*), 35, 37, 100, 171; incomes of, 62; increased autonomy of, 81, 82, 83–84, 216; and reorganization of provincial system, 76–77, 78, 79; retinues of, 165
Governors, provincial (*sancakbeyis*), 37–38; decline in power of, 63, 78, 80, 82–84; incomes of, 62; retinues of, 165
Grand viziers, 60; appointments of, 201n.21; checks on power of, 33; as consolidators, 203; role of, 238; and suppression of bandits, 201. *See also specific grand viziers*
Great Anatolian Rebellion, The (Griswold), 215n.60
Griswold, William J., 197, 206, 215n.60, 216
Guilds, 41

Habsburgs: peace with, 208, 209, 217; war against, 45, 46, 69, 70
Hafız Pasha (grand vizier), 223, 226

Hassa lands, 94
Haydaroğlu, 182–83
Hisba, 42
Hobsbawm, Eric J., 21, 178, 179
Holy War (*gaza*), 27
Howard, Douglas, 61, 63n.13
Hüseyin Pasha, 73, 75
Hüsrev Pasha (grand vizier), 224, 225

Iltizam. See Tax farming
Ilyas Pasha, 167n.58
Imperial council, decision making by,
   33–34
Inalcık, Halil, 28, 41n.59, 102, 125; on enrollment of mercenaries, 173, 198; on
   firearms, 151–52; on independence of
   peasants, 108–9; on rotation system, 39–
   40, 106; on ruling classes, 29n.12, 30
Incorporation strategy, of bandits by state,
   237, 239–40, 241–42
Inheritance, and landholdings, 65–66,
   96–98
Intermediaries: in tax collection process,
   16; and weakening of patron-client relationship, 100–101, 102. *See also* Tax
   farming
Iran (Persia): Shah of, 128, 211, 214; Shah
   Abbas, 202, 207, 209, 217; Shi'ite sect of,
   126, 154; wars with, 45–46, 51, 160, 162,
   201, 209, 219
Islam, 27, 116, 124
Islamic law (*şer'iat*), 29
Islamic scholars (*ulema* class), 30, 38–39,
   60, 124
Islamoğlu-Inan, Huri, 148–49, 150–51

Janissary army, 33, 173; and assassination of
   Osman II, 220, 221–22, 223; attempt to
   restrict power of, 34–35, 73; conflicts
   with mercenary armies, 174, 222, 223,
   224; empowerment of, 69–70, 71,
   172n.76, 206
Judges (*kadıs*), 38, 96, 100; abuse of peasantry by, 105, 106; for nomadic populations, 123; peasant and state ties of, 89,
   103–4; rotation of, 39–40, 103, 106,
   157–58
Justice: circle of, 27–28, 85, 233; decree on
   peasant militarization, 170; and social
   banditry, 179; of Süleyman, 46–47

Kadıs. See Judges
Kadı sicilleri (court records), 253–54
Kafadar, Cemal, 29n.9, 34n.30, 41,
   48n.80, 52

Kalenderoğlu, 167n.58, 208, 210–11, 217
Kanun (sultanic law), 29, 38
Kapıkulu army (central army), 29, 34, 35,
   79; organization of, 173–74; rivalry with
   mercenaries, 186–87
Karahaydaroğlu, 225, 226
Karayazıcı Abdülhalim, 166, 182, 199n.18,
   203, 204–6
Kemerbaşılar, 161
Khazanov, A. M., 116
Kinship ties, among peasants, 133, 138–39
Kitab-i Müstatab (anonymous), 187
Koçi Bey, 61
Köprülü, Fuad, 124, 127
Köroğlu, 180, 181–82
Kuhn, Philip A., 175, 236
Kuls (slaves), 29, 187
Kunt, Ibrahim Metin, 54, 59, 79, 80–81, 83
Kuyucu Murad Pasha (grand vizier), 166,
   219; defeat of Canboladoğlu by, 190, 217;
   war on bandits by, 153, 203, 208, 209–10,
   213–14, 217–18, 220

Land (*tımar*) holders, 36–37, 184n.102;
   competition with bandits, 185; and court
   system, 39, 104, 234; decline of, 70, 89,
   225; dismissal of, 203, 204; household
   demands on, 93–94; impact of firearms
   on, 68–70, 75; military obligations of,
   95–96; and peasants, 89, 91–92, 95, 99,
   144, 147; profile of, 62, 64; and reorganization of *tımar* system, 61–62, 74; special
   lands for, 94; tax collection duties of,
   93, 95–96, 111; and tax farming, 61, 68,
   76, 101
Land ownership: and disempowerment
   of elites, 89; lack of, 93; state monopoly on, 36, 140. *See also* Land (*tımar*)
   holders
Land (*tımar*) system, 36, 60–76; competition and conflict in, 66–67; flexibility
   in, 47; lack of inheritance in, 65–66,
   96–98; reorganization of, 60–62, 63–65,
   67–68, 70, 71–72, 73–76; rotation policy
   of, 65, 96, 98; and *ruznamçe* registers,
   251–52; spatial organization of holdings
   in, 94–95; and tax reform, 72–73
Law: Islamic (*şer'iat*), 29; review of legislative code, 202; secular (*kanun*), 29, 38.
   See also Decrees
Legal services, 138–39
Legitimacy, state as arbitrator of, 12, 239
Lepanto, battle of, 46, 201, 215n.60
Local officials: competition with bandits,
   185; and state centralization, 3

Manisa, 129, 136–37, 246, 247
Mann, Michael, 6, 7
Markets: in peasant villages, 133–34; regulation of, 41–42, 43, 135, 136n.125
Marriage, as means of state co-optation, 191–92
Medrese (religious school), 106, 124, 151; job shortage for students from, 156, 157, 158, 162
Mehmed I (1402–21), 117
Mehmed II (1451–81), 28, 42; currency debasement by, 34; and forced settlement of nomads, 117; militarization of peasants by, 170, 171; and rotation policy, 97n.27
Mercenaries, 156, 200; as bandits, x, 12, 142, 176; as bargaining tool with state, 193–94; competition for, 197; demobilization of, 5, 12, 163–64, 171–72, 174, 236; impact of, on rural life, 235–36; organization of, 197–98; peasants as, 12, 66–67, 235; permanent status desires of, 186–87; and regional officials, 161, 164–67, 228; state as client for, 172, 203, 207, 209, 227; vagrant peasants as, 151, 163, 167, 168, 171, 172. *See also Sekban/sarıca* armies
Meritocratic system: and military class, 32; and provincial officials, 79–80; rotation system perceived as, 37, 40
Mezra'a (temporary settlements), 113–15
Mezö-Keresztes, battle of, 70, 203, 204
Migration, 90, 147–49; causes of, 150–51, 219
Militarization: in China, 15–16, 175, 236; and elites, 164–67; of nomads, 119–20; of peasants, 70, 152, 154–56, 163–64, 167–70, 175, 235; in response to student disturbances, 159–61, 162; and rise of banditry, 13, 16, 154–56
Military, structure of, 25. *See also* Army
"Military and Fiscal Transformation" (Inalcık), 173
Military campaigns, 45–46; as constraints on landholder's life, 95–96
Military class (*askeri*): peasant mobility into, 164; and slave-servant system, 30–31, 32, 33, 233–34
Military officers, 100; appointments of, as governors, 83; *condottieri*, 5n.8, 172, 198, 208; landholdings granted to, 64, 67
Militia (*ileri*) organizations, 167–69, 170, 172–73; state bargaining with, 236
Minorities, autonomy of, 43
Mobility, upward, for peasants, 47, 156, 157, 164, 184

Monetary crisis, 98–99
Monetary fluctuations, 49–50
Mongol invasion (1221–60), 116
Moral Economy arguments, 87
Mosques, 123
Mühimme registers, 120, 254
Murad III (1574–95), 35, 160, 161, 170, 171
Murad IV (1623–40), 202, 222, 224; consolidation efforts by, 226–28; provincial system reorganization by, 62, 63–64, 73; tax reform under, 72–73; *tımar* system reorganization by, 71–72, 73–76
Murphey, Rhoads, 29n.10, 75, 191
Musketeer armies, 12, 204; and decline of cavalry, 68–70; land rewarded to, 66–67; state need for, 172. *See also Sekban/sarıca* armies
Muslu Çavuş, 211
Mustafa I (1617–18) (1622–23), 202, 220, 222
Mystic leader (*şeyh*), 124, 131

Nagata, Yuzo, 247–48
Nahr (official price setting), 41
Naima, Mustafa, 72, 166n.55, 200, 205
Nasuh Pasha, 166, 183n.97, 202, 218, 219
Networks, in villages, 132–33, 139–40; and central town, 134–36; in China, 133–34; kinship ties and legal services, 138–39; trade relations, 133, 136–37
Nobility and peasant relations, in Europe, 7
Nomads and the Outside World (Khazanov), 116n.76
Nomads (*yürüks*), 121, 150; and dervish convents, 125; forced settlement of, 117, 118–19, 120, 234; origins of, 115–16; paramilitary organization of, 119–20; and peasants, 115, 116, 118, 121–23

Orthodox Islam, 27, 116, 124
Osman II (1618–22), 71, 202; assassination of, 220–23
Ottoman Empire, The (Inalcık), 28n.7
"Ottoman *Timar* System, The" (Howard), 63n.13

Palace intrigues, 60, 221
Pamphleteers, 58, 67, 79; critique of state by, 47–48; on militarization of peasants, 155, 164; on *tımar* system reorganization, 74–75
Paramilitary organization, of nomads, 119–20
Parry, V. J., 60

Pastoralism, 116n.76
Patrimonial system, 34, 191; and bureaucracy, 25, 26, 27; and centralization, 10,
11, 32, 230
Patronage, 27, 100
Patron-client relations, 89, 91; and class
alliances, 234, 235; court-peasant relations, 102–7, 146, 234; dervish convents
and peasants, 131–32; dilution of, 139–40;
exploitation in, 100; and inheritance of
timar lands, 96–98; and monetary crisis,
98–99; personal contact in, 92; and rebellion, 107, 143; and rotation policy, 96,
98; and structure of *timar* system, 93–95
"Peasant and the Brigand, The" (Blok),
184n.101
Peasant rebellion: bandits as impediment
to, 184, 187–88; class alliance for, 91, 143,
230, 232; lack of, 21, 22, 86, 115; and role
of religious institutions, 124; social banditry as, 180; social structures to inhibit,
88–89; state action as cause of, 86–88
Peasants (*reaya*), 11, 30, 39; alternatives for,
90; and bandits, 177, 178, 179, 183–85;
bandits' abuse of, 145–46, 182, 183, 187–
88; and circle of justice, 233; and court
system, 102–7, 146, 234; and dervish convents, 131–32; and elites, 11, 91, 143, 235;
European and Ottoman compared, 9;
independence of, 108–9, 137; kinship ties
of, and legal services, 138–39; and landholders, 89, 91–92, 95, 99, 144, 147; as
mercenaries, 12, 66–67, 235; militarization of, 70, 152, 154–56, 163–64, 167–70,
175, 235; and nomads, 115, 116, 118, 121–23;
organization of, 89–90, 108–13, 133, 139–
40, 175; protection from bandits, 12–13;
provincial officials' abuse of, 85–86, 99–
101, 143–45, 167, 169–70; religious student attacks on, 158, 167; responses to
abuse of, 47, 146–48; state alliance
against nobility, 6–7; and taxation, 52,
85–86, 100, 111–13, 147; and temporary
settlements, 113–15; upward mobility of,
47, 156, 157, 164, 184; and village-town
relationship, 134–36. See also Patron-
client relations; Vagrant peasants
Period narratives. See Pamphleteers
Perry, Elizabeth J., 15, 177
Persia. See Iran
Personal pledging, in court cases, 138n.128
Pious foundations (*vakıf*), 130
Political rhetoric, of bandits, 225
Population, 135; growth of, 49, 51, 52;
movement of, 90, 147–49, 150–51, 219;

surveys and *tapu tahrir* registers, 250–51;
and temporary settlements, 113–14
Power, elites' struggle for, 32–34, 60,
209, 221
Prebendal system. See Rotation system
Price revolution, 51–52
Private property, absence of, 40
Protectionist trade policy, lack of, 53
Provincial officials: arming of, against students, 158–59, 161, 162; autonomy of, 26,
228, 241; and bandit leaders compared,
197; exploitation of peasants by, 85–86,
99–101, 143–45, 167, 169–70; retinues of,
164–67, 171–72, 228; rotation of, 36, 65,
214–15. See also Governor-generals; Governors, provincial
Provincial system, 26, 37; and fodder
money, 80, 81, 82–83; meritocracy in,
79–80; reorganization of, 63–64, 73–84.
See also Land (*timar*) system

Qalandariya (Kalenderis), 127

Reaya. See Peasants
Rebellions, 7, 59, 90; by bandits, 50, 142,
153, 203, 240; of cavalry, 35, 206, 226;
class alliance for, 9, 11; against European
states, 4–5; following assassination of
Osman II, 22; primitive, 193; of Prince
Beyazid, 168. See also Bandit leaders;
Collective action; Peasant rebellion
Receb Pasha (grand vizier), 72
Redistributive ethos, of bandits, 177
Regional officials. See Provincial officials
Religion, state, 27, 29, 116, 124
Religious affiliation, in rural communities,
123–26; dervish convents, 129–32; and
wandering dervishes, 126–27, 128
Religious and ethnic minorities, autonomy
of, 43
Religious class (*ulema*), 30, 38–39, 60,
124, 221
Religious education, 106, 124, 151; job
shortage for students of, 106, 156, 157–
58, 162
Religious (*şer'iat*) law, 29
Religious orders: dervishes, 123, 125–32;
Sufi, 39, 124, 125–26, 129, 132
Religious students (*suhtes*), 106, 156–63,
200; scarcity of jobs for, 106, 156, 157–58,
162; state co-optation of, 159, 160, 161–62
Renomadization, by peasants, 90
Retinues, of regional officials, 164–67,
171, 228
Robin Hoods, 179, 183

Rodrigue, Aron, 43n.65
Rotation system, 26–27, 36; and demobilization of mercenaries, 174, 236; and land (*tımar*) holders, 65, 96, 98; meritocratic aspects of, 37, 40; and peasant-elite alliances, 92, 93, 103, 106; and peasant organization, 140; and state-judge relations, 39–40
Rural movements. *See* Population
Rural society: bandits as detriments to, 20–21; dervish convents in, 129–32; religious affiliations in, 123–28
Russian Empire, state centralization in, 13–15
Rüstem Pasha (grand vizier), 68, 69
Ruznamçe registers, 251–53

Sancaks (districts), 38, 77
Saruhan, province of, 243, 244, 246–48
Secession attempt, by Canboladoğlu Ali Pasha, 195, 213, 214–17
Secular (*kanun*) law, 38
Sekban/sarıca armies, 142, 155, 174–75, 199, 211; creation of, 202–3; rivalry with janissary army, 222, 223, 224. *See also* Mercenaries
Selâniki, Mustafa Efendi, 205
Şer'iat (Islamic law), 29
Serradcızade Ahmed Bey, 217
Settlements, temporary (*mezra'a*), 113–15
Şeyh (mystic leader), 124, 131
Şeyh Celal, 153–54
Shah Abbas, 202, 207, 209, 217
Shah of Iran (Persia), 128, 211, 214
Shamanism, 125
Shi'ite sect, 124, 126, 154
Shinder, Joel, 28n.6
Silver, influx of, 49, 52
Sipahis. See Cavalry army; Land (*tımar*) holders
Skinner, G. William, 133–34
Skocpol, Theda, 193
Slave-servant system (*kul system*), 31–33, 233–34
Social banditry, 178–83
Social structures: as hindrance to collective action, 88–89; and state centralization, 9–10, 11; and state-society relations, 231–32
Sofu Sinan Pasha, 208
State: and changing *tımar* system, 67–68; decline of, 19–20, 58, 93n.7, 238–39; escape from, 90, 115; formation of, 229–30; as institution, 238; and judges, 38–40; and nomads, 115, 117, 118–21;

officials, 71, 80–81, 156, 199, 234; patrimonial-bureaucratic system of, 25, 26, 27–28; and peasants, 12–13, 89, 90, 175; religion, 27, 29, 116, 124; tax farm revenues for, 101–2. *See also* Centralization
State actions: and militarization of peasants, 155, 156; regarding religious students, 158–63; as spur to peasant rebellion, 86–88; and state-society relations, 231–32
State-bandit relations, 8, 141–42, 176–77; bargaining, 2, 3, 9, 12–13, 17, 181, 192, 203–8; Canboladoğlu's negotiation with sultan, x, 189–91, 213, 218, 242; co-optation of bandit leaders, 192–93, 200, 210, 211, 212; co-optation of bandits, 22, 194–95, 205, 206–7, 208, 217, 218; incorporation strategies for, 239–40, 241–42; and janissary-mercenary rivalry, 222, 223, 224; Kuyucu Murad Pasha's war on bandits, 153, 203, 208, 209–11, 213, 217–18, 220; mercenary armies as bargaining tool, 193–94; policy of sending rebels to frontier, 212; reorganization by Murad IV, 226–28; and state officials' illegal activities, 199; suppression attempts by state, 200–201
State-elite relations: changing power balance in, 59–60; decline of provincial governors, 78, 80, 82–84; divisiveness and competition, 56–57; inability of elites to oppose state, 55–56; and power of governor-generals, 76–77, 78, 79, 81; and *ruznamçe registers*, 251–53
State policy: of crisis-management (1550–1650), 57–58, 59; decentralization resulting from, 240–41; of incorporation, France and Ottoman state compared, 241–42
States and Social Revolutions: A Comparative Analysis of France, Russia, and China (Skocpol), 193n.7
State-society relations, 90; bandit uprisings, 20–21; and centralization, 9, 17, 26, 229; and circle of justice, 27–28, 233; and dominance of state, 43–44, 59; involuntary process of, 15–16; key elements of, 231–32; and local militarization, 236; overview of, 21–22; rivalry within, 35–36; 17th century transformation of, 24–25, 233
Students, religious (*suhtes*), 156–63, 200; scarcity of jobs for, 106, 156, 157–58, 162; state co-optation of, 159, 160, 161–62

Sufi orders, 39, 124, 125–26, 129, 132
Süleyman the Magnificent (1520–66), 28, 29, 44–48, 160, 191n.3, 201; centralizing decree of 1531, 63
Sultan, authority of, 28, 30–31, 238. *See also individual sultans*
Sultanic decrees, 29; to control vagrant peasants, 170, 171; *Mühimme* registers, 120, 254; ordering peasants to leave Istanbul, 219; regarding religious students, 160, 161
Sultanic law (*kanun*), 29, 38
Sultan's Servants, The: The Transformation of Ottoman Provincial Government, 1550–1650 (Kunt), 59
Sunni religious establishment (*ulema*), 30, 38–39, 60, 124, 221
Syria, secession attempt by, 214–15

Tapu tahrir registers, 250–51
Tarih-i Selâniki (Selâniki), 205
Tavil Halil, 206, 207–8, 211
Taxes: and bandit-peasant relations, 185; collection of, 16, 50, 52, 100, 105; to finance military retinues, 171; on peasants, 85–86, 100, 111–13, 147; reform of, 53, 72–73; *tımar* holders' collection of, 93, 95–96
Tax farming (*iltizam*), 73, 83, 99, 100; dependence of state revenues on, 101–2; and land (*tımar*) holders, 61, 68, 76
Tax officials, court cases against, 105
Temporary settlements (*Mezra'a*), 113–15
Tilly, Charles, 4, 20n.25, 87; on European centralization, 6–11, 18, 87
Tımar holders. *See* Land (*tımar*) holders
Tımar system. *See* Land (*tımar*) system
Tire, 248, 249
Trade, 27; in peasant villages, 133, 136–37; policy, 52–53; routes, 50, 215
Treaty of Sitva Torok (peace with Habsburgs), 202, 208
Turcoman tribes, 115–16, 125, 127, 128
Türkmen shaiks (babas), 125

Ulema (religious) class, 30, 38–39, 60, 124; restriction of, by Osman II, 221. *See also* Judges
Urbanization, 90, 114, 153
Usury, court cases about, 143n.2

Vagrant peasants (*levends*), 142, 144, 167; as bandits, 156, 176, 177, 187; decrees for control of, 170, 171; as mercenaries, 151, 163, 167, 168, 171, 172; migration of, 147–48, 150, 152–53; in regional officials' retinues, 165, 166
Vakıf (pious foundation), 130
"Veliyyuddin *Telhis*" (Murphey), 73, 75, 79
Village networks, 132–33, 139–40; and central town, 134–36; in China, 133–34; kinship ties and legal services, 138–39; and periodic settlements, 113–15; trade relations, 133, 136–37

War: with Habsburgs, 45, 46, 69, 70; with Iran (Persia), 45–46, 51, 160, 162, 201, 209, 219
Warfare, 45, 46, 212; changing nature of, 50–51; and consolidation of state, 201–2; firearms used in, 12, 51, 68–70, 172; land as reward for service in, 66; provincial officials' participation in, 78
Weber, Max, 10n.16, 32, 237
Women: in palace intrigues, 60; as usurers, 143n.2

Yemişçi Hasan Pasha (grand vizier), 203, 206
Yürüks. See Nomads
Yusuf Pasha, 166n.55, 211

Zagorin, Perez, 4
Zaviyes (dervish convents), 129–32
Zeamets (tenures), 64, 66, 76. *See also* Land (*tımar*) holdings
Zilfi, Madeline, 38

The Wilder House Series in Politics, History, and Culture

Language and Power: Exploring Political Cultures in Indonesia
   by Benedict R. O'G. Anderson
Bandits and Bureaucrats: The Ottoman Route to State Centralization
   by Karen Barkey
*Reclaiming the Sacred: Lay Religion and Popular Politics in
Revolutionary France*
   by Suzanne Desan
*Divided Nations: Class, Politics, and Nationalism in the
Basque Country and Catalonia*
   by Juan Díez Medrano
*Manufacturing Inequality: Gender Division in the French and
British Metalworking Industries, 1914-1939*
   by Laura Lee Downs
*State and Society in Medieval Europe: Gwynedd and Languedoc
under Outside Rule*
   by James Given
New Voices in the Nation: Women and the Greek Resistance, 1941-1964
   by Janet Hart
The Rise of Christian Democracy in Europe
   by Stathis N. Kalyvas
The Presence of the Past: Chronicles, Politics, and Culture in Sinhala Life
   by Steven Kemper
True France: The Wars over Cultural Identity, 1900–1945
   by Herman Lebovics
*Unsettled States, Disputed Lands: Britain and Ireland, France and Algeria,
Israel and the West Bank–Gaza*
   by Ian S. Lustick
Communities of Grain: Rural Rebellion in Comparative Perspective
   by Victor V. Magagna
Hausaland Divided: Colonialism and Independence in Nigeria and Niger
   by William F. S. Miles
*"We Ask for British Justice": Workers and Racial Difference in
Late Imperial Britain*
   by Laura Tabili
Gifts, Favors, and Banquets: The Art of Social Relationships in China
   by Mayfair Mei-hui Yang